Decision in the Atlantic

Decision
in the
Atlantic

*The Allies and the
Longest Campaign of
the Second World War*

Edited by Marcus Faulkner
and Christopher M. Bell

andarta books
an imprint of the University Press of Kentucky

Brécourt
Academic

Published by Andarta Books
An imprint of The University Press of Kentucky

Scholarly publisher for the Commonwealth,
serving Bellarmine University, Berea College, Centre
College of Kentucky, Eastern Kentucky University,
The Filson Historical Society, Georgetown College,
Kentucky Historical Society, Kentucky State University,
Morehead State University, Murray State University,
Northern Kentucky University, Transylvania University,
University of Kentucky, University of Louisville,
and Western Kentucky University.
All rights reserved.

Editorial and Sales Offices: The University Press of Kentucky
663 South Limestone Street, Lexington, Kentucky 40508-4008
www.kentuckypress.com

Library of Congress Cataloging-in-Publication Data

Names: Faulkner, Marcus, editor. | Bell, Christopher M., editor.
Title: Decision in the Atlantic : the Allies and the longest campaign of the
    Second World War / edited by Marcus Faulkner and Christopher M. Bell.
Description: Lexington, Kentucky : Andarta Books, an imprint of The
    University Press of Kentucky, [2019] | Series: New perspectives on the Second
    World War | Includes index.
Identifiers: LCCN 2019007774| ISBN 9781949668001 (hardcover : alk. paper) |
    ISBN 9781949668025 (pdf) | ISBN 9781949668032 (epub)
Subjects: LCSH: World War, 1939–1945—Campaigns—Atlantic Ocean. | World
    War, 1939–1945—Naval operations, British. | World War, 1939–1945—Naval
    operations, American.
Classification: LCC D770 .D364 2019 | DDC 940.54/293—dc23
LC record available at https://lccn.loc.gov/2019007774

 Member of the Association
of University Presses

Contents

Introduction

Winston Churchill coined the term "Battle of the Atlantic" in March 1941. He explained in his memoirs that this measure, "like featuring 'the Battle of Britain' nine months earlier, was a signal intended to concentrate all minds and all departments concerned upon the U-boat war."[1] Churchill often used evocative terms like "battle" not only to focus minds and actions at the time, but also to instill drama into his accounts. This is underlined by the often-quoted statement after the war that it was only the threat of U-boats that had kept him awake at night. Contemporaries understood that when Churchill wrote and spoke of a Battle of the Atlantic, he was referring to the German attack on Britain's imports and maritime communications. In many respects, however, the term is misleading. To begin with, the Battle of the Atlantic was not a "battle" in the conventional sense. It was actually a protracted campaign—the longest of the Second World War—that ran from 3 September 1939 until Nazi Germany finally collapsed in May 1945. Within hours of the Anglo-French declarations of war on Germany, the British passenger liner SS *Athenia* was sunk by *U-30,* evoking memories of Germany's devastating unrestricted U-boat campaign of 1917–18. The last operational U-boats were taken out of action in May 1945 only hours before the German surrender came into effect.

The so-called "battle" also involved little in the way of actual fighting. There is a natural tendency to focus on the dramatic clashes between U-boats and convoy escorts, but this is only part of the tale. Britain and its allies were always happy to destroy U-boats, but the main objective was to ensure the "safe and timely arrival" of convoys and unescorted merchant ships in British ports. Avoiding U-boats was the most practical means to achieve this. Convoy escorts only saw action if all other measures to protect the convoy had failed. The vast majority of trans-Atlantic convoys completed their voyages without making contact with enemy forces, and even at times of crisis most merchant vessels reached their destinations unharmed.

The term "Battle of the Atlantic" is also geographically inaccurate. When Churchill devised the label, the Atlantic Ocean was indeed the main area of operations, but as the war progressed and Allied defenses improved, this theater became increasingly perilous for the Germans. The *Kriegsmarine's* surface raiders, followed

---

[1] Winston S. Churchill, *The Second World War,* 6 vols. (London: Cassell, 1948–53), Vol. III, p. 106.

later by U-boats, were increasingly compelled to seek easier targets in other seas. The campaign gradually spilled over into the Indian Ocean, the Arctic, and the Pacific. Dönitz's favored strategy of *Tonnagekrieg* (tonnage warfare) dictated only that Allied ships be sunk—it did not matter where or how this was accomplished. The war on shipping therefore became a struggle of global dimensions. Merchant vessels passed through the Atlantic on to other destinations, while British factories consumed raw materials from around the globe. Naval forces constantly moved between theaters, and escorts were pulled periodically from the convoy routes for other tasks, such as protecting Britain from invasion in the summer of 1940 or covering the landing of expeditionary forces later in the war.

Popular understanding of the Battle of the Atlantic has been distorted by the tendency to focus on the activities of Admiral Karl Dönitz's U-boats. Submarines were undeniably Germany's most effective commerce raiders, accounting for approximately sixty-nine percent of British, Allied, and neutral merchant ship losses in 1940–1944.[2] But Allied shipping was also constantly at risk from aircraft, mines, and surface ships of all sizes, including fast torpedo boats, auxiliary cruisers, battle cruisers, "pocket battleships," and, most famously, the battleship *Bismarck*. Nor could the British afford to ignore the potential danger to shipping posed by the formidable battleship *Tirpitz* or, more remotely, by the aircraft carrier *Graf Zeppelin*. The modest assistance provided by the Italian Navy is usually overlooked, too. However, it was the interaction of these different methods of attack that made the conduct of the campaign such a complex undertaking for the Allies. Across the war, fifty-five percent of all Allied merchant ship tonnage was lost in the North Atlantic.[3] The Allies had no choice but to adopt a wide range of measures to reduce the impact of the Axis attack on shipping. When Churchill declared the "Battle of the Atlantic" in March 1941, he did not expect to secure a complete victory over the U-boats in the short-term. His most pressing need at the time was to reduce shipping losses and increase the capacity of the merchant fleet in order to maintain British imports at levels necessary to sustain the war effort. The "Battle" of 1941 might more accurately have been termed the "Battle of the Imports" had Churchill not intuitively opted for the more inspiring label. But for all its imperfections, the term Battle of the Atlantic stuck. It quickly became a convenient shorthand for Germany's attempt to starve Britain of essential supplies and Allied efforts to safeguard shipping.

The complexity of the Allied response to the Axis attack on shipping has not always been appreciated. At the tactical level, of course, convoys had to be protected. This required a substantial force of well-trained and well-equipped escort

---

[2]   Eric J. Grove, ed., *The Defeat of the Enemy Attack upon Shipping, 1939–1945: A Revised Edition of the Naval Staff History* (Aldershot: Ashgate/Navy Records Society, 1997), plan 14.

[3]   S. W. Roskill, *The War at Sea, 1939–1945*, Vol. II, Part III (Uckfield: Naval & Military Press, 2004), p. 479.

vessels and aircraft. Ideally, these would destroy the U-boats and other commerce raiders they encountered, although this was not essential. At the operational level, good intelligence was necessary to route convoys and shipping away from danger. As the war progressed, it also enabled the Allies to concentrate hunter-killer forces where they could inflict the greatest damage on the enemy. But there was also a range of problems stemming from what historian Kevin Smith calls the "managerial" aspects of the campaign—the organizational, industrial, and diplomatic measures that could be employed to ensure that Britain's imports did not drop to critical levels even when shipping losses were at their highest.[4] At the top level of decision-making, British and Allied leaders had a variety of tools at their disposal to alleviate the effects of the German attack on shipping. Tactical and operational failures at sea could be offset, if necessary, by building new ships faster than the enemy could sink them. Import levels could be boosted by expedients like the faster loading and unloading of ships in ports. The amount of shipping available could be increased by speeding up the repair of damaged merchant vessels in British shipyards. However, these measures required the commitment of scarce resources that were always urgently needed for other elements of the Allied war effort. As vital as the Atlantic was to the Allies, its needs had to be balanced against the requirements of other theaters. From Britain's perspective in particular, the allocation of resources for the defense of shipping was always at tension with the desire to take offensive action against the Axis powers. It was also the subject of frequent, and sometimes intense, inter-service and intra-Allied conflict. Thus, events and factors far removed from the North Atlantic could and did influence the campaign.

Curiously, given the length and complexity of the campaign, historians have often been content with simple explanations for the Allied victory. A dominant feature within the historiography is the idea that the spring of 1943 was the moment when the Battle of the Atlantic was decisively won. And in hindsight, we can see that May 1943 was a turning point. A seemingly-imminent Allied defeat in March gave way to a dramatic collapse of the U-boat campaign in "Black May," which resulted in Dönitz's temporary withdrawal of his boats from the North Atlantic trade routes. Operations did not cease though, and U-boats continued to be deployed in other areas. This reversal was not the product of short-term operational or technological factors, but rather the culmination of numerous developments. In reality, the course of the campaign ebbed and flowed on both sides throughout the war.

Although the spring of 1943 was a crucial moment in the campaign, the Allies were apprehensive of a resurgent German assault on maritime trade when newer U-boat designs became available. This finally occurred in late 1944, and the

---

[4]   Kevin Smith, "Maritime War: Combat, Management, and Memory," in Thomas W. Zeiler, ed., *A Companion to World War II,* 2 vols. (Malden, MA: Wiley-Blackwell, 2013), Vol. 1.

Germans switched to inshore operations around the British Isles. Allied anti-submarine warfare superiority was soon called into question and the new operational challenges were not fully mastered before the end of the war.[5] The Ultra revelations of the 1970s focused attention on the impact of signals intelligence on the campaign, and for a time it was widely accepted that this had been the decisive factor in the Allied victory.[6] However, as W. J. R. Gardner has argued, the linking cause and effect is a far more multifaceted affair, and the impact of signals intelligence, while important, needs to be seen in a wider context.[7]

This volume seeks to highlight the complexity of the Battle of the Atlantic by reassessing its place within Allied grand strategy and by examining some of its lesser-known aspects. While the general narrative of the campaign and many of its facets are well known, much remains to be addressed. The volume begins with chapters by Marc Milner and Christopher Bell that explore the campaign's role in the context of the wider Allied war effort and provide a new understanding of its place within the Second World War. Kevin Smith's and Tim Benbow's chapters illustrate the choices and tensions concerning the allocation of scarce resources the British faced in waging the campaign. Far from being a concentrated effort, the multitude of actors and changing priorities had at times as much impact as German action. James Goldrick, Ben Jones, Harry Bennett, and Marcus Faulkner address a range of operational issues that have hitherto been sidelined or left unexplored. These contributors show that the campaign was far less about convoy battles in the mid-Atlantic than has been portrayed. Furthermore, the scale of the German assault required the development of new organizations and approaches to waging the campaign. David Kohnen and Kevin Smith's second chapter show how the Battle of the Atlantic spread beyond the ocean itself both in military and economic terms.

---

[5] Malcolm Llewellyn-Jones, *The Royal Navy and Anti-Submarine Warfare, 1917–1949* (New York: Routledge, 2006).

[6] Jürgen Rohwer and Eberhard Jäckel, eds., *Die Funkaufklärung und ihre Rolle im 2. Weltkrieg* (Stuttgart: Motorbuch Verlag, 1979); David Syrett, *The Defeat of the German U-Boats: The Battle of the Atlantic* (Columbia: University of South Carolina Press, 1994).

[7] W. J. R. Gardner, *Decoding History: The Battle of the Atlantic and Ultra* (Basingstoke: Macmillan, 1999).

1

The Atlantic War, 1939–1945

The Case for a New Paradigm

Marc Milner

In the first volume of his magisterial *England in the Seven Years War*, Sir Julian Corbett summarized his conception of sea power and maritime war in one paragraph. The passage was so germane to the debate over the proper functioning of sea power, the role of battles at sea, and the way in which historians have traditionally written about naval war, that Donald Schurman quoted it at length in his seminal work, *The Education of a Navy*, in 1965. Since Corbett's words inform this historian's understanding of the Atlantic war between 1939 and 1945, they are worth repeating here, too.

> . . .there may be moments in the most complex war when the destruction of the enemy's main fleet and the securing of the command of a certain sea may be of an importance so great and pressing that naval action may rightly be left free to concern itself with nothing else. . . .. When such rare moments occur, they are invariably so dazzling in their intensity as to dull our vision of what they really mean and how they were brought about. The imagination comes naturally to concentrate itself upon such supreme catastrophes and to forget that war is not made up of them. Historians, greedy of dramatic effect, encourage such concentrations of attention, and the result is that the current conception of the functions of a fleet is dangerously narrowed, and our best minds cramp their strategical view by assuming unconsciously that the sole purpose of a fleet is to win battles at sea. That this is the supreme function of a fleet is certain . . . but on the other hand it must not be forgotten that convenient opportunities of winning a battle do not always occur when they are wanted. The great dramatic moments of naval history have to be worked for, and the first preoccupation of the fleet will almost always be to bring them about by interference with the enemy's military and diplomatic arrangements.[1]

---

[1]   Julian Corbett, *England in the Seven Years War*, Vol. I, pp. 3–4, as quoted in D. M. Schurman, *The Education of a Navy: The Development of British Naval and Strategic Thought, 1867-1914* (London: Cassell, 1965), p. 165. This chapter was originally published in *Global War Studies* 14:1 (2017).

When Corbett penned those words he was, of course, engaged in battle against the orthodox navalism engendered by the great American prophet of sea power, Captain Alfred Thayer Mahan. Mahan, rather reductionist in his approach, had argued that "the history of sea power . . . is largely a military history." He said that explicitly on page 1 of his most influential book, *The Influence of Sea Power Upon History 1660–1783*, while the rest of that book is a series of parables about the importance of battles at sea in determining the fate of nations.[2] Crudely put: navies in the late 17th and 18th centuries sparred aimlessly for years before a great battle took place which decided the war. Ideally then, a direct drive to a decisive battle was a shortcut to victory.

Whether because of Mahan's lingering influence, or simply because historians remain "greedy of dramatic effect," much of the ink spilt over what is generally known as the Battle of the Atlantic also focuses on battles. It does not help that Winston Churchill's sobriquet of "battle," coined for one particular phase of the Atlantic war in the spring of 1941, supports the Mahanian interpretation, and so, too, did wartime propaganda. All the might-have-beens revolve around combat at sea: What if the Germans had had 300 submarines in 1939?; What if German torpedoes had worked properly?; What if the Allies had not penetrated German naval codes?; What if the Allies had not perfected 10cm radar and ship-borne HF/DF?— if, if, if . . . it all would have turned out differently, better, sooner.

But Allied victory in the Atlantic war was not determined by a single cause, and the great "battle" of the spring of 1943 did not, in the end, decide the issue. The victory of spring 1943 was—as Corbett suggested it should be—the culmination of a long process of interfering with the enemy's "military and diplomatic" arrangements. In many ways, to continue the Corbett paradigm a little further, victory in May 1943 was like Nelson's victory on 21 October 1805 off Cape Trafalgar. Admiral Karl Dönitz's U-boat fleet was no more prepared to fight a decisive naval engagement in 1943 than Admiral Villeneuve's fleet was in 1805. In both cases, victory was the result of a long campaign that ultimately forced the enemy to fight a battle which he could not possibly win, in a naval war he had already lost. The British Admiralty seems to have understood this by 1940 or early 1941, and certainly by 1943. It is not clear if, during the war, the Americans ever did.

In a modern analogy, everything prior to January 1943 might be seen as a "shaping operation," preparing the enemy for destruction. That assumes, of course, that the British actually thought it was possible to "defeat" the U-boats in any meaningful way. Certainly they tried to defeat them in 1939 with hunting operations that proved a dismal failure. After that the objective of British strategy and operations in the Atlantic was entirely Corbettian: interfere with the enemy in

---

[2]   Alfred Thayer Mahan, *The Influence of Sea Power Upon History 1660–1783* (Boston: Little, Brown, 1890).

order to allow trade to flow with acceptable losses.[3] Success was measured in tonnage delivered and strategy for the wider war advanced, not in U-boat kills. Victory over the U-boat, when it lay within easy reach in May 1943, was then sudden, stunning, and crushing in its effects. It was, in the end, a modern Trafalgar. But like Trafalgar, it did not end the war—at sea or elsewhere.

Back to Basics

It is important to understand that the basis of British, and therefore Allied, victory in the Atlantic was—except for the spring of 1943—avoidance of the enemy. Wartime public relations rhetoric (and subsequent historians) described the destroyers, frigates, and corvettes around escorted convoys as the first line of defense against the U-boats, but that was a necessary falsehood. The first line of defense of trade was always the main battle fleet. As small and as thinly-stretched as it was, the Royal Navy's main fleet provided the cover under which trade protection operated. It made the North Atlantic untenable for major German surface units (generally!), and therefore safe for small ships of the flotilla to operate effectively. In the Atlantic war, the main fleet played a key operational role directly in trade defense more often and with greater importance than is generally assumed. The ill-fated sortie of *Bismarck* in May 1941 is the classic example of this. But she was simply the last in a long line of German cruisers, battlecruisers, and pocket battleships that prowled the North Atlantic from 1939 to 1942. In particular, *Scharnhorst, Gneisenau, Hipper, Prinz Eugen*, and *Scheer* were all on the loose in the North Atlantic from December 1940 to March 1941. The presence of these large raiders along with very long range FW 200 Condor patrol aircraft and U-boats meant that North Atlantic trade in the second winter of the war was under a combined arms assault. The enemy did not sink much shipping, but it disrupted movements and posed a very serious threat. *Scharnhorst, Gneisenau*, and *Prinz Eugen*, it needs emphasizing, remained in French ports throughout 1941. *Bismarck's* mistake was to emerge in the late spring, into almost twenty-four hours of Arctic daylight, and into a theater now patrolled by radar-equipped aircraft: she really had no place to hide. *Bismarck's* sister ship, *Tirpitz*, was ready to sortie by the fall. So the surface threat even in the third winter of the war remained very real. Historians do not focus on the surface threat after the *Bismarck* sortie because nothing of "dramatic effect" happened, but those charged with the defense of trade in the North Atlantic did not have that luxury and so the work of the small escort ships was entirely predicated on the stand-off between powerful main

---

[3]   This idea is hardly new, but it has never gained much traction. A revised edition of D. W. Waters' critical naval staff history, Eric J. Grove, ed., *The Defeat of the Enemy Attack upon Shipping, 1939–1945: A Revised Edition of the Naval Staff History* (Aldershot: Ashgate/ Navy Records Society, 1997), makes a Corbettian case for the Atlantic war. The author of this chapter does so as well in Marc Milner, "The Battle of the Atlantic," *The Journal of Strategic Studies* 13:1 (1990), pp. 45–66.

fleets. Even when the main German surface fleet redeployed to operational bases in Norway, sorties into the broad North Atlantic remained a possibility. As a result, the Allied battle fleet remained the first line of trade defense.

Naval intelligence came a close second, and not just the special stuff. Ultra was unquestionably valuable, and the lure of "reading the other guy's mail" has been almost like an opiate for historians. But the hum-drum of more conventional forms of operational intelligence, such as traffic analysis and direction finding of radio transmissions, played fundamental roles which historians have yet to fully explore. The great advantage of naval operational intelligence was that it allowed a strategy of avoidance to be effective, permitting safe routing of trade away from known enemy concentrations. Naval intelligence, therefore, went hand-in-hand with the third key component of trade defense: Naval Control of Shipping (NCS). NCS operated like modern air traffic control, allowing merchant ships to be effectively managed, routed, and escorted. It allowed the convoy system to function and it kept high-speed and high-value ships out of harm's way—most of the time. Routing authorities and escort forces did not need to know where the enemy or their own main fleet were, they simply needed to know where not to be.[4]

The final line of defense was, therefore, the escort itself: it fought if all else failed. For most of the war, it was less important that the escort be tactically competent than that it simply be there. How else can one explain the ill-prepared, barely-trained, and poorly-equipped Canadian escorts of the Newfoundland Escort Force (NEF) in 1941? Everyone, except perhaps Captain Donald Macintyre, RN, understood that the NEF was largely incapable of protecting a convoy from serious attack.[5] Certainly the Admiralty, the Royal Canadian Navy (RCN), and the routing authorities did. When the RCN was asked in the spring of 1941 to use its burgeoning fleet of corvettes to form the NEF and to begin immediate operations, the Canadian Naval Staff protested that the ships and their crews were utterly unprepared. The Admiralty insisted that the system was more important than the efficacy of the escorts and the NEF started operations in June. As a result, Canadian-escorted convoys often fared poorly in late 1941. One of them, SC 52, was sent back to Canada in October 1941 after it was intercepted by U-boats virtually within sight of Newfoundland: the only north Atlantic convoy turned back by the mere threat of enemy attack.[6]

---

[4]   For a discussion of the functioning of NCS, see Marc Milner, "Naval Control of Shipping and the Atlantic War, 1939–1945," *The Mariner's Mirror* 83:2 (1997), pp. 169–84.

[5]   See Donald Macintyre's memoir, *U-boat Killer: Fighting the U-boats in the Battle of the Atlantic* (London: Weidenfeld and Nicolson, 1956).

[6]   See Marc Milner, *North Atlantic Run: The Royal Canadian Navy and the Battle for the Convoys* (Toronto: University of Toronto Press, 1985), ch. 2 for a discussion of the formation of the NEF. For a fully detailed analysis, see the RCN official history, W. A. B. Douglas, Roger Sarty, and Michael Whitby, *No Higher Purpose: The Official Operational History of the Royal Canadian Navy in the Second World War, 1939–1943*, Vol. II, Part I (St. Catharines: Vanwell, 2002), ch. 3.

The essential point in all this is that it was the trade defense *system* that mattered in the North Atlantic, not the drama of battle. The system had been nurtured in the interwar years by the British Empire precisely because it was both essential in wartime and relatively inexpensive to maintain. Considerable effort had been made in the 1930s when Admiral Sir Eldon Manisty was sent on a global tour to coordinate naval intelligence and NCS matters. Manisty had been involved in the establishment of ocean convoys in 1917, and by 1939 he ensured that the British Empire and Commonwealth had a superb system of tracking merchant shipping, routing it, and passing information around the world. This, in turn, was netted into the larger operational intelligence picture so that pieces which appeared to be out of place could be treated with caution and so that failures to arrive at port on schedule could trigger a search for raiders. It did not always work, as the loss of HMAS *Sydney* in November 1941 indicates, but it was exceptionally effective. This British system became the bedrock of Allied merchant shipping monitoring, control, and defense throughout the war.[7]

Doctrine and Tactics, 1941–42

While it is true that the Royal Navy tinkered, disastrously, with hunter-killer operations for U-boats in the very early stages of the war, the imperative of simply rendering U-boat operations less effective—and therefore manageable—started early. The ultimate manifestation of this approach is evidenced in the progressive expansion of the oceanic convoys system after 1940 and in the Western Approaches Convoy Instructions (WACIs) issued by the Royal Navy in the spring of 1941 which governed those operations. WACIs placed "safe and timely arrival of the convoy" at the very top of the escort's responsibilities. WACIs (and their Allied variant adopted in 1942, Atlantic Convoy Instructions)[8] became the guiding doctrine of British Commonwealth escort and anti-submarine operations in the Atlantic war.

Not everyone was happy with WACIs: Captain Johnny Walker, RN, certainly was not.[9] But most of the initial opposition to WACIs' emphasis on safe and timely

---

[7]   For a more detailed discussion of the development of the British Commonwealth NCS system, see Marc Milner, *Canadian Naval Force Requirements in the Second World War* (Ottawa: Operational Research and Analysis Establishment, NDHQ, Extra-mural Paper no. 20, 1981).

[8]   ACIs blended American tactics and doctrine in the North Atlantic (i.e. not forces south of the Gulf of Maine) with those of the British Commonwealth navies, and included a common phonetic alphabet to facilitate voice radio communications.

[9]   Admiral Sir Peter Gretton confided to the author in 1985 that Walker got away with his disregard for WACIs because he was so skilled at U-boat killing. Gretton preferred to get the shipping through, as did most British escort commanders.

arrival came from the North American navies. The reasons for the subtle but profoundly different views of the Battle of the Atlantic on either side of the ocean early in the war have also never been fully explored by historians.[10] The American view was unquestionably Mahanian: sea power as a function of battles. The United States Navy entered the Atlantic war in the fall of 1941 to escort ships, but its "Escort of Convoy Instructions" (Lantft 9A) issued in November 1941 placed safe arrival of the convoy dead last on the priorities of the escort. The job of an American escort was to sink U-boats. The idea was simple enough: every ship was safe from a dead U-boat. But as the British knew well, it was not the job of the U-boat to stand and fight, and they would simply run away if pursued. The U.S. Navy went after them all the same.

In 1941–42 so, too, did the burgeoning RCN, and for several discernible reasons. First, most of the RCN's escort forces operated beyond the reach of the British in 1941 and 1942. Once the U.S. entered the shooting war in September 1941, all escort operations west of Iceland became their responsibility, with a "Change of Operational Control" Line (CHOP Line) running down the middle of the North Atlantic. The Anglo-Canadians retained responsibility for naval control of shipping and convoy routing, but Western Approaches Command's writ stopped at the CHOP Line. This left the rapidly expanding Canadians in the American zone, beyond reach of the British trainers, British control, and British tactical orthodoxy. The Americans, for their part, assumed no responsibility for the struggling RCN escort fleet: that was a British imperial "problem." When the eastern terminus of escort operations shifted from Iceland to Ireland in February 1942, the Royal Navy was able to influence the portion of the RCN which took convoys across the midocean. But for a critical period in the middle of the war, the RCN was free to follow its instincts and predilections.

Secondly, like the Americans, Canadians believed they had gone to war to fight the Germans. The notion that one's task was to push the enemy away and then run like hell was a hard sell to Canadians. Moreover, for Americans and Canadians alike the Atlantic was a war zone. It was the place where the enemy was found, and where the shooting commenced. Fighting the Germans seemed to define the job. For the British, in contrast, the North Atlantic was a rear area, an LOC: securing it was always the paramount task. This difference between British and North American attitudes can be read clearly in the assessments of convoy actions by staffs on either side of the Atlantic in 1942.[11] As long as the escort was aggressive, Canadian and American staff officers were content. The British often despaired that the North Americans buzzed about to little effect. Indeed, Admiral Sir Max Horton's biographer described the Canadian method of convoy defense as akin to cowboys

---

[10]   See Milner, *North Atlantic Run,* p. 104.

[11]   The author's *North Atlantic Run* explores this theme a little, but more could certainly be done.

riding aimlessly around the herd, keeping things well stirred up.[12] Better they should keep the convoys safe and get them home.

The North American navies may have shared a penchant for tactical aggressiveness, but they did not share the same understanding of the fundamental nature of the Atlantic war. The RCN, for its part, fully subscribed to the view that convoys, escorts, and evasive routing were the bedrocks of Allied success in the Atlantic. When the war expanded westward in early 1942, the Canadians established local convoys almost immediately and continued to extend that system as needed through the year. Only in the Gulf and River St. Lawrence were losses in Canadian waters dramatic. Most of these came off the Gaspé Peninsula, where the river was too narrow for effective evasive routing and the U-boats were able to ambush the convoys. Even so, and despite the domestic political mayhem losses in the St. Lawrence caused in 1942, the rate of losses to convoys in the area was negligible: roughly 1.2 percent.

Anglo-American historians have missed this story, presumably because they assume that nothing much of importance happened in the Canadian Atlantic zone. While U-boats slaughtered merchant shipping in the mid-ocean and along the U.S. eastern seaboard, the 500–600 Allied ships per month plying the Great Circle route between Cape Cod and the Grand Banks apparently slipped through a 1,500 mile gap in the space-time continuum like a starship through a wormhole! Or perhaps U-boat captains simply avoided the area so they would not get stuck in the *ennui* of a Canadian story. It is more likely, however, that the reason that no history critical to the existing Atlantic narrative emerged from the Canadian zone in 1942 is because most ships moving through it were convoyed and effectively routed. The Germans complained about cold weather off Canada—but also the empty seas. They would not have abandoned the Canadian zone (much closer to their bases in France and Norway than any part of the U.S. coast) for warmer climes if targets had been plentiful and easy.[13]

Effective naval control of shipping and convoy routing was one of the unheralded victories of Canada (and the British Commonwealth) in the northwest Atlantic in 1942. This was no accident. Canada was an integral part of the global British NCS and naval intelligence system. In fact, NCS and routing west of 40 degrees and north of the equator, including American ports, was run from Ottawa from August 1939 until late July 1942 when Washington took over the western hemisphere NCS duties. That was why Canadians were able to establish their own coastal convoys so easily, why they were able to establish the first convoys in the U.S. Eastern Sea Frontier, and why the RCN could even run tanker

---

[12]   Rear Admiral W. S. Chalmers, *Max Horton and the Western Approaches: A Biography of Admiral Sir Max Kennedy Horton* (London: Hodder and Stoughton, 1954), p. 147.

[13]   See Roger Sarty, *War in the St Lawrence: The Forgotten U-Boat Battle on Canada's Shores* (Toronto: Penguin, 2012).

convoys to the Caribbean through the American zone in the spring and summer of 1942 without loss and despite German attempts to mount at least one Wolf Pack operation against them.[14]

Carnage off America, 1942

The American failure to establish a system of coastal convoys in early 1942 is therefore primarily reflective of how they viewed the Atlantic war: as essentially a tactical problem of finding and sinking the attacker. The report of the Board on the Organization of East Coast Convoys in March makes this clear. Effective convoying, they wrote, "depends upon the escort being in sufficient strength to permit their taking offensive action against attacking submarines. . . Any protection less than this simply results in the convoy's becoming a convenient target."[15] British naval officers pulled their hair out in dismay at this folly; it seemed that nothing they told the Americans about the primacy of convoys registered. But the British are wont to forget (then and now) that the American reluctance to convoy was also based on their own recent operational experience in the North Atlantic. Since September 1941 they had escorted convoys between Newfoundland and Iceland, and convoys in that area (most often the slow, weakly-escorted RCN ones) were occasionally overwhelmed and suffered heavy losses.

In the fall of 1941, North Atlantic convoys were also frequently and successfully attacked well inshore. Not surprisingly, and as the American "tactical" approach to the problem reveals, in 1942 they made no clear distinction between inshore and oceanic U-boat operations: they were all the same. The British and Canadians did make that distinction. They understood that inshore convoys, moving under air escort, were generally safe from pack attacks. Air power normally kept the packs from forming and the U-boats from operating with impunity on the surface.[16] Consequently, inshore attacks were typically by Lone Wolves. They could sink ships, but they could never overwhelm a convoy and losses would be sustainable.[17]

---

[14]   Rob Fisher, "'We'll Get our Own': Canada and the Oil Shipping Crisis of 1942," *The Northern Mariner* 3:2 (1993), pp. 33–40.

[15]   Milner, *North Atlantic Run*, p. 99.

[16]   See the correspondence from the Assistant Chief of Naval Staff (Trade), Rear Admiral E. L. S. King, RN, to the First Sea Lord, Admiral Sir Dudley Pound, in the "Battle of the Atlantic Review" for May 1942, ADM 1/12062, The National Archives, London, and the discussion in Milner, *North Atlantic Run*, pp. 109–11.

[17]   Marc Milner, "Inshore ASW: The Canadian Experience in Home Waters," in W. A. B. Douglas, ed., *The RCN in Transition, 1910–1985* (Vancouver: University of British Columbia Press, 1988), pp. 143–58.

However, not all coastal zones were free of pack attacks, and here, too, recent operational experience supported American caution about convoys in early 1942. The northwest Atlantic situation was anomalous; the persistence of fog on the Grand Banks allowed Wolf Packs to operate almost within sight of Newfoundland despite air patrols reaching 400 miles to seaward. Early airborne metric wavelength radars were no solution to this problem, since they could not distinguish between a towering iceberg and a ship. Attempts to do a visual classification of a target at low altitude in dense Grand Banks fog could be fatal! In the fall of 1941, Wolf Packs regularly operated as close as 200–300 miles of Newfoundland and on one occasion, SC 52, they intercepted a convoy close enough to the coast to force the Allies to abandon attempts to push it across the Atlantic.

So the fog of the Grand Banks probably contributed to the fog of war that engulfed the American reaction to the U-boat in 1942. Certainly their response to the U-boat problem is more explicable if one considers the U.S. Navy's own experience in the North Atlantic prior to the spring of 1942. This experience west of Iceland was shared primarily with the RCN, not the British. There are, of course, a whole host of other problems and issues which complicate the American response to the U-boat in early 1942, from command and control confusion, to lack of a clear doctrine and basic drills for ASW, and the distraction of a catastrophic situation in the Pacific. But all of the U.S. Navy's focus on defending shipping by sinking U-boats makes it clear that that service thought of the U-boat as a tactical and technological problem, not one which could be managed by structures and systems.

So, what happened off the U.S. coast from January to the late summer of 1942 dumbfounded the British (and Canadians) at the time and has perplexed historians ever since. In the first six months of that year, some 2.34 million tons of shipping (397 ships) were lost in the Eastern, Gulf, and Caribbean Sea Frontiers: nearly the equivalent of total U.S. registered shipping losses for the entire war. In May and June, when nineteen U-boats operated in American coastal zones, more than one million tons were sunk there: nearly half the annual totals for the first two years of the war in just two months. Put another way, in May and June 1942, fully eighty-five percent of global Allied shipping losses occurred in American waters.

And this happened with very modest damage inflicted on the enemy, despite intense efforts to find and sink them—in accordance with the U.S. Navy's stated doctrine. In all, ten U-boats were sunk by American forces in the Eastern, Gulf, and Caribbean Sea Frontiers between January and September 1942. As the U.S. Navy's official historian, Samuel Eliot Morison, pointed out, this was about two weeks of submarine production in Germany that year. A year later, at the height of the crisis in the spring of 1943, the British considered an exchange rate of two merchant ships for every U-boat sunk acceptable. In the first nine months of 1942 in U.S. waters, the exchange rate was thirty-nine to one.

Much ink has been spilt trying to explain what happened. Morison blamed the U.S. Navy for sitting on its duff and failing to learn the obvious lessons, particularly the need for escorted convoys.[18] Eliot Cohen ascribed the disaster to that service's more general failure to get the operational command, control, and inter-service organization right for dealing with a submarine problem.[19] The solution, Tenth Fleet, had to await 1943. Michael Gannon argued that the misapplication of U.S. destroyer strength, the failure to plan ahead for the small craft needed, and the intractability of Admiral Ernest J. King, the American Chief of Naval Operations, were the real culprits for what he calls the single biggest defeat at sea in United States history.[20]

Whatever the cause, we do know with certainty what drove the U-boats out of the American zone: convoys. Once again, the convoy system did two crucial things; it made the U-boat problem manageable, and it forced Dönitz to find a more profitable place to deploy what was, by late 1942, a massive fleet of conventional, fairly short-ranged Type VII 740-ton U-boats. By the fall of that year, there was really only one place they could go: back to the mid-Atlantic air gap.

By then, the Germans had effectively lost the naval war. Although they sank some nine million tons of Allied merchant shipping in 1942, Germany could not stop the curve of new construction from surpassing losses in November. At that point, Michael Salewski concluded decades ago, the Battle of the Atlantic had been lost.[21] All Dönitz could hope to do now was embarrass the development of Allied strategy. What he did not know was that the Allies had not even really been trying to win the Atlantic war.

The Great Dramatic Moment

As catastrophic as the losses in Allied merchant shipping were in 1942, Winston Churchill remained unfazed by the Atlantic war until the fall. With so very much going wrong, Churchill preferred to focus on British import projections rather than shipping losses.[22] Through much of 1942, these projections remained acceptable, and with the flood of new construction now pouring from American yards— originally ordered by the British under lend-lease—there seemed no reason to

---

[18]   S. E. Morison, *History of United States Naval Operations in World War II,* Vol. I (Boston: Little, Brown, 1956), pp. 200–01.

[19]   Eliot Cohen and John Gooch, eds., *Military Misfortunes: The Anatomy of Failure in War* (New York: Free Press, 1990).

[20]   Michael Gannon, *Operation Drumbeat: The Dramatic True Story of Germany's First U-Boat Attacks along the American Coast in World War II* (New York: Harper and Row, 1990).

[21]   Michael Salewski, *Die deutsche Seekriegsleitung 1939–1945,* Vol. 2 (Frankfurt am Main: Bernard und Graefe, 1975).

[22]   Christopher M. Bell, *Churchill and Sea Power* (Oxford: Oxford University Press, 2013), ch. 9.

believe that losses to shipping would not be made good. Then at the end of 1942, several things happened to focus the attention of senior Allied leaders on the Atlantic for the first and only time during the war. Not all of these things were the result of enemy action.

The first factor shaping the critical winter of 1942–43 in the North Atlantic was Operation Torch, the Allied landing in North Africa on 9 November. To find the escorts to mount and sustain Torch, the British shut down convoys in the south and east Atlantic. The lack of convoys in the south-central Atlantic led to the highest loss rates of the war off West Africa in October and November, exacerbating an already critical shortage of British-controlled shipping. Shutting down shipping routes in the east Atlantic meant that all shipping in and out of the UK now went westward, across the Atlantic and through the convoy routes of the western hemisphere. This circuitous routing, especially for far eastern shipping, sharply reduced the carrying capacity of what British-controlled shipping remained. All this, and an unexpected extra drawdown of ships and supplies to support the North African campaign, pushed the whole import profile for 1943 into crisis by late November. Despite Churchill's desperate pleas, it took President Roosevelt four months to pry merchant ships from the hands of his flag officers and generals who wanted them for the Pacific war.

With Britain teetering on the brink of disaster in late 1942, and its link to the outside world now down to the embattled North Atlantic route, U-boats began to flood into the mid-ocean. By early 1943, nearly 100 trolled the main convoy routes. But it was not Britain's fate that finally prompted action, it was the fate of preparations for a second front in Europe. In January 1943, Allied senior staffs met in Casablanca to discuss future strategy and found that everything hinged on sorting out the Atlantic war. Their most important decision was to close the air gap in the mid-ocean. In a stroke, this would eliminate the surface maneuverability upon which the U-boats depended for their success. This would be done through an infusion of VLR (Very Long Range) aircraft—only fifty were needed, the equivalent of losses on the Ploesti raid alone—and by the provision of both small aircraft carriers and more radar-equipped escorts. It took months for the effects of those decisions to be felt, but the cards had been played.

While the resources were being mustered, losses to North Atlantic convoys spiked over the winter and especially in the first three weeks of March 1943. During that period, Ultra special intelligence failed completely and, as a result, 100 percent of trans-Atlantic convoys were intercepted by U-boats, fifty-four percent were attacked, and fully twenty-two percent of all shipping in those convoys was sunk.[23] There seemed to be no clear solution. There were too many U-boats to avoid, and too many to stop from swarming the escort and getting into the convoys. British oil supplies plummeted and some in Britain toyed with abandoning convoys

---

[23] Jürgen Rohwer, *The Critical Convoy Battles of March 1943: The Battle for HX229/SC122* (Annapolis: Naval Institute Press, 1977).

altogether. However, the seeds of Allied victory had already been sown. Just as shipping to and from Britain was now dangerously concentrated and vulnerable, so, too, were the U-boats. The mid-ocean was like a pond on the Serengeti late in the dry season: the predators and the prey were heavily concentrated and there was no place else left to go. In this instance, however, the predators were weak and the prey had the power to bite back.

In late March, Ultra intelligence came back on line just as the weather improved. In the days to follow, air and naval reinforcements arrived. In late April, command and control arrangements were fixed and, in the process, the British came in for the kill. Spring weather always improved things for North Atlantic convoys, with flatter seas and more daylight U-boats were easier to spot, especially with 10cm radar. The restoration of Ultra not only allowed convoys to be routed safely again, it also revealed the precarious morale of the U-boat fleet. Dönitz was now admonishing his reluctant captains to be brave in the face of strengthening naval and air escorts, and to press home their attacks. There was enough of this radio traffic for the British to smell blood in the water, and so the Admiralty moved swiftly to crush the U-boat fleet with a well-orchestrated offensive. While most convoys were routed safely away from the waiting packs, selected convoys were heavily reinforced and driven into the waiting submarines. Escort carriers and new support groups reinforced convoys at the crucial moment, just before contact was made, while air power descended on the waiting Wolf Pack. It was a battle German submariners could not win. In military terms, they had been "fixed," and were now ripe for defeat.

In April 1943, the British had to manage this offensive carefully. Operational control of convoys west of 35 degrees was still in American hands and they failed to see clearly the opportunity for a crushing defeat of the U-boats. Admiral Ernest J. King, for example, responded to the surge of Allied shipping losses in the mid-Atlantic in March with an appeal for concentration on safe and timely arrival. The British had other ideas, but in April they had to bide their time. In early March, the major Allied navies had met in Washington, at Canadian urging, to sort out the muddled command and control structure in the North Atlantic. The Canadians had been pushing for this for some time.[24] At one point in 1942, there were no less than nine separate national and service commands operating in the northwest Atlantic, while the U.S. Navy admiral at Argentia, Newfoundland, (who had virtually no ships of his own) exercised operational control over virtually the entire Canadian Navy. Meanwhile, convoys in the mid-ocean still changed overall operational control in the middle of their passage—and often in the midst of intense battle. The British wanted to reassert their control over mid-ocean escort operations, while the Canadians consolidated their own commands in the northwest

---

[24]   For the best discussion of the Washington Convoy Conference, see Douglas, Sarty, and Whitby, *No Higher Purpose,* ch. 11.

Atlantic and increasingly ignored the American admiral in notional command. The Washington Convoy Conference of March 1943 restructured command relationships and responsibilities in the North Atlantic for the balance of the war. As of 30 April 1943, the Northwest Atlantic became a Canadian Operational command, with which complete control of mid-ocean escort operations reverted to the British. The Americans retained strategic control west of the CHOP Line, but the struggle against the U-boats was once again a British Commonwealth campaign.

The new arrangements gave Western Approaches Command (WAC) operational control of the convoy system westward to the Grand Banks of Newfoundland (47 degrees west). Their first major battle, and one of the decisive convoy battles of the war, ONS 5, ran down the touch line from Greenland southward, just inside the British zone. In May, WAC abandoned safe and timely arrival of the convoy as a guiding principle and intensified the offensive. Two merchant ships lost for one U-boat killed was considered an acceptable rate of exchange. Operational staffs still picked their battles carefully, arranging for heavy naval and air reinforcement to join the convoy just before contact with the U-boats was made. Fairer weather and the arrival of even more resources, including enough VLR aircraft to eliminate the air gap, helped immensely. So, too, did the elimination of the need to coordinate all this with Washington. The offensive reached a devastating pitch in May when forty-seven U-boats were sunk. Mobile hunting and killing forces, including escort carriers and radar-equipped VLR aircraft, shifted from convoy to convoy. It was the U-boats which came to the killing ground, and it was German submariners—including Karl Dönitz's only son—who died.[25]

By the time this was all over, the mystique of the Wolf Pack was broken: 100 U-boats had been sunk in five months, nearly half of those in May alone. The offensive continued over the summer. Air power and hunter-killer groups, some of them U.S. Navy and all directed by superb intelligence, harried the U-boats wherever they appeared: transiting the Bay of Biscay, reaching to the depth of the Caribbean, or patrolling off the Azores. Dönitz was left with a massive fleet of outdated submarines which could not stay at sea safely, except perhaps while submerged. When he tried to renew the offensive in the fall with heavier anti-aircraft armament and new acoustic homing torpedoes, his U-boats suffered miserably. Air power swarmed the German submarines, which tried to fight it out on the surface and suffered further dreadful losses. Meanwhile, Canadians solved the riddle of the acoustic homing torpedo within hours of its first use during the battle for ONS 18/ON 202 in September. Even while the battle still raged in the mid-ocean, scientists in Halifax designed, tested, and distributed blueprints for the astonishingly simple "Canadian Anti-Acoustic Torpedo" (CAT) gear. Fifty sets of CAT gear were

---

[25]   See Marc Milner, *The U-Boat Hunters: The Royal Canadian Navy and the Offensive Against Germany's Submarines* (Toronto: University of Toronto Press, 1993), ch. 1, for a discussion of this topic.

waiting on the wharf in St. John's when the escorts of ONS 18/ON 202 arrived from the battle.[26]

Conclusion

The submarine problem lingered for the balance of the war. Finding U-boats and sinking them became harder as the war went on. Submariners became more wary and skilled at survival. The *Schnorkel,* introduced in 1944, helped, as did the sharp reduction in U-boat signal traffic. But U-boats became fugitives in the ocean, trying simply to complete a patrol safely. By 1944, Allied shipping losses were negligible.

By 1943, the Allies had more shipping, thanks to the defeat of the Wolf Packs, American production, and the opening of the Mediterranean, than they knew what to do with. Virtually all of the new ships were American, however, and the need to charter shipping from the U.S. cost the ailing British economy more than it could afford. The British and the Americans never did find common ground over the handling of merchant tonnage during the war, and it remained a sore point to the bitter end. By 1945, the British complained that American mismanagement of merchant shipping cost the Allies nine million tons in lost carrying capacity annually: more than losses to all causes in 1942 and triple the U.S.' war losses for the entire war.[27]

There is no indication that the shipping situation adversely affected the development of Allied strategy. In fact, quite the contrary. New merchant ship construction peaked as victory in the Atlantic and the Mediterranean was achieved in 1943, and also just as the great wave of new equipment and new American Army formations were getting ready to move overseas. Much of the latter was carried by special U.S. military convoys that went straight across the North Atlantic from New York and appears to have moved without loss. Operation Bolero, the build-up of forces in the UK for the assault on France, met its target. Overlord was launched in the

---

[26]   The Atlantic war literature remains fixated on the British solution to the acoustic torpedo, the "Foxer" towed noise maker. Foxer was a complex and heavy device that allowed two pipes to rattle together to draw the torpedo away from the ship. Royal Navy practice called for two Foxer gear to be streamed at the same time. Keeping them apart required minesweeping kites on very heavy cables on either quarter, and thirty minutes of hard work with davits and hoists to launch and a steam winch to recover. CAT gear was simply two five-foot-long 1.25-inch pipes fitted in brackets that allowed one pipe to rattle against the other, the brackets were attached to a light wire cable with a wire yoke. Launching CAT required one man to pick it up and throw it into the sea: recovery required a hand-winch. The U.S. Navy adopted CAT gear. See Milner, *The U-Boat Hunters,* pp. 72–76.

[27]   C. B. A. Behrens, *Merchant Shipping and the Demands of War* (London: HMSO, 1955), p. 415.

spring of 1944, and the vast weight of the Great Republic was soon swarming ashore in northwest Europe.

Allied victory in the north Atlantic in the spring of 1943 was, in the end, no hollow success. It did mark a turning point in both the war and in the development of modern anti-submarine warfare. It rendered obsolete virtually the entire U-boat fleet in a matter of weeks. The slaughter of German submariners in 1943 is stark testimony to the weakness of the weapon which Dönitz wielded: more rapier than cutlass. The Allied victory of 1943 was, as Corbett would describe it, one of the great dramatic moments of naval history. It would be idle to suggest that it was irrelevant, but it is not yet clear what, if anything, it did to influence the outcome of the war. Operation Bolero was already moving ahead, with comparatively fast trans-Atlantic military convoys under U.S. Navy escort (the UC-CU series). By the fall, the opening of the Mediterranean to Allied shipping and the sharing of the massive surge in new American construction (fourteen million tons in 1943) left the Allies, including the British, with a surfeit of tonnage. Indeed, the tonnage war had been lost in the fall of 1942, the British import crisis of 1942–43 was an issue of allocation. As with previous years, the bottlenecks in Allied strategic planning and execution remained elsewhere.

That said, the victory of 1943 had to be worked for. It was dramatic, and it was the culmination of a process that forced battle onto an enemy who was incapable of fighting it. The Admiralty understood that in the spring of 1943. While the Americans pleaded with them to guard the convoys and push them through, the British seized the moment, threw caution to the wind, and achieved a brilliant victory at sea. And as Corbett would have suspected and as Michael Salewski concluded decades ago, it probably did not matter to the outcome of the war. Sea power, even in the 20th century, was always about more than battles.

2

The View from the Top

Winston Churchill, British Grand Strategy, and the Battle of the Atlantic

Christopher M. Bell

In the second volume of his influential Second World War memoirs, Winston Churchill wrote that "The only thing that ever really frightened me during the war was the U-boat peril."[1] Britain's wartime prime minister provided another pithy statement on this subject in a subsequent volume. "The Battle of the Atlantic," he declared, "was the dominating factor all through the war. Never for one moment could we forget that everything happening elsewhere, on land, at sea, or in the air, depended ultimately on its outcome, and amid all other cares we viewed its changing fortunes day by day with hope or apprehension."[2] These are some of the most frequently quoted words from Churchill's memoirs, and for obvious reasons. They convey succinctly, and on unimpeachable authority, the importance of sea-borne trade to the Allied war effort, and the severity of the threat from Germany's U-boats. But "sound bites" do not necessarily make for good history, and these brief statements must be treated with caution. There is no doubt that Churchill was keenly aware of the importance of protecting Britain's maritime supply lines; and there were times when he was genuinely alarmed by the severity of Allied shipping losses. But as Prime Minister and Minister of Defence, Churchill took less interest in the day-to-day management of the anti-U-boat war than his memoirs suggest. There were only two periods in his premiership when he felt his personal intervention was necessary to avert a disaster. And even when heavy shipping losses compelled him to take notice, Churchill viewed the campaign through the lens of British grand strategy, which meant that he frequently differed from his naval advisers over the necessity of committing resources to mastering the U-boat threat. For Churchill, victory in the Atlantic campaign was never simply a question of achieving tactical superiority at sea, however desirable that might be. The most important challenge, as he saw it, was to ensure an adequate level of imports for

---

[1]   Winston S. Churchill, *The Second World War,* 6 vols. (London: Cassell, 1948–53), Vol. II, p. 529.

[2]   Ibid., Vol. V, p. 6.

Britain with the smallest possible commitment of resources to the Royal Navy and the Royal Air Force's Coastal Command. He was, therefore, prepared at times to suffer heavier-than-necessary shipping losses if doing so would free up resources for what he deemed "offensive" purposes, such as the dispatch of ground forces to North Africa or the strategic bombing campaign against Germany.

The First Phase (June 1940–July 1941)

Germany's rapid conquest of Norway and France in 1940 transformed the Battle of the Atlantic by providing Hitler with new bases from which his navy and air force could intensify their assault on Britain's maritime communications. In the summer of 1940, the long-term threat to British shipping and ports was overshadowed by the danger of invasion, which might have brought a decisive German victory long before the attack on British shipping could become serious. Churchill naturally focused on the most immediate threat to Britain's survival. To bolster Britain's defenses, he supported the Admiralty's decision to strip the Royal Navy's home fleet and the Atlantic convoys of destroyers, corvettes, and other light craft in order to maintain the strongest possible anti-invasion patrols along the south east coast of England. "All round the coasts," he told the War Cabinet in July, "were some hundreds of armed trawlers, motor-torpedo boats and mine-sweepers which could take part in the melee, if invasion were attempted." He was confident that these forces, supported if necessary by the heavy units of the home fleet, would make any German invasion "a most hazardous and even suicidal operation."[3] The anti-invasion patrols had one additional benefit that Churchill was eager to exploit. If the Navy could be counted on to keep the Germans away from Britain's shores, the British Isles could safely be denuded of land forces to allow for offensive operations in the Middle East.

From Churchill's perspective, this was too good an opportunity to pass up. Even as Britain's fortunes reached their lowest point in the summer of 1940, he was determined not to let British strategy become completely defensive. There were few opportunities, however, to strike directly at the Germans. Churchill was eager to launch amphibious raids along the coast of occupied Europe, although in the short-term these could be little more than an inconvenience to the enemy.[4] The Royal Air Force (RAF) would eventually provide the means to deliver powerful blows on the Continent, but this capability would also take time to develop. The

---

[3]   The National Archives, London (hereinafter TNA), Cabinet records (hereinafter CAB) 65/14/9, War Cabinet minutes (hereinafter WM) (40) 198, Confidential Annex (hereinafter CA), 9 July 1940. See also TNA, Admiralty records (hereinafter ADM) 205/6, Churchill to Generals Ironside and Dill, 10 July 1940; Churchill, *Second World War,* Vol. II, pp. 252–53.

[4]   Churchill's views on combined operations in 1940–41 are outlined in Christopher M. Bell, *Churchill and Sea Power* (Oxford: Oxford University Press, 2012), pp. 206–14.

best chance of scoring a meaningful victory against the Axis powers in 1940 was to concentrate on Italian forces in North Africa. With Germany actively preparing for an invasion, the dispatch of British troops and equipment to the Middle East was a bold step, and one that came at a price. Stripping the convoys of escorts resulted in a sharp increase in losses to U-boats during the second half of 1940, and even Churchill admitted that the shipping situation might eventually become critical. As he remarked to one of his private secretaries in August, the "startling shipping losses in the North West Approaches" contained "the seeds of something that might be mortal if allowed to get out of hand."[5] But this was a problem for the future. Britain was in a good position to absorb heavy shipping losses in 1940. Its merchant fleet was still the largest in the world, and its strength had recently been augmented by nearly two million tons of shipping acquired from Continental states overrun by the Germans.

Churchill was nevertheless eager to prevent the shipping situation getting out of hand. He encouraged the Admiralty to maintain a large and steady building program for escort vessels, and lobbied U.S. President Franklin D. Roosevelt for the loan of First World War-vintage U.S. destroyers.[6] When his initial approaches to the President met with no encouragement, Churchill briefly toyed with the idea of offering to exchange one of Britain's battleships for thirty-five American destroyers, an idea that was quickly shot down by the Admiralty.[7] But as long as there appeared to be any danger of invasion, Churchill was reluctant to divert warships from anti-invasion patrols to trade defense. His professional advisers took a more alarmist view of British shipping losses. In early October 1940, the Admiralty and the Chiefs of Staff Committee (COS) decided that additional escorts were urgently needed in the North Western Approaches. When this proposal was considered by the War Cabinet's Defence Committee (Operations) on 3 October, with Churchill in the chair, the Prime Minister's views prevailed. Even though the danger of invasion had decreased, the committee concluded that "we could afford for some time to come to sustain a heavy rate of sinkings, [but] we could not afford to give the enemy an opening to launch his attack [on land]." The continued movement of British land forces to the Middle East provided "an added reason," in their view, "for not unduly weakening ourselves at sea on the decisive front." The twelve destroyers and thirty anti-submarine trawlers the Admiralty wanted to divert to trade defense were therefore reduced to four and ten respectively.[8] On 15 October,

[5]   Colville diary, 30 August 1940: John Colville, *The Fringes of Power: 10 Downing Street Diaries, 1939–55* (New York: Norton, 1985), p. 232.

[6]   Philip Goodhart, *Fifty Ships that Saved the World* (London: Heinemann, 1965).

[7]   ADM 205/7, "Minutes of Meeting held in Upper War Room, Admiralty," 21 June 1940.

[8]   TNA, CAB 69/1, Defence Committee, Operations (hereinafter DO) (40) 33, 3 October 1940.

Churchill informed the War Cabinet that since German preparations for invasion were continuing, the Navy could not yet be allowed "to withdraw any more of their forces from the invasion front in order to strengthen shipping escorts in the north-west approaches."[9] It was only at the end of the month that the danger of invasion receded to the point that Churchill and the Defence Committee agreed "to reduce to a minimum the light naval forces allotted to anti-invasion duties."[10]

The diminished danger of invasion was also a green light to divert aircraft from attacks on invasion ports to strategic targets inside Germany. The RAF's Bomber Command offered virtually the only means at Churchill's disposal in 1940 to strike directly at Germany, and he was resolved to strengthen its capabilities, even at the expense of aircraft for the protection of merchant shipping. The Admiralty's first wartime attempt to secure a large increase in resources for Coastal Command in November 1940 was brusquely dismissed by the Prime Minister, who criticized the Admiralty in the Defence Committee for putting forward "extravagant demands ... which could not possibly be met at a time when we were engaged on the task of increasing our power to bomb Germany."[11] As long as the shipping situation was not actually critical, Churchill consistently opposed the diversion of air resources from strategic bombing to trade protection, which he regarded as a purely defensive task. It was nevertheless clear that the shipping situation could not be wholly neglected. By the beginning of 1941, German attacks on British trade and ports had significantly reduced import levels, which in turn threatened Britain's ability to sustain offensive operations in the Middle East.

Churchill was evidently satisfied that the Navy was making good use of its limited resources in the anti-U-boat war, and his efforts over the winter of 1940–1941 were concentrated on ensuring that optimal use was being made of Britain's shipping resources. His first major step was taken in January 1941 with the establishment of the Import Executive, under the chairmanship of the Minster of Supply.[12] Continuing heavy losses eventually convinced Churchill that more drastic measures were needed. He informed the War Cabinet on 27 February that "the highest possible priority must be given to the measures necessary to deal with the double menace to our shipping constituted by submarines and Focke-Wulf aircraft, acting in combination. Our effort against this renewed danger must, for the moment, be our supreme exertion."[13] On 6 March, Churchill issued his famous "Battle of the Atlantic" directive outlining various measures that he believed would improve the

---

[9]   CAB 65/9/33, WM (40) 271, 15 October 1940.

[10]   CAB 69/1, DO (40) 39th meeting, 31 October 1940; F. H. Hinsley et al., *British Intelligence in the Second World War*, 5 vols. (London: HMSO, 1979–90), Vol. I, pp. 188–90.

[11]   CAB 69/1, DO (40) 40, 5 November 1940.

[12]   Churchill, *Second World War*, Vol. II, pp. 532–34, Vol. III, pp. 98–102.

[13]   CAB 65/17/21, WM (41) 21, 27 February 1941.

situation.[14] To protect convoys from long-range German aircraft, he directed that "extreme priority" be given to fitting out merchant ships to carry fighter aircraft. Coastal Command's resources would be concentrated in the vital North Western Approaches, and both Fighter Command and Bomber Command were expected to provide support on Britain's east coast. Priority was also given to the provision of anti-aircraft guns to merchant ships, and the strengthening of anti-aircraft defenses at Britain's main western ports. To obtain the best results from Britain's merchant fleet, Churchill called for a drastic reduction in the amount of shipping awaiting repair, a faster turn-round time for ships in port at home and abroad, and a possible reduction in the minimum speed necessary for ships allowed to travel outside convoy.[15]

Churchill also created a new Cabinet sub-committee, the Battle of the Atlantic Committee, with himself as chair, to bring together the departments and individuals most concerned with the shipping and supply situation.[16] Over the next few months, the Committee achieved some notable successes. By July 1941, the amount of shipping requiring repair had been decreased by nearly a million tons; the turn-round time of merchant ships was significantly reduced; and congestion in British ports was brought under control. Other measures were less successful. Under pressure from Churchill, and against the advice of the Admiralty, ships capable of sailing at twelve knots or more were allowed to travel independently starting in March 1941. This resulted in increased losses, however, and after reviewing the Admiralty's statistics it was decided in June that the lower limit for convoy should be increased to fifteen knots.[17] The plan to support convoys with merchant ships capable of launching fighter aircraft at sea, known as Catapult Aircraft Merchantmen, also fell far short of expectations. The first ships equipped with catapults entered service at the end of April 1941, but disagreement soon emerged over how the vessels should be employed. Churchill wanted them dedicated to protecting convoys in waters beyond the range of land-based air cover, even if it meant they would no longer carry cargoes to British ports. When the Committee decided that these vessels should continue to operate as regular merchant ships, Churchill quickly lost interest in the project.[18]

---

[14]   Churchill, *Second World War*, Vol. III, p. 106; see also his secret session speech to the House of Commons, 25 June 1941, Robert Rhodes James, ed., *Winston S. Churchill: His Complete Speeches*, 8 vols. (New York: Chelsea House, 1974), Vol. VI, p. 6434.

[15]   CAB 86/1, Churchill directive, "The Battle of the Atlantic," 6 March 1941; Churchill, *Second World War*, Vol. III, pp. 107–09; Stephen Roskill, *The War at Sea*, 3 vols. (London: HMSO, 1954–61), Vol. I, pp. 609–11.

[16]   On the work of the Committee, see Max Schoenfeld, "Winston Churchill as War Manager: The Battle of the Atlantic Committee, 1941," *Military Affairs* 52 (1988).

[17]   CAB 86/1, Battle of the Atlantic Committee (41) 10th meeting, 5 June 1941; CAB 65/18/40, WM (41) 61, 19 June 1941.

[18]   Schoenfeld, "Churchill as War Manager," pp. 123–25.

Churchill also lobbied for additional assistance from the United States. His suggestion that American warships and aircraft should maintain a presence in the central Atlantic, where Britain was as yet unable to provide convoy escorts, was rewarded in April 1941 when Roosevelt informed him that the United States would extend its patrol areas in the north Atlantic and report any Axis raiders operating west of 25°.[19] Britain's other pressing need at this time—one that would become increasingly urgent—was for new merchant ships. Britain's shipbuilding industry was incapable of replacing all the vessels being sunk by the Germans. According to historian Kevin Smith, by June 1941 Britain had lost 4,491,000 tons of shipping, only thirty percent of which had been replaced by new construction.[20] To make good this deficit, Churchill believed it would be necessary to harness the American shipbuilding industry to the British war effort. "Nothing is of more importance than the shipping problem," he wrote to the First Lord of the Admiralty on 10 March, "and the key to its solution lies largely in America."[21] To increase the supply of American shipping, Churchill dispatched a special mission to Washington in March 1941 under Sir Arthur Salter to bring home to the Roosevelt administration the seriousness of Britain's import situation. "The battle of the Atlantic has begun," he wrote to Salter before his departure. "The issue may well depend on the speed with which our resources to combat the menace to our communications with the Western Hemisphere are supplemented by those of the United States of America."[22]

At the time, the prospects for American assistance looked good. Churchill reported to the War Cabinet on 17 March that John Winant, the American ambassador, and Averell Harriman, Roosevelt's special envoy, had informed him that the United States was planning "a very big merchant shipbuilding programme, which would mature in 1942."[23] Churchill was confident that Britain would eventually benefit from the expansion of the United States' shipbuilding industry, so much so that on 27 March he ordered a reduction in British merchant ship construction for the coming year in order to concentrate more domestic resources on repairing ships. "It is to the United States building that we must look for relief in 1942," he

---

[19]   Roosevelt to Churchill, 11 April 1941, Warren Kimball, ed., *Churchill and Roosevelt: The Complete Correspondence,* 3 vols. (Princeton: Princeton University Press, 1984), Vol. I, pp. 166–67.

[20]   Kevin Smith, *Conflict Over Convoys: Anglo-American Logistics Diplomacy in the Second World War* (Cambridge: Cambridge University Press, 1996), p. 65.

[21]   Churchill College Archives Centre, Cambridge, Churchill papers (hereinafter CHAR) 20/21B/134, Churchill to A. V. Alexander, 10 March 1941.

[22]   CHAR 20/21B/143–45, Churchill to Salter, 12 March 1941.

[23]   CAB 65/18/8, WM (41) 29, 17 March 1941.

announced.[24] These hopes were fueled on 9 May when Salter reported that Roosevelt had decided to increase U.S. "shipbuilding to a level at which it will enable the enemy's current destruction to be outmatched before the end of the next year." Salter predicted that by the latter half of 1942, U.S. production alone, which then stood at an annual rate of 800,000 GRT, would reach a rate equivalent to four million tons per annum. British, Canadian, and American output combined was expected to reach 5¾ million GRT.[25] Roosevelt himself was even more optimistic. On 25 June, he informed Churchill that he was asking Congress to increase U.S. merchant ship production to "a minimum of five to five and [a] half million tons in 1942 and seven million tons in 1943."[26]

Production on this scale would alleviate most, if not all, of Britain's shipping problems. When Churchill provided a secret session of the House of Commons with a review of the Battle of the Atlantic on 25 June 1941, he noted that even with the heavy shipping losses suffered between March and June, Britain was still on track to meet the government's import target of thirty-one million tons in the coming year.[27] He soon had additional grounds for optimism. During the second half of 1941, shipping losses decreased sharply. Between February and June, an average of 125 ships had been lost each month. From July to November, the figure was 50.4.[28] There were numerous factors that contributed to the sudden improvement, including increases in the number of escort vessels, improved equipment and training, the growing effectiveness of Coastal Command aircraft, a decrease in the number of ships sailing independently, and intelligence breakthroughs that

---

[24]   TNA, CAB 66/15/42, War Cabinet paper (hereinafter WP) (41) 69, Churchill directive, "Naval Programme 1941," 27 March 1941. The output of new merchant ships for 1942 had been set at 1,250,000 tons. Churchill now directed that the figure be changed to 1,100,000, and that "we should not at the present time proceed with any merchant vessels which cannot be completed by the end of 1941."

[25]   TNA, Ministry of Transport records (hereinafter MT) 59/2206, Salter to Churchill, 9 May 1941. See also Churchill to Wendell Willkie (unsent), 19 May 1941, Kimball, ed., *Churchill and Roosevelt,* Vol. I, pp. 189–90.

[26]   Roosevelt to Churchill, 25 June 1941, Kimball, ed., *Churchill and Roosevelt,* Vol. I, p. 212. These predictions continued to climb. In his 6 January 1942 State of the Union address, Roosevelt announced the construction of "merchant ships so rapidly that in this year, 1942, we shall build 6,000,000 deadweight tons as compared with a 1941 completed production of 1,100,000 . . . so that next year, 1943, we shall build 10,000,000 tons of shipping." David Kohnen, "Commander in Chief, U.S. Navy: Reconsidering Ernest J. King and his Headquarters of the Second World War," Ph.D. dissertation, King's College London, 2013, p. 34.

[27]   Speech to the House of Commons, 25 June 1941, Rhodes James, ed., *Complete Speeches,* Vol. VI, p. 6444.

[28]   Eric J. Grove, ed., *The Defeat of the Enemy Attack upon Shipping, 1939–1945: A Revised Edition of the Naval Staff History* (Aldershot: Ashgate/Navy Records Society, 1997), Vol. 1B, table 13.

allowed, at least temporarily, the decryption of U-boat signals. The drop in ship-ping losses was all the more remarkable in view of the large expansion of the Ger-man U-boat fleet in 1941. Taken together, these developments appear to have convinced Churchill that the U-boat threat had been permanently reduced to manageable proportions. In August 1941, he told General Hastings Ismay that "he was inclined to think that the corner had been turned in the Battle of the Atlantic and that the drop in the rate of sinkings might be maintained."[29]

The Second Phase (July 1941–May 1943)

Churchill's optimism was not shared by the Admiralty, which correctly assumed that the U-boat threat was still far from mastered. Captain A. J. Power, an Assistant Chief of Naval Staff, warned Admiral Sir Dudley Pound, the First Sea Lord, in August 1941 that "Any suggestion that the Battle of the Atlantic has turned the cor-ner in our favour is not supported by facts." Power attributed the recent decline in shipping losses primarily to the availability of Ultra intelligence, which could be cut off at any time. In his view, which proved to be accurate, Britain had "not yet even felt the full weight of [Germany's] offensive against our trade. To relax our preparations at the present moment is courting disaster."[30] In the months to come, Pound and A. V. Alexander, the First Lord of the Admiralty, lobbied for more escort vessels, long-range aircraft, and auxiliary aircraft carriers to provide air cover to convoys. The greatest challenge was obtaining additional aircraft for Coastal Com-mand. Once the first crisis in the Battle of the Atlantic had passed, Churchill decided that Britain's air resources should be concentrated as far as possible on the bombing of Germany. During the latter half of 1941, he sought on several occa-sions to divert long-range aircraft, including American-built B-24 Liberators, from Coastal Command to Bomber Command.

The distribution of long-range aircraft became the subject of heated debate between the Admiralty and the Air Ministry beginning in February 1942, when the latter proposed to expand its strategic bombing campaign against Germany.[31] This would entail an immediate reduction in the number of heavy bombers target-ing enemy warships at Brest, and the Admiralty rightly feared that fewer aircraft would be allocated to the war at sea over the long term if the Air Ministry's plans were implemented. The First Lord advised the Defence Committee on 14 February that priority should be given instead to meeting the Navy's air needs. He proposed strengthening Coastal Command with six and a half Wellington squadrons from Bomber Command, and eighty-one new long-range bombers (either B-17 Flying

---

[29] ADM 205/8, Ismay to Portal, 20 August 1941.

[30] ADM 205/8, Power to Pound, 21 August 1941; Roskill, *War at Sea*, Vol. I, p. 467.

[31] CAB 69/4, DO (42) 14, Sinclair memorandum, "Bombing Policy," 9 February 1942.

Fortresses or B-24 Liberators) from the United States. The Admiralty also hoped to divert two squadrons from Bomber Command to protect communications in the Indian Ocean.[32] When the Air Ministry objected to these proposals, Pound prepared a more forceful memorandum for the Defence Committee. "If we lose the war at sea," he wrote on 5 March, "we lose the war." The First Sea Lord now proposed an even more substantial increase in Coastal Command's strength: from 519 aircraft to 1,940.[33]

The RAF mounted a determined opposition. Senior air force officers believed that the protection of maritime communications was an inherently defensive task that should absorb as few resources as possible, while strategic bombing, a purely "offensive" measure, was regarded as the most effective means to strike at the heart of German power.[34] Air Marshal Sir Arthur Harris, the Air Officer Commanding-in-Chief (AOC-in-C) Bomber Command, was perhaps the most extreme advocate of this viewpoint. In June 1942, he confidently predicted that the concentration of British air resources on strategic bombing would knock Germany "out of the War in a matter of months." Coastal Command, he charged, was "merely an obstacle to victory."[35] Air Marshal Sir Charles Portal, the Chief of the Air Staff, took a more moderate view, but still deprecated the diversion of aircraft to what were derisively labeled "defensive" tasks. The Air Ministry's priorities were outlined in a memorandum for the Defence Committee by Sir Archibald Sinclair, the Secretary of State for Air, who insisted that the Admiralty's proposed diversion of resources from Bomber Command "to an uneconomical defensive role would be unsound at any time": "It would be doubly so now when we are about to launch a bombing offensive with the aid of a new technique [the navigational aid 'Gee'] of which we have high expectations and which will enable us to deliver a heavy and concentrated blow against Germany at a moment when German morale is low and when the Russians are in great need of our assistance."[36]

---

[32]   CAB 69/4, DO (42) 15, Admiralty memorandum, "Bombing Policy," 14 February 1942.

[33]   CAB 69/4, DO (42) 23, Pound memorandum, "Air Requirements for the Successful Prosecution of the War at Sea," 5 March 1942.

[34]   Duncan Redford, "Inter- and Intra-Service Rivalries in the Battle of the Atlantic," *The Journal of Strategic Studies* 32:6 (December 2009), pp. 918–24.

[35]   Harris to Churchill, 17 June 1942, cited in Charles Webster and Noble Frankland, *The Strategic Air Offensive Against Germany, 1939–1945*, 4 vols. (London: HMSO, 1961), Vol. I, pp. 340–41. For Harris' views, see also CAB 66/28/4, WP (42) 374, "Note by Air Marshal Sir Arthur Harris, K.C.B., O.B.E., A.F.C., on the Role and Work of Bomber Command," 28 June 1942.

[36]   CAB 69/4, DO (42) 24, Sinclair memorandum, 8 March 1942; Webster and Frankland, *Strategic Air Offensive*, Vol. I, p. 326; J. R. M. Butler et al., *Grand Strategy*, 6 vols. (London: HMSO, 1964), Vol. III, Part 2, p. 535.

This line of argument appealed strongly to Churchill's own offensive instincts. He told the Defence Committee on 18 March that "the bombing of Germany was the only offensive action we could take and he hoped that, in the next few months, we should give the Germans treatment on a scale that they had never received before."[37] He did not, however, subscribe to the views of those like Harris who believed that strategic bombing alone could achieve decisive results. In September 1941, for example, he had warned Portal that it was "very disputable whether bombing by itself will be a decisive factor in the present war. . . . The most we can say is that it will be a heavy and, I trust, a seriously increasing annoyance."[38] The RAF's heavy losses and inability to hit its targets had undermined Churchill's faith in the bomber offensive in the autumn of 1941, but his optimism revived early the following year after the Air Ministry's bold predictions about the impact of an expanded bomber offensive were endorsed by his close friend and scientific adviser, Lord Cherwell. Cherwell's views, though notoriously erratic, were nevertheless highly regarded by Churchill. An influential memorandum by Cherwell in late March 1942 drastically overestimated the impact that "dehousing" would have on German morale. "Investigation seems to show," he wrote, "that having one's house demolished is most damaging to morale. People seem to mind it more than having their friends or even relatives killed."

Cherwell estimated that with a greatly expanded force of 10,000 heavy bombers, Bomber Command could render roughly a third of the German population homeless by the middle of 1943. "There seems little doubt," he concluded, "this would break the spirit of the people."[39] Even though these calculations were badly flawed, Churchill's support for strategic bombing steadily increased over the next few months.[40] Portal noted in June 1942 that the Prime Minister was "subconsciously but no less thoroughly aware of the principle that the minimum necessary force should be put into the defensive and the maximum possible into the offensive."[41] However, Churchill was still not convinced that bombing alone could

---

[37]   CAB 69/4, DO (42) 8, 18 March 1942.

[38]   Churchill to Portal, 27 September 1941, Martin Gilbert, ed., *The Churchill War Papers*, 3 vols. (New York: Norton, 1993–2001) (hereinafter CWP), Vol. III, p. 1270; see also Churchill to Portal, 7 October 1941, CWP, Vol. III, pp. 1313–14.

[39]   TNA, Prime Minister's office records (hereinafter PREM) 3/11/4, Cherwell to WSC, 30 March 1942; Webster and Frankland, *Strategic Air Offensive*, Vol. I, pp. 331–32.

[40]   On Cherwell's faulty calculations, see P. M. S. Blackett, *Studies of War* (Edinburgh: Oliver & Boyd, 1962), pp. 223–28; Paul Crook, "The Case against Area Bombing," in Peter Hore, ed., *Patrick Blackett: Sailor, Scientist and Socialist* (London: Frank Cass, 2003), pp. 167–86; Stephen Budiansky, *Blackett's War* (New York: Alfred A. Knopf, 2013), pp. 200–02.

[41]   Christ Church Library, Oxford, Portal papers, Portal to Joubert, 11 June 1942.

win the war. The campaign, he wrote to Sinclair, "is not decisive, but better than doing nothing, and indeed is a formidable method of injuring the enemy."[42]

With Churchill firmly committed to strategic bombing, Coastal Command continued to go short of resources. In mid-April, the Air Ministry agreed to transfer four squadrons from Bomber Command to Coastal Command, but this was far short of what the Admiralty believed was necessary to meet its essential needs. Pound and Alexander continued to press for the allocation of more aircraft to trade defense in the weeks that followed, but Churchill and the Air Ministry were unwilling to budge. A meeting of naval commanders-in-chief at the Admiralty on 1 June revealed how frustrated naval leaders had become with inadequate air support. Admiral Tovey, C-in-C of the Royal Navy's home fleet, maintained that the "situation at sea was now so grave that the time had come for a stand to be made, even if this led to Their Lordships [of the Admiralty] taking the extreme step of resignation. I was supported in my contention by Admiral of the Fleet Sir Charles Forbes and Admiral Sir Andrew Cunningham."[43]

With service opinion demanding action, Pound prepared to take another stand, this time in the COS. In a memorandum dated 16 June, the First Sea Lord drew his colleagues' attention to recent heavy shipping losses, which averaged over 677,000 tons per month during the previous three months. Losses were still outstripping new construction, he warned, and Germany was building twenty new U-boats each month. An expanded shipbuilding effort later in the year might eventually cover these losses, he conceded, but this could not be guaranteed if the rate of sinkings also increased. And even if losses could be replaced with new construction, the heavy drain this effort imposed on Allied resources would threaten their offensive plans for 1943. The allocation of additional aircraft for trade protection was therefore a matter of "supreme urgency."[44] At a meeting of the COS the same day, Pound argued that the bombing of Germany should continue, but "that priority should now be given to the improvement of our position at sea which, in his opinion, was more vital and of greater urgency."[45]

These efforts succeeded in forcing the Air Ministry to reopen the question of air support for the war at sea. Direct negotiations with the Admiralty produced a compromise proposal to transfer two Lancaster squadrons from Bomber Command to Coastal Command, but this arrangement was flatly rejected by Portal,

---

[42]   Churchill to Sinclair and Portal, 13 March 1942, Ian Hunter, ed., *Winston and Archie: The Letters of Sir Archibald Sinclair and Winston S. Churchill, 1915–1960* (London: Politico's, 2005), p. 344.

[43]   Tovey dispatch, 30 June 1942, Grove, ed., *Defeat of Enemy Attack,* p. 354; see also the amended minutes of this meeting, ADM 205/23.

[44]   TNA, CAB 80/63, Chiefs of Staff Committee (hereinafter COS) (42) 171(O), Pound memorandum, "The Bombing of Germany," 16 June 1942.

[45]   ADM 205/15, COS (42) 180, 16 June 1942.

Cherwell, and Churchill.[46] Not surprisingly, the final agreement that emerged in mid-July made only modest concessions to the Navy. No Bomber Command squadrons were to be transferred to Coastal Command, although the latter's strength would be expanded gradually through the allocation of new American-built Fortresses and Liberators. To meet the Admiralty's immediate requirements, Bomber Command would temporarily divert some of its Whitley and Lancaster bombers for long-range patrols in the Bay of Biscay. Portal estimated that Bomber Command aircraft would make an average of fifty sorties a week in support of the war at sea, although he warned that the precise number would fluctuate from week to week.[47]

Opinion within the Admiralty was mixed. P. M. S. Blackett, the Admiralty's Chief Adviser on Operational Research, and Captain George Creasy, Director of the Anti-Submarine Warfare Division, allowed that this deal "would provide a substantial increase over our present A/S [anti-submarine] air effort," but also noted that it would still fall "a long way below" the original compromise worked out with the Air Ministry, "which, in our view, is the absolute minimum required to cope with the present critical position."[48] However, this was clearly the best deal the Admiralty could expect. Rear Admiral Patrick Brind, Assistant Chief of the Naval Staff (Home), urged Pound to take it. In his opinion, the Admiralty had won two important admissions from Portal and the Air Ministry: that the RAF had an obligation to assist the Navy in securing the nation's maritime communications, and that immediate assistance was required. He was confident, moreover, that the CAS (Chief of the Air Staff (Portal)) was genuinely committed to making the new arrangement work. Perhaps most tellingly, he observed that by "accepting this proposal we shall get going at once without any further arguments."[49] Pound was also clearly eager to move on. He informed senior members of the Naval Staff a few days later that "Having come to an agreement with CAS about the air for War at Sea, I have not the slightest intention of asking for further help at the present time."[50] The First Sea Lord put a positive spin on the deal he had accepted. Writing to a senior admiral on 21 July, Pound claimed "that the battle over the Air, which

[46]   CAB 80/37, COS (42) 332, memorandum by Brind and Slessor, "General Policy for the Employment of Aircraft," 2 July 1942; PREM 3/97, WSC minute to Alexander, Sinclair, 14 July 1942; ADM 205/24, Chief of the Air Staff (Portal) draft memorandum, "Provision of Long Range Aircraft for Anti-Submarine Patrols," 9 July 1942.

[47]   CAB 66/26/32, WP (42) 302, COS memorandum, "Provision of Aircraft for the War at Sea," 18 July 1942; Correlli Barnett, *Engage the Enemy More Closely* (New York: Norton, 1991), pp. 467–68.

[48]   ADM 205/14, Blackett and Creasy memorandum, 10 July 1942.

[49]   ADM 205/24, Brind to Pound, 12 July 1942.

[50]   ADM 205/24, Pound minute to VCNS, ACNS(F) and ACNS(H), 23 July 1942.

has been in progress for several months, has now been concluded satisfactorily from our point of view." He admitted that the only improvement in the short-term would be in the number of aircraft available for Biscay patrols, but, like Brind, he emphasized that the Admiralty had won important concessions of principle. "There has," he wrote, "been a real change in heart on the part of the Air Ministry, which has possibly been brought about by the general feeling that the sea war was not getting its fair share. However, whatever may be the reason, I feel that it is genuine."[51]

Although Churchill accepted the Air Ministry-Admiralty deal, he was eager to put a halt to the continuous demands being made on Bomber Command's resources. This concern emerged clearly in a lengthy memorandum he submitted to the War Cabinet on 21 July outlining his views on Britain's strategic priorities.[52] Churchill again rejected the idea that strategic bombing alone could win the war, as Harris and others argued, and he was unwilling to give bombing absolute priority. But he was determined not to divert any more aircraft from Bomber Command than were absolutely necessary to meet the minimum essential demands of either the Army or the Navy. The bomber offensive, he wrote, must be given priority "second only to the largest military operations which can be conducted on the Continent until [Germany's] war-will is broken. Renewed, intense efforts should be made by the Allies to develop during the winter and onwards ever-growing, ever more accurate and ever more far-ranging Bomber attacks on Germany. In this way alone can we prepare the conditions which will be favourable to the major military operations on which we are resolved."

Churchill was not oblivious, however, to the potential impact of these priorities on British imports. Depriving Coastal Command of long-range aircraft for the Battle of the Atlantic would inevitably mean heavier shipping losses. "It might," he wrote, "be true to say that the issue of the war depends on whether Hitler's U-boat attack on Allied tonnage, or the increase and application of Allied Air power, reach their full fruition first." The risk was a carefully calculated one. Churchill's decision to support Bomber Command over Coastal Command ultimately was based on three assumptions. First, that strategic bombing would be more effective than it actually was. Second, that the United States would be able and willing to supply enough new merchant shipping tonnage to meet both American and British needs. As in 1941, Churchill was willing to rely on new construction to replace heavy shipping losses. "There is no reason," he wrote, "to assume that we cannot get through the present year or that the tonnage position in 1943 will not steadily improve as a result of the prodigious American shipbuilding." The difficulty with this approach, of course, was that most of the necessary ships would be built by the

---

[51]   ADM 205/22A, Pound to Drax, 21 July 1942.

[52]   CAB 66/26/41, WP (42) 311, WSC memorandum, "A Review of the War Position," 21 July 1942; Churchill, *Second World War*, Vol. IV, pp. 781–84.

United States rather than Britain. It was therefore essential, Churchill concluded, "not to let our position deteriorate to an unmanageable degree before we have a clear understanding with the United States as to the future. With this object we must now in the next few weeks come to a solemn compact, almost a treaty, with the United States about the share of their new building we are to get in 1943 and 1944." Churchill's third assumption was that air resources could be shifted to the war at sea in time to avert a disaster in the event that the import situation did start to become critical. Viewed from this perspective, the most likely result of Churchill's priorities would be tighter rationing for the British people and the depletion of existing stocks. In Churchill's opinion, this was a reasonable price to pay to intensify the air campaign against Germany, an investment that could potentially pay huge dividends.

Churchill was eager, therefore, to do more than just stop the drain of aircraft from strategic bombing. On 17 September, he instructed Sinclair and Portal that Bomber Command's operational strength should be increased from thirty-two squadrons to fifty squadrons by the end of 1942. Once a concrete plan had been developed by the Air Ministry, he proposed to take it to the War Cabinet for approval. "It will then become binding," he noted, and for the balance of the year would have "priority over every other competing claim."[53] While the Air Staff was developing expansion plans, the Admiralty's frustration continued to mount. As the Deputy First Sea Lord observed on 28 September, "the feeling throughout the Navy is that we are not getting a fair deal and that without this we may well lose the war."[54] Unaware of the Prime Minister's intention to expand Bomber Command, the Naval Staff launched a new appeal for a greater share of the nation's resources. On 5 October, Pound submitted a memorandum to the Defence Committee (Supply) outlining the Admiralty's case. At present, he noted, "the proportion of the National effort devoted to the Navy is much smaller than that to the sister Services." Britain had therefore

> lost a measure of control over the sea communications. This has already had, and is having a far-reaching effect not only on the maintenance of the United Kingdom but on our ability to take the offensive. It is manifesting itself in the realms of supply and production, our blockade of the enemy, our control over the sources of raw materials and our freedom to dispose all our forces at will. In fact, we have reached the point at which we are unable to carry out concurrently those operations which the present state of the war so urgently demands.

---

[53]   CAB 66/30/11, WP (42) 481, "Strength of Bomber Command."

[54]   ADM 205/15, Draft memorandum by Admiral Sir Charles Kennedy-Purvis, 28 September 1942.

Pound warned that the whole basis of British grand strategy was in danger of col-lapsing: "Unless steps are taken urgently to relieve the situation in which the Navy finds itself, our ability to secure our sea communications and hence to win the war, regardless of the type of offensive chosen, will be impaired."[55]

The First Sea Lord's memorandum recommended a far-reaching reallocation of the nation's manpower and industrial resources in order to increase the Navy's supply of warships and long-range aircraft for the war at sea.[56] Churchill was unmoved. "Everyone knows that the U-boat menace remains our greatest danger," he wrote to Pound on 19 October. But even though he was "certainly prepared to assist you in specific needs which you state," he doubted "very much whether the overriding priorities which you ask for . . . should be accorded."[57] This could hardly have come as a surprise to the Admiralty, as Churchill had three days earlier revealed his plans to expand Bomber Command.[58] Once again, naval leaders were dismayed. Brind advised Pound that the proposed expansion of Bomber Com-mand, which would include the transfer of two squadrons from Coastal Com-mand, should "be resisted with all the vigour at the disposal of the Admiralty." He added, "It seems there can be no conception of what is being undertaken now at sea. Far from accepting any reduction in Coastal Command it is essential that our maritime aircraft should be strongly reinforced with the right sort of aircraft to meet the new circumstances in the Atlantic and Mediterranean."[59] Pound wrote to the Prime Minister on 25 October to plead the Navy's case one more time. "[T]he situation generally at sea is so serious," he warned, "that the Cabinet should be informed and the urgency of the Navy's needs re-assessed."[60]

Churchill had no intention of being deflected from his plans. The previous day he had submitted a new memorandum to the War Cabinet justifying the immediate expansion of Bomber Command. Again, he was willing to concede the seriousness of the situation at sea. "There preys upon us," he wrote, "as the greatest danger to the United Nations, and particularly to our Island, the U-boat attack." He nevertheless rejected the Admiralty's recommendations: "The Navy call for greater assistance from the Air. I am proposing to my colleagues that we try for the present to obtain this extra assistance mainly from the United States, and that we encroach as little as possible upon our Bomber effort against Germany, which is of peculiar importance during these winter months. I have, on the contrary, asked for an

---

[55]   CAB 70/5, DO (S) (42) 88, Pound memorandum, "The Needs of the Navy," 5 October 1942.

[56]   Ibid.

[57]   ADM 205/15, Churchill to Pound, 19 October 1942.

[58]   CAB 80/65, COS (42) 317 (O), "Strength of Bomber Command," 16 October 1942.

[59]   ADM 205/26, Brind to Pound, 18 October 1942.

[60]   ADM 205/15, Pound to WSC, 25 October 1942.

increase in the Bomber effort, rising to 50 squadrons by the end of the year. Thereafter our bombing power will increase through the maturing of production." Churchill went on to reassure his colleagues that air resources could be reallocated to the war at sea if the situation continued to decline. "It may be," he wrote, "that early in 1943 we shall have to damp down the Bomber offensive against Germany in order to meet the stress and peril of the U-boat war. I hope and trust not, but by then it will be possible at any rate to peg our bomber offensive at a higher level than at present. The issue is not one of principle, but of emphasis. At present, in spite of U-boat losses, the Bomber offensive should have first place in our air effort."[61]

Remarkably, this commitment to strategic bombing was made even as shipping losses continued to increase and the import situation deteriorated. By October 1942, Churchill had to admit that it would be unwise to count on the American shipbuilding industry acting as a sort of safety net for British imports. When the United States entered the war in December 1941, British and American leaders had agreed that their shipping resources should be pooled and allocated according to need by a Combined Shipping Adjustment Board.[62] This should have guaranteed that Britain's needs would automatically be met, but American leaders had not anticipated the heavy demands that global war would place on American shipping resources. The United States' armed forces soon began to monopolize the new tonnage that British leaders were counting on, and by mid-1942 alarm bells were beginning to sound in Whitehall. The government's interdepartmental Shipping Committee had calculated in June 1942 that without substantial American assistance, British stocks might be exhausted within a year.[63] When the War Cabinet discussed this problem on 28 July, Churchill set Britain's "irreducible minima" for imports at twenty-five million tons in 1942, and twenty-seven million tons in 1943.[64] But in the months that followed, British diplomats were unable to secure a firm commitment from the United States to meet these requirements, and by late October it was clear that the minimum figures set by Churchill in July were unlikely to be met.[65] The Shipping Committee advised the War Cabinet that even if existing

---

[61]   CAB 66/30/13, WP (42) 483, Churchill memorandum, "Policy for the Conduct of the War," 24 October 1942. Churchill made a similar comment to the COS a day earlier, noting that "It might, of course, be necessary, if sinkings became bad, to postpone the still greater expansion plan for Bomber Command in 1943 by diverting, early in the year, added resources to Coastal Command," CAB 79/23, COS (42) 297th meeting, 23 October 1942.

[62]   Smith, *Conflict over Convoys*, pp. 68–70; C. B. A. Behrens, *Merchant Shipping and the Demands of War* (London: HMSO and Longmans, Green and Co., 1955), pp. 287–88.

[63]   Behrens, *Merchant Shipping*, pp. 304–06.

[64]   CAB 65/27/14, WM (42) 98, 28 July 1942.

[65]   Smith, *Conflict over Convoys*, pp. 91–96.

stocks were run down by four million tons in the first half of 1943 as planned, Britain would still need a massive infusion of shipping from the United States to meet its minimum needs.[66]

The expansion of Bomber Command was only viable as long as Churchill could avert, or at the very least delay, an import crisis. He took two important steps to accomplish this. First, he stepped up British efforts to obtain a "solemn compact" with the United States over the allocation of new shipping. In early November 1942, a new emissary, Lord Lyttelton, was dispatched to Washington to secure for Britain a greater share of merchant ships and escort vessels from American shipyards. Second, Churchill resurrected the Battle of the Atlantic Committee. This body, now renamed the Anti-U-Boat Warfare Committee, began meeting weekly on 4 November with Churchill as chair. The goal, once again, was to bring together the departments with a stake in the Battle of the Atlantic in order to identify and expedite measures to improve the situation at sea. However, this did not mean that the war against the U-boats was now being given the highest priority. At the Committee's first meeting, Churchill acknowledged that additional air support would be required to deal with the U-boats, but he warned those present that "he was most anxious that this should not be achieved at the expense of our night-bombing effort against Germany." In particular, he gave notice that Bomber Command's Lancaster bombers were off limits. This meant that additional air support could only come from American-built aircraft deemed "unsuitable for night-bombing."[67]

Churchill himself had no strong views on what should be done. His suggestions were limited to strengthening convoy escorts and assigning fast merchant ships, which still sailed independently, to convoys for added protection. The Admiralty had a much clearer idea of what was needed. With the return of the U-boats to the mid-Atlantic in mid-1942, the most serious hole remaining in Allied defenses was the "air gap" south of Greenland, where air cover could seldom be provided to convoys. German "wolf packs" could operate on the surface in this area with considerable freedom, which greatly increased their effectiveness. As Pound told the Anti-U-Boat Warfare [AU] Committee, "there was a blind spot in the centre of the North Atlantic where no air cover was provided, and it was here that our heaviest losses occurred."[68] When this problem first developed in July 1942, the Admiralty and Coastal Command had hoped that small aircraft carriers, known as escort carriers, would be capable of providing convoys with a mobile "air umbrella" as they passed through the area beyond the reach of land-based aircraft. However, by September 1942 it was clear that even with the first American-built escort carriers

---

[66]   CAB 66/30/27, WP (42) 497, "Third Report by the Shipping Committee," 31 October 1942.

[67]   TNA, CAB 86/2, Anti-U-Boat Warfare Committee (hereinafter AU) (42) 1, 4 November 1942.

[68]   CAB 86/2, AU (42) 1, 4 November 1942.

entering service in the Royal Navy, delays caused by repairs, conversions, and other operational requirements would prevent them closing the air gap in the short-term. The Admiralty was therefore pursuing other solutions, including the conversion of merchant ships into "Merchant Aircraft Carriers" with a flight deck capable of operating a handful of Swordfish aircraft, and the acquisition of aircraft with extended endurance capable of operating over the air gap from Coastal Command's existing air bases. Little progress had yet been made, however, by early November.[69]

The AU committee looked at both land-based and sea-borne aircraft as potential means to solve this problem. Merchant Aircraft Carriers did not seem to offer the quick fix the Committee was looking for, and it was quickly decided that the most promising solution would be land-based aircraft. The key requirement here was very-long-range (VLR) aircraft with a range of around 2,500 miles. At the AU Committee's first meeting, Air Chief Marshal Sir Philip Joubert de la Ferté, Air Officer Commanding-in-Chief (AOC-in-C) Coastal Command, estimated that only forty such aircraft would be required to cover the air gap. In mid-1941, Coastal Command had reequipped its 120 Squadron with American-built Liberator I bombers, which were capable of the necessary range, but there were not enough of these machines to close the air gap. Unfortunately, the Liberators supplied to Coastal Command in 1942 were different models, which did not possess nearly the same range. The AU Committee decided at its second meeting, on 13 November, to begin withdrawing Coastal Command's Liberator IIIs from the Biscay patrols in order to convert them to VLR status for use over the mid-Atlantic.[70] The importance of these aircraft was also recognized by the Anglo-American Combined Chiefs of Staff, which decided at the Casablanca conference in January 1943 that eighty VLR aircraft should ultimately be provided to close the air gap. But even though the flow of new Liberators to Britain increased in early 1943, the process of converting them to VLR status was painfully slow. By the beginning of February 1943, only two of the thirty-three Liberators designated for modification in November had become operational.[71]

Meanwhile, the import situation continued to deteriorate. At the end of November 1942, Roosevelt reassured Churchill that the United States would increase its shipbuilding program to ensure that Britain's minimum import requirements for 1943 were met.[72] But while this might eventually make good

---

[69]   Christopher M. Bell, "Air Power and the Battle of the Atlantic: Very Long Range Aircraft and the Closing of the 'Air Gap,'" *The Journal of Military History* (July 2015).

[70]   CAB 86/2, AU (42) 2, 13 November 1942.

[71]   Richard Goette, "Britain and the Delay in Closing the Mid-Atlantic 'Air Gap' during the Battle of the Atlantic," *The Northern Mariner* 15:4 (October 2005), p. 36; Michael Howard, *Grand Strategy*, Vol. IV, p. 310.

[72]   Roosevelt to Churchill, 30 November 1942, Kimball, ed., *Churchill and Roosevelt*, Vol. II, pp. 44–45.

Britain's deficiencies, in the short-term the import situation would only worsen. On 30 December, Churchill warned the President that imports between November 1942 and March 1943 would likely be at a level equivalent to only seventeen million tons a year, far below Britain's minimum requirements. "This," he remarked, "is indeed a grim prospect, and one which means for us dangerous and difficult decisions between military operations, food and raw materials."[73] To make matters worse, American aid showed no sign of catching up to British expectations. Roosevelt's pledge to maintain British imports had been made without consulting his advisers, and without ensuring that measures were taken to implement it. The American military continued to make huge demands on American resources, and the United States' War Shipping Administration, the civilian agency responsible for overseeing American shipping, informed the British on 18 January that the figures promised by the President were being "taken as estimate only, and not as commitment to allocate a precise amount of shipping."[74] British leaders now had to acknowledge that the additional shipping they had been counting on might not materialize in time to avert a crisis.

On the basis of figures provided by the Shipping Committee, John Anderson, the Lord President of the Council, informed the War Cabinet on 10 March that to meet import requirements for the first half of 1943 "it would be necessary during May and June for our food imports to be at a monthly rate nearly twice as great as, and for our material imports to be at a monthly rate more than twice as great as, the average monthly rate likely to be achieved for the first four months. It is improbable that so great an improvement will occur."[75] Churchill's confidence that the United States could produce enough new tonnage to replace Allied losses had not been misplaced, however. Cherwell calculated in March that American construction alone had exceeded overall Allied losses in 1942 by 2.7 million tons. The problem was that Britain was not receiving enough of this output to replenish its losses. Despite the boom in American shipyards, British shipping had decreased by around two million tons in 1942.[76] With no reason to expect the U.S. armed services to reduce their shipping demands, Churchill finally decided to appeal directly to Roosevelt. Antony Eden, the Foreign Secretary, was dispatched to Washington with instructions "to bring home to our friends in the United States that our minimum imports must be considered an absolute first charge on Allied shipping; that they are as vital to the war effort as supplies to the various theatres."

---

[73]   Churchill to Roosevelt, 30 December 1942, Kimball, ed., *Churchill and Roosevelt,* Vol. II, p. 95.

[74]   Smith, *Conflict over Convoys,* pp. 113–14.

[75]   CAB 66/35/5, WP (43) 105, John Anderson memorandum, "The United Kingdom Import Programme," 10 March 1943.

[76]   CAB 66/34/50, WP (43) 100, Cherwell memorandum, "The Shipping Position," 7 March 1943.

Our own [merchant] fleet is diminished by operating before and after America came into the war, in the most dangerous waters. We have undertaken arduous and essential operations encouraged by the belief that we could rely on American shipbuilding to see us through. But we must know where we stand. We cannot live from hand to mouth on promises limited by provisos. This not only prevents planning and makes the use of ships less economical, it may, in the long run, even imperil good relations. Unless we can get a satisfactory long-term settlement, British ships will have to be withdrawn from their present military service even though our agreed [military] operations are crippled or prejudiced.[77]

Churchill reinforced this message with a personal appeal to Roosevelt on 24 March. British imports in 1943 had "been at such a low rate," he observed, "that even with increasing allocations already notified for forward months, it is going to be extremely difficult to make up leeway." An increased supply of shipping from the United States had therefore become an "urgent and immediate necessity."[78]

With Britain's import program now approaching the crisis point, Churchill began to look more favorably on Admiralty requests for air support. Faced with delays in converting Liberators to VLR status for the mid-Atlantic, naval leaders could not resist asking for Bomber Command aircraft to hit the U-boats in other areas. In January, the First Lord proposed to bomb German U-boat bases in France and the cities surrounding them. Harris protested strongly against this diversion of resources from strategic bombing, and for once he had a strong case. Previous attacks on these bases by the U.S. Eighth Air Force had little or no impact, and the Admiralty's call for larger and less-discriminate attacks reflected the Navy's growing desperation.[79] When the idea was initially raised, Churchill and the War Cabinet had hesitated to take this step, which would produce heavy French civilian casualties, but they, too, were eager to obtain even a small measure of relief. The subject was debated by the AU Committee at the end of March, and Churchill insisted that the bombers be given a chance, even if it came at the expense of strategic bombing. He observed, however, that "he was sceptical whether the damage done in these ports was commensurate with the results achieved by bombing

---

[77] Ibid.

[78] Churchill to Roosevelt, 24 March 1943, Kimball, ed., *Churchill and Roosevelt,* Vol. II, p. 167.

[79] Josef W. Konvitz, "Bombs, Cities, and Submarines: Allied Bombing of the French Ports, 1942–1943," *The International History Review* 14:1 (February 1992), pp. 28–30; CAB 66/33/11, WP (43) 11, Alexander memorandum, "U-Boat Bases in the Bay of Biscay," 7 January 1943.

targets in Germany. Nevertheless," he concluded, "we must work to dislocate the U-boats as much as possible and check them coming in and out of their bases."[80]

The Admiralty also lobbied for the diversion of long- and medium-range aircraft from Bomber Command to strengthen anti-submarine patrols in the Bay of Biscay. This proposal was also contentious. Statistical analysis showed clearly that aircraft were much more likely to locate U-boats in the vicinity of a threatened convoy than in the Bay. Air Marshal John Slessor, the recently-appointed AOC-in-C Coastal Command, reported that convoy support produced on average one U-boat sighting for every twenty-nine hours of flying, while "on the Bay patrols the figure was one sighting per 164 hours in the period June to September 1942, and one sighting per 312 hours from October to February 1943."[81] Cherwell and the Air Ministry were therefore strongly opposed to the diversion of Bomber Command aircraft to the Bay Offensive, which would entail a large commitment of resources in return for what could only be a small payoff. However, the Bay patrols appealed strongly to naval leaders, who were instinctively attracted to measures that were deemed "offensive." On 31 March, Admiral Harold Stark of the U.S. Navy advised the AU Committee that increasing the Biscay patrols would allow the Allies "for the first time, to carry out an all-out offensive against the U-boats." This, in his opinion, would "break the back of the U-boat campaign." Pound was also confident that the concentration of U-boats in this area represented a "great opportunity to initiate attacks." The First Sea Lord argued, moreover, that even when full protection was afforded to mid-Atlantic convoys, the U-boat threat could not be decisively beaten without also strengthening the Bay offensive. Additional aircraft were needed, therefore, "as an absolute necessity and not a luxury in the anti-U-boat campaign."[82]

Churchill's views were mixed. He harbored doubts of his own about the value of the Bay Offensive, and deprecated "any reduction of the bomber offensive at . . . an extremely critical moment." The shipping situation was now so serious, however, that even a modest decrease in the U-boat fleet was desirable. He was therefore unwilling to reject the Admiralty's request out of hand. "Even if the Bay of Biscay patrols resulted in sinking only three or four U-boats a month," he remarked, "this must be regarded as a very important objective." He concluded that "something more could . . . be done to provide additional aircraft for the Bay patrols, without impairing the effectiveness of the bomber offensive."[83] Churchill encouraged the Air Ministry to "examine this point very carefully," and it was decided in April to assign an additional thirty medium- and long-range aircraft to the patrols.[84]

---

[80]   CAB 86/2, AU (43) 13, 31 March 1943.

[81]   CAB 86/3, AU (43) 84, Slessor memorandum, "The Value of the Bay of Biscay Patrols," 22 March 1943.

[82]   CAB 86/2, AU (43) 13, 31 March 1943.

[83]   Ibid.

[84]   CAB 86/2, AU (43) 15, 14 April 1943.

This decision, together with the bombing of U-boat bases in France, shows that Churchill's commitment to Bomber Command was beginning to waver in early 1943. However, he had still not reached the point where he was prepared to undertake a large-scale reduction of the bomber offensive against Germany for the sake of the Battle of the Atlantic. Even as he began to hedge his bets in late March, Churchill expressed confidence that the steadily increasing air protection being provided to convoys would soon begin to bring shipping losses under control.

This confidence was not misplaced. Beginning in April 1943, the United States began to supply VLR aircraft to the Royal Canadian Air Force (RCAF) to operate over the air gap from the western side of the Atlantic.[85] This measure, along with the steady conversion of the Liberators in Coastal Command to VLR status, allowed the Allies to operate forty-one VLR aircraft over the mid-Atlantic by mid-May, effectively closing the air gap. Churchill's faith in Roosevelt was also justified. In late March, the President overruled his own military leaders and gave British imports top priority.[86] By the end of May 1943, the tide had turned decisively in the Battle of the Atlantic. The air gap was now covered not just by land-based aircraft, but also by Allied escort carriers and the first converted merchant aircraft carrier. The dramatic reversal in the air situation, together with the Allies' ability to read U-boat signals and improvements in the efficiency of aircraft and convoy escorts and their equipment, swung the tactical balance at sea in favor of the Allies. Convoys were now able to fight their way through the mid-Atlantic wolf packs and inflict a heavy toll on their adversaries. The Battle of the Atlantic continued right up to the end of the European war in May 1945, but the U-boats were never again able to pose a decisive threat to Britain's war effort.

Churchill's Impact on the Battle of the Atlantic

Churchill's Second World War memoirs appear to have played a major role in shaping popular views on his part in the Battle of the Atlantic. It is easy to assume, based on his oft-quoted declaration that the U-boat threat was the thing he feared most during the war, that he must have done everything in his power to give the Navy the resources it needed to defeat the German attack on shipping. Churchill was also fortunate that he was not censured by Captain Stephen Roskill in the British official history, *The War at Sea*. In the first volume of this series, published in 1954 while Churchill was again Prime Minister, Roskill was openly critical of Churchill's role in the Norwegian campaign of 1940 and for the decision to despatch *Prince of Wales* and *Repulse* to Singapore in 1941. However, in the second volume (1956), Roskill chose not to draw attention to Churchill's decision to keep Coastal Command short of aircraft during 1941 and 1942—probably to avoid a

---

[85] Howard, *Grand Strategy*, Vol. IV, p. 305; Goette, "Air Gap," pp. 37–38.

[86] Howard, *Grand Strategy*, Vol. IV, pp. 297–98; Smith, *Conflict over Convoys*, pp. 173–76.

renewal of the controversy generated by his criticisms in the previous volume. His comments on Churchill's role in the Battle of the Atlantic were therefore relegated to a proposed "Confidential Annex," which would not be made available to the general public. According to this document, which was never distributed in any form, "The priority given to the bombing of North-West Germany at a time when lack of long-range aircraft was causing great losses in the Atlantic seems to have been largely attributable to the Prime Minister's insistence on this 'offensive' measure against the enemy."[87]

This was a surprisingly mild rebuke, and one that Churchill fully deserved. But without the official historian pointing the way, the first generation of post-war historians was neither inclined nor equipped to challenge Churchill's account of his role in the Battle of the Atlantic. Roskill did, however, focus attention on the Admiralty's competition with Bomber Command. The second volume of *The War at Sea* concluded that the shortage of air resources had been a serious problem throughout the Battle of the Atlantic, and, most importantly, that disaster had nearly resulted from delays in providing VLR aircraft for the "air gap." Roskill stated his view "that in the early spring of 1943 we had a very narrow escape from defeat in the Atlantic; and that, had we suffered such a defeat, history would have judged that the main cause had been the lack of two more squadrons of very long range aircraft for convoy escort duties."[88] This judgement, now widely accepted, did not blame Churchill for the shortage of air support, although Roskill would go on to make the connection in a later work, *Churchill and the Admirals*, published in 1977.

In this later volume, the former official historian, now free from government oversight, charged that the diversion of air resources to strategic bombing "was, perhaps, the most far-reaching and tragic strategic error which can, at any rate in part, be laid at Churchill's door, since it was shortage of shipping that delayed every offensive by the United Nations in every theatre up to mid-1944, and so prolonged the struggle at the cost of inestimable suffering to the peoples of the occupied countries."[89] But Roskill was still unwilling to place all the blame on Churchill. Much of the problem, in his view, had been the exaggerated claims made by the Air Ministry and advocates of strategic bombing like Harris and Cherwell, and their excessive influence on British policy-making. This was compounded by the weakness of the Admiralty, and particularly the First Sea Lord, Dudley Pound, who had failed, in Roskill's opinion, to put forward the Navy's case with sufficient vigor. In addition, Roskill admitted that the Admiralty had made important mistakes of its

---

[87]   CAB 140/109, Roskill letter to Sir James Butler, 20 January 1954, and enclosed draft, "Confidential Appendix to 'The War at Sea' Volume I: Mr. Churchill's views on Maritime Strategy and his Relations with Prominent Sea Officers in the War of 1939–45."

[88]   Roskill, *War at Sea*, Vol. II, pp. 370–71.

[89]   Roskill, *Churchill and the Admirals*, pp. 229–30.

own, particularly by diverting aircraft to the bombing of U-boat bases in France and the Biscay offensive.

Churchill's exaggerated faith in strategic bombing and consequent neglect of Coastal Command are now well-established themes in the literature on the Battle of the Atlantic.[90] There is no doubt that his intervention resulted in the loss of more merchant ships than would otherwise have been the case, although only, it should be stressed, in areas outside the air gap. Some writers have suggested that Coastal Command's shortage of aircraft in 1942 resulted in a significant delay in mastering the U-boat threat. Roskill, for example, claimed that if the Admiralty's broad views had prevailed, the Battle of the Atlantic might have been won six months sooner.[91] John O'Connell claims that victory could have been achieved a full year earlier if the British had employed their Liberators more effectively.[92]

The question of whether the U-boats could have been defeated sooner is a complicated one, but a decisive victory ultimately depended on driving U-boats out of the air gap. This might have been achieved before May 1943 if VLR aircraft had been allocated to the task much sooner. This delay was not Churchill's fault, however. Historians who have suggested otherwise frequently claim that the Admiralty repeatedly asked for VLR aircraft between February and October 1942, and that the Air Ministry, backed by Churchill, regularly denied them. In fact, the air gap was not a concern for the Admiralty until July 1942, and it did not begin seriously considering modified land-based aircraft as a solution until September-October. Moreover, naval leaders were slow to alert Churchill specifically to the need for VLR aircraft. Pound's memorandum of 5 October 1942 for the Defence Committee, for example, provided a long list of Admiralty requirements for the war at sea, but did not specifically note the importance of closing the air gap, and contained only a single oblique reference to the need for "specially long range aircraft."[93] Nor did Pound draw attention to this subject in his correspondence with the Prime Minister during the remainder of October.

The first time the problem was brought to Churchill's attention was the initial meeting of the Anti-U-Boat Warfare Committee on 4 November 1942. Some accounts claim that Churchill continued to resist the diversion of Liberators to trade defense after this date, but these are also mistaken. Most of the aircraft

---

[90]   Redford, "Inter- and Intra-Service Rivalries," pp. 918–24; Goette, "Britain and the Delay in Closing the Mid-Atlantic 'Air Gap'"; Tim Benbow, "Brothers in Arms: The Admiralty, the Air Ministry, and the Battle of the Atlantic," *Global War Studies* 11:1 (2014); Bell, *Churchill and Sea Power*, ch. 9.

[91]   Roskill, *Churchill and the Admirals*, pp. 139, 229–30.

[92]   John F. O'Connell, "Closing the North Atlantic Air Gap: Where did all the British Liberators go?," *Air Power History* (Summer 2012), pp. 32–43.

[93]   CAB 70/5, DO (S) (42) 88, Pound memorandum, "The Needs of the Navy," 5 October 1942.

needed to close the air gap were already operating in Coastal Command. Churchill therefore had no cause to object to their conversion for use in the mid-Atlantic, and he immediately gave the proposal his full backing.[94] This was, after all, precisely the sort of solution the Anti-U-Boat Warfare Committee had been created to find: one that promised big results without diverting long-range aircraft from the bombing of Germany. The Admiralty and Air Ministry would probably have produced VLR aircraft for the air gap eventually if they had been left to pursue a solution on their own, but it should be recognized that the process was accelerated considerably by Churchill's decision to create a special high-level committee to focus attention on the Battle of the Atlantic and expedite solutions.

Conclusion

No simple verdict is possible with respect to Churchill's impact on the Battle of the Atlantic. Popular perceptions of the wartime Prime Minister watching anxiously as shipping losses rose and imports fell only tells part of the story. Churchill was clearly alarmed at times by the U-boat threat, but he did not frighten easily, and he did not frighten often. He only shifted his full attention to the Battle of the Atlantic when disaster seemed a real possibility—in the spring of 1941 and again in late 1942. But even during these periods, Churchill was prepared to run risks at sea and accept heavy losses if doing so would enable him to pursue other important or desirable objectives. A case could be made that the decision to accept higher shipping losses in 1940–41 in order to take the offensive in North Africa was justifiable on strategic grounds. However, Churchill's commitment in 1942 to a grand strategy that favored strategic bombing over trade protection was both reckless and misguided. The problem was not his willingness to run risks with British shipping, but that he did so to bolster a strategic air offensive that contributed little in 1941–43 to weakening Germany. However, in other respects Churchill's assessment was accurate. Britain was able to withstand very heavy shipping losses, and resources could be redirected in time to avoid a decisive defeat at sea. Thus, while Churchill's priorities brought Britain closer to disaster in 1943 than was necessary, there was probably never a serious danger of a complete collapse of the British war effort due to heavy shipping losses.

Churchill was temperamentally predisposed to support strategic bombing as long as this appeared to offer the best means to strike directly at Britain's enemies, and this frequently led him to listen to the wrong advisers. His preoccupation with "offensive" measures undoubtedly came at a cost. The provision of additional

---

[94]   For claims that Churchill and Bomber Command continued to block the allocation of Liberators to Coastal Command, see Terry Hughes and John Costello, *The Battle of the Atlantic* (New York: Dial Press, 1977), pp. 230–31; Malcolm Murfett, *Naval Warfare, 1919–1945* (London: Routledge, 2009), p. 240.

aircraft to Coastal Command would have reduced the number of ships lost to U-boats, although how many might have been saved is incalculable. This must be balanced, however, against his part in finally closing the air gap. There are no grounds to claim that he specifically denied VLR aircraft to Coastal Command throughout 1942 and early 1943, and that he was therefore responsible for prolonging this hole in Allied defenses. In fact, Churchill could not have denied these aircraft, because he had not been asked for them. When the Admiralty finally raised the issue with the AU Committee in November 1942, Churchill immediately backed the request and threw his weight behind efforts to supply the modified aircraft needed for the air gap. Without Churchill's intervention, the provision of VLR aircraft would have been delayed still further. In this respect, at least, Churchill had a positive impact.

3

"Immobilized by Reason of Repair" and by the Choice "Between Lithgow and Hitler"

Class Conflict in Britain's Wartime Merchant Shipping Repair Yards

Kevin Smith

Britain's survival in the Second World War depended upon maintaining its lines of maritime communications for overseas supplies. In order to keep those lines open, the U-boat menace had to be contained, but Britain also had to utilize its remaining merchant ships in the most efficient manner possible. British officials could not control every aspect of this process; they were unable, for example, to ensure that overseas cargoes arrived in overseas ports at the same time that British-controlled cargo ships were there and ready to load them. These officials, however, could exercise more direct influence over the movement of goods and the preparation of ships in Britain itself. Obsession with anti-submarine warfare, both at the time and in the years since, has generated a legacy of disproportionate attention to combat at sea on the part of operations research analysts, veterans, and historians.

While descriptions of strategic discussions provide essential context and the review of tactical struggles is exciting, attention to the mundane aspects of maintaining the logistical infrastructure in good working order is necessary in constructing a balanced perspective concerning how victory in the Battle of the Atlantic, as well as the entire supply struggle, was achieved. Yet British efforts in Britain itself to maximize merchant shipping capacity—especially through the particularly key aspect of rapid and thorough repair of damaged ships—were and are generally overlooked. Far more merchant shipping capacity was out of service at any given time, either "immobilized by reason of repair" or "undergoing repairs while working cargo," than the U-boats knocked out of service in any given month, even after American repair of damaged British merchant vessels under Lend-Lease complemented an overdue reordering of merchant ship repair priorities that partially unclogged dockyards. Even allowing for the reality that the consequences of U-boat sinkings were cumulative, whereas damaged ships were eventually released from repair yards and put back into service, throughout the first three years of war the loss of shipping capacity due to day-to-day ship-repairing delays was comparable to that inflicted by submarines.

Throughout the era of Allied obsession with the U-boat—as well as over the years since—Britain's repair yards certainly deserved more attention than they received. C. B. A. Behrens, author of the official British account of merchant shipping management, argued in a private letter in 1947 that more carrying capacity was lost due to tonnage immobilized for repairs than as a result of submarine attack. This chapter seeks to modify that argument and rescue it from the dustbin of history to which it has been consigned.[1] One important aspect of the effort to prepare ships for moving cargo following repair will be explored more thoroughly than in this author's previous publications: the role of class conflict in impeding productivity. A review of attitudes on both sides of this societal gulf will illustrate the significant contribution of unresolved class conflict in slowing wartime repairs.

Shipping Capacity Management and the Rise of British Dependence

When *Conflict over Convoys* was published in 1996 and was subsequently reviewed in the standard journals, the comparative effect of submarine attack and repair delays was not subjected to scrutiny in any review.[2] Inattention has continued; historians have been even less interested in British management of merchant shipping than Winston Churchill, who was notoriously obsessed with combat while, at the same time, he recognized the need for a Cabinet-level committee to oversee this shortcoming. There have been a few exceptions; most notably, Jock Gardner, in seeking to synthesize the economic and industrial aspects with the tactical and

---

[1]   Central Statistical Office, *History of the Second World War: United Kingdom Civil Series, Statistical Digest of the War* (London: HMSO, 1951), Table 115. Behrens' official account of merchant shipping management is *Merchant Shipping and the Demands of War* (London: HMSO and Kraus Reprints, 1978; first edition 1955); The National Archives, London (hereinafter TNA), Cabinet Office File (hereinafter CAB) 102/424, Behrens to M. M. Postan, 26 February 1947.

[2]   The argument below builds on the discussion of shipbuilding and ship repair in Kevin Smith, *Conflict over Convoys: Anglo-American Logistics Diplomacy in the Second World War* (Cambridge: Cambridge University Press, 1996), pp. 13–27, 58–63. Related issues such as delays in discharging cargo and stagnation in shipbuilding are also discussed therein. See further exploration of the broader strategic significance in "Logistics Diplomacy at Casablanca: The Anglo-American Failure to Integrate Shipping and Military Strategy," *Diplomacy & Statecraft* 2:3 (1991), and "Constraining OVERLORD: Civilian Logistics, TORCH, and The Second Front," in Theodore A. Wilson, ed., *D-Day 1944* (Lawrence: University Press of Kansas, 1994). For an overview of recent scholarship, see "Maritime War: Combat, Management, and Memory," in Thomas Zeiler, ed., *A Companion to the Second World War* (Malden, MA: Wiley-Blackwell, 2013), pp. 262–77.

strategic and to view Ultra's impact more modestly, concluded that "there was considerably more to the shipping balance than convoy warfare in the narrow sense" and "performance at sea cannot be considered the sole arbiter of Allied progress."[3] The role of technological developments has certainly been integrated into historians' analyses, the best known examples of these being code-breaking, HF/DF, weapons advances (e.g., Hedgehog and Leigh Light), and radar. But other developments also affected maritime warfare. For example, as German forces gained bases on the English Channel, cargo ships had to be rerouted from unloading most cargoes in east coast ports to discharging them in west coast ports. Preparation for this rerouting was haphazard and management of the adjustment was chaotic since swiveling movement along Britain's domestic rail network to reorient to the west coast ports slowed the turnaround of ships and reduced overall shipping capacity. Also, Britain's desperate efforts to increase steel imports in 1940 caused damage to ships that were not designed to carry steel, which is an example of the adverse effects on shipping capacity due to the loss of access to nearby European markets and the difficulty in wedding the right kind of ships and cargoes to new global routes. Still another example of these various unfavorable developments is the attempt of British diplomats to allocate American merchant shipbuilding to British control, only to have their efforts complicated once the United States entered the war because British demands then had to compete with the demand of the U.S. Army that priority be given to troop deployment over civilian imports.

Thus, delays in repair and the resulting loss of shipping capacity did not merely affect Britain's import program; the geographical realities that the Axis controlled the European continent and that the Allies were separated from one another, and from the enemy, by oceans dictated that Allied offensives of every sort and in every theater demanded ever-increasing allocations of cargo shipping capacity. Contextualizing maritime management and diplomacy with reference to grand strategy is, therefore, essential since offensive operations not only demanded cargo shipping, but they also stripped escort vessels from other routes for use in protecting military convoys while simultaneously immobilizing some cargo vessels in Northwest and Northeast African and South Pacific bases that lacked adequate port facilities because the ships had to be used as floating warehouses. Traditional habits in the British shipbuilding industry also deterred modernization; output remained static. Cargo shipping capacity shortages, whatever the cause, influenced strategic debate, helped generate Anglo-American friction, and would eventually help shape the development of critical offensives, including the Second Front in France.[4]

---

[3]   W. J. R. Gardner, *Decoding History: The Battle of the Atlantic and Ultra* (Annapolis: Naval Institute Press, 1999), p. 46.

[4]   David Reynolds emphasized Anglo-American wartime competition in *Creation of the Anglo-American Alliance: A Study in Competitive Co-operation* (London: Europa, 1981), as did Christopher Thorne in *Allies of a Kind: The United States, Britain, and the War against*

These managerial issues must not be isolated from examination of combat; yet a truly comprehensive history of the Battle of the Atlantic that integrates its martial and managerial aspects still eludes historians. This chapter brings forward the issue of ship repair for further scrutiny as one representative domestic example (others include shipbuilding and dockworkers' handling of cargo) in hopes of stimulating an overdue discussion about the role of managerial expertise in achieving—or rather delaying—victory in the Battle of the Atlantic. Perhaps this may also stimulate re-examination of how the construction of memory obscures reality: the 2013 anniversary commemoration of victory in the Battle of the Atlantic, for example, emphasized praise for the "all-out, round-the-clock effort" of local laborers.

Britain's independence was also at stake. The United Kingdom could only sustain a total war of indeterminate length if procurement of needed food and raw materials from America and elsewhere could be funded by Lend-Lease and moved in ships maintained by Britain or provided by the United States. Britain's dependence upon the United States extended from supplies and finance to ships. Thus, the failure of Britain's ship repairers to unclog British repair yards and contribute satisfactorily to British cargo shipping capacity enhanced dependence upon the United States, subjecting Britain's import lifeline to potential interdiction by American decisions as well as by German submarines. The examination of this issue, therefore, provides yet another angle from which to examine the transition to American global dominance at mid-century.[5] Britain's failure to build and repair ships led inexorably to dependence upon the United States for allocations of newly-built merchant ships in competition with the United States military. British imports suffered a cumulatively aggravated decline by 1941 to about one-half the pre-war average of about fifty-five million tons of dry-cargo imports (thirty-one million tons) and to about one-third by late 1942 (twenty-three million tons in 1942; seventeen million tons on a per annum basis during the winter of 1942–43). British dependence upon the United States increased even as British leaders sought to influence Allied strategy—and, therefore, by extension the use of cargo ships that Americans controlled.

Japan, 1941–1945 (London: Hamish Hamilton, 1978). For the impact of American logistics upon grand strategy, see Richard Leighton and Robert Coakley, *Global Logistics and Strategy*, 2 vols. (Washington, DC: Office of the Chief of Military History, 1955, 1968). See Mark Stoler, *Allies and Adversaries: The Joint Chiefs of Staff, the Grand Alliance, and U.S. Strategy in World War II* (Chapel Hill: University of North Carolina Press, 2000).

[5]   Some historians have challenged the prevailing narrative of British decline and American ascent during the Second World War; David Edgerton, *Britain's War Machine: Weapons, Resources, and Experts in the Second World War* (Oxford: Oxford University Press, 2011) is a prime recent example. While he offers important objections, Britain's maritime industries do not provide useful support for his argument.

Table 3.1:   **Dry Cargo Imports, Britain, 1940–1944**

Month	1940	1941	1942	1943	1944
Jan	3811	2413	2006	1177	1966
Feb	3598	2152	1867	1267	2126
Mar	3856	2386	1943	2015	2073
Apr	4207	2360	2099	2378	1992
May	4177	2767	2214	2064	2345
Jun	4054	2776	2091	2723	2352
Jul	3389	2648	2167	2748	2060
Aug	3936	2712	1919	2368	2102
Sep	2974	2816	2149	2661	2000
Oct	3208	2930	2023	2569	2216
Nov	2602	2140	1300	2186	2371
Dec	2547	2680	1235	2327	1923
Total	**41859**	**30478**	**22891**	**26372**	**25147**

Digest, Table 161. All import figures expressed in thousands of tons and include the Ministry of Food program, the Ministry of Supply program (later Ministry of Production), munitions, and other minor miscellaneous imports.

Introducing Britain's Repair Crisis, 1940–41

The congestion in Britain's west coast repair yards owed its existence to a variety of causes. As described in *Conflict over Convoys,* the German conquest of continental Europe and the ensuing Blitz added externally-imposed challenges to pre-existing problems plaguing the British shipbuilding and ship-repairing industry. The deteriorating strategic situation of 1940 created a new set of challenges for ship repair that in turn hindered the pursuit of British and, by extension, Allied strategic objectives: fewer repair yards were available to handle a greater volume of repairs thanks to defeat in Scandinavia and the threat to the British east coast resulting from German occupation of the Low Countries; the Blitz threatened the safety of workers on both coasts and damaged yet more ships; and the Admiralty struggled to devise and impose an effective system to govern repairs.[6]

---

[6]   The ensuing discussion briefly summarizes the argument in Smith, *Conflict over Convoys,* pp. 58–60, before focusing attention on the role of class conflict between laborers and employers, laborers and the Admiralty Controller of Merchant Shipbuilding and Repair, and even within the government between that Controller and the Minister of Labour.

Naval vessels damaged in the Dunkirk evacuation and in operations off Norway required extensive repairs; these had to be prioritized in preparation for the expected imminent cross-channel invasion. Britain had to defend Egypt for reasons of domestic and imperial politics, but Italian entry into the war endangered Mediterranean convoys and redirected the transportation and resupply of troops around the Cape of Good Hope. More ships would be needed, and many would need alterations to carry different types of cargo. Making these alterations would further clog repair yards. Meanwhile, German conquests forced merchant vessels to sail unfamiliar routes in order to evade U-boats while carrying unaccustomed or heavy cargo. They often experienced severe damage as a result. Enemy attacks generally inflicted greater damage in individual engagements, requiring longer repairs, but ships commencing repair for "marine damage" on "ordinary" passages also filled the repair yards. The latter outnumbered ships commencing repairs for damage incurred by enemy action by at least four to one in March-June 1941, for example, a ratio that increased tremendously thereafter. The U-boat was, therefore, only indirectly responsible for the damage to many of the British merchant ships laid up for repair. Also, while some American ships had been purchased, needed repairs had been delayed in order to save dollars as the German conquest of continental Europe again forced Britain to devote scarce resources to other aspects of rearmament, an example being the degaussing of European ships that had escaped Nazi control in order to protect them against magnetic mines. Fewer facilities were available to handle this deluge after the spring of 1940. Ships deemed too valuable to risk passage to east coast ports that were located too close to German bases just across the English Channel could neither discharge cargo nor await repair there. European shipyards were unavailable and British shipowners initially disdained inefficient, unknown, and costly foreign repairers elsewhere. In addition to all of these difficulties, repair workers were plagued by equipment shortages.[7]

While the above discussion summarizes how German conquest of continental Europe added to Britain's repair burden, these problems were superimposed upon existing issues that the war aggravated. The workers in Britain's shipbuilding and (necessarily related) ship-repairing yards had suffered through years of hardship that poisoned labor attitudes toward management and government; suspicion even embittered interaction between government ministries interested in enhancing shipping capacity for the Battle of the Atlantic. Thus class conflict was not suspended for the war's duration, but was rather enhanced in this arena.

---

[7]   National Maritime Museum, Greenwich, Shipbuilding Employers Federation (hereinafter NMM/SEF), SRNA/5/H/3/1, Sir Amos Ayre, "Merchant Ship Repairs During the Earlier Period of the War," p. 6; TNA, CAB 86/1, Battle of the Atlantic Committee (hereinafter BA) (41) 100, 15 July 1941; Lord Cherwell speaking at BA (41) 15th meeting, 10 September 1941; BA (42) 6, 16 May 1942, Table 6.

The Impact of Declining Competitiveness and the Great Depression

British shipbuilding production fell eighty-nine percent between 1927 and 1933, resulting in sixty percent unemployment among British shipbuilding workers.[8] While much of the following discussion emphasizes the situation in the British shipbuilding industry, the allocation of labor and materials for building and repair overlapped in both the pre-war and wartime eras. Builders' reluctance to embrace new methods had been reinforced by workers' fear that efficiencies would undermine demarcation lines between trades that preserved jobs. Even as builders overseas had become more competitive, the Great Depression demolished both the carrying trade and the incentives to build new ships generated by it. Shipbuilders finally responded to years of stagnation by concluding that British production would not return to former levels and that some yards must no longer build ships so that others might survive. Sir James Lithgow coordinated this downsizing effort on behalf of his fellow shipbuilders, organizing National Shipbuilders Security Ltd. (hereinafter NSS) to buy yards, to impose restrictive covenants, and to remove yards from the industry permanently. While Lithgow's adoring biographer describes the reduction in capacity as unavoidable and correct and Lithgow himself claimed that the unions approved, workers' resentment at the institutionalization of mass unemployment festered and endured.[9] One of the most important symbols of Depression-era suffering in Britain had been the Jarrow March of October 1936, in which "Red Ellen" Wilkinson led a deputation of workers made redundant by the closing of Palmer's Shipyard on an unsuccessful month-long sojourn to London to seek redress. A retrospective report commissioned as part of the wartime effort to increase shipyard productivity, the Barlow Report of 1942, summarized the effect of the Depression:

> No other vital industry suffered such an eclipse, and its effect upon the present position is three-fold: men skilled in the industry had . . . to seek work elsewhere and a substantial number were permanently lost to it; in

---

[8]   University of Glasgow, Sir James Lithgow Papers (hereinafter LP), File 59, "Report to the Minister of Production of the Committee set up by him to enquire into conditions of Labour in shipyards," 24 July 1942, p. 1. This was and will be referred to in this chapter as the Barlow Report. Robert Barlow chaired the committee; the two most important members of the committee were H. B. Robin Rowell, President of the Shipbuilding Employers' Federation, and Gavin Martin, General Secretary of the Confederation of Shipbuilding and Engineering Unions.

[9]   J. M. Reid, *James Lithgow, Master of Work* (London: Hutchinson, 1964), pp. 133–36, 199–200; LP, File 45, Lithgow response to Barlow Report, 29 July 1942: NSS activities "deprived no Shipyard operative of his opportunities for employment in Shipbuilding. . . . The whole operation was undertaken following advice from the trade Union side."

addition there was a stoppage of new entrants into the industry; a not unnatural reluctance on the part of the workpeople readily to admit a further great expansion of the people employed in the industry; the industry in general has not been able to maintain its equipment in the state of efficiency needed for maximum war production.[10]

Bevin's Role

In May 1940, Prime Minister Winston Churchill recognized that he needed to construct a more inclusive coalition government. His effort to maximize the contribution of labor to the fighting of a total war included an invitation to join the Cabinet for Ernest Bevin, Britain's leading trade unionist and head of the Transport and General Workers' Union. Accounts of Bevin's career emphasize his role as pre-war General Secretary and post-war Foreign Secretary; during the war years, they emphasize his successes in controlling and mobilizing manpower, especially in manning the coal mines. Even as industrial productivity languished in certain sectors and absenteeism continued, Robert Pearce praises his adroit and "remarkably restrained" allocation of manpower; Bevin used his "powers of coercion sparingly." Alan Bullock, his most famous biographer, lauds Bevin's understanding that the manpower budget would be "the basis of the wartime planning of the country's resources and the ultimate limit on its mobilization" and his consequent success in gaining and maintaining control while disturbing "every established practice and vested interest in the country" on the path to increased output. Bullock praises both this achievement and Bevin's restraint in administration, delaying the deployment of compulsory powers on the grounds that "when it came, compulsion and direction would be accepted by working-class opinion if voluntary methods of recruitment for industry had been exhausted first." Bullock concluded that Britain's extraordinary level of mobilization of men and women "had been achieved on a basis of consent, with the minimum of coercion."[11]

Bevin's extraordinary successes are not diminished in their importance by recognition of their limitations. An area in which Bevin particularly struggled to mobilize manpower throughout the Battle of the Atlantic was the shipyards. An influenza outbreak in autumn 1940 temporarily cut the workforce by 5,000 men; this "closely coincided with the peak point of gross tonnage undergoing or awaiting repair."[12] The rapid changes in the broader war situation in autumn 1940 created artificial local

---

[10]   LP, File 59, Barlow Report, p. 1.

[11]   Robert Pearce, "Ernest Bevin," in Kevin Jeffreys, ed., *Labour Forces: From Ernie Bevin to Gordon Brown* (London: I. B. Tauris, 2002), p. 15; Alan Bullock, *Ernest Bevin: Foreign Secretary, 1945–1951* (New York: Norton, 1983), pp. 853–54. See also Peter Weiler, *Ernest Bevin* (Manchester: Manchester University Press, 1993).

[12]   NMM/SEF, SRNA/5/H/3/1, Ayre, "Merchant Ship Repairs," pp. 11–12.

labor shortages and surpluses. The Blitz crippled London facilities and discouraged east coast repairs while, at the same time, priority for naval repairs drained labor from merchant repairs. Bevin began with an appeal for voluntary movement into the shipbuilding industry, but parochial resistance to migration created labor shortages and surpluses. His appeal elicited a Tyneside complaint: "I don't know what they want more men for. There are too many doing nothing in the yards already." But while there were too many workers sitting idle in underused east coast yards, there were too few available on the west coast. And when Tyneside did need workers, Bevin refused to compel London electricians who were unemployed to migrate there "on the grounds that Tyneside pay would be lower and the men, if directed, would only make trouble."[13] This was a sensible concern: "many of the reports of slacking . . . relate to men who have been sent back to the industry and are trying to get away again."[14] Bevin faced the challenge of managing a theoretically national pool of manpower in a nation with stark regional differences in pay scales. And recruiting Irish workers for shipbuilding also posed a challenge: "How can I expect to recruit labour from Eire for this low standard wage when at the same time I have to recruit them for other industries at higher standards?"[15] Moreover, the yards struggled to find skilled workers because men in certain trades were also in high demand elsewhere. For example, several dozen electricians left Cammell Laird's in Birkenhead despite efforts to retain them simply because they could make more money building airplanes.[16] More traditional problems also arose. The most serious single labor dispute of 1941 in any field occurred in February and March (exactly as Churchill's Government was beginning to grapple with ship-repairing productivity) when "25,000 apprentices in the shipbuilding and engineering industries in Scotland, Belfast, Barrow, and Manchester stopped work in support of a claim for increased wage."[17]

---

[13]   CAB 102/424, "The Crisis of the Winter of 1940/41," p. 7, CAB 102/439, "Manpower Problems: Dunkirk to Pearl Harbour," p. 4. The CAB 102 files (and the LAB 9 files below) were prepared in the final months of the war and immediately thereafter for use in writing what would become the UK Civil Series. They were often more opinionated than the volumes which were published over the next decade; as will be noted, some drafts were indeed written in response to other drafts. Generally, these are useful in illuminating the ideas of civil servants engaged in wartime controversies.

[14]   TNA, Ministry of Labour and National Service File (hereinafter LAB) 8/588, minutes of meeting of Ministry of Labour Director General of Man-Power (D. Pointon) with Shipbuilding Employers Federation, 4 March 1942.

[15]   LAB 8/588, Minister of Labour and National Service Ernest Bevin to First Lord of the Admiralty Albert V. Alexander, undated (April 1942).

[16]   CAB 102/439, "Manpower Problems: Dunkirk to Pearl Harbour," p. 2.

[17]   LAB 76/29, E. C. Bowley, "Internal War History: Strikes and Lock-outs, 1939–45," p. 5. This document included a table (drawn from the Ministry's Report for the years 1939–1946, Appendix XXVIII, pp. 385–86) that indicated that for 1941–44, shipbuilding and engineering (not always related, of course) disputes that involved stoppages of work constituted

Bevin turned his attention to improvements in working conditions that might help retain workers, but struggled to devise terms for compulsion. Shipyard management needed a reliable workforce, but they wanted to discard traditional regulations that preserved jobs but slowed completion of work. Bevin, for his part, demanded concessions in return for imposing compulsion, but he could not move the unions to accept change. While Admiralty official R. K. Duncan could, in 1945, describe the introduction of the Essential Work Order for Shipbuilding and Shiprepairing [sic] in March 1941 as a step taken by the Ministry of Labour (with the approval of the Admiralty, management, and unions) "towards a better co-operative spirit in the Industry which would lead to increased production,"[18] the rest of his description of industrial strife clearly exhibits the kind of attitude that prevailed on both sides, an attitude that restrained innovative efforts to boost productivity. Meanwhile, only factories that met certain conditions, such as providing washrooms and canteens, were eligible for inclusion in the Essential Work Order that directed workers to them. Bevin continued to doubt that the yard managers could make full use of the labor supplied. He shared the workers' critique of management, arguing "that the work is not properly organized, that there is too much regard paid to the interests of individual establishments, and that there is a considerable amount of wasted time forced upon the men." Thus, "the experience of the men of what they regard as inefficient organization and management . . . makes it difficult to persuade them that under present conditions the changes for which they are being asked are not only to suit the interests of private employers." The solution was to "make it clear that the men are working for the nation and not in the interests of particular employers."[19]

But Bevin did not merely passionately empathize with workers, befitting his long career as a trade unionist. He took a broader view as well, understanding that dwelling on past struggles did not build ships in wartime. He was palpably frustrated with the workers' obsessive refusal to adapt to changes in working conditions that were designed to increase productivity. Stalemate between employees and employers prevented effective progress on any issue related to increasing the size of the workforce, including shifting workers between trades, reducing the number of skilled men needed to complete a task, and shifting workers between yards and regions. Employees would not consider changes that might risk their

---

20–27 percent of the overall total of disputes, 20–35 percent of the workers involved, and 26–40 percent of the working days lost in all industrial disputes. In each case, 1941 marked the high-water mark of trouble, and the coal industry always remained the most difficult.

[18] LP, File 59, R. K. Duncan of the Directorate of Merchant Shipbuilding and Repairs, "Shipbuilding and Shiprepairing: A Criticism of Industrial Relations within the Industry," 30 January 1945, p. 1.

[19] LAB 76/9, Bevin to Alexander, 16 January 1941, Chapter XI, "The Break-up of the Labour Market," p. 224.

future employment; employers would not consider trying to innovate without prior agreement to do so. Bevin acknowledged both the crippling effect of union stubbornness on this issue and of shipbuilders' determination to capitalize on wartime necessity in order to bypass union regulations. His response: "Can anything be done to create a machinery by which there can be real movement? I know all about the fifteen years. Heaven knows we are paying quite enough for it now. I cannot undo the fifteen years, that is the trouble. I cannot go back."[20]

Lithgow's Role: "Deliberately Lowered"?

Bevin disliked the influence of shipbuilders upon the Admiralty's oversight of shipbuilding and repair. Then First Lord of the Admiralty Winston Churchill had chosen Sir James Lithgow in early 1940 as Controller of Merchant Shipbuilding and Repair. Since workers blamed him for pre-war unemployment, this was a divisive choice. Lithgow's web of connections with those same shipbuilders with whom he had colluded in the previous decade to reduce building capacity and to select certain yards for survival led workers (and Bevin) to suspect that employers influenced Government policy. Lithgow's actions reinforced that view, while his private rhetoric as displayed in his papers confirms his disdain for disgruntled workers who resisted efforts to expand the pool of skilled labor, preferring archaic demarcation rules that preserved jobs and reduced efficiency. These workers feared that expansion of the workforce in wartime would lead to post-war unemployment when demand subsided, as had been the case after World War One.

Lithgow and his brother Henry had assumed control of Fairfield Govan in 1935, and his confrontation with shop stewards there illustrates his utter disregard for the sentiments of shipyard workers. A major complaint of the men concerned the operation of a new canteen that had been built in compliance with Bevin's Essential Work Order. They requested the withdrawal of public notices about alleged theft of cutlery. They also charged that different menus were available for the same price to different clientele (unsubtly implying class discrimination) and that the workers did not have access to trays whereas other users did. Finally, they sought to open the canteen five minutes earlier at lunchtime in order to ease the transition from work to lunch. Here in his very own yard, Lithgow demonstrated his contempt: he "categorically refute[d]" the shop stewards' claims about differentiated menus and rejected their requests point by point. He then brought a complaint that appears frequently in his papers, connecting it to the operation of the canteen in a manner that clearly indicates that the canteen had been introduced

---

[20]   LAB 76/9, Bevin speaking at a joint meeting with Alexander, representatives of the Shipbuilding Employers' Federation, and Gavin Martin, the General Secretary of the Confederation of Shipbuilding and Engineering Unions, on 28 February 1941, referenced in Chapter XI, "The Break-up of the Labour Market," p. 242.

against his will, implying that any concession to workers was a concession wrought by wartime exigency that would be withdrawn as soon as possible:

> We would draw attention to the deplorable state of affairs within these Works in respect to the manner in which a very large percentage of our employees are stopping work a very considerable time before the official hour of closing for the lunch-time break. . ... The canteen was introduced as a facility which, it was represented, would be much appreciated by the employees. The trouble in respect of stopping work before the time has been much aggravated since the opening of the canteen, which was certainly not the intention when it was opened. This deplorable practice, as associated with the opening of the canteen, immediately accentuated the habit of men leaving their work before the official stopping time.[21]

Lithgow's disdain for workers was reciprocated:

> The present position of . . . Lithgow is acting as a deterrent to production in the West of Scotland Shipyards. Rightly or wrongly, he is referred to locally as the King of Scotland; he is said to have complete control of the Shipping Industry, the Steel Industry, and Admiralty Orders; and he is considered to be the cause of all the unemployment and evil times from which the Clydeside Shipping Industry has suffered during the last fifteen years. Mistrust is so deep that enthusiasm for the war effort is not possible so long as the choice seems to lie between Lithgow and Hitler.[22]

While this could be seen merely as a politically motivated attack lobbed by an anonymous coward on "Red Clydeside," the fact that this letter was written to a Labour member of the wartime coalition serving as Parliamentary Secretary in the Ministry of War Transport indicates that this sentiment was real, deep-rooted, and that it existed elsewhere.[23] Indeed, Gavin Martin, General Secretary of the

---

[21] LP, File 57, Fairfield Shop Stewards Committee (A. Bickerstaff and R. Saunders) to Lithgow, 13 January 1942, and Lithgow's response, 15 January 1942.

[22] Churchill College Archives, Cambridge University, Philip Noel-Baker Papers (hereinafter CCACU/PNB) 3/213, unsigned to Noel-Baker, (Labour) Parliamentary Secretary to the Minister of War Transport, undated (early 1942).

[23] Class consciousness was pervasive. On an unrelated issue, in an internal history, a civil servant refers to the removal of policemen from the list of reserved occupations (and therefore available for work deemed more vital to the war effort) in these words: "another privileged bastion had fallen before the attack of the Ministry of Labour" (LAB 76/9, Chapter XI, "The Break-up of the Labour Market," p. 256).

Confederation of Shipbuilding and Engineering Unions, insisted on including a minority report in the "Barlow Report" to the Minister of Production that examined the continued shortfall in shipyard output in summer 1942. His scathing critique of NSS was direct and personally aimed at Lithgow:

> The policy of this Company was based upon a contraction of the building capacity of the Industry for profit . . . workpeople, who had given a lifetime of service to the firms so closed, and left without any prospect of again finding employment in the Industry . . . were lost to the Industry for all time. In the carrying out of their policy they deliberately lowered the building capacity of the Industry without regard to the nation's needs, either in peace or war. After the war commenced the Merchant Shipbuilding Control was created. The Chairman and Vice-Chairman of National Shipbuilders Security Ltd. were appointed members of such Control. Notwithstanding the need to extend the building capacity . . . to build a mercantile marine fleet capable of meeting the nation's requirements and of replacing shipping losses incurred by war wastage, no new shipbuilding yards have been opened, nor have established firms extended the number of building berths in their yards. The need of the nation for new tonnage is greater today than at any time in history and as adequate measures have not been taken by the Merchant Shipbuilding Control to meet these needs, it leads one to the conclusion that it is primarily concerned with the post-war policy of National Shipbuilders Security Ltd., and not with the requirements of the nation today.[24]

Martin concluded by calling for joint oversight of the industry by shipbuilders, the government, and the relevant unions. While Lithgow "quite candidly resent[ed] the implied criticism of the Department for faults that lie in other quarters"[25] elsewhere in the report, he was incensed by the minority report. He demanded that "Mr. Martin should be called upon to substantiate or withdraw the statements."[26] George Hall, Financial Secretary in the Admiralty, sought to smooth over the *contretemps*. He spoke to Martin, and conveyed that "Mr. Martin had no intention of singling out either Sir Amos Ayre or yourself, but . . . his criticism was directed to the activities of National Shipbuilders Security Ltd. as a whole."[27] This explanation was at complete variance with the plain language of Martin's minority report, and no one could reasonably have been convinced otherwise.

---

[24]   LP, File 59, Barlow Report, p. 8. Amos Ayre served as Director of Merchant Shipbuilding under Lithgow at the Admiralty.

[25]   LP, File 59, Lithgow to Rowell, 1 August 1942.

[26]   LP, File 59, Lithgow to Alexander, 24 August 1942.

[27]   LP, File 59, Hall to Lithgow, 3 September 1942.

Bevin's disdain was only slightly better restrained. When H. B. Robin Rowell, President of the Shipbuilding Employers' Federation, informed Lithgow of his continuing opposition to paying workers per accomplished task (piece work) rather than a set wage, Bevin exploded. Writing to First Lord of the Admiralty Albert V. Alexander, he complained of "how difficult and backward the shipbuilding industry has been from the labour point of view ever since I have been in office." He specifically targeted Lithgow, telling Alexander that "the conservatism of the industry . . . runs from your own Controller's Department right down through the managerial side."[28]

Lithgow reciprocated Bevin's personal hostility. Ignoring his own ambivalence about employing more men, he critiqued the Essential Work Order for his industry. He charged Bevin with shirking his responsibility for the proper control and discipline of labor and its condition and with handing the task to the Admiralty: "The formidable nature of this task can be judged from the fact that the Labour Minister himself has taken no effective step towards its fulfillment during all the months when we have endeavoured to get him to face up to it."[29] This statement ignored months of negotiations in which Bevin sought to overcome the obstacles thrown up by labor and management, as well as Bevin's successes in other industries. Lithgow did possess enough self-awareness to acknowledge that Admiralty control of shipbuilding and ship-repairing labor would be made more difficult by his presence and offered his resignation, which was not accepted as the initial draft of the Essential Work Order was modified to limit his role in controlling the workforce. Lithgow continued to perceive and record Bevin's personal hostility: "statements that have reached me to the effect that the Minister of Labour has been suggesting that the Admiralty have 'slept in.'"[30] He referred to another message from Bevin as "merely another danger signal" of interference with Lithgow's policy of limiting the number of open yards in the absence of wholesale capitulation on working conditions.[31]

In Duncan's 1945 report on industrial relations, he summarized the view from Lithgow's office: the Ministry of Labour's "weakness" in failing to prosecute illegal strikers diminished the Order's deterrent value. "The historical record of illegal strikes throughout the War years is a damning picture of irresponsibility on the part of the Trade Unions, and of the Ministry of Labour and National Service." The

---

[28]   LAB 8/572, Bevin to Alexander, undated (April 1942), in response to Alexander to Bevin, 22 April 1942.

[29]   Churchill College Archives, Cambridge University, Albert V. Alexander Papers (hereinafter CCACU/AVA) 5/5/12, Lithgow to Alexander, 11 March 1941.

[30]   With regard to building a new shipyard for electric welding (LP, File 45, Lithgow to C. C. Jarrett of the Admiralty, 14 July 1942).

[31]   LP, File 45, Lithgow to Amos Ayre, 24 June 1942.

gap in attitudes and expectations between workers and management, between workers and the Admiralty Controller of Merchant Shipbuilding and Repair's office, and between that office and the Ministry of Labour was too wide to bridge, even in a national emergency.[32]

Wartime efforts to build or repair more ships by embracing new methods, by reopening yards, or by recruiting additional workers collided with this unfortunate history and these personal tensions. Examples of the obstacles created appear early in the war. British builders had been involved in the 1940 efforts to increase British shipping capacity by placing orders in American shipyards. In early 1941, these builders proposed that a Newcastle yard be reopened and that it be run along "American lines," building welded ships. Builders immediately demanded an assurance from the Ministry of Labour "that trade union arrangements would not be allowed to prejudice the adoption of new methods of manning and construction."[33] Lithgow echoed these concerns in his analysis for the First Sea Lord, adding his own concern that "dissipating" the few remaining trained men across more yards would "retard rather than accelerate production." He states further that because "the prospects of fully manning the existing yards with men capable of producing ships by normal methods are not bright" and that diluting the workforce by supplementing the existing number of skilled men with others who would learn alongside them while being paid equally would slow down output, then "nothing but trouble and harmful repercussions upon our normal programme will result unless we have the wholehearted support of the shipyard Unions and the complete backing of the Ministry of Labour."[34]

Jarrow also resurfaced. Even though Lithgow resisted expansion of production into new or disused yards, rumors persisted that the Admiralty would reopen yards. As late as 1943, Sir Alexander Russell (Conservative MP for Tynemouth) asked Lithgow to receive a deputation to "present to you once again the local point of view" as they had also done two years before. The MP cited "a rather persistent rumour that the Government had decided to open a yard at Jarrow." While he admitted that the previous deputation had been "impressed" and "satisfied," he believed that "a few facts about the shipbuilding position generally, and

---

[32]   LP, File 59, R. K. Duncan of the Directorate of Merchant Shipbuilding and Repairs, "Shipbuilding and Shiprepairing: A Criticism of Industrial Relations within the Industry," 30 January 1945, pp. 3–4.

[33]   LP, File 45, Memorandum from the Shipbuilding Conference (trade organization) on "Proposal to reopen Low Walker Shipyard of Sir W. G. Armstrong Whitworth & Co (Shipbuilders) Ltd., Newcastle-on-Tyne," 23 January 1941.

[34]   LP, File 45, Lithgow to Alexander, 27 January 1941. Illustrating both the divide in the Labour movement and the natural tendency to identify with the organization to which he belonged, Alexander recommended full support for Lithgow's position to Bevin (LP, File 59, 4 February 1941).

their application to local circumstance in particular" would settle the issue. But Russell's closing point illustrated the tenacity of local sentiment: "Of course, if you can tell them it is the intention of the Government to open the shipyard in the near future, so much the better."[35]

Thus, while Lithgow's place on the Board of Admiralty gained employers' confidence, it aroused hostility among workers. "Putting . . . official authority in the hands of their employers in this way" was unpopular with shipyard workers throughout the war.[36] This controversial appointment did not improve labor-management relations that were already fragile at best. The conflict between workers and Lithgow, as well as between Bevin and Lithgow, is a reminder that the constructed memory of "all-out effort" so popular today obscures the class divide that lingered in wartime Britain. Scholars have challenged the notion of a "People's War" that eroded class distinctions amid shared suffering; this discussion contributes one more example to the literature.[37]

The Admiralty also moved slowly to implement a sensible plan to prioritize ships for repair; decisions that had to be made quickly could not be centrally coordinated. The Senior Naval Officer (hereinafter SNO) in each port determined priorities without any clear avenue of appeal, but without access to all relevant facts. As Lithgow acknowledged, the SNO decided "from the point of view of operational control and if he judges that postponement of naval work would jeopardise operations he gave it priority."[38] Admiralty Licensing Surveyors working with the SNO also exercised inadequate supervision, failing to ensure that only the essential repairs they had licensed were indeed executed. The Ministry of Shipping, which was naturally interested in prioritizing repair for merchant vessels, criticized Lithgow's refusal to force naval vessels to adhere to clearly phrased austerity standards for merchant shipping. The result of his refusal was what some observers judged to be non-essential repairs being allocated equipment and manpower that essential short-term repairs lacked. Sometimes badly damaged vessels unworthy of repair on technical merits received undue attention in a misguided effort to raise morale. Thus, in spring 1941, "labour and facilities were inadequate, everyone was putting forward maximum claims, and who got satisfied and who left out was settled in a largely arbitrary way."[39]

---

[35]   LP, File 45, Russell to Lithgow, 5 January 1943, and Lithgow to Russell, 8 January 1943.

[36]   J. D. Scott and Richard Hughes, *History of the Second World War: United Kingdom Civil Series, The Administration of War Production* (London: HMSO, 1955), p. 146.

[37]   Angus Calder, *The People's War: Britain, 1939–45* (London: Jonathan Cape, 1969); a notable commentary on developments fifty years after the war is Jose Harris, "War and Social History: Britain and the Home Front during the Second World War," *Contemporary European History* 1:1 (1992), pp. 17–35.

[38]   CAB 102/424, "The Crisis of the Winter of 1940/41," p. 4.

[39]   Ibid., p. 5.

Resolution and its Limitations

The crisis crested in February 1941. Nearly 2,600,000 GRT (gross registered tons) of British-controlled merchant shipping awaited or was undergoing repair in British ports; the dry-cargo vessels among them amounted to one-quarter of Britain's active full-time importing fleet. Nearly two-thirds of these ships were immobilized— unable to discharge cargo and needing more than seven days to repair.[40]

Churchill turned his attention to this issue and other problems that were reducing shipping capacity. As Christopher Bell describes elsewhere in this volume, he convened the Battle of the Atlantic Committee, a weekly gathering of whichever officials Churchill thought most relevant to define, discuss, and tackle emerging problems. In addition to certain enhancements in anti-submarine warfare, the Committee also considered other managerial initiatives such as sailing ships capable of making twelve knots independently (a counterproductive move), reducing turnaround time in ports by loading and unloading cargo more quickly, and accelerating ship repair.[41]

In response to the crisis, HM Treasury agreed to remove an important financial obstacle to clearing the backlog of repairs by agreeing to pay all of the difference in cost between British and foreign repairers. Initially, the Treasury had in January 1941 authorized reimbursement to ship owners equal to eighty percent of the difference in cost between repairs at home and abroad, but revised its policy to 100 percent for repairs undertaken from 1 October 1941.[42] This step relieved congestion in British yards by encouraging owners to seek repairs abroad. It also worsened Britain's dollar imbalance and dependence upon the United States. Such an action could only be considered because Lend-Lease aid was on the horizon. As with every other aspect of the Battle of the Atlantic, the American role must be considered. Also, since "tonnage losses and enforced concentration on repairs" would "constitute the crux of the Battle of the Atlantic," Churchill had demanded "concerted attack by all Departments involved . . . upon the immense mass of damaged shipping now accumulated in our ports." Special lighting permitted work during blackout, and the working of double day shifts was implemented where possible. Workers objected that these innovations risked their safety and earnings: dock areas were well-defined air targets, and the altered work schedule reduced

---

[40]   *Digest*, Table 115; CAB 86/1, BA (42) 6, Table 6, 16 May 1942; TNA, Ministry of War Transport (hereinafter MT) File 65/28, "Estimate of United Kingdom Dry Cargo Imports for 1943," compiled 21 December 1942, Appendix B.

[41]   TNA, CAB 66/15/35, War Cabinet (hereinafter WP) (41) 62, 18 March 1941; Max Schoenfeld, "Winston Churchill as War Manager: The Battle of the Atlantic Committee, 1941," *Military Affairs* 52:3 (1988), pp. 122–27.

[42]   LP, File 55, Memorandum on Ship Repairs circulated by Ministry of Shipping, 9 April 1941.

overtime pay. Prioritization was also improved by cutting back on planned merchant shipbuilding (again increasing reliance on American building), stopping long-range merchant building (ships not scheduled to complete in 1941), and halting heavy warship building. Also, non-essential repairs were eliminated, and labor and facilities were transferred from long-term repair work (those expected to exceed six weeks). Ten thousand men were sought from merchant and naval shipbuilding to work on merchant repairs.[43] Several of these approaches helped remedy the short-term crisis, but they aggravated Britain's long-term shortage of ships by delaying construction of new vessels.

As has been noted, Bevin led the Ministry of Labour's effort to put more men in the yards. An Industrial Registration Order required men who had worked in shipbuilding and repairing in the preceding fifteen years to register so as to facilitate the transfer to the shipyards of those men currently employed in non-essential areas. While sixty thousand registered between March and October, workers were reluctant to return from vital war work elsewhere to an industry that paid lower wages, had limited long-term prospects, and that they perceived to be controlled by a shipbuilder who had helped destroy it for personal profit. Only eleven thousand moved into shipping industries; of thirteen thousand who registered as marine engineers, just 465 transferred. In operating compulsion, the restraint which Bullock praised as so successful elsewhere was condemned by builders and Lithgow's office as lenient, weak, and ineffective.

Limited expansion, re-prioritization, postponement of long-term repairs, and diversion of repairs abroad helped achieve a reduction in tonnage awaiting repair in British ports. By July 1941, tonnage awaiting repair in British ports had fallen nearly forty percent to 1,600,000 GRT, while tonnage completely immobilized awaiting repair was reduced by forty-five percent. Despite seasonal fluctuations, repair congestion never again threatened in British ports.[44] Thus it appeared that the repair backlog had been resolved, and the issue did not receive Cabinet-level attention again. Churchill and the Battle of the Atlantic Committee had grasped that this was one of several managerial problems requiring attention—but they could not grasp its complete scope.

This essential reduction in the number and tonnage of ships immobilized by reason of repair in British ports certainly was a vital prerequisite to improving the

---

[43]   CAB 86/1, Import Executive meeting, 28 February 1941, BA (41) 18, 15 April 1941, BA (41) 83, 30 June 1941; NMM/SEF, SRNA/5/H/3/1, Edwards, "Report," p. 8; CAB 102/424, "Outline of History of Ship Repair," p. 10. This last document was written in preparation for the official history due to dissatisfaction with a previous draft which ignored the transfer of repairs abroad. Thus those civil servants directed to prepare the history of these events struggled to grasp a cohesive vision of the factors affecting maritime warfare.

[44]   *Digest*, Table 115; CAB 86/1, BA (41) 3rd meeting, 2 April 1941, BA (41) 141, 21 October 1941; NMM/SEF, SRNA/H/3/1, Edwards, "Report," p. 20.

movement of cargo into British ports, but important shortcomings were camou-flaged by this apparent statistical achievement. Some ships' repairs were so limited and rushed that they soon returned for further repairs. Some workers were diverted to naval construction. Additions to the repair workforce also did not produce long-term results. Indeed, per capita productivity dropped steeply from March to May 1941 in the midst of a steady and consistent decline between January 1941 and June 1942. British repairers thus became less efficient in response to the crisis. Most importantly, the problem was transferred abroad to American and Dominion yards once Lend-Lease opened U.S. yards to British merchant ships. Records in the archives concerning overseas ports only date from August 1941. Indeed, the relevant table in the official *Statistical Digest of the War* only includes ships under repair in British ports, thereby masking the extent of the ongoing problem for post-war researchers who could not ascertain the continuing nature of the crisis. Throughout the war, two-thirds of British-controlled tonnage immobilized for repairs lay in ports abroad. Military planners' allowances for shipping undergoing repair when considering potential operations rose from nine percent of carrying capacity in August 1940 to thirteen percent in March 1943.[45] The repair backlog had been redistributed from clogged British ports, but the lost shipping capacity had not been restored.

The Comparative Toll on British Shipping Capacity: Repair Delays versus Submarines

The consequences of Britain's inability to provide ship-repairing productivity suffi-cient to mitigate its shipping capacity crisis are best illustrated by a comparison between the impact of U-boats and of repair congestion upon British shipping capacity. The dreaded U-boat accounted for two-thirds of British-flagged vessels

---

[45]   W. Averell Harriman Papers, Library of Congress, Box 159, Chronological File April 1–14, 1941, PURSA 245 Admiralty to Sir Arthur Salter, 7 April 1941; Chronological File May 7–21, 1941, Harriman Memo for Personal File of Battle of the Atlantic Committee meeting, 17 May 1941; CAB 102/424, "Outline of History of Ship Repair," p. 12, Appendix 3; CAB 86/1, BA (42) 6 of 16 May 1942, Table 8; BA (42) 1st meeting, 11 February 1942; TNA, Prime Minister's Papers (hereinafter PREM) 4/2/5, Enclosure 43, Ministry of Shipping report, 1 August 1940 and Shipping Committee (hereinafter SC) (43) 54, Appendix II, cited in Behrens, *Merchant Shipping*, Appendices XVIII and LX. On a related issue, as she began in 1945 to assess the rea-sons for improved turnaround of ships in port as they discharged cargo (which included but was not limited to ships under repair), Behrens believed the most important factor was the amalgamation of the Ministry of Shipping and the Ministry of Transport into the Ministry of War Transport in spring 1941. She wrote to the chief Statistician in the Ministry, W. P. Elderton (MT 65/163, 11 October and 17 November 1945), that she "thought it unnecessary to explain the real position [regarding the decrease in time spent in port] which might seem unduly com-plicated to the layman." This indicates a lack of confidence in the reader more than an attempt to deceive, and it points to one of the problems posed by the use of official histories.

Table 3.2:   Tonnage of British-Controlled Ships Lost to Submarines, 1939–1945

Date	1939	1940	1941	1942	1943	1944	1945
Jan		11.3	105.1	124.4	66.9	51.7	30
Feb		73	171.7	207.5	148	53.8	26.8
Mar		19.1	174.3	195.5	327.9	41.8	27.6
Apr		14.6	188.6	151.5	185.1	13.5	43.9
May		25	234	203.1	119.1	24.4	2.9
Jun		134.9	203.8	182.4	38.7	24.9	
Jul		139.2	71.9	192.7	101.7	25.1	
Aug		188.2	60.7	245.2	47	68.2	
Sep	137.1	223	156.6	249.4	42.2	26.4	
Oct	74.9	257.4	106.4	389.8	35.8	0	
Nov	22.9	110.7	55.2	403.7	21.8	10.1	
Dec	31.4	163.3	34.4	216.5	40.9	25.5	
Year	266.3	1359.7	1562.6	2761.7	1175.3	365.5	131.2

Digest, Table 158. Includes tankers and non-tankers. Includes all vessels with gross tonnage capacity of under 1600 GRT as well as those exceeding 1600 GRT. All figures are expressed in thousands of GRT.

lost to enemy action throughout the war, and for about one-half in 1940–41.[46] While the repair burden was reasonably consistent after 1941 (with a backlog each winter), code-breaking and tactical successes combined with North Atlantic weather to cause fluctuations in the U-boats' toll of British ships. During their best two consecutive months (October-November 1942), the U-boats sank about 396,000 GRT monthly; in no extended period did the U-boats average more than 270,000 GRT per month. In 1942 as a whole—the worst calendar year—the U-boats averaged 230,000 GRT each month. During the year July 1940–June 1941, the U-boat toll often fell below 200,000 GRT per month and averaged 259,000 GRT monthly.

During this same period, the repair crisis was tackled and supposedly reduced to "manageable" proportions—at least in British ports. Yet the global monthly total for British ships under repair from August 1941 through the end of the U-boat

---

[46]   Submarines were by no means the cause of all ship losses, but their proportional toll increased *vis-à-vis* losses to weather, mines, aircraft, and surface raiders as the war progressed. The wartime and post-war obsession with the submarine dictates the comparative focus here; these figures and the analysis derived will exclude losses due to mines, aircraft, and surface raiders, though the relative proportion of losses is clarified in the following note.

Table 3.3:   British-controlled Merchant Ships under Repair Compared with British-controlled Merchant Ships Lost to Submarines, monthly

Date	World Total *British ports only until July 1941	Ships Lost to Subs
Sep39 to Jan41		1731
Jan–41	*	105.1
Feb–41	2394	171.7
Mar–41	2275	174.3
Apr–41	1901	188.6
May–41	1952	234
Jun–41	1755	203.8
Jul–41	1579	71.9
Aug–41	**2823**	**60.7**
Sep–41	**2973**	**156.6**
Oct–41	**2885**	**106.4**
Nov–41	**2871**	**55.2**
Dec–41	**3385**	**34.4**
Jan–42	**3236**	**124.4**
Feb–42	**3404**	**207.5**
Mar–42	**3052**	**195.5**
Apr–42	**3102**	**151.5**
May–42	**2977**	**203.1**
Jun–42	**3040**	**182.4**
Jul–42	**3018**	**192.7**
Aug–42	**2889**	**245.2**
Sep–42	**2844**	**249.4**
Oct–42	**3073**	**389.8**
Nov–42	**3053**	**403.7**
Dec–42	**3403**	**216.5**
Jan–43	**3607**	**66.9**
Feb–43	**3464**	**148**
Mar–43	**3283**	**327.9**
Apr–43	**3396**	**185.1**

May–43	3101	119.1
Jun–43	2742	38.7
Jul–43	2551	101.7
Aug–43	2616	47
Sep–43	2566	42.2
Oct–43	2783	35.8
Nov–43	2665	21.8
Dec–43	3048	40.9
Jan–44	3039	51.7
Feb–44	2865	53.8
Mar–44	2585	41.8
Apr–44	2736	13.5
May–44	2801	24.4
Jun–44	2360	24.9
Jul–44	2404	25.1
Aug–44	2472	68.2
Sep–44	2306	26.4
Oct–44	2799	0
Nov–44	2962	10.1
Dec–44	2842	25.5
Jan–45	3010	30
Feb–45	3120	26.8
Mar–45	3076	27.6
Apr–45	3113	43.9
May–45	2970	2.9

Digest, Table 115, 116, 158; CAB 102/424, Behrens letter to M.M. Postan, 26 February 1947; CAB 86/1, BA (42) 6, 16 May 1942, Tables 6-8. All figures are expressed in thousands of GRT and figures for losses to submarines include all vessels. For ships under repair, only ships of 1600 GRT or more were included so as to utilize statistics that differentiated between ships under repair in Britain and abroad. For statistics that include all ships under repair, see *Digest*, Table 115.

crisis in summer 1943 ranged between 2,800,000 and 3,600,000 GRT, averaging about 3,100,000 GRT (see Tables 3.3 and 3.7). Thus the very numbers which when tabulated in Table 3.2 appear so enormous, shrink in significance when compared (on the right in Table 3.3) with disruption due to delays for repair (on the left in Table 3.3). In any given period, therefore, at least seven times more shipping was out of service "immobilized by reason of repair" or "undergoing repairs while working cargo" as compared to the U-boats' contemporaneous efforts to eliminate them from service.

Even allowing for the reality that there will always be a number of ships laid up for repair at any given time, however, this disparity is significant. The contrast was usually greater. More frequently, the ratio of ships under repair to those being sunk exceeded ten to one, and was occasionally as high as fifty or one hundred to one (August, November, and December 1941). On a day-to-day basis, therefore, the real shipping crisis was in British shipyards.

The task of venturing a cumulative assessment is challenging but necessary. Certainly a longer-term view partly redresses the balance for four reasons. First, the U-boats' toll of Allied (not just British) ships was detrimental to British interests because it deprived Britain of subsequent reinforcement, though there were specific and severe diplomatic and strategic consequences imposed by Britain's loss of shipping capacity, regardless of cause, as American strategists moved inexorably toward exercising greater influence over Allied decision-making. Second, while the relative impact of submarine action in the Battle of the Atlantic on shipping capacity has always been overemphasized *vis-à-vis* other causes of loss, the very real impact on the crews and their families of their ship's loss regardless of cause was catastrophic.[47] Third, though only a small percentage of the repair load resulted from the failure of U-boats to sink ships, those few ships often took far longer to repair. Of course, some U-boat triumphs were partly attributable to Britain's desperate expedient of returning unseaworthy ships to duty after inadequate repairs. Thus, the U-boats' psychological and material importance in waging war (and the need to improve anti-submarine warfare) should not be dismissed in any study of the war. Nor should the interaction between U-boat depredations and the repair crisis be ignored. Nor should the importance of adequate repair facilities be overrated, particularly in comparison to the overall toll of sinkings from all causes. Certainly the repair crisis removed less shipping capacity from availability than total British (let alone Allied) sinkings from all causes. Further study and statistical analysis could provide additional conclusions.

But a fourth caveat deserves particular statistical analysis. Carrying capacity lost to U-boat action was lost permanently and cumulatively. The loss of a ship to

---

[47]   Losses of British-flagged ships due to submarines in 1940–41 were fifty-five percent of all losses; as aircraft were diverted to the Eastern Front and surface ships became unavailable, submarines accounted for seventy-nine percent of the total in 1942–43 (*Digest*, Table 158).

Table 3.4: Cumulative Comparison, 1941–1943

Date	Known Cumulative Ton-Months Lost to Repair (World Total for British Ships)	Cumulative Ton-Months Lost to Subs
Jan–41	*	12007.4
Feb–41	2394	13910.2
Mar–41	4669	15987.3
Apr–41	6570	18253
May–41	8522	20752.7
Jun–41	10277	23456.2
Jul–41	11856	26231.6
Aug–41	14679	29067.7
Sep–41	17652	32060.4
Oct–41	20537	35159.5
Nov–41	23408	38313.8
Dec–41	26793	41502.5
Jan–42	30029	44815.6
Feb–42	33433	48336.2
Mar–42	36485	52052.3
Apr–42	39587	55919.9
May–42	42564	59990.6
Jun–42	45604	64243.7
Jul–42	48622	68689.5
Aug–42	51511	73380.5
Sep–42	54355	78320.9
Oct–42	57428	83651.1
Nov–42	60481	89385
Dec–42	63884	95335.4
Jan–43	67491	101352.7
Feb–43	70955	107518
Mar–43	74238	114011.2
Apr–43	77634	120689.5
May–43	80735	127486.9
Jun–43	83477	134323

Digest, Table 115, 116, 158; CAB 102/424, Behrens letter to M.M. Postan, 26 February 1947; CAB 86/1, BA (42) 6, 16 May 1942, Tables 6-8. All data for losses to submarines include all vessels. For ships under repair, only ships of 1600 GRT or more were included so as to utilize statistics that differentiated between ships under repair in Britain and abroad. Thus this table underrepresents the total repair burden, even though ships undergoing repair while unloading cargo are included. Combining the two operations inevitably slowed both cargo discharge and ship repair. For statistics that include all ships under repair, see *Digest*, Table 115. All figures are expressed in "ton-months," which expresses the cumulative loss of tonnage in terms of months of service lost. Thus the permanent loss of tonnage capacity to submarines is correctly weighted in comparison to the temporary loss of tonnage capacity while immobilized in repair yards.

repair congestion for, say, June to September 1941 did not deprive Britain of that capacity subsequently, whereas a ship sunk in June 1941 deprived Britain of that capacity permanently. The longer the war lasted, the greater would be the U-boat's cumulative impact. When the cumulative monthly reduction of carrying capacity induced by U-boat attack is compared with the segmented monthly impacts of repair congestion for the months where statistics are available, the data indicates that shipping capacity lost due to repair delays totaled about eighty-eight percent of the capacity lost due to sinking between February 1941 and May 1942. The loss of shipping capacity is expressed in Table 3.4 in "ton-months": ship tonnage unavailable for usage in a given month (and beyond).

The gap in relative impact grew in the second half of 1942 as the cumulative impact of shipping losses mounted. Only in 1943 did the defeat of the U-boats, U.S. shipbuilding, and hard-won American shipping allocations to British needs begin to relieve pressure upon British shipping capacity.[48]

As Table 3.4 depicts, Britain only began keeping detailed records for ships under repair in British ports in February 1941, and, as noted, did not maintain complete worldwide records for British ships under repair until August 1941. This statistical oversight reflects political and bureaucratic delays in recognizing the problem rather than its sudden appearance in 1941. Ships had been unavailable due to repair delays in 1940 as well. Tables 3.5 and 3.8 include a conservative estimate of repair congestion for earlier months. While the data is an estimate, it avoids the pit-fall of the previous table in ignoring the impact of the loss of shipping capacity due to repair delays in the war's first seventeen months, a period which included the chaos following Dunkirk. By adding the third column representing the additional estimated ton-months of capacity lost to repair, the cumulative impact of repair delays is seen as more significant than losses to submarines throughout 1941 and most of 1942. Only in the months immediately preceding the defeat of the U-boats did their long-term cumulative activity actually deprive Britain of more ship-ping capacity than did Britain's ship-repairing congestion. Throughout the era of Allied obsession with the U-boat, Britain's shipyards certainly deserved greater and continuing attention, especially after Lend-Lease transferred a significant propor-tion of the repair burden overseas—out of sight, but no less damaging to British shipping capacity. The conscious and fateful decision to avoid domestic labor disputes by pressing for effective compromise between labor and management in order to increase both shipbuilding and ship-repairing output meant, therefore, that

---

48   Given the evidence that repair congestion was present as early as the winter of 1939–40 and then increased after Dunkirk, the author has conservatively assumed an initially mod-erate, then swelling tide of ships under repair by the time statistics were first kept in Febru-ary 1941. Also, troopships and hospital ships which consistently accounted for a repair load of another 300,000 GRT were excluded from these statistics. CAB 102/424, Behrens letter to M. M. Postan, 26 February 1947; *Digest*, Tables 115, 152, 158; CAB 86/1, BA (42) 6, 16 May 1942, Table 6–8.

Britain would depend on American goodwill and the skill of British diplomats to extract the shipping allocations necessary to achieve British as well as Allied strategic objectives later in the war. Thus, while Allied losses mattered enormously to victory, this comparison of British losses to submarines with British ships immobilized by repair influences our understanding of how that victory would be achieved. American shipbuilding would, as is well known, far outpace the consequences of both German attacks and wasteful use of shipping for the Allies as a whole in 1942 and 1943. But the Americans would decide who used those ships, not only because of their tremendous production and the effects of submarine attack, but also because of the deficiencies in British ship-repairing.

Conclusion

British ship-repairing's illusory triumph in 1941 had retrieved ships at a rate sufficient only to maintain British imports at around thirty million tons annually; when U-boat depredations compounded British trials while shipping was devoted to supporting overseas operations, British imports sank once again. This failure forced the premier maritime nation inexorably toward a humiliating logistical dependence upon the United States. Britain's laggard response to this crisis needlessly irritated relations. American belligerency, which forced attention to be paid to U.S. military transport needs, diminished aid to Britain even as the war's global scope stretched Britain's shipping resources. Churchill's decision to place complete reliance upon the Americans for provision of the necessary shipping capacity ("It is to the United States building that we must look for relief") meant that Britain's survival and her influence upon war-winning strategy would depend upon American decision-makers.[49]

Integration of our understanding of how combat, diplomacy, technological change, intelligence, internal rail transit, labor relations, port and shipyard management, class conflict, and other factors contributed to the provision of enough shipping capacity to win the war—and to the decision of whose strategy could be implemented at what point—is therefore the challenge facing the next generation of historians of the Battle of the Atlantic.

---

[49] CAB 66/15/42, WP (41) 69, 26 March 1941, "The Import Programmes," Annex II, Naval Programme 1941, 27 March 1941, p. 6.

Table 3.5: Cumulative Estimated Comparison, 1941–1943

Date	Known Cumulative Ton-Months Lost to Repair (World Total for British Ships)	Cumulative Ton-Months Lost to Subs	Estimated Cumulative Ton-Months Lost to Repair (World Total for British Ships)
Jan–41	*	12007.4	25600
Feb–41	2394	13910.2	27994
Mar–41	4669	15987.3	30269
Apr–41	6570	18253	32170
May–41	8522	20752.7	34122
Jun–41	10277	23456.2	35877
Jul–41	11856	26231.6	37456
Aug–41	14679	29067.7	40279
Sep–41	17652	32060.4	43252
Oct–41	20537	35159.5	46137
Nov–41	23408	38313.8	49008
Dec–41	26793	41502.5	52393
Jan–42	30029	44815.6	55629
Feb–42	33433	48336.2	59033
Mar–42	36485	52052.3	62085
Apr–42	39587	55919.9	65187
May–42	42564	59990.6	68164
Jun–42	45604	64243.7	71204
Jul–42	48622	68689.5	74222
Aug–42	51511	73380.5	77111
Sep–42	54355	78320.9	79955
Oct–42	57428	83651.1	83028
Nov–42	60481	89385	86081
Dec–42	63884	95335.4	89484
Jan–43	67491	101352.7	93091
Feb–43	70955	107518	96155
Mar–43	74238	114011.2	99838
Apr–43	77634	120689.5	103234
May–43	80735	127486.9	106335
Jun–43	83477	134323	109077

Footnotes 47 and 48 provide the data and the assumptions guiding the estimated data. The estimates for tonnage under repair before January 1941 (made necessary by the lack of statistics) are conservative.

Table 3.6: Total Wartime British Imports

Month	1939	1940	1941	1942	1943	1944	1945
Jan		3811	2413	2006	1177	1966	1841
Feb		3598	2152	1867	1267	2126	1830
Mar		3856	2386	1943	2015	2073	2013
Apr		4207	2360	2099	2378	1992	1926
May		4177	2767	2214	2064	2345	2130
Jun		4054	2776	2091	2723	2352	2658
Jul		3389	2648	2167	2748	2060	2608
Aug		3936	2712	1919	2368	2102	2438
Sep	2831	2974	2816	2149	2661	2000	
Oct	3091	3208	2930	2023	2569	2216	
Nov	3529	2602	2140	1300	2186	2371	
Dec	3690	2547	2680	1235	2327	1923	
Total	**13141**	**41859**	**30478**	**22891**	**26372**	**25147**	**17444**

Digest, Table 161. All import figures expressed in thousands of tons and include the Ministry of Food program, the Ministry of Supply program (later Ministry of Production), munitions, and other minor miscellaneous imports.

Table 3.7:   British-Controlled Merchant Ships under Repair Compared with British-Controlled Ships Lost to Submarines, Monthly

Date	Undergoing Repair while working cargo	Immobilized by reason of repair	Total in British Ports	Abroad Total	World Total	Ships Lost to Subs
Sep39–Jan41	N/A	N/A	N/A	N/A	N/A	1731
Jan	N/A	N/A	N/A	N/A	N/A	105.1
Feb	927	1467	2394	N/A	N/A	171.7
Mar	897	1378	2275	N/A	N/A	174.3
Apr	650	1251	1901	N/A	N/A	188.6
May	875	1077	1952	N/A	N/A	234
Jun	914	841	1755	N/A	N/A	203.8
Jul	813	766	1579	N/A	N/A	71.9
Aug	843	756	1599	1224	**2823**	**60.7**
Sep	953	640	1593	1380	**2973**	**156.6**
Oct	988	637	1625	1260	**2885**	**106.4**
Nov	927	658	1585	1286	**2871**	**55.2**
Dec	1141	652	1793	1592	**3385**	**34.4**
Jan–42	1015	722	1737	1499	**3236**	**124.4**
Feb	1067	759	1826	1578	**3404**	**207.5**
Mar	921	611	1532	1520	**3052**	**195.5**
Apr	835	679	1514	1588	**3102**	**151.5**
May	811	665	1476	1501	**2977**	**203.1**
Jun	812	541	1353	1687	**3040**	**182.4**
Jul	798	572	1370	1648	**3018**	**192.7**
Aug	739	597	1336	1553	**2889**	**245.2**
Sep	874	684	1558	1286	**2844**	**249.4**
Oct	910	641	1551	1522	**3073**	**389.8**
Nov	770	659	1429	1626	**3053**	**403.7**
Dec	712	663	1375	2028	**3403**	**216.5**
Jan–43	885	722	1607	2000	**3607**	**66.9**
Feb	865	726	1591	1873	**3464**	**148**
Mar	802	790	1592	1691	**3283**	**327.9**

Apr	947	876	1823	1573	**3396**	**185.1**
May	935	734	1669	1432	**3101**	**119.1**
Jun	853	639	1491	1251	**2742**	**38.7**
Jul	811	571	1383	1168	**2551**	**101.7**
Aug	832	580	1412	1204	**2616**	**47**
Sep	996	633	1629	937	**2566**	**42.2**
Oct	951	636	1587	1196	**2783**	**35.8**
Nov	896	665	1560	1105	**2665**	**21.8**
Dec	964	676	1640	1408	**3048**	**40.9**
Jan–44	941	700	1641	1398	**3039**	**51.7**
Feb	920	662	1582	1283	**2865**	**53.8**
Mar	871	669	1540	1045	**2585**	**41.8**
Apr	972	639	1611	1125	**2736**	**13.5**
May	979	646	1625	1176	**2801**	**24.4**
Jun	854	565	1420	940	**2360**	**24.9**
Jul	870	585	1455	949	**2404**	**25.1**
Aug	829	768	1597	875	**2472**	**68.2**
Sep	799	732	1531	775	**2306**	**26.4**
Oct	1023	806	1828	971	**2799**	**0**
Nov	1098	851	1949	1013	**2962**	**10.1**
Dec	1072	769	1841	999	**2842**	**25.5**
Jan–45	1145	830	1975	1035	**3010**	**30**
Feb	1185	883	2068	1052	**3120**	**26.8**
Mar	1036	860	1896	1180	**3076**	**27.6**
Apr	1049	820	1868	1245	**3113**	**43.9**
May	1051	872	1923	1047	**2970**	**2.9**

Digest, Table 115, 116, 158; CAB 102/424, Behrens letter to M.M. Postan, 26 February 1947; CAB 86/1, BA (42) 6, 16 May 1942, Tables 6-8. All figures are expressed in thousands of GRT and figures for losses to submarines include all vessels. For ships under repair, only ships of 1600 GRT or more were included so as to utilize statistics that differentiated between ships under repair in Britain and abroad. For statistics that include all ships under repair, see *Digest*, Table 115.

Table 3.8:   British-Controlled Merchant Ships under Repair Compared Cumulatively with British-Controlled Ships Lost to Submarines, 1939-1943

Date	Known Cumulative Ton-Months Lost to Repair (World Total for British Ships)	Cumulative Ton-Months Lost to Subs	Estimated Cumulative Ton-Months Lost to Repair (World Total for British Ships)
Sep–39	N/A	137.1	400
Oct	N/A	349.1	1100
Nov	N/A	584	2100
Dec	N/A	850.3	3500
Jan–40	N/A	1127.9	5000
Feb	N/A	1478.5	6400
Mar	N/A	1848.2	7500
Apr	N/A	2232.5	8700
May	N/A	2641.8	10400
Jun	N/A	3186	12000
Jul	N/A	3869.4	13600
Aug	N/A	4741	15300
Sep	N/A	5835.6	17000
Oct	N/A	7187.6	18800
Nov	N/A	8650.3	20800
Dec	N/A	10276.3	23100
Jan–41	N/A	12007.4	25600
Feb	2394	13910.2	27994
Mar	4669	15987.3	30269
Apr	6570	18253	32170
May	8522	20752.7	34122
Jun	10277	23456.2	35877
Jul	11856	26231.6	37456
Aug	14679	29067.7	40279
Sep	17652	32060.4	43252
Oct	20537	35159.5	46137
Nov	23408	38313.8	49008

Dec	26793	41502.5	52393
Jan–42	30029	44815.6	55629
Feb	33433	48336.2	59033
Mar	36485	52052.3	62085
Apr	39587	55919.9	65187
May	42564	59990.6	68164
Jun	45604	64243.7	71204
Jul	48622	68689.5	74222
Aug	51511	73380.5	77111
Sep	54355	78320.9	79955
Oct	57428	83651.1	83028
Nov	60481	89385	86081
Dec	63884	95335.4	89484
Jan–43	67491	101352.7	93091
Feb	70955	107518	96155
Mar	74238	114011.2	99838
Apr	77634	120689.5	103234
May	80735	127486.9	106335
Jun–43	83477	134323	109077

Digest, Table 115, 116, 158; CAB 102/424, Behrens letter to M.M. Postan, 26 February 1947; CAB 86/1, BA (42) 6, 16 May 1942, Tables 6-8. All data for losses to submarines include all vessels. For ships under repair, only ships of 1600 GRT or more were included so as to utilize statistics that differentiated between ships under repair in Britain and abroad. Thus this table underrepresents the total repair burden, even though ships undergoing repair while unloading cargo are included. Combining the two operations inevitably slowed both cargo discharge and ship repair. For statistics that include all ships under repair, see *Digest*, Table 115. All figures are expressed in "ton-months," which expresses the cumulative loss of tonnage in terms of months of service lost. Thus the permanent loss of tonnage capacity to submarines is correctly weighted in comparison to the temporary loss of tonnage capacity while immobilized in repair yards. Also, the estimates for tonnage under repair before January 1941 (made necessary by the lack of statistics) are conservative.

4

Brothers in Arms

The Admiralty, the Air Ministry, and the Battle of the Atlantic

Tim Benbow

Those interested in the history of inter-service disputes between the Royal Navy and the Royal Air Force are presented with an embarrassment of riches. This relationship has from the very start journeyed through rough waters—and, to be properly balanced, stormy skies. The most notorious and bitter periods of the conflict were in the interwar years and then again in the mid-1960s. In both of these eras, the intensity of the struggle and the perceived significance of the issues at stake for one or both services were so great that the conflict flowed over the walls of discretion surrounding Whitehall to impact on the public consciousness. In fact, there is more continuity in the relationship than this depiction would suggest. The early and mid-1950s saw a remarkable level of bureaucratic infighting and political skulduggery that is all the more striking for not spilling over into the public arena. Similarly, the disputes were by no means put in abeyance during the Second World War. While there was a great deal of very effective cooperation between the services, particularly at the level of those conducting operations, the relationship at the top of the hierarchy was anything but harmonious. There were many serious clashes between the leaderships of the two services, which perhaps do not get the attention they deserve due to being eclipsed by the comforting knowledge that the result was victory. Perhaps the most enduring as well as the most significant concerned the allocation of aircraft between the competing claims of the strategic air offensive and the campaign against the U-boats.

This chapter examines this wartime argument between the two services and explores the reasons underlying it.[1] It begins with a brief overview of the parallel development of the two campaigns, to provide a broad chronology and to set the

---

[1] I would like to thank Christina Goulter and David Jordan for invaluable guidance through the literature on the air war, and two anonymous reviewers for their hugely constructive comments on an earlier draft of this chapter. I alone am responsible for the interpretations and arguments that it contains. This chapter was originally published in *Global War Studies* 11:1 (2014).

analysis that follows in its wider context. It then summarizes the conceptual background and the central contention of the interwar air theorists that the proper use of air power lay in bombing the heart of the enemy's power, which would by itself bring victory. It argues that the Royal Air Force was fixated on implementing this approach during the Second World War, and held to it tenaciously despite the shortcomings that rapidly became apparent. The chapter explores in some detail the attempts of the Admiralty to secure additional aircraft for the war at sea and the resistance of the Air Ministry to providing them at the expense of the strategic air offensive against Germany. The focus is on the issue of transferring aircraft from Bomber Command to Coastal Command; the related issue of the effectiveness of Bomber Command when it was used in the war at sea is unfortunately beyond the scope of what is already a long chapter. Finally, it examines the failure of the government, and in particular of Winston Churchill (who combined the roles of Prime Minister and Minister of Defence), to mediate effectively on this vitally important question.

This subject has received a growing amount of attention in the academic literature. John Buckley argues that the inability of Coastal Command to perform the role allocated to it, as a result of interwar neglect by both the Air Ministry and the Admiralty, brought Britain close to disaster between 1940 and 1941. During the war, he suggests, the Admiralty, which had previously been confident that the U-boat problem had been resolved, quickly realized the vital role for land-based maritime air power, but their efforts to get it committed were blocked by the focus of the Air Ministry on strategic bombing. This policy choice, exacerbated by the policies of the U.S. services, brought about a second, entirely avoidable crisis between 1942 and 1943.[2] Marc Milner is one of many historians who identify the mid-Atlantic air gap as the key problem in winning the campaign, going so far as to state that "The failure of the Allies to close the air gap before 1943 remains one of the great unsolved historical problems of the war." He notes that closing it required Very Long Range (VLR) aircraft and argues that but for misplaced priorities, these could have been provided earlier.[3] Richard Goette—who identifies a general lack of attention to the issue of maritime air power in the literature on the Battle of the Atlantic—argues that the crisis caused by the air gap "could and should have been avoided." He continues, "the British had the resources to close the air gap in 1942, but they failed to do so. This was a clear failure of Britain's military

[2]   John Buckley, *The RAF and Trade Defence, 1919–1945: Constant Endeavour* (Keele: Keele University Press, 1995); for the more offensive role of Coastal Command, see Christina J. M. Goulter, *A Forgotten Offensive: Royal Air Force Coastal Command's Anti-Shipping Campaign, 1940–45* (London: Frank Cass, 1995).

[3]   Marc Milner, "The Battle of the Atlantic," *The Journal of Strategic Studies* 13:1 (1990), pp. 45–66; quotation, p. 59. Milner plays down the importance of Ultra signals intelligence, assessing it as secondary to the air gap, ibid., pp. 57–58.

and political leadership."[4] John O'Connell also concludes that the campaign could have been won a year earlier, in 1942, if the RAF had allocated the B-24 Liberators it acquired from the U.S.[5] Even historians who approach the subject area from a perspective more sympathetic to air power tend to acknowledge that the Air Staff might have been wrong in its attitude towards the campaign against the U-boats. Malcolm Smith accepts this point,[6] and Richard Overy writes, "Why the RAF remained resistant for so long to the idea of releasing bombers to work over the ocean defies explanation."[7]

There is therefore some degree of consensus that the decisions made in British interwar and, in particular, wartime policy created huge problems for the Battle of the Atlantic which were by no means inevitable. The main issue is therefore to understand why this was the case. Some recent work has sought to explain why British policy took the shape that it did. Duncan Redford considers the balance in British policy between the bombing campaign and the Battle of the Atlantic, arguing that it was weighted too heavily towards the former. He explains this imbalance as being the result of wider strategic and alliance concerns—including the U.S. brand of inter-service rivalry—and also the corporate culture of the RAF.[8] Christopher Bell adds that Churchill's role in the shortfalls of aircraft for the Battle of the Atlantic has generally been overlooked, partly because the great man's own memoirs draw a veil over it whilst also giving the impression that his concern over shipping losses was greater than it actually was. In practice, often swayed by Lord Cherwell, he instinctively sided with the Air Ministry over the Admiralty and also the War Office. While he never wholly swallowed claims that bombing could win the war alone, he was prepared to give the airmen the priority they demanded, over the needs of the Battle of the Atlantic.[9]

This chapter aims to explore more deeply the failure to provide the aircraft which, it is generally acknowledged, were urgently needed for the maritime campaign yet were not forthcoming. It identifies as the key factor the core ideology of

[4]   Richard Goette, "Britain and the Delay in Closing the Mid-Atlantic 'Air Gap' during the Battle of the Atlantic," *The Northern Mariner* XV:4 (October 2005), pp. 19–41; quotations pp. 21, 40.

[5]   John F. O'Connell, "Closing the North Atlantic Air Gap: Where Did All the British Liberators Go?," *Air Power History* 59:2 (Summer 2012), pp. 32–43.

[6]   Malcolm Smith, "The Allied Air Offensive," *The Journal of Strategic Studies* 13:1 (1990), pp. 67–83, especially pp. 80–81.

[7]   Richard J. Overy, *Why the Allies Won* (London: Pimlico, 1996), p. 60.

[8]   Duncan Redford, "Inter- and Intra-Service Rivalries in the Battle of the Atlantic," *The Journal of Strategic Studies* 32:6 (December 2009), pp. 899–928.

[9]   Christopher M. Bell, *Churchill and Sea Power* (Oxford: Oxford University Press, 2013), especially chapter 9.

the Royal Air Force which led it to focus on strategic bombing to the exclusion of properly resourcing other equally valid roles for air power. It argues that the Air Staff—including Portal, its Chief—was excessively focused on demonstrating that strategic bombing could win the war on its own. The result was that it was blind to the requirements of Britain's most vital campaign during the critical period of mid-1940 to early 1943. At this time the RAF and Churchill had abundant evidence both that the costly strategic bombing campaign was failing to deliver what had been promised, and also that long-range aircraft were desperately needed for the Battle of the Atlantic. Nevertheless, they refused to accept even the small diminution of the effort devoted to the bombing offensive that would have turned the campaign against the U-boats decisively in Britain's favor. The chapter concludes that to characterize disputes such as this one as "inter-service squabbling" risks overlooking the fundamental—and enduring—intellectual differences on which they rest.

Overview: A Tale of Two Campaigns

First, however, a brief overview of the two related and competing campaigns—the struggle against the U-boats and the strategic bombing campaign—will provide some context for what follows.[10] The early stages of the war were in some ways

---

[10]   For general works on the war at sea and the Battle of the Atlantic, see S. W. Roskill, *The War at Sea, 1939–45*, 4 vols. (London: HMSO, 1954 to 1961); S. W. Roskill, *The Navy at War, 1939–1945* (London: Collins, 1960); Corelli Barnett, *Engage the Enemy More Closely: The Royal Navy in the Second World War* (London: Hodder and Stoughton, 1991); Marc Milner's article, "The Battle of the Atlantic," cited in full above, and the same author's *Battle of the Atlantic*, second edition (Stroud: History Press, 2011); John Terraine, *Business in Great Waters: The U-Boat Wars, 1916–1945* (London: Leo Cooper, 1989); and V. E. Tarrant, *The U-Boat Offensive, 1914–1945* (London: Cassell, 2000). For the air war in general and the strategic air offensive in particular, see Richard J. Overy, *The Air War, 1939–1945* (London: Europa, 1980); John Terraine, *The Right of the Line: The Royal Air Force in the European War, 1939–1945* (London: Sceptre, 1988); Smith, "The Allied Air Offensive"; Charles Webster and Noble Frankland, *The Strategic Air Offensive Against Germany, 1939–45*, 4 vols. (London: HMSO, 1961); Tami Davis Biddle, *Rhetoric and Reality in Air Warfare: The Evolution of British and American Ideas About Strategic Bombing, 1914–1945* (Princeton: Princeton University Press, 2002); and Peter W. Gray, "The Strategic Leadership and Direction of the Royal Air Force Strategic Air Offensive against Germany from Inception to 1945," Ph.D. thesis, University of Birmingham, October 2009. The official history of the RAF in the maritime war was written but never published; with the exception of the official history of the strategic air offensive, the Air Ministry was reluctant to cede to the Cabinet Office oversight and the final say over what might be written, as was the practice with the official histories, for fear that the result might be critical of the RAF. See Gray, "Strategic Leadership and Direction of the Royal Air Force Strategic Air Offensive," p. 20, also Christina J. M. Goulter, "British Official Histories of the Air War," in Jeffrey Grey, ed., *The Last Word: Essays on Official History in the United States and British Commonwealth* (Westport, CT: Praeger, 2003).

different to what had been anticipated. There were no air attacks on Britain, while the British Expeditionary Force deployed in France found things remarkably quiet, hence the "phoney war" soubriquet. The use of this term was quite inappropriate to the war at sea, however, where the war was far more intense from the outset. Fortunately for Britain and the Allied cause, Germany was notably ill-prepared for war at sea, her ambitious naval expansion plans assuming that war would begin only in 1944. German warships were used for commerce raiding, compelling Britain to divert scarce capital ships and causing much disruption to shipping in addition to the vessels they sank. Moreover, in stark contrast to the hesitancy that characterized the campaign in the First World War, U-boats conducted attacks without warning almost from the beginning of hostilities. However, on the outbreak of war, Germany only had thirty-nine operational U-boats; production was expanded, but with the needs of the land forces still being strongly prioritized, only thirteen more were commissioned by April 1940.[11] In contrast to the First World War, Britain adopted a convoy and escort system from the outset (though it was far from comprehensive and most convoys had minimal escorts)—yet also wasted effort and lost valuable warships in supposedly "offensive" patrolling. During this first phase, as Tarrant put it, the U-boat campaign was "little more than a nuisance" yet it was also just "a preliminary skirmish."[12] Both sides suffered from a lack of preparation, limited initial numbers of platforms, inadequate training, mechanical failures, and technological shortcomings. Both would ascend a steep learning curve, with the balance of advantage shifting repeatedly over the following years as the campaign ebbed and flowed.

For the RAF in particular, the war did not begin as had been expected. Instead of launching strategic attacks on the enemy heartland, a policy of restraint was pursued in which great care was taken to avoid hitting civilian targets. This was partly in order to avoid provoking air attacks on British cities and partly due to a desire not to alienate neutral opinion, especially in the U.S.[13] Bomber Command was used for some attacks against the German fleet and for dropping propaganda leaflets. Coastal Command contributed to the campaign against the U-boats, but the degree of focus on strategic bombing in doctrine, planning, development, and procurement meant that anti-submarine warfare, one of the key roles of the air power which the RAF insisted it must control in its totality, was gravely neglected.[14]

The course of the war took an abrupt turn for the worse from the British perspective with the German invasion of France in summer 1940. In addition to knocking Britain's most powerful ally out of the war—alongside several smaller

---

[11]   Tarrant, *U-Boat Offensive*, p. 81.

[12]   Ibid., p. 88.

[13]   Gray, "Strategic Leadership and Direction of the Royal Air Force Strategic Air Offensive," pp. 155–57.

[14]   Milner, *Battle of the Atlantic*, pp. 14–15.

ones—the campaign brought Italy into the conflict on the opposing side as well as allowing the principal adversary to advance to the Channel coast. With Britain forcibly evicted from the continent, air power inevitably took on a more central role in British strategy. Strategic bombing became the principal potential means of striking against Germany and putting direct military pressure against it, with the maritime blockade and the use of subversion in a secondary position. For RAF Bomber Command, now the tip of the spear for British strategy, the gloves were off and the campaign began in earnest, with bombing of industrial targets in the Ruhr beginning in May, though there were also pressing demands to support the Army in France, and then to target shipping that could be used in any invasion of Britain. The RAF thus now had a golden opportunity to indulge its obsession and to make good on all its previous claims. Two major problems swiftly emerged. First, to the initial disbelief and growing discomfort of the airmen, the impact of bombing proved to be vastly less than had been claimed beforehand. Bombers proved far more vulnerable to enemy air defenses than anticipated, with daylight bombing swiftly proving to be prohibitively costly while, partly as a result, their attacks were woefully inaccurate. Further, German industry and morale both proved to be more resilient targets than had been assumed. Much of this was the inevitable result of initial teething problems that could be tackled given time and resources. However, the second problem was that the strategic air campaign was not the only call on Britain's scare resources. While the fall of France increased the centrality of strategic bombing to British strategy, it also tipped the balance of the maritime war very strongly against her, vastly increasing the threat to the sea communications on which Britain's war effort (including any air operations) were utterly dependent.

During the First World War, the U-boat threat had been barely contained despite the advantage of the British Isles acting as a geographical cork in the bottle for the German fleet, severely restricting its access to the Atlantic. In mid-1940, however, Germany occupied the Channel and Atlantic coasts of France, as well as the coast of Norway. Naturally, it was quick to build submarine bases and air bases in these areas. The U-boats now enjoyed much easier and safer access to Britain's maritime lifelines. Shorter-range vessels could join the campaign while all U-boats could reach their patrol areas more quickly and could therefore spend more time there. As Germany benefited from this enormous force multiplier, Britain faced the opposite effect as evacuations from the continent cost many destroyers either sunk or damaged and then precautions against invasion tied down significant numbers of escorts. The remaining British anti-submarine forces faced a far greater tactical challenge than had been expected; the general confidence—arguably complacence—that Asdic had solved the U-boat problem was blown apart when the attackers adopted the technique of attacking on the surface, at night, when escorts could neither detect them nor match their speed. At the same time the convoy escorts, pitifully weak at this early stage of the war, were overwhelmed by "wolf pack" tactics (U-boats concentrating before attacking). Despite the low number of U-boats in service, the period from the summer of 1940 to early 1941 saw the toll of sunk merchant ships rapidly rise during what the U-boat crews labeled the "happy time." The threat, moreover, was growing as the increased priority given to U-boat production began to have an effect in the form of the rising number in commission.

The anti-submarine campaign benefited from a number of improvements during 1940 and 1941. Signals intelligence, at first direction finding and then the breaking of naval cyphers, for a time helped with evasive routing. Significant enhancements in the control of shipping and the management of ports allowed Britain to use her merchant tonnage more efficiently. The number of escorts grew, as did the training and the experience of their British and Canadian crews. The growing expertise of Coastal Command provided much needed air cover, but only relatively close to land, as the Air Ministry strongly resisted the increasingly desperate appeals of the Admiralty (and indeed Coastal Command) to reallocate very-long-range (VLR) aircraft to the Battle of the Atlantic. The useful impact of these efforts was much reduced by their tendency to push the U-boats farther out into the mid-Atlantic air gap, where the medium-range aircraft that the Air Ministry would allow Coastal Command could not reach.[15] As will be explored in more detail below, Bomber Command was periodically ordered to focus on maritime targets, but used the considerable latitude it was allowed to interpret such directives so as to allow it to pursue what it saw as strategic bombing in its proper sense rather than be "diverted" to the war at sea. The Air Ministry declined to attack the U-boat pens while they were being constructed in France (and later objected to further appeals to bomb them on the grounds that they were too well protected!),[16] arguing that its best contribution to dealing with the U-boat threat lay in bombing the factories making components in Germany. They maintained this line in the face of abundant evidence that their preferred approach was not having a significant effect.

Grand strategy brought a mixed blessing; Germany's invasion of the Soviet Union dispersed German efforts, yet the costly Arctic convoys to take supplies to the surly and barely cooperative new ally represented a heavy commitment for British naval and maritime air forces. More helpfully, the diversion of U-boats to the Mediterranean during the last two months of 1941 brought a much-needed respite in the Atlantic; yet on the other hand, between April and December 1941,

---

[15]   Goette recounts how one squadron of nine Liberators was passed to Coastal Command in June 1941 but as they went out of service, they were not replaced, leaving only the shorter-ranged aircraft. He cites the effective operating radius of the Liberator as 700–1000 miles compared to the Catalina (600 miles), Sunderland (440 miles), Wellington and Whitley (both 340 miles), and Hudson (250 miles). Goette, "Britain and the Delay in Closing the Mid-Atlantic 'Air Gap,'" pp. 25–26.

[16]   Redford argues that the failure of Bomber Command to attack the U-boat pens while they were under construction "is possibly one of the key failures of the war," Redford, "Inter- and Intra-Service Rivalries," p. 925.

the number of U-boats in commission more than doubled, to 250.[17] The end of the year, of course, brought the greatest grand strategic twist of the war with the entry of the United States.

The U.S. had its own vocal corps of air power enthusiasts who were just as keen as their British counterparts to seize their moment in the sun. Their impact during 1942 was limited as their numbers involved in the campaign grew only slowly. Further, the U.S. Army Air Force insisted on climbing the same painful learning curve as the RAF, discovering for itself the appalling vulnerability of bombers conducting daylight attacks. Bomber Command, in turn, continued to argue for top priority in resources and, now under the command of Arthur Harris, chafed at any "diversion" from the true path. Its capabilities improved as ever more four-engined heavy bombers joined the front line and notable advances in technology and technique began to enhance navigation and the accuracy of bombing. While the British were conducting area attacks against industrial and population areas, the U.S. nominally focused more on precision strikes; in practice, however, the distinction between the two was limited. The weight of what became the Combined Bombing Offensive grew steadily, but results remained limited, in absolute terms and even more in relation to the bold promises that had been made—and the question of the right allocation of resources remained.

As in the earlier stages of the Battle of the Atlantic, the balance of advantage was mixed. Despite the shift to belligerent status of the U.S. (whose forces had previously had a far greater involvement in the anti-submarine campaign than was fully consistent with neutrality), 1942 saw the number of merchant ships sunk by U-boats climb dramatically. In part this was due to the loss of Ultra intelligence for eleven months from February, when a fourth rotor wheel was added to the Enigma machine.[18] It also resulted from the abject failure of the Americans to learn from British experience by introducing convoying or even a coastal blackout, resulting in the U-boats enjoying their "second happy time" off the eastern coast of the U.S. Losses could have been worse still but for Hitler shifting U-boats to the Mediterranean, and to the north to guard against the phantom menace of an Allied invasion of Norway. Conversely, the formidable U.S. industrial potential began to make itself felt in terms of production of merchant ships and also of escorts and escort carriers—though the Atlantic was by no means the only call for shipping and escorts, with much effort committed to the Pacific or the Mediterranean (notably escort carriers to support the Torch landings). Bomber Command was not the only service that had grounds for complaints about diversions.

As the U.S. belatedly introduced coastal convoys, the U-boats returned to the mid-Atlantic air gap once again, and in ever-increasing numbers—there were in

---

[17] Tarrant, *U-Boat Offensive*, p. 96.

[18] For a general account of signals intelligence in the campaign, see W. J. R. Gardner, *Decoding History: The Battle of the Atlantic and Ultra* (Basingstoke: Macmillan, 1999).

service 358 in August 1942 and then 420 in May 1943,[19] albeit not all operational at once. Some additional Liberator aircraft were commissioned into Coastal Command, but they were used "offensively" in the Bay of Biscay rather than over convoys where they would have been more effective—in part because they were a later mark of Liberator which lacked the full range of the Mark I.[20] The key problem was the shortage of VLR aircraft in Coastal Command. Those responsible for protecting sea communications continued to be frustrated by the determined resistance of the Air Ministry to seeing their precious strategic bombing campaign weakened by the small number of VLR aircraft that could have closed the air gap. Important technological advances assisted the anti-submarine campaign, such as the wider availability of radio direction finding equipment for escorts and for aircraft; Leigh lights on aircraft; better air-dropped depth charges; and an improved, forward-firing depth charge launcher for escorts. On the other hand, radar receivers helped U-boats avoid air attack. Similarly in signals intelligence, Britain broke the German cyphers again late in 1942 (only for another gap to emerge in early 1943), but the advantage this provided was offset by Germany benefiting from its own penetration of British signals. In November 1942, Britain finally decided to increase the allocation of VLR aircraft to Coastal Command. Putting this decision into practice (which required conversions of Liberators) proved a surprisingly slow business.[21]

At the 1943 Casablanca conference, the Allies finally made the defeat of the U-boats their top priority, though the strategic air offensive was also retained as a central element of Allied strategy. March 1943 saw some of the highest shipping losses of the war, but by the spring various factors and trends finally came together to result in a decisive shift in the balance of advantage. Ever greater numbers of escorts came into service and were increasingly effective due to radar, countering the advantage enjoyed by U-boats when attacking on the surface at night, and to the improving tactics and growing experience of commanders and crews (while those with experience among the U-boat crews became ever fewer). More support groups were formed to assist convoys that came under heavy attack and to hunt down the U-boats that were located while the convoy continued its voyage. There were improvements in signals intelligence that endured. Crucially, the much-needed air support finally became available, belatedly allowing the mid-Atlantic gap to be closed, with the commitment of escort carriers and converted merchant aircraft carriers to Atlantic convoys and also, at last, sufficient numbers of very-long-range land-based maritime patrol aircraft. The decisive point in the campaign against the U-boats came in May 1943, when their losses became so high that Dönitz temporarily withdrew them from the Atlantic. This respite was only temporary and further

---

[19]   Tarrant, *U-Boat Offensive*, p. 108.

[20]   Buckley, *RAF and Trade Defence, 1919–1945*, chapters 5–7; Goette, "Britain and the Delay in Closing the Mid-Atlantic 'Air Gap,'" pp. 29–30.

[21]   Ibid., pp. 33–35.

offensives were launched, and the protection of the vast shipping requirements needed for the build-up of U.S. forces in Britain continued to demand considerable resources, but the crisis point had passed. Major German technological break-throughs that could have caused far greater problems (notably the "*schnorkel,*" which allowed U-boats to recharge their batteries while submerged) came too late and in too small numbers to have a decisive effect—not least due to the mining campaign of Bomber Command disrupting the training of crews and work-up of new boats.

The strategic bombing offensive continued to enjoy comparatively lavish resources. During the campaigns of 1943, the leaders of the RAF and USAAF were finally forced to accept that the interwar air theorists had been wrong to believe that, unlike the older services, the air force could ignore its opposite number to concentrate directly on putting pressure on the heart of the enemy's will and power. This was no minor correction to air power theory, but rather struck at the heart of its "offensive" mantra. The solution was to pursue true air supremacy; the Pointblank directive of June 1943 made the German fighter force the first priority for the bombing campaign. The decisive shift came with the advent of long-range fighters capable of escorting the bombers throughout their missions; the German fighters had to give battle and were shot down in increasing numbers. As command of the air started to become a reality, other developments in navigation and bombing accuracy, as well as better techniques for bombing, improved the impact of attacks. As Overy put it, "During the last year of the war the bombing campaign came of age."[22] There were still tensions over the priorities for the campaign (with debates continuing to rage over oil production versus transportation targets or population centers). The bomber forces were to some extent brought to heel and pulled back within Allied strategy to provide broad support for Overlord, ending the remaining hope that strategic bombing could make it at best unnecessary, at worst, a mere occupation. In the closing stages of the war, as it became clear that the resources of the Allies were simply overwhelming Germany, the bombing campaign continued to expand. "In the month of March 1945, for instance, the total tonnage dropped by the Anglo-American air forces was, amazingly, just shy of the total tonnage dropped during the year 1943."[23]

The strategic air campaign eventually inflicted enormous damage and disruption, directly and indirectly eroding the capacity of Germany to wage war. However, the results were far less in magnitude and far slower to accrue than had been promised by the bombing proponents on either side of the Atlantic. Moreover, their campaign came at a huge opportunity cost; a very small proportion of the long-range bombers lost over Germany (at a stage in the war when their impact was very limited) could have had a decisive effect on the Battle of the Atlantic. At

---

[22]   Overy, *Why the Allies Won*, p. 124.

[23]   Tami Davis Biddle, "Winston Churchill and Sir Charles Portal: Their Wartime Relationship, 1940–1945," in Peter W. Gray and Sebastian Cox, eds., *Airpower Leadership: Theory and Practice* (London: The Stationery Office, 2002), p. 191.

first glance, it seems inexplicable that there should be such reluctance to transfer air power from strategic bombing, which was delivering so little, to provide desperately needed support in a campaign that was genuinely critical for Britain's very survival. To understand this, we need to consider the conceptual backdrop that created the intellectual baggage that so distorted British strategy.

The Conceptual Background: Bombing to Win

The interwar period was a remarkably fruitful one for new ideas about how to wage war. The experience of the Great War resulted in a widespread conviction that a better way of fighting had to be found. Conversely, a wide range of new military technologies had seen their major debut during the war, including tanks, submarines, and air power. Although none of these exerted a decisive influence on the course or outcome of the war, their initial uses hinted that much more might be expected if they were used differently. The result was that a range of thinkers sought to answer the problems of strategy by setting their fertile imaginations to extrapolate the future capabilities of these new technologies.[24] While the conceptual debate raged, the armed forces faced the practical challenge of evaluating the current capabilities of multiple new military systems and—even more exacting—their possible future potential. This task would have been difficult at the best of times, but in this instance, was made even harder by the uncertainty over British strategy—what sort of war might be fought, where, against whom?—as well as by financial pressures. The principal concern of the Royal Air Force was to retain its hard-won status as an independent service in the face of suspicion and even hostility from the two older services. The desire of the Air Staff to carve out a distinctive niche for the fledgling RAF forged a role in colonial policing and, for major war, in strategic bombing—that is, bombing not conducted in close or deep support of the other services, but rather aimed directly at the heart of the enemy war-making potential; not working alongside the other services, but operating entirely independently.[25] This latter role in particular rested on theoretical foundations provided by

---

[24]   In the British context, J. F. C. Fuller and Basil H. Liddell Hart are the best known examples. For their influential interwar works, see J. F. C. Fuller, *The Reformation of War* (London: Hutchinson, 1923), *On Future Warfare* (London: Sifton Praed, 1928), and *Machine Warfare* (London: Hutchinson, 1942); Basil H. Liddell Hart, *Paris or the Future of War* (London: Kegan Paul, Trench, Trubner & Co, 1925) and *The British Way in Warfare* (London: Faber and Faber, 1932).

[25]   For general accounts of British air policy, see H. Montgomery Hyde, *British Air Policy Between the Wars* (London: Heinemann, 1976); Malcolm Smith, *British Air Strategy Between the Wars* (Oxford: Clarendon, 1984). For a recent account of the British and U.S. development and then application of ideas about strategic bombing, see Biddle, *Rhetoric and Reality in Air Warfare*. See also Gray, "Strategic Leadership and Direction of the Royal Air Force Strategic Air Offensive."

a vocal group of air theorists. While the views of senior British airmen did not always coincide with those of the air theorists,[26] there was considerable common ground between them especially on the fundamental issue of the ability of strategic air power to win wars alone, and hence, the need to focus on strategic bombing as far as possible to the exclusion of other roles.[27]

For the air theorists in Italy, Britain, and the United States, the navy was a particular target for their polemics. Their arguments and the challenge they posed to navies lay on three different levels of strategy.[28] First, at the tactical level, it was argued that aircraft could always and easily locate warships, which would then be helpless targets for attack. Aircraft carriers (always the subject of bitter criticism since they represented the dangerous heresy of air power not controlled by the air force) were dismissed out of hand on the grounds that their aircraft would inevitably be inferior to land-based aircraft. Second, at the operational level of warfare, the air theorists argued that land-based aircraft could more effectively and more efficiently perform the traditional roles of the navy, from countering the enemy battle fleet to protecting against invasion. There might, in the short term, be some areas where land-based aircraft could not reach, where navies temporarily retained a residual role, but these were shrinking and would soon vanish. Finally, at the strategic level, the central proposition of the interwar air enthusiasts was that air power was not best used in support of the navy and army against their counterparts on the enemy side. Rather, it should be used from the outset of the war against the heart of the enemy's military and industrial strength. The advantage in air warfare lay with the offensive rather than the defensive; command of the air would be gained quickly and would then allow rapid victory by destroying the will and ability of the enemy to fight. The logical result of this principle was that there was little or no need to devote resources to the older services, who could not

---

[26]   For example, Marshal of the RAF Sir John Slessor, who as Chief of the Air Staff in the early 1950s was still a true believer in strategic bombing and also remarkably hostile to naval aviation, told a correspondent in 1968 that he had never read Douhet. The National Archives, London (hereinafter TNA), Air Ministry files (hereinafter AIR) 75/86, Slessor to Major William Giffen, Department of History, USAF Academy, 20 July 1968. Both Harris and Slessor insisted to another author that they had never either read or even heard of Douhet before the war, Tony Mason, *Air Power: A Centennial Appraisal* (London: Brassey's, 1994), pp. 44–45. Harris did cite Seversky approvingly in his account of the strategic bombing campaign, Arthur Harris, *Bomber Offensive* (London: Collins, 1947), p. 264.

[27]   For a general account of the influences on interwar air thinking, including a review of the literature, see Gray, "Strategic Leadership and Direction of the Royal Air Force Strategic Air Offensive," pp. 69–81, also 107–16, 146–52.

[28]   This analysis is developed at greater length in Tim Benbow, "Navies and the Challenge of Technological Change," *Defence Studies* 8:2 (June 2008), especially pp. 210–15.

operate without dominant air power and were not really necessary with it.[29] These multi-level challenges to the ability of—and even need for—the navy to perform its traditional roles set the stage for what was to follow.

The central claim of the interwar air theorists was that offensive action (bombing the enemy's air bases and the factories producing his aircraft) would swiftly gain command of the air, which could and should then be exploited to shatter his will and ability to continue fighting. This point bears emphasis: they were not, as is often suggested, simply predicting that air power would be important in future war—this claim would be so self-evident as to be banal. Their hypothesis was more specific and far more ambitious, namely that air power properly used would on its own bring rapid and low-cost victory, obviating the necessity to accept the costly slogging matches entailed by fighting at sea or on land. There would be no need to undergo the slow and exhausting process of waiting for the naval blockade to bite or for the army to painstakingly push back the opposing army inch by bloody inch. Unlike the older services, air forces were not compelled to undergo the time-consuming attrition of their enemy counterpart; rather they could immediately and directly attack the heart of his power and thereby win the war. For the Royal Air Force, just as for the interwar air theorists, strategic bombing was the unique selling point of air power. This role, and its corollary of an independent, centralized air force owning everything that flies, went to the very heart of its institutional identity and was the centerpiece of its claim to exist as a single service. The vision of the interwar theorists was taken up by the leaders of the RAF for whom strategic bombing became more than a matter of policy or doctrine—it seems to have resembled something between ideology and theology, an article of faith that transcended reason. It would be unfair and inaccurate to impute to the RAF leadership (which in any case contained a range of opinions) the more ludicrous excesses of all the theorists. However, the two groups had a great deal in common in terms of the direction of travel, even if they differed in terms of just how far down the road they went. Not all senior airmen believed that bombing alone could win the war, and many moderated their views in the light of experience; however, the conviction that it was possible and the aspiration to make it a reality were sufficiently

---

[29]   For overviews of the interwar air theorists, see Edward Warner, "Douhet, Mitchell, Seversky: Theories of Air Warfare," in Edward M. Earle, ed., *Makers of Modern Strategy: Military Thought from Machiavelli to Hitler* (Princeton: Princeton University Press, 1943); also David MacIsaac, "Voices from the Central Blue: The Air Power Theorists," in Peter Paret, ed., *Makers of Modern Strategy from Machiavelli to the Nuclear Age* (Oxford: Oxford University Press, 1986). The key works of the major air theorists are: Giulio Douhet, *Command of the Air* (London: Faber and Faber, 1943—original 1921); William Mitchell, *Winged Defense: The Development and Possibilities of Modern Air Power—Economic and Military* (New York: Putnam's, 1925) and *Skyways* (Philadelphia: Lippincott, 1930); Alexander P. de Seversky, *Victory Through Air Power* (New York: Simon and Schuster, 1942).

widely held in the Air Staff for long enough to have a decisive and highly detrimental impact on wartime strategy.

Theory into Reality: The Strategic Air Offensive and Victory

According to the RAF Air Historical Branch, at the start of the war the Air Force expected that the strategic offensive "would produce significant and perhaps even decisive results within six months."[30] The core belief that strategic bombing would produce victory appears time and again in Air Ministry papers. The Chief of the Air Staff, Air Chief Marshal Sir Charles Portal, stated in May 1941: "At the moment therefore we are working to a clear strategic plan. We aim to win the war in the air, not on land. Undoubtedly, we must build up land forces as well within the priorities already assigned but as far as the Continent is concerned these forces will be used as an Army of Occupation *after* the bombing offensive has crushed the enemy's will to resist." Before British land forces returned to the continent, he argued, "there is one indispensable prerequisite, namely, that the Air Force as a whole must establish decisive air superiority, and that the Bomber Force in particular must cripple the enemy's will to resist."[31] He repeated the point the following month: "The war can only be won by the development of our air offensive on a scale which, together with the effects of economic pressure and propaganda, will break the German will to continue fighting."[32] Portal's biographer denies that he believed the war could be won by bombing alone and praises his "balanced outlook";[33] as will be shown below, his approach to the war at sea tends to contradict this sympathetic assertion. General Sir Alan Brooke, Chief of the Imperial General Staff, was clear where Portal's views about strategy lay: "Spent afternoon in the office battling with Portal's latest ideas for the policy of conduct of this war. Needless to say it is based on bombing Germany at the expense of everything else."[34] Again: "A heated COS [Chiefs of Staff Committee meeting] at which I had a hammer and tongs argument with Portal on the policy for the conduct of the war. He wants to devote all efforts to an intensive air bombardment of Germany on the basis that a decisive result can be obtained that way. I am only prepared to look on the bombing of Germany as

---

[30]   AIR 8/1452, RAF Air Historical Branch draft paper, "Bomber Command in the war at sea, 1939–1945," p. 8.

[31]   TNA, Cabinet Office files (hereinafter CAB) 80/57, COS(41)83(O), Chief of the Air Staff, "The Air Programme," 21 May 1941, paras. 4, 9, emphasis original.

[32]   CAB 80/58, COS(41)119(O), Chief of the Air Staff, "Army Air Requirements," 26 June 1941.

[33]   Denis Richards, *Lord Portal of Hungerford* (London: Heinemann, 1977), pp. 338, 199.

[34]   Alex Danchev and Daniel Todman, eds., *Field Marshall Lord Alanbrooke: War Diaries, 1939–1945* (London: Weidenfeld & Nicolson, 2001), entry for 29 September 1942, p. 325.

one of the many ways by which we shall bring Germany to her knees."[35] Portal's views on the potential of air power might indeed have been more moderate and nuanced, "more provisional" than those of Lord Trenchard or Arthur Harris,[36] but this was not saying a lot: he laid an emphasis on strategic bombing that was every bit as overwhelming and single-minded as might be expected of a former head of Bomber Command.

From the very beginning, however, the British air offensive ran into the sort of practical difficulties that the interwar theorists had overlooked. Numerous and deep flaws in the theory became apparent, not least an exaggeration of the accuracy and destructive power of bombing, a massive underestimation of the potential of air defense, a surprising neglect of issues relating to targeting, and the assumption that command of the air would be swiftly achieved. In practice, the campaign was initially constrained for fear of German retaliation; when the bombers were unleashed, their ability to find their targets and to bomb them accurately was far less than had been anticipated and losses were far higher.[37] The impact of bombing on the German war effort was hugely disappointing because its industry was far more resilient than was assumed, while its economy proved to have considerable slack which could still be devoted to increased production. The effects of the air offensive were slower to be felt and much less in magnitude than had been expected: according to its official historians, the damage inflicted on the German economy in 1940–41 was "negligible," while in 1942, "some substantial damage was done if not such as had any appreciable effect on war production."[38] Although it would eventually show marked improvement, at no point in the war did it meet the claims of the interwar enthusiasts or the promises of the airmen. Strategic bombing was not a quick way to win wars on its own; rather it would be one more means of exerting pressure on the enemy alongside more traditional campaigns—it was not a revolution, simply one additional technique to use.

Judged against the bold predictions made on its behalf, the strategic air offensive was a great disappointment. At times, even Prime Minister Winston Churchill,

---

[35]   Ibid., entry for 22 October 1942, p. 332. In May 1943, Brooke commented that Portal still believed that bombing could win the war, ibid., p. 411.

[36]   Richards, *Lord Portal*, p. 225.

[37]   In August 1941, the Butt Report revealed that of the aircrews who claimed to have attacked their targets, only one-third actually managed to get as close as five miles; this figure was better for French ports at two-thirds, and worse for the Ruhr at one-tenth. Charles Webster and Noble Frankland, *The Strategic Air Offensive Against Germany, 1939–45*, Vol. I, *Preparation* (London: HMSO, 1961), pp. 178–79; the report itself is reproduced in Vol. IV, *Annexes and Appendices* (London: HMSO, 1961), pp. 205–13. Webster and Frankland also drily note, "Crews who failed to find their bases on return were 'nearly always' convinced that they had found their targets," *Strategic Air Offensive*, Vol. I, p. 228.

[38]   Ibid., p. 473.

who found the concept singularly attractive, showed signs of doubt. When told by Portal in 1941 that four months of focused attacks could end production in Germany's seventeen main oil plants, he remarked that he "was sceptical of these cut and dried calculations which showed infallibly how the war could be won," such as claims earlier that attacks on the Ruhr would "shatter the German industry. . . but there had only been a fractional interruption of work in the industries of the Ruhr." Yet Portal insisted that "the forecasts made were not unduly optimistic."[39] A few months later, the Chief of the Air Staff had to admit that: "Oil targets were not so vulnerable as had previously been supposed and there had been difficulty in attacking them during the summer months," that "experience showed that oil targets were difficult to find on any but very good nights of which there might be only three or four in a month."[40] The inaccuracy of bombing led to a shift in rationale towards a greater emphasis on morale, which had been a major theme of the interwar theorists. In one of his occasional Olympian missives to the Prime Minister, Lord Trenchard, the godfather of the RAF, advocated morale as a target: "All the evidence of the last war and of this shows that the German nation is particularly susceptible to air bombing. . .. The ordinary people are . . . virtually imprisoned in their shelters or within the bombed area, they remain passive and easy prey to hysteria and panic without anything to mitigate the inevitable chaos and confusion. There is no joking in the German shelters as in ours."[41] Yet experience would show the German population to be no more wobbly under bombing than the British had been.

Despite the failure of the strategic offensive to achieve the promised results, Britain persisted with it. For the RAF leadership, it was their big chance for the service to make its mark as a war winner. It was equally attractive to the political leadership. Having been brutally pushed out of the continent and with no realistic prospect of an imminent return, it seemed to offer perhaps the only opportunity to take offensive action against Germany. This was of some value in the longer term strategic balance, and of even greater importance as a boost to morale at home and to impress the Americans, showing that the country was hitting back. After the German invasion of the Soviet Union, it also became a significant way to provide concrete military support to the hard-pressed Russians, a useful placatory card to play in the face of ever more strident demands for a second front. So despite the poor return, ever more resources were poured into the campaign. It was always given another chance, with more aircraft and a different set of targets; success was always just around the corner, and despite his occasional scepticism, Churchill

---

39   CAB 69/2, DO(41)4th Meeting, 13 January 1941.

40   CAB 69/2, DO(41)41st Meeting, 16 June 1941 and DO(41)52nd Meeting, 21 July 1941.

41   CAB 80/57, COS(41)86(O), Lord Trenchard, "The present war situation mainly in so far as it relates to air," 19 May 1941. Trenchard's source of such remarkably detailed intelligence on the behavior of the German population in air raid shelters is not identified.

kept returning to the irresistible promise of a shortcut to victory,[42] which the Air Staff was happy to keep offering him. It is difficult not to sympathize with the motivations of those airmen who had embraced strategic bombing in the hope of avoiding a repeat of the trench warfare they had witnessed in the Great War. However, there is considerable irony in the way that they lapsed into the same patterns of behavior of the generals that they criticized: in both cases senior officers clung to their faith in a particular approach, repeatedly doing the same thing only on a larger scale and at higher cost. In both cases, there was, over time, a huge attritional effect on the enemy. The problem was that the attrition affected Britain too, and there were other calls on resources that might have earned a better return.

This was the point where the hopes of theory hit the brick wall of reality: once strategic bombing could not provide the promised rapid victory, Britain was compelled once again to face the sordid reality of also fighting traditional campaigns on the sea and on the land, both in order to prevent defeat and to provide further avenues for putting military pressure on the enemy—and these campaigns would also require the support of air power. The question was not, therefore, simply whether it was worth pressing on with the strategic bombing campaign, but rather the extent to which it should enjoy priority in resource allocation over other needs.

In part, this debate concerned production and manpower for the RAF as opposed to the Navy and the Army, but it also extended to the allocation of RAF resources between the strategic bombing campaign and the various competing uses of air power. The leading interwar theorists had seen any suggestion that air power should be used in support of land or naval forces as a dangerous and wasteful diversion of effort. Douhet, for example, insisted that these "auxiliary uses" of air power were "worthless, superfluous and harmful": without command of the air, they could not achieve anything; with command of the air, they would be pointless; and devoting effort to them would detract from and perhaps jeopardize the effort to gain command of the air.[43] This issue was the biggest gap between the ideas of the theorists and the senior airmen who led the RAF during the war. Significant effort was devoted to the air defense of Britain, to support of the Army and the Navy and—as will be discussed below—to Coastal Command. However, the

---

[42]   The Commander-in-Chief of RAF Coastal Command from June 1941 to February 1943, Air Marshal Philip Joubert de la Ferté, noted this appeal and its effect: "Mr Churchill's one wish was to hit at Germany in Germany and so Bomber Command was his favourite child. Any suggestion that some of the resources becoming available should be directed towards winning the air/sea war met with considerable resistance and a determination that the bombing offensive against the German homeland should have pride of place." Philip Joubert de la Ferté, *Fun and Games* (London: Hutchinson, 1964), p. 122.

[43]   Douhet, *Command of the Air,* p. 81. He makes it quite clear that this is his real opinion, in contrast to the more benign view he expressed for tactical reasons in his earlier work (reproduced in the same volume) that such uses might have value.

attachment to strategic bombing at the top of the RAF was considerably greater than its achievements merited with the result that the allocation of resources was skewed and the other, equally vital roles for air power were slow to receive the attention that they deserved.[44]

To be clear, the strategic bombing offensive did achieve a great deal: in slowing the increase in German war production; in causing the diversion to air defense of many fighters, guns, and men that would otherwise have been deployed elsewhere; in the psychological boost it provided to the home front; in helping the Allies to gain air supremacy; and then in the direct disruption it caused to oil production and transport (albeit achieved in the face of determined resistance from the bomber barons to such "panacea" targeting). However, these very real and very significant accomplishments were not only much less than had been promised and much slower to appear, they also came at a huge cost in blood and treasure—not least, in the opportunity cost of what those resources might have achieved in other areas. If it is appropriate to consider the wider benefits of the strategic air offensive, then it is equally appropriate to count the wider costs, which include Coastal Command aircrew who died in obsolescent aircraft and many merchant ships, their crews, and cargoes—as well as lost warships and lost opportunities that might have been available had the Fleet Air Arm not been so starved of resources or had better shore-based support been available to the Navy. (Perhaps the principal ethical dilemma concerning strategic bombing should not be seen as the hoary debate over bombing enemy civilian targets, but rather the obstinate refusal of the RAF leadership to "divert" a relatively tiny number of long-range aircraft from largely ineffective attacks over Germany to maritime operations, where they could have prevented the needless sacrifice of so many sailors, ships, and cargoes.) It is at least possible to question whether some proportion of the resources devoted to the strategic air offensive between 1941 and 1943 might have been better directed to other ends.

The Airmen Make Their Case

Trenchard, in another epistle to the Prime Minister that was circulated to the War Cabinet in August 1942, set out the case for focusing strongly on the air offensive. "Once a major plan has been decided on in war," he wrote, "nothing should be

---

[44]   An Air Historical Branch paper about the campaign reveals the centrality of the bombing offensive to the self-image of the RAF, noting that the strategic options for the RAF were either to join the land forces in defense of France and naval forces in defense of sea communications, or to take the offensive against Germany. "The choice between an offensive and defensive policy for Bomber Command was therefore also the choice between an independent or auxiliary role." Should they attack German warships and ports, "then their action would be auxiliary to that of the navy and equally defensive." In other words, cooperation with the other services was anathema and only an independent role was worthwhile. AIR 8/1452, RAF Air Historical Branch draft paper, "Bomber Command in the war at sea, 1939–1945," pp. 6–7.

allowed to interfere with it or to divert elsewhere the means of carrying it out. *Compromise in war plans is fatal.*" Britain must focus its efforts on the strategic bombing of Germany and not waste air power on other diversions, nor attempt to land in Europe, which "is to play Germany's game—it is to revert to 1914–18." He could not have been clearer about the extent to which bombing should be the overriding priority: "The risk is that we shall try to go down two roads and that our Air Power will be inextricably entangled in large schemes and protracted operations of two dimensional warfare.... There is no realisable limit to the power we can achieve in this arm *if we concentrate our efforts on a policy which realises what we can do—and do quickly.* . . . We have in our possession the opportunity of producing decisive effects if we realise *now* that air power has already been proved to be the *dominant, deciding and final* power in the warfare of today and the future."[45] The proposition that Bomber Command was the only means to achieve victory was, not surprisingly, asserted strongly by its Commander-in-Chief, Air Marshal Sir Arthur Harris. In a paper for the War Cabinet, he wrote:

> To sum up, Bomber Command provides our only offensive action yet pressed home directly against Germany. All our other efforts are defensive in their nature, and are not intended to do more, and can never do more, than enable us to exist in the face of the enemy. Bomber Command provides the only means of bringing assistance to Russia in time. The only means of physically weakening and nervously exhausting Germany to an extent which will make subsequent invasion a possible proposition, and is therefore the only force which can in fact hurt our enemy in the present and in the future secure our victory.[46]

The key themes in these two papers reappeared again and again: only strategic bombing could lead to victory and other uses of air power were dangerous deviations from its proper use; it is striking how often air proponents used loaded terms such as "diverted" or even "plundered"[47]—Harris once complained of

---

[45]   CAB 66/28/29, WP(42)399, Lord Trenchard, "Note on our War Policy," 29 August 1942, emphases original.

[46]   CAB 66/28/4, WP(42)374, Air Marshal Sir Arthur Harris, "The Role and Work of Bomber Command," 24 August 1942, para. 17.

[47]   While their account is in some respects one of the more balanced, it is striking that this latter term is from Webster and Frankland, *Strategic Air Offensive*, Vol. I, p. 310. Terraine lists the "diversions" that Bomber Command complained about, noting "it will be seen that in effect they add up to the war itself." Terraine, *The Right of the Line*, pp. 227–28, 691. Biddle concurs: "What he called 'diversions' was the war itself"—and also points out that his approach risks overlooking the valuable work done by Bomber Command in other roles, Tami Davis Biddle, "Bombing by the Square Yard: Sir Arthur Harris at War, 1942–1945," *The International History Review* XXI:3 (September 1999), p. 664.

"robbery"[48]—rather than, say, "reallocated." The Secretary of State for Air joined in this refrain, complaining that the "most serious brake in the past on Bomber expansion has been the extraneous commitments"[49]—that is, anything other than the strategic air offensive.

There were a number of problems with this line of argument. First, it underrated the fundamental, even predominant importance for the British war effort of the Battle of the Atlantic. Others on the Chief of Staff Committee were aware of this inescapable reality: "the Battle of the Atlantic must at present remain our chief preoccupation: after that our effort should be employed against the most profitable targets in Germany.. . . The Battle of the Atlantic should have overriding priority." Thereafter, there could be a bomber offensive to achieve the air superiority that will be required before operating on the continent, "But we must be clear that, before any overriding priority is given to the building of a bomber force to achieve this end, adequate provision must first be made for the security of this country and of those areas overseas which are essential to the maintenance of our war effort." It is all the more noteworthy that the author of these words was not a naval officer, but rather General Sir John Dill, Chief of the Imperial General Staff.[50] Success in the Battle of the Atlantic was necessary not only for Britain's survival, but also for all military operations—including the air offensive. In the words of a senior Admiral, "It is pertinent here to emphasize that Air Power cannot be exercised if sea communications are cut, as it is by those sea routes that, among other things required by the RAF, come the petrol and oil which allow aircraft to function."[51]

---

[48] Harris to Portal, 11 May 1942, cited in Dudley Saward, *Bomber Harris: The Story of Marshal of the Royal Air Force Sir Arthur Harris* (New York: Doubleday, 1985), p. 142. In the same memo he complained that other RAF Commands "regard Bomber Command as a milch cow whenever they feel the slightest pangs of hunger or even mere inconvenience within their own organisations." Harris' single-mindedness is further demonstrated in his own account of the campaign, in which he objected to the fact that "I was required to attack targets of immediate strategic importance—a euphemism for targets chosen by the Navy." Harris, *Bomber Offensive*, p. 90.

[49] CAB 66/30/11, Secretary of State for Air to Prime Minister, 9 October 1942, appendix to WP(42)481, Note by Secretary, "Strength of Bomber Command," 23 October 1942.

[50] CAB 80/57, COS(41)95(O), Comments by CIGS on Lord Trenchard's Paper, 2 June 1941. His successor as CIGS (who replaced him in December 1941) felt the same way, referring to the anti-submarine war, "on which our very existence depended," Danchev and Todman, *Alanbrooke: War Diaries*, p. 238.

[51] TNA, Admiralty File (hereinafter ADM) 205/15, Second Sea Lord to First Sea Lord, "Remarks on Bombing Policy called for by First Sea Lord," 26 February 1942. This dependence was recognized in parts of the RAF: "Ultimately everything, including of course the strategic bombing offensive, depended upon British success in this struggle," AIR 8/1452, RAF Air Historical Branch draft paper, "Bomber Command in the war at sea, 1939–1945," p. 8. The official historians of the strategic air offensive noted that Bomber Command

This point draws attention to a related flaw in the Air Ministry case, namely its appropriation for strategic bombing alone of the adjective "offensive." Only bombing Germany was truly "offensive"; all other uses of air power (let alone operations on land or at sea) were pejoratively labeled "defensive," and thus should be demoted way behind in second priority. This approach was taken particularly with regard to naval campaigns, but was also applied to the Army. Thus, after referring to aircraft for cooperation with the Navy and Army, the Secretary of State for Air wrote, "It is, therefore, vital that we should allot the minimum proportion of our resources to the strictly defensive roles."[52] Portal even went so far in 1941 as to assert that "The Army has no primary offensive role."[53]

By this contorted logic, operations aimed by the Royal Navy against enemy forces in their bases would be "defensive," but attacks by Bomber Command against the industrial foundations of the opposing air force were "offensive." Similarly, the campaigns on land in North Africa or at sea in the Mediterranean, where Axis land, naval, and air power were ground down, were merely defensive, and any use of air power there was a "diversion" from its proper use against Germany. In fact, many of the operations that the Navy wished to undertake were "offensive" by any reasonable definition. The Admiralty repeatedly pointed out that lack of air support in the form of reconnaissance and fighter cover was not only detrimental to the anti-submarine campaign, but also hindered its ability to take offensive action against the enemy fleet, to attack his sea communications by blockade, and to support amphibious operations. Proper air support could also free up capital ships from the Mediterranean for offensive operations against Japan in the Indian Ocean.[54] Heavy shipping losses in the "defensive" campaign against the U-boats also reduced Britain's ability to transport and supply land and air forces for offensive operations overseas as well as to bring in the fuel that was needed by all branches of the forces, not least Bomber Command. As one Admiralty paper put it, pointing out that the second front in Europe would require vast shipping support, "Every ship that the U-boats can sink is therefore a blow against our offensive

---

depended on fuel from overseas, and to some extent on crew training there: "Thus, even in its defensive phases, the Battle of the Atlantic had an ultimately offensive purpose." Webster and Frankland, *Strategic Air Offensive*, Vol. I, p. 167.

[52]   CAB 66/13, WP(40)454, Secretary of State for Air, "Coastal Command," 21 November 1940, p. 3.

[53]   CAB 80/57, COS(41)83(O), Chief of the Air Staff, "The Air Programme," 21 May 1941, para. 2.

[54]   ADM 205/15, Director of Plans to First Sea Lord, "Sea and air power in future developments: Paper B," 27 February 1942, paras. 19–21. Churchill seemed sympathetic to this argument, stating that: "The use of the fighter aircraft in larger proportions by our carriers is not a defensive symptom, since its object is to enable the Fleet to take bolder offensive action." CAB 66/32, WP(42)580, Prime Minister, "Air Policy," 16 December 1942, para. 14.

strength."[55] Of course, assisting other services cut both ways: in May 1941, Admiral Sir Dudley Pound, the First Sea Lord, sought approval for the carrier HMS *Victorious* to be released from the (defensive?) role of ferrying RAF fighter reinforcements to the Mediterranean and Middle East: "When *Victorious* had carried her present load of Hurricanes to the Mediterranean they felt it was essential that she should return to her proper role as an offensive weapon against enemy raiders."[56] The very day that this request was made, *Bismarck* was sunk by Royal Navy warships after being slowed by an air strike launched from HMS *Ark Royal*—which at the time the German battleship put to sea "was 1,500 miles away ferrying aircraft to Malta."[57] Thankfully she was able to switch from a defensive role ferrying RAF aircraft to an offensive role in the war at sea remarkably quickly.

In his paper cited above, Harris described the heavy and medium bombers of Bomber Command as "our only offensive weapon against Germany"—this was written, it should be emphasized, in 1942—and stated, "One cannot win wars by defending oneself."[58] An internal Admiralty paper disputed this statement, suggesting that on the contrary: "The history of our country shows that we have often been successful in maintaining a prolonged defensive until the enemy had exhausted himself, and only then turning to the offensive to bring the matter to a conclusion." The defense of the United Kingdom and protection of sea communications "indicate a strategic defensive, but they should be implemented by offensive tactics. Although the 'Battle of Britain' was part of this defensive strategy it inflicted a very heavy defeat on the enemy's air force. The strategic defence of our sea communications inevitably involves destroying the enemy's armed forces which attack them, while it also allows us to blockade the enemy, which is strategically offensive."[59] This analysis seems to demonstrate a rather more nuanced understanding of the fluctuating interconnection between offense and defense than appears in bald statements that strategic bombing is offensive and other campaigns are defensive. It might well be good bureaucratic politics to seek to dominate the terminology used in debates,[60] not least

---

55   ADM 205/30, Naval Assistant to First Sea Lord, cover note to paper on "U-boat bases in the Bay of Biscay," 26 March 1943, para. 4.

56   CAB 69/2, DO(41)35th Meeting, 27 May 1941.

57   Geoffrey Till, *Air Power and the Royal Navy, 1914–1945* (London: Jane's, 1979), p. 177. For a detailed account of this action, see Admiralty Tactical and Staff Duties Division (Historical Section), BR1736(3/50), *Battle Summary No. 5, The Chase and Sinking of the 'Bismarck'* (1949).

58   CAB 66/28/4, WP(42)374, Air Marshal Sir Arthur Harris, "The Role and Work of Bomber Command," 24 August 1942, para. 1.

59   ADM 205/15, "Admiralty comments on Lord Trenchard and Air Marshal Harris' papers," 9 September 1942, paras. 7–8.

60   The Air Staff would do this again after the war, contrasting their "medium bombers" (clearly a restrained, minimal, and entirely responsible use of resources) with the Admiralty's "heavy carriers" (evidently wastefully luxurious over-provision).

because it was targeted so effectively to appeal to Churchill and his desire to hit back against Germany, yet in this case, it was as mendacious a misuse of language as it was bad strategy.

The War Over the War at Sea

For the Air Ministry, the one priority that eclipsed all others was the strategic offensive against Germany. This resulted in a determination not to "divert" resources to Coastal Command—which, as we have seen, was dismissed as a merely "defensive" use of air power.[61] The Admiralty consistently pressed for more air power to be allocated to the war at sea. It is important to be clear what was sought: this was not a request for resources to be switched from producing aircraft for the RAF to building warships for the Navy, but rather for production and allocation to shift between two Commands of the RAF, from the one bombing Germany to the one cooperating with the Navy in maritime operations.

This approach was in stark contrast to the antediluvian opinions about the role of air power often attributed to the Navy. Air enthusiasts liked to claim that the Admiralty did not understand air power, did not value it, and sought jealously to keep the naval war to itself. A few choice quotations could be dredged up from retired officers writing during the interwar period to show what dinosaurs these nautical fellows were. A fine example would be Bernard Acworth, who was roundly sceptical about air power in general and air power at sea in particular. In his 1930 book, he wrote that unless seaplanes could be operated from cruisers and battleships, he "would advocate the total abolition of aeroplanes from the future British Navy as being, by any other means of employment, of insufficient importance to justify the present disproportionate effort that their utilisation involves."[62] Digging

---

[61]   This neglect pre-dated the outbreak of war: "Not all sections of the Royal Air Force benefitted from the injection of defence funding after 1933, and just as maritime aviation was to suffer proportionately greater cuts in relation to other branches of the air force in the period of disarmament after the First World War, the maritime aspect grew most slowly when expansion of the air force occurred." Goulter, *A Forgotten Offensive*, p. 72. This book explains how Coastal Command, because of the RAF's doctrinal and financial neglect of maritime tasks in the interwar period, had to painfully and expensively relearn many lessons from the First World War.

[62]   Bernard Acworth, The *Navies of Today and Tomorrow: A Study of the Naval Crisis from Within* (London: Eyre & Spottiswoode, 1930). His later works included *The Navy and the Next War: A Vindication of Sea Power* (London: Eyre & Spottiswoode, 1934); *The Restoration of England's Sea Power* (London: Eyre & Spottiswoode, 1935); and *Britain in Danger: An Examination of Our New Navy* (London: Eyre & Spottiswoode, 1937). He also wrote books attacking the theory of evolution. His views on air power bear striking resemblance to those of an earlier, pseudonymous author who in 1927—when Acworth was still a serving officer—dismissed the idea that air power could be decisive in war: "Cool and dispassionate consideration of the

up such quotations is entertaining, but opinions such as his were utterly different to those directing the policy of the Navy—which, indeed, Acworth criticized as being far too air-oriented.[63] Such views do not bear comparison with those of the interwar air theorists in terms of their closeness to the official views of the respective services during the Second World War. Time and again, the Admiralty demonstrated a keen awareness of the value of air power in the war at sea, expressed the belief that the defense of sea communications was now a role for the RAF as well as for the Navy, and sought additional land-based air support for maritime operations.

They could not have been clearer on this point. In some ways, of course, close cooperation with another service was not new. As the Second Sea Lord noted, defending sea communications "is not and never has been a matter that concerns the Navy alone, although naturally the Navy takes the preponderating role at sea. Many of the Army's campaigns in the last 300 years have been fought with the sole object of helping the Navy to obtain and hold command at sea."[64] A similar partnership was now needed with the RAF. In the words of the Admiralty Director of Plans: "The security of sea communications must be a joint responsibility between the Navy and the Air Force. Neither, whether in attack or defence, can operate without the other and the two Services are essentially complementary." His paper went on to express concern about the attrition that the Navy was facing as a result of "the necessity of operating our surface forces in areas where we have inadequate air support against naval forces of the enemy operating in close co-operation with powerful air forces."[65]

This should have been music to the ears of the Air Staff, with the Admiralty abandoning any previous scepticism and now warmly endorsing the role of the RAF in the war at sea. In some ways, however, their bluff had been called. Having long proclaimed the willingness of airmen and the ability of land-based air power to take over much of the war at sea, they now faced calls to do so. Far from being greeted with relief or pleasure, such invitations were evidently most unwelcome.

---

facts will show, however, that 'air power' is illusory and 'air supremacy' a will-o'-the-wisp. The development of aircraft for war purposes is a sheer waste of men and money." Neon, *The Great Delusion: A Study of Aircraft in Peace and War* (London: Ernest Benn, 1927), p. xxxvii.

[63] For example, he criticized the attention and resources that the Admiralty was devoting to naval aviation as encouraging delusions about the impact of air power: "With one voice the Navy proclaims (pianissimo) the ridiculous exaggeration that surrounds all aerial propaganda, and with the same voice (fortissimo) it proclaims the dawn of the Air Age at sea and the outstanding importance of the Naval Air Arm!," Acworth, *The Navy and the Next War*, p. 163.

[64] ADM 205/15, Second Sea Lord to First Sea Lord, "Remarks on Bombing Policy called for by First Sea Lord," 26 February 1942.

[65] ADM 205/15, Director of Plans to First Sea Lord, "Sea and air power in future developments: Paper A," 27 February 1942.

First, they involved requests to reallocate aircraft from Bomber Command to Coastal Command, particularly the long-range types that were as ideally suited to patrolling distant waters as they were to bombing distant cities. Second, there were demands to use Bomber Command against targets directly related to the war at sea rather than against the German industrial heartland. Such proposals seemed to imply that the other services should have a say in how aircraft should be designed and the priorities for aircraft production, as well as in how air power should be used. These were areas jealously guarded by the Air Ministry as part of the doctrine of central control of all air power by the Air Force. In a related concern, they also threatened to compel the Air Ministry to reduce the effort dedicated to strategic bombing, the role that was core to its self-identity as an institution, offering the potential to show they could win the war alone, and therefore, guarantee a central role for the future.[66] These issues were not treated as minor matters of allocation of assets, but rather as serious challenges to the institution of an independent air force.

There had been serious blemishes on the Navy's interwar record of appreciating the potential of air power, both hostile and friendly.[67] If some in the Admiralty had once underestimated either the potential threat or the potential benefits from air power, they now proved remarkably fast learners.[68] Unfortunately, their willingness and ability to challenge previously held conceptions and to accept the need for a

---

[66]   Joubert, as head of Coastal Command, was under no illusions about the relative importance that the Air Ministry placed on his Command, which he described as: "a link between the RAF and the Navy—coveted by the latter and rather despised by the former." Joubert, *Fun and Games*, p. 120. In his autobiography, he wrote that the Air Ministry was well aware of the desperate need of Coastal Command for VLR aircraft, "But at every point the requirements of Bomber Command and the priority that was given to its needs thwarted our desires and intentions." Philip Joubert de la Ferté, *The Fated Sky: An Autobiography* (London: Hutchinson, 1952), p. 208. Or again: "Bomber Command always won, though a few crumbs would be thrown to Coastal. It is almost incredible that it took months of argument and discussion to allocate the 27 Very Long Range aircraft needed for the U-boat war." Philip Joubert de la Ferté, *Birds and Fishes: The Story of Coastal Command* (London: Hutchinson, 1960), p. 150. It is tempting to conclude that it was his heretical efforts on behalf of the maritime campaign that saw him replaced as Commander-in-Chief of Coastal Command by Slessor, who was far more in tune with the strategic bombing orthodoxy.

[67]   A good account of these failings can be found in Till, *Air Power and the Royal Navy*. For greater detail on the interwar Royal Navy, see S. W. Roskill, *Naval Policy Between the Wars*, Vol. I, *The Period of Anglo-American Antagonism, 1919–1929* (London: Collins, 1968) and *Naval Policy Between the Wars*, Vol. II, *The Period of Reluctant Rearmament, 1930–39* (London: Collins, 1976).

[68]   General Alan Brooke noted this on 26 July 1940, "The attitude of the representatives of the Naval Command brought [out] very clearly the fact that the navy now realises fully that its position has been seriously undermined by the advent of aircraft." Danchev and Todman, *Alanbrooke: War Diaries*, p. 95.

different approach was not matched by those who clung to the dream of strategic bombing winning the war on its own long after this particular aspiration had been shown to be unachievable and also to have a heavy cost. During the Second World War, the attitude of the Admiralty was far from sceptical of the potential contribution of land-based aircraft in the war at sea—on the contrary, their complaint was that there was not enough of it. Time and again the Navy requested that greater RAF effort be devoted to the maritime campaign; time and again they were rebuffed because to do so was not compatible with the focus of the Air Staff on the attempt to achieve their Holy Grail of winning the war through strategic bombing. As regards the utility of aircraft at sea, the problem was not that the Admiralty did not get the principle; rather that, despite repeated efforts, they could not get the aircraft.

As early as November 1940 the Admiralty went to the War Cabinet with a request for an improvement in air support for reconnaissance over the North Sea, air patrols against minelayers, and defense against enemy aircraft attacking merchant shipping or guiding in U-boats. They were not criticizing Coastal Command, but rather urging that it be better resourced: "It is observed that whilst the Coastal Command has given the Navy every possible assistance with the forces at their command, no means of meeting the Navy's urgent requirements can be within reach on the present Coastal Command strength."[69] At the meeting that discussed this paper, A. V. Alexander, First Lord of the Admiralty, requested that fifteen of the planned 100 new RAF squadrons should be for Coastal Command—hardly a massively disproportionate share—and coined a term that has often been used for this neglected command: "They felt that the Coastal Command had always been the 'Cinderella' of the Royal Air Force." The Secretary of State for Air rejected the Cinderella label and replied that such an allocation would be an "undue diversion of aircraft to Coastal duties [which] would hinder the building up of Bomber Command for offensive operations." The situation then dramatically worsened for the RAF when Lord Beaverbrook (Minister of Aircraft Production) suggested that the Navy should take over control of Coastal Command; his proposal, a great shock to the Air Ministry, got a sympathetic response from Churchill, who knew from his time as First Lord of the Admiralty about the problems with the existing situation: "there was no doubt that there would be advantages in having the whole protection of trade under one operational control. The Coastal Command had not received the scale of equipment that they should have had." Portal fell back on the familiar refrain: "In principle, all our efforts ought to go towards hitting the enemy and only the bare minimum should go for protective duties." Interestingly, the First Sea Lord did not back the proposal, stressing that the urgent need was for short-term assistance which could only come from the Air Ministry.[70]

---

[69]   CAB 66/13, WP(40)434, First Lord, "Strengthening Coastal Command," 4 November 1940.

[70]   CAB 69/1, DO(40)40th Meeting, 5 November 1940.

The subject was reconsidered a fortnight later. Beaverbrook pushed the case hard, arguing: "It is not a satisfactory answer to say that the Royal Air Force can fulfil the task of supplementing the surface craft of the fleet. It has failed to do so. The Coastal Command of the RAF is quite inadequate." The Secretary of State for Air denied that it was starved of resources: "The figures showed that there had been relatively a much greater increase in the strength of the Coastal Command than in any other Command of the Royal Air Force." (Of course, the fact that an additional 150 aircraft since September 1939 represented a doubling of its strength only showed how small it had been on the outbreak of war.) The First Lord of the Admiralty and the First Sea Lord made clear their complaints about the existing system, notably their lack of say in design and equipment of the aircraft or the training of the crews that cooperated with the Navy, and also the fact that "Although the number of aircraft in Coastal Command is totally inadequate, the Air Ministry can under present arrangements deflect even the small force that exists from its naval purposes without even consulting the Admiralty." Yet although they were broadly positive about the proposed change of control—Alexander more than Pound—their support was no more than lukewarm. The Admiralty representatives made it clear that their concern was rapid expansion, now; thus, they offered to delay the formation of two Fleet Air Arm squadrons for the Mediterranean to equip two land-based Coastal Command torpedo bomber squadrons in the UK—that is, they volunteered to weaken the naval air arm in order to strengthen part of the RAF—and repeated their request that by June 1941, fifteen of the 100 expansion RAF squadrons should be in Coastal Command. Churchill concluded that the change of control might have been desirable in peacetime, but it "would be disastrous at the present moment to tear a large fragment from the Royal Air Force." The Defence Committee decided that the RAF would retain administrative control of Coastal Command, though operational control should pass to the Admiralty. The Air Ministry managed to find a number of squadrons of bombers, torpedo bombers, and long-range fighters to transfer to Coastal, and promised that they would do what the Admiralty requested and allocate fifteen of the 100 new squadrons to Coastal Command; indeed, the Air Ministry "will accord the highest priority" to achieving this by June 1941.[71]

---

[71] For minutes of the meeting, see CAB 69/1, DO(40)47th Meeting, 4 December 1940. The papers circulated for it can be found in CAB 66/13 and comprise WP(40)439, Minister of Aircraft Production, "A Naval Air Force," 11 November 1940; WP(40)454, Secretary of State for Air, "Coastal Command," 21 November 1940; WP(40)455, First Lord, "Coastal Command," 20 November 1940; WP(40)459, First Lord, "Coastal Command," 22 November 1940. There was a similar dispute raging over the aircraft allocated to Army Co-operation Command, with the Army complaining they were inadequate and arguing that each Corps and Army should have reconnaissance, bomber, and fighter squadrons as "an integral part of these formations," CAB 80/57, COS(41)89(O), CIGS, "Army Air Requirements," 30 May 1941; also CAB 69/4, DO(42)24, Secretary of State for Air, "Requirements in Long-range General Reconnaissance Aircraft," 8 March 1942 and DO(42)34, Secretary of State for Air,

Of course, making commitments and fulfilling them were two different things. In March 1941, the First Lord complained to Churchill: "We understand that only 6 of the 15 new operational squadrons promised for Coastal Command have yet been formed and urge all possible acceleration."[72]

Two points emerge from this episode. First, the Admiralty did not seize this opportunity presented on the initiative of Lord Beaverbrook to push hard for full control of Coastal Command, focusing instead on the practical issue of improving the cooperation provided by the existing arrangements. After the war, one of the senior civil servants involved recalled that the Chief of the Air Staff and First Sea Lord had agreed with each other on the practical matters involved, while Slessor (in 1940, RAF Director of Plans) commented that the Naval Staff had declined to support "this Beaverbrook baboonery"[73]—thereby challenging his own distinctly paranoid view of naval intentions. Second, it is significant that matters had become so serious that the RAF faced losing one of its commands—its greatest nightmare being dismemberment of this sort—and that it took such a danger to push it to promise more aircraft to Coastal Command, memorably described by Harris as achieving "nothing essential to either our survival or the defeat of the enemy" and being "merely an obstacle to victory."[74] (This description, all the more damaging for appearing in a personal note to Churchill, is less suggestive of cool analysis than of someone in thrall to an obsessive ideology.)

The ongoing dispute intensified during 1942. Shipping losses to U-boats continued at a high level, the Chiefs of Staff concluding that the result was a "very serious situation" in which Britain could not adequately reinforce the Middle East, India, the Indian Ocean, and Far East.[75] A report suggested that from the beginning of 1942 to mid-1943, there would be a shortage of 8.4 million tons (or 20%) in non-tanker imports. It concluded that the resulting cut-backs "might damage national morale and limit our capacity to carry on the war with full vigour and

---

"Air Forces for Co-operation with the Army and the Navy," 1 April 1942. The head of the Admiralty Naval Air Division remarked that the "Army's arguments are very much parallel to our own . . . the General Staff do not ask for the disintegration of the Royal Air Force, but that greater attention must be paid to the needs of those Air Forces operating with the Army, and that fuller co-operation is necessary on the part of the Air Ministry." ADM 205/15, Director of Naval Air Division to First Sea Lord, 5 May 1942.

72   First Lord to Prime Minister, 11 March 1941—part of CAB 66/15, WP(41)62, "The Battle of the Atlantic," 18 March 1941.

73   AIR 75/17, Maurice Dean to Slessor, 30 June 1949, Slessor to H. Saunders, RAF Historian, 21 June 1949.

74   AIR 8/405, Harris to Churchill, 17 June 1942, cited in Redford, "Inter- and Intra-Service Rivalries," pp. 915–16. See also Terraine, The Right of the Line, p. 426.

75   CAB 69/4, DO(42)16, Chiefs of Staff, "Shipping Situation," 15 February 1942.

efficiency."[76] Ironically, this was just the effect that the British strategic bombing campaign was intended to have on Germany.

Admiral Pound submitted a paper stating explicitly in its opening words the harsh reality that Portal and the Air Ministry refused to acknowledge: "If we lose the war at sea we lose the war." The requirements he set out for the war at sea included sufficient land-based aircraft that "the enemy, whenever they come within the range of our shore-based aircraft, are subjected to attack by air forces which are at least as numerous, as suitable and as well trained for operations over the sea as are those of our enemies." He also identified the need for aircraft to protect convoys and shipping, a torpedo bombing force, and bombing of U-boat yards. The numbers of aircraft he sought were large, but hardly outrageous, including 100 long-range General Reconnaissance aircraft for Home use (250 altogether) and a strike force of 160 aircraft at Home (a total of 390, plus seventy Navy aircraft). In all, this would amount to 1,940 aircraft.[77] To put this figure in context, the RAF "Target Force E" of June 1941 envisaged a Bomber Command in which heavy bombers alone would number 4,000.[78] The Admiralty was asking no more of the RAF than that it do what it had always claimed it could. Its request represented a small number of aircraft relative to those the Air Ministry was losing over Germany to arguably less important ends, given the meager results of the strategic air offensive to this point; as Pound commented to Churchill, "If I could get the number of bombers we lose in a few days [over Germany] we could make a great start."[79] The Air Ministry, however, continued to reject shifting long-range aircraft from Bomber Command to Coastal, arguing that it would be "a dispersion of our bombing resources in an attempt to contribute defensively to the control of sea communications over immense areas of oceans where targets are uncertain, fleeting and difficult to hit." Better, they argued, to weaken the U-boats by attacking industrial areas in Germany.[80] Again, in the Defence Committee, Portal rejected

---

[76]   CAB 66/26, WP(42)294, Lord President of the Council, "The Shipping Situation," 14 July 1942.

[77]   CAB 69/4, DO(42)23, First Lord, "Air requirements for the successful prosecution of the war at sea," 6 March 1942.

[78]   Terraine, *The Right of the Line*, p. 289.

[79]   Pound to Churchill, 19 April 1942, cited in Till, *Air Power and the Royal Navy*, p. 191. During the month that Pound wrote this memo, Bomber Command lost 143 aircraft destroyed with a further 533 damaged, Webster and Frankland, *Strategic Air Offensive*, Vol. IV, pp. 432, 435. Pound might have had in mind Harris' well-publicized "1000 bomber raid" on Cologne of 30/31 May, in which sixty-two long-range aircraft were lost and thirty-three more seriously damaged. He only reached his magic number by pulling in aircraft from Coastal Command, among other sources. Terraine, *The Right of the Line*, p. 487.

[80]   CAB 69/4, DO(42)24, Secretary of State for Air, "Requirements in Long-range General Reconnaissance Aircraft," 8 March 1942.

Pound's appeal for more land-based aircraft for anti-submarine patrolling, on the grounds that it would mean a "considerable reduction in the strength of Bomber Command. The question was whether the war effort would be best assisted, and the maximum help to Russia given, by maintaining the maximum offensive against Germany or by diverting resources to defensive patrolling over the sea."[81] Any suggestion that the bombing campaign should give any ground to other needs was anathema to the RAF, which generally had the support of Churchill. As Brooke put it, "With PM in his present mood, and with his desire to maintain air bombardment of Germany, it will not be possible to get adequate support for either the Army or the Navy."[82]

The Air Ministry frequently argued that the problem was not any lack of will to support the maritime campaign, but rather a lack of resources—that is, the problem was the shortage of aircraft relative to the many demands on them.[83] There was undoubtedly some justice in this. Strategists will never have all the resources that they might wish, and Britain's position in the early years of the war was particularly grim. However, there were still real questions over the allocation of those scarce resources that were available. The Admiralty commented that they appreciated that there was a general shortfall in aircraft, but felt that "the effect has fallen rather more heavily on Coastal Command types than on others."[84] The problem was not, as the Air Staff argued, solely the result of insufficient aircraft; while this was a factor, it was greatly exacerbated by the policy of the Air Staff, which in design and production of aircraft, training of crews, and allocation of effort consistently over-emphasized the strategic air offensive at the expense of other commitments.

The First Sea Lord returned to the issue in June 1942, underlining the gravity of the situation with sinkings averaging over 677,000 tons per month over the

---

[81]   CAB 69/4, DO(42)8th meeting, 18 March 1942.

[82]   Danchev and Todman, *Alanbrooke: War Diaries,* entry for 19 March 1942, p. 240. Brooke repeatedly engaged on this subject. On 11 March he complained that the belief of many in the RAF that Germany could be defeated by bombing alone led to a focus on heavy bombers: "As a result the army was being starved of any types suitable for the direct support of land forces . . . All Air Force eyes were trained on Germany and consequently all the personnel trained for long distance raids, and little interest was displayed in close cooperation with land forces." Ibid., p. 238. It is interesting that CIGS perceived much the same problem as the Admiralty, for example: "It is a depressing situation and the Air Ministry outlook is now so divorced from the requirements of the army that I see no solution except an Army Air Arm." 19 May 1942, ibid., p. 258. For other comments in a similar vein, see also pp. 127, 138, 157, 247, 253, 312, 327, 331.

[83]   See, for example, CAB 69/4, DO(42)34, Secretary of State for Air, "Air Forces for Co-operation with the Army and the Navy," 1 April 1942, para. 9.

[84]   ADM 205/15, DO(42)34, "Summary of Criticisms by the Naval Staff."

previous quarter, while Germany was commissioning twenty new U-boats per month. In response, Portal not only rejected the plea for more aircraft, but even refused the suggestion of a study of the issue by the Joint Planning Staff (which was proposed by Pound, but also backed by Brooke). He offered the extraordinary argument that new production of shipping would shortly rise above the level of sinkings, and that Pound's paper was "not conclusive" on whether the situation at sea was grave, and "unassailable arguments should be forthcoming before a severe curtailment of the air offensive could be accepted."[85] This approach characterized the debate: hundreds of thousands of tons of shipping lost, with all the wasted resources of building the ships and their cargoes, let alone the deaths of their crews, did not constitute an "unassailable argument" for reconsidering resource allocation, while the most modest transfer of aircraft is "a severe curtailment of the air offensive." As noted above, such an approach appears to be little different in terms of callous refusal to reconsider assumptions to the tactics of the First World War generals whom the Air Staff were so quick to criticize.[86]

As a result of the on-going dispute, the Assistant Chief of the Naval Staff (Home) and Assistant Chief of the Air Staff (Policy) wrote a joint report. It began by noting that British strategy had agreed priorities placing "Minimum necessary allocations for securing our vital communications and interrupting those of the enemy" ahead of "Maximum possible provision for the offensive, both direct and in support of land operations." The "minimum necessary" for sea communications was defined as: "Prevent our losing the war by the cutting of our sea supply lines; or suffering unacceptable delay in the development of our capacity to win it by the reduction of supplies, or by the sinking of unfinished war material." The compromise report noted that the Admiralty saw the situation at sea as critical, with the number of sinkings "a deadly menace" resulting in waste of war effort and offensive potential. The Air Ministry, however, perceived the same situation as grave, but not critical: "a relatively small proportion of our war material is being sunk and no action we can take in the next few months would make a substantial difference to the amount of shipping available for WS [Britain to Suez Canal] convoys in the near future." Nonetheless, despite this vastly different appreciation of the situation, the two authors agreed that the planned expansion in Coastal Command would not come fast enough, and so recommended that two squadrons of Lancasters be

---

[85]   CAB 80/63, COS(42)171(O), First Sea Lord, "The Bombing of Germany," 16 June 1942 and COS(42)183(O), CAS, "The Bombing of Germany," 23 June 1942.

[86]   During June 1942, Bomber Command lost 201 aircraft destroyed, and another 488 damaged, Webster and Frankland, *Strategic Air Offensive*, Vol. IV, pp. 432, 435. It is rather sobering that in his May 1941 memo advocating absolute priority for a bombing offensive against Germany, Trenchard accepted that his bomber force might suffer casualties of up to seventy percent of front line strength *each month*, CAB 80/57, COS(41)86(O), Lord Trenchard, "The present war situation mainly in so far as it relates to air," 19 May 1941.

loaned from Bomber Command for reconnaissance for the fleet and for anti-U-boat patrolling.[87] It is striking that the two officers who thus concluded that the situation at sea was grave enough to merit transferring long-range aircraft from Bomber Command were Rear Admiral E. J. P. Brind and Air Vice Marshal John C. Slessor, who at other times proved himself to be a fervent believer in the bomber offensive.

The latter's argument did not go down well with his chief: where the report states that the effects of the bomber offensive "are just as much open to speculation as those of the blockade," the copy stamped "CAS PERSONAL COPY" has the pencil annotations, "No" and "Rot."[88] Slessor defended the proposal in a briefing to Portal, arguing that although Britain was not in danger of losing the war due to the shipping situation, "I do not feel that we can allow the present rate of sinkings to go on." He even went as far, behind closed doors in the Air Ministry, as to concede that the number of very-long-range aircraft forces in Coastal Command was unacceptable "on any standards" and that "I do not think the Admiralty requirements are at all unreasonable." He believed it was right to lend the Lancasters, though in his defense, he pointed out that the two-squadron loan was "very short" of the Navy's initial demands and that failing to agree might have led to more being transferred.[89] Portal, however, remained immoveable and insisted that the aircraft envisaged might at best sink five U-boats and damage a dozen more or could instead drop 800 tons of bombs on Germany and lay 600 mines. (It is an extraordinary indication of how he continued to overstate the impact of bombing that he rated dropping 800 tons of bombs on Germany higher than sinking five U-boats and putting a dozen more out of action.) They would make a greater contribution to the war effort by remaining in Bomber Command: "I am so strongly convinced of this that I regard the loss of these two squadrons to Bomber Command as unacceptable." His counter-offer was that some training squadrons (albeit without any maritime training) might conduct some flights in the desired patrol zone and an unspecified number of Lancasters might be switched from mining to anti-submarine operations. Reconnaissance would be conducted by Bomber Command aircraft as needed.[90]

The Chiefs of Staff acknowledged that "the Navy is already stretched to the utmost and that the shipping losses are dangerously high," which would take up

---

[87] AIR 8/991, COS(42)332, ACNS(H), and ACAS(P), "General Policy for the Employment of Air Forces," 2 July 1942.

[88] AIR 8/991, COS(42)332, margin annotations next to para. 14.

[89] AIR 8/991, ACAS(P) brief for CAS on COS(42)332, 2 July 1942.

[90] AIR 8/991, COS(42)341, CAS, "Provision of long range aircraft for anti-submarine patrols," 14 July 1942. That month, Bomber Command lost 190 aircraft destroyed, 373 damaged, Webster and Frankland, *Strategic Air Offensive*, Vol. IV, pp. 432, 435.

much Allied production, harm the ability to reinforce and supply forces overseas, and "also hamper dangerously our future strategy." Nevertheless, they went along with this minimal and grudging concession;[91] once again, the Admiralty was unwilling or unable to prevent the Air Staff putting its preferences first. For Harris, even such marginal reallocations as Portal was prepared to concede were too much to bear. In a long paper written for the War Cabinet, he referred to those "who advocate the breaking-up of Bomber Command for the purpose of adding strength to Coastal and Army Co-operation Commands," comparing them to amateur politicians who would divide the national wealth among the entire population, giving each person a tiny sum while wrecking the overall economy.[92] This was a rather extreme interpretation of a fairly modest redistribution of long-range aircraft.

This small promised reallocation was, once again, not fulfilled and the Admiralty returned to the issue in October. It pointed out that "the minimum target figures of shore-based aircraft agreed with the Air Ministry for operations over the sea will only be met to the extent of 75 per cent by 1st November 1942." The result was that in the six months to August, the average loss of merchant shipping per month was 685,000 tons, resulting in a waste of labor and resources in the ships and their cargoes, a shortage of tankers, the loss of trained merchant seamen, and lower morale for the survivors. The lack of air support was also limiting the ability of the Navy to undertake offensive operations, as well as halting convoys and holding up overseas reinforcements, and restricting the ability to interfere with enemy sea communications. Priorities for air production which stood while Allied air power was inferior to the enemy should be reassessed now that this was no longer the case. The First Lord, therefore, sought a greater proportion of the national effort for naval production, including making up arrears in production for the Fleet Air Arm, not least new aircraft to reduce the proportion of obsolescent aircraft on carriers. He also recommended that more long-range aircraft should be committed to maritime operations, including types suitable for anti-shipping work, and that shore-based maritime aircraft should "have priority second only to the needs of the fighter defence of the United Kingdom."[93] This was a fairly modest

---

[91]   CAB 66/26, WP(42)302, Chiefs of Staff, "Provision of Aircraft for the War at Sea," 18 July 1942.

[92]   CAB 66/28, WP(42)374, Air Marshal Sir Arthur Harris, "The Role and Work of Bomber Command," 24 August 1942. An earlier version of the paper of 28 June 1942, in AIR 8/991, referred to "amateur socialists"; presumably this was altered in the circulated version to "amateur politicians" out of sensitivity to the members of the national unity government from the Labour Party. His book about the campaign repeats this questionable zero-sum approach, complaining that demands from the Middle East and other places, "and of course, the inordinate demands of the Admiralty for every conceivable thing to be turned to their use, would bring any bomber force offensive to a standstill," Harris, *Bomber Offensive*, p. 75.

[93]   AIR 8/991, DC(S)(42)88, First Lord of the Admiralty, "The Needs of the Navy," 5 October 1942.

proposal; meeting the backlog in previously agreed numbers for the Fleet Air Arm and temporarily raising the priority of Coastal Command above that of Bomber Command in order to meet the long-standing shortfall compared to what had been agreed, as well as shifting some resources into naval production.

Just like Harris in relation to the previous proposal, Slessor as ACAS (Policy) reacted in an extreme fashion—which perhaps suggests that he had learned the lesson from having his wings clipped after his compromise of a few months before. He strongly opposed the suggestion, characterizing the Admiralty's attitude as "their requirements must invariably be met as a matter of first priority and without regard for any other commitments"; the recommendations of the paper "could be summarised in one sentence 'Never mind Bomber Command—give all the long-range bombers to Coastal.'"[94] Just like Harris before him, Slessor was robustly objecting to an argument that no one was actually making, a ridiculous straw man. The Admiralty was not advocating the abolition of Bomber Command, nor calling for the termination of the strategic bombing campaign, nor even for a temporary halt, nor demanding huge chunks of the long-range bomber force be moved over to Coastal. What was sought was an increase in the number of long-range aircraft in Coastal Command at the expense of a relatively far smaller slowing of the pace of expansion of Bomber Command; that is, of the increasing resources pouring into the RAF, a little more than planned should go to Coastal Command. Indeed, the attitude Slessor described of "their requirements must invariably be met as a matter of first priority and without regard for any other commitments" would be a more accurate description of the approach of the Air Ministry than that of the Admiralty.

The remarkable hyperbole of the reaction to this proposal suggests that there had been something of a loss of perspective in parts of the Air Ministry to the extent that advocating the transfer of a few aircraft from one RAF Command to

---

[94] AIR 8/991, ACAS(P), "Comments on DC(S)(42)88 and DC(S)(42)90," 13 October 1942. Slessor held to this line after the war as Chief of the Air Staff. He wrote to the First Sea Lord in 1952 to complain that the draft Admiralty history of the Battle of the Atlantic suggested that Bomber Command had enjoyed too high a priority and a greater proportion of resources should have gone to Coastal Command. The sort of sentiments that he expressed within the Air Ministry during the war now erupted in his communication with a fellow chief of a service, as he complained that "the implication is that the strategic offensive against Germany should have taken second place to the maritime battle" and criticized "the narrowness of vision which pre-suppose that the first claim of the RAF's available long range aircraft should always be awarded to the maritime war." He objected that the bombing offensive "could not be turned on or off like a tap, even to take part in the Battle of the Atlantic." Air 8/1701, CAS to First Sea Lord, 1 September 1952. His letter was accompanied by ten pages of deletions, substitutions, and additions requested for the Naval Staff History, *The Defeat of the Enemy Attack on Shipping*. The Air Ministry perspective on the dispute over the Staff History can be found in AIR 8/1701; that of the Admiralty in ADM 1/25446.

another was interpreted as an existential threat. The Admiralty was not questioning whether there should be a strategic bombing campaign. There was an acceptance that it had a central role in British strategy, albeit not one that would be decisive on its own as some of the senior airmen believed. As a note discussing papers by Trenchard and Harris put it: "In the Admiralty's view the bombing of Germany is analogous to the blockade. Both contribute considerably to the undermining of the enemy's resources and morale, and thereby weaken the fighting power of his armed forces; but neither of them are substitutes for their defeat but only contributions thereto."[95] They were not trying to stop the bombing offensive, but rather were questioning the extent of the priority it was receiving and the cost that resulted in terms of Britain's ability to conduct other important campaigns. They were seeking not an end to strategic bombing, but a modest rebalancing of resources towards other needs. There were times of particular crisis when it would have been entirely sensible for the air offensive to continue, but to be temporarily put in second place behind ensuring victory in the Battle of the Atlantic, which was necessary first for Britain's survival and then for any "offensive" operations, including strategic bombing. It is a huge leap to move from this contention to saying that there should be no strategic air offensive, but this sort of proposal, frequently railed against by the Air Staff, was pure fiction, and not one that the Admiralty ever made. Another internal Admiralty paper from 1942 argued for some long-range aircraft to be released from Bomber Command, but was quite clear that the forces moved would be small: "This should mean only a reduction in the scale of the bombing offensive. It is not suggested that there should be any relaxation of a continued bombing offensive."[96]

Even a modest reduction was too much to ask. The Air Staff continued to insist that the best way that the RAF could contribute to the Battle of the Atlantic was to attack German industrial power, which would destroy the factories that built components for U-boats and the yards that assembled them. Typical of this approach was Harris: ". . .Bomber Command attacks the sources of all Naval power, rather than the fringes of the one type of enemy Naval operation which obviously menaces us— the submarine."[97] There were two problems with this approach. First, at least up until early 1943, the strategic air offensive did little or nothing to stem the flow of U-boats into the German Navy. In the middle of 1941, Churchill for a while attached absolute priority to the Battle of the Atlantic (covered in more detail below). The Air Staff chafed against this but did carry out some attacks on bases and yards. This effort was

---

[95]   ADM 205/15, "Admiralty comments on Lord Trenchard and Air Marshal Harris' papers," 9 September 1942, para. 9.

[96]   ADM 205/18, "Air Requirements for the Successful Prosecution of the War at Sea," summer 1942, para. 10.

[97]   CAB 66/28, WP(42)374, Air Marshal Sir Arthur Harris, "The Role and Work of Bomber Command," 24 August 1942, para. 16.

ineffective: "Post-war records make it clear that, in fact, it had a negligible effect on the large number of U-boats now building."[98] In late 1942, an Admiralty paper noted that even on Harris' own evidence—"some of it of the flimsiest character"—out of 360 U-boats completed and 260 building, only "22 boats have been directly affected" by strategic bombing.[99] The official historians of the strategic air campaign conclude that from 1941 to January 1943: "Submarine construction continued to rise and the effect of the large number of attacks on the ports concerned was negligible. That this was the case was realised by MEW [the Ministry of Economic Warfare], whose estimates of the number of submarines built in the year and the gradual rise of the monthly average was very accurate. The claim of Bomber Command that it could do more to help the Battle of the Atlantic by bombing submarine construction yards rather than the ports from which they set out was not substantiated." In other words, not only was Bomber Command failing to damage U-boat production, but the British government knew it to be failing.[100] This represents a devastating indictment of RAF policy from a well-informed and sympathetic source.

The second problem was that available evidence strongly suggested the allocation of resources should have been different. Operational analysis, which played an important role in the Battle of the Atlantic, showed that a very-long-range aircraft operating with convoys could save at least half a dozen merchant ships during its operational lifetime; alternatively, if used instead over Germany, it could drop less than 100 tons of bombs on Berlin. As Professor P. M. S. Blackett concluded, "No-one would dispute that the saving of six merchant vessels and their crews and cargoes was of incomparably more value to the Allied war effort than the killing of some two dozen enemy civilians, the destruction of a number of houses, and a certain very small effect on production."[101] In this respect, of course, he was quite wrong; Portal, Harris, Trenchard, Slessor, and all too often, Churchill, did dispute this.

---

[98]   S. W. Roskill, *The War at Sea, 1939–45*, Vol. I, *The Defensive* (London: HMSO, 1954), p. 459.

[99]   ADM 205/15, Appendix C of "Admiralty comments on Lord Trenchard and Air Marshal Harris' papers," 9 September 1942; it refers to CAB 66/28, WP(42)374, Air Marshal Sir Arthur Harris, "The Role and Work of Bomber Command," 24 August 1942, Appendix C.

[100]   Webster and Frankland, *Strategic Air Offensive*, Vol. I, p. 481. They further note: "The submarine construction industry itself, MEW thought, was not a very rewarding target because the yards were difficult to destroy and easy to rebuild quickly." Charles Webster and Noble Frankland, *The Strategic Air Offensive Against Germany, 1939–45*, Vol. II, *Endeavour* (London: HMSO, 1961), p. 216. Even as bombing in general improved, the impact on U-boat production showed little progress: in the whole of 1943, the bombing of Germany caused the loss of fifteen U-boats in production and sank one. Webster and Frankland, *Strategic Air Offensive*, Vol. IV, p. 524.

[101]   P. M. S. Blackett, "Operational Research: Recollections of Problems Studied, 1940–45," in *Brassey's Annual 1953* (London: William Clowes and Sons, 1953), p. 104. Blackett was Director of Operational Research for the Admiralty.

"Hard and fast priorities unintelligently interpreted"[102]

By the summer of 1943, the worst period of crisis in the Battle of the Atlantic had passed and the situation was improving markedly. In part, the Allies' ever-growing productive capacity meant that a relative bounty of resources could resolve many strategic dilemmas. More long-range aircraft slowly yet steadily became available— suggesting what might have been achieved earlier. This, together with the crucial advent of escort carriers, finally closed the mid-Atlantic air gap. The results achieved by the bombing campaign also improved with new navigation aids, greater experience, and better techniques. This is not to argue that the claims of the airmen to be able to win the war alone could ever have been achieved—much of the great eventual effect of strategic bombing was realized as it became, against the determined resistance of Harris and other such purists, ever more closely tied into an avowedly all-arms strategy that explicitly saw bombing as assisting the opposed invasion of the continent, not making it unnecessary. However, the fact that the Chiefs of Staff did not adequately resolve the problem of the provision of air support for the war at sea during the critical period between 1940 and early 1943 was a glaring failure of the system which needlessly lengthened the period of crisis in the Battle of the Atlantic.

Fully accounting for this failure is beyond the scope of this chapter, but some contributing causes can be identified. One major factor was the intransigence and dogmatism displayed by Portal. According to his biographer, Portal gave a speech at the Mansion House in London in June 1946, where referring to the Chiefs of Staff, he asserted that "there was no axe-grinding by any particular service."[103] His reluctance to countenance any reduction in the bombing of Germany regardless of the air power needs of his fellow Chiefs suggests that he might have been flattering himself a little. Portal put his undoubtedly formidable intellectual and bureaucratic talents solidly behind the Air Ministry's preoccupation with the strategic

---

[102]   In response to Trenchard's paper cited above (CAB 80/57, COS(41)86(O), Lord Trenchard, "The present war situation mainly in so far as it relates to air," 19 May 1941), Pound agreed that air superiority would be needed before a British return to the continent, but stressed the need for some provision of aircraft for support of naval and land operations. The paper, he argued, was an overstatement: "we must not go to extremes. The danger of hard and fast priorities unintelligently interpreted has often been exemplified." CAB 80/57, COS(41)96(O), First Sea Lord, "Lord Trenchard's Memorandum," 2 June 1941.

[103]   Richards, *Lord Portal,* p. 345. Even in an account so friendly to its subject, at times bordering on the hagiographic, it is surprising to read the assertion that Portal was "doing all he humanly could to increase and improve the air forces directly cooperating with the Army and the Royal Navy"; ibid., p. 206. Other writers have made similarly positive comments about Portal, which in the light of this issue seem equally questionable—for example, "Lacking dogmatism . . . he remained open to the evidence before him." Biddle, "Winston Churchill and Sir Charles Portal," p. 198.

bombing campaign, which was not necessarily in the best interests of the country or even the RAF. Portal was by no means the worst case in the Air Staff of a prisoner to dogma: later in the war he would strongly back the use of Bomber Command in support of Operation Overlord.[104] He was criticized for this after the war by some former colleagues, including Slessor.[105] Nevertheless, during the critical period up to the spring of 1943, he repeatedly refused to meet the needs of the war at sea in favor of persisting with the strategic air offensive, which he and the government were well aware was failing to deliver on its promises.

Why was the implacable Portal allowed to get away with so much? Part of the explanation must be the reasonable reluctance of the other Chiefs of Staff to take on the bitter conflict that would have been necessary to prise more aircraft from the Air Staff for the war at sea. There were good reasons to wish the usually collegiate working of the Chiefs of Staff Committee to continue, not least because the Chiefs were often drawn together by the common need to resist some of Churchill's more colorful brainwaves. The understandable tendency of the Chiefs to seek consensus and compromise allowed those with the most extreme opinions to stick to their views. It could also manifest itself in a lack of clarity. Thus, Portal could accept that absolute priority should go to the bomber force only after "the minimum force of aircraft (e.g. fighter, general reconnaissance, Fleet Air Arm, etc.) essential for our security has been provided";[106] yet as time would prove, he and his counterparts would have a very different idea of just what would constitute this "minimum." The Chiefs of Staff as a body could agree that offensive bombing against transportation and morale should be conducted, "Subject therefore to the requirements of security (including of course the Battle of the Atlantic),"[107] but again, this apparent consensus masked fundamental disagreements.

It is also hard to avoid the conclusion that Pound's poor and declining health made him less able and willing to take on Portal than perhaps he should have

---

[104] Portal himself explained to the War Cabinet that due to the evidence from the North Africa campaign and the persuasive powers of Air Chief Marshal Tedder, one of his most trusted subordinates, he did come around to the plan to attack German communications in the run-up to Overlord, having previously opposed it. See CAB 69/6, DO(44)5th meeting, 5 April 1944.

[105] Slessor wrote, "if we had given the necessary priority to the Bombers and their equipment, Germany's economy (and hence ability to sustain the war) *could* have been destroyed before the Normandy invasion. The Armies would still have had subsequently to go in, to restore order and occupy enemy territory till a peace settlement; but on a much smaller scale and without a massive operation like Overlord." AIR 75/86, Slessor to Major William Giffen, Department of History, U.S. Air Force Academy, 20 July 1968, emphasis original.

[106] CAB 80/57, COS(41)94(O), Note by the Chief of the Air Staff, 2 June 1941, para. 2.

[107] CAB 80/58, COS(41)114(O), Chiefs of Staff, "The present war situation mainly in so far as it relates to air," 21 June 1941.

been.[108] As Chief of the Imperial General Staff, Brooke noted Pound's frequent ineffectiveness in meetings: "I always felt nervous lest the naval aspect of our problems should not be adequately represented owing to his being so often asleep."[109] The saga of the failure to devote the necessary resources to the war at sea suggests that this was indeed the case, and a different First Sea Lord might have offered Portal a more robust challenge.

The entrenched position of Portal, and the unwillingness and inability of the other Chiefs of Staff to confront him, meant that this vital matter was allowed to fester while the Air Staff resisted, delayed, and dismissed attempts to reallocate resources in favor of waging what amounted at times to its own private war. Given that the Air Ministry failed to behave in a very fraternal fashion over the Battle for the Atlantic, the resolution should have come from its political masters. When the Chiefs of Staff cannot agree on such issues—which are by any standard genuinely complicated—then the War Cabinet needs to step in and make a decision on priorities. That this was not done is an indictment of the government, and to a considerable extent of the Prime Minister, not least since he had also taken on the role of Minister of Defence. Churchill's approach to this matter was characterized by a maddening inconsistency. As First Lord of the Admiralty, he had stressed the importance of air power for the Navy, for reconnaissance and anti-submarine warfare, arguing that the needs of the Fleet Air Arm "though small comparatively,

---

[108]   Brian Farrell criticizes Pound for allowing "the all-important struggle to secure more effective support from the Royal Air Force to drag on so long as to threaten the whole war effort," Brian P. Farrell, "Sir (Alfred) Dudley Pickman Rogers Pound," *Oxford Dictionary of National Biography* (Oxford: Oxford University Press, 2004–12). He also questions whether Pound's health was adequate for him to take on the position of First Sea Lord. Pound's biographer notes that although the First Sea Lord's colleagues generally believed him to be fit for office when he was appointed, his health then steadily declined until he died of a brain tumor on Trafalgar Day 1943, Robin Brodhurst, *Churchill's Anchor: The Biography of Admiral of the Fleet Sir Dudley Pound* (Barnsley: Leo Cooper, 2000), pp. 113–16, 279–80. Brodhurst also notes that due to the structure of the Admiralty, Pound had weighty operational responsibilities that his colleagues on the Chiefs of Staff committee did not share—which was the pretext given for Churchill replacing him as its chairman with Brooke. Ibid., pp. 211–12.

[109]   Danchev and Todman, *Alanbrooke: War Diaries,* entry for 28 August 1943, pp. 449–50. The diaries contain repeated critical and often irritable references to Pound's slowness and ineffectiveness at Chiefs of Staff Committee meetings and his tendency to fall asleep, see ibid., pp. 143, 181 (particularly interesting for its comparison of the Committee to the tea party in *Alice in Wonderland,* with Pound as the dormouse and Portal as the Mad Hatter), 207, 221, 230, 241, 244, 280, 315, 334, 356, 357. On 3 February 1942, Brooke commented that Pound "looked like an old parrot asleep on his perch," p. 226. Here and on pp. 316 and 450 he later noted that he was unaware how ill Pound was and expressed regret at his harsh comments that he had written in ignorance.

cannot cede priority in any respect."[110] He wrote to Prime Minister Neville Chamberlain that he agreed that "Air Power stand foremost in our requirements, and indeed I sometimes think that it may be the ultimate path by which victory will be gained." However, he continued, the Air Ministry "seems to peg out vast and vague claims, which are not at present substantiated, and which, if accorded absolute priority, would overlay other indispensable forms of war effort."[111] This was precisely what would happen when he was later in a position to prevent it.

As Prime Minister, Churchill proved unable to resist the Air Ministry's extravagant claims on behalf of air power; whilst at times expressing scepticism as a result of their failure to realize these claims in practice, he tended to favor the strategic air offensive over other campaigns.[112] Yet his support did not always preclude pushing other competing calls on resources. One of the most egregious examples of this is a memorandum he wrote in September 1940: "The Navy can lose us the war, but only the Air Force can win it. Therefore our supreme effort must be to gain overwhelming mastery in the air. The Fighters are our salvation, but the Bombers alone provide the means of victory.... In no other way at present visible can we hope to overcome the immense military power of Germany.... The Air Force and its action on the larger scale must therefore, *subject to what is said later,* claim the first place over the Navy or the Army." So, bombing should have priority, but not at the expense of all other activities. The same memorandum ordered the Navy to plan "aggressive schemes of war" against enemy coasts: "The production of anti-U-boat craft must proceed at the maximum until further orders.... The decision to raise the Army to a strength of 55 divisions as rapidly as possible does not seem to require any reconsideration.... Intense efforts must be made to complete the equipment of our Army at home and of our Army in the Middle East.. ... We must expect to fight in Egypt and the Soudan, in Turkey, Syria or Palestine, and possibly in Iraq and Persia." Also, radar and associated scientific developments must be regarded as "ranking in priority with the Air Force."[113] He was apparently unaware of the old saying that if everything is a priority, then nothing is.

The problem was not any reluctance to set priorities; on the contrary, they were set too many times in a contradictory fashion, and difficult issues were shirked rather than give a clear lead that would be unacceptable to one of the services.

---

[110]   CAB 66/1, WP(39)36, Report of the First Lord of the Admiralty to the War Cabinet, 17 September 1939, para. 6.

[111]   First Lord to Prime Minister, 18 September 1939, reproduced in Winston S. Churchill, *The Second World War,* Vol. I, *The Gathering Storm* (London: Cassell, 1948), p. 411.

[112]   For his contribution to the dispute, see in particular Bell, *Churchill and Sea Power.*

[113]   Memorandum by the Prime Minister, 3 September 1940, Winston S. Churchill, *The Second World War,* Vol. II, *Their Finest Hour* (London: Cassell, 1949), pp. 405–08, emphasis added.

What is the most pressing concern for strategy will naturally change frequently over the course of a war lasting nearly six years, especially one characterized by so many ebbs and flows of fortune. It is to be expected that priorities will evolve. However, the frequency with which priorities changed is nonetheless startling.

At times Churchill did, it is true, give the maritime campaign a prominent place in his rhetoric; however, his record of following this through into policy decisions and prioritization was quite abysmal. After the war, he famously wrote: "The only thing that ever really frightened me during the war was the U-boat peril . . . our life-line, even across the broad oceans, and especially in the entrances to the Island, was endangered. I was even more anxious about this battle than I had been about the glorious air fight called the Battle of Britain."[114] This ringing retrospective declaration of concern was not at all a reflection of his actual policy during the war. There was little "glorious" about the campaign against the U-boats—in stark contrast to the well-publicized activities of Bomber Command (never knowingly undersold), and the even more extravagant promises of future achievement that were never fulfilled. Again, according to his memoirs, "this mortal danger to our life-lines gnawed my bowels," so in March 1941 he formally proclaimed "the Battle of the Atlantic," instituted the "Battle of the Atlantic Committee," and issued his "Battle of the Atlantic Directive." Offensive action was to be taken against the U-boats and land-based aircraft supporting them, as well as their bases; "extreme" priority should go to ships capable of launching fighters, Coastal Command should get the support of Fighter and Bomber Commands, and labor would be reallocated to repair and building of merchant shipping, among other measures.[115]

The directive issued by the RAF to Bomber Command putting the Prime Minister's instructions into practice demonstrates the limited impact of such worthy statements.[116] Churchill's directive suggested that Britain "should" be able to defeat the threat in four months; the Air Ministry directive putting his instructions into effect interpreted this conveniently to mean that the shift in effort would only last for four months. It also stated that operations should be directed against the mandated targets "when circumstances permit" while pointing out that this "does not entirely exclude attacks on the primary objectives," to which some effort should still be devoted; moreover, clinging to the overall ideology, priority was to be given not to those targets that would most influence the Battle of the Atlantic, but rather to "those in Germany which lie in congested areas where the greatest moral effect is likely to result."[117] The target list included not only the operational bases of the

---

[114]   Ibid., p. 529.

[115]   Winston S. Churchill, *The Second World War,* Vol. III, *The Grand Alliance* (London: Cassell, 1950), pp. 106–10, which includes the full text of the 6 March 1941 directive.

[116]   Air Chief Marshal Sir Wilfrid Freeman (Vice Chief of the Air Staff), to Air Marshal Sir Richard Peirse, 9 March 1941, in Webster and Frankland, Vol. IV, Appendix 8, p. xiv.

[117]   Ibid., paras. 1, 3–5.

submarines and U-boats, but also targets that would only have at best an eventual and indirect effect, hardly ameliorating the current crisis, such as U-boat construction yards as well as engine and aircraft factories; a subsequent directive watered down the focus on naval targets even further, adding submarine battery and engine factories in the Ruhr and in Southern Germany—the latter, it was emphasized, "are suitable as area objectives and their attack should have high morale value."[118] Clearly there is a need for some form of transmission mechanism to put prime ministerial intentions into operational orders, but a more egregious case of the phenomenon of "consent and evade" would be difficult to find.[119]

Four months to the day from the first directive, Bomber Command was once again ordered "to direct the main effort of the bombing force, until further instructions, towards dislocating the German transportation system and to destroying the morale of the civil population as a whole and of the industrial workers in particular," though important naval units and submarine building yards and bases were still to be "attacked periodically."[120] It could hardly be argued that by July 1941 the crisis in the Battle of the Atlantic had passed, yet as so often, Churchill did not follow through on his earlier words.

It is therefore easy to exaggerate the significance of the March 1941 "Battle of the Atlantic" directive. First, it was only one of a stream of directives to Bomber Command which were often mutually contradictory and swiftly superseded. Second (assisted by the multiple directives), there was always room for interpretation in how the directive was put into practice—and here there was a frequent tendency to violate the spirit and even the letter of what had been requested. Exacerbating this was the Prime Ministerial failure to follow through with such worthy

---

[118]   Air Vice Marshal A. T. Harris (Deputy Chief of the Air Staff) to Air Marshal Sir Richard Peirse, 18 March 1941, in Webster and Frankland, Vol. IV, Appendix 8, p. xv. Redford explains how the Air Staff would "interpret" agreements and directives in a way that fitted their preferences. For example, when ordered to attack naval targets, they refused to attack the U-boat pens, but rather focused on the construction yards; and even with these targets, the aim points would not be the docks, but rather the built-up areas of the port cities. "In other words, the RAF might have told the Admiralty (or indeed anyone else) they were attacking submarine construction yards, but the bombs were aimed elsewhere." Redford, "Inter- and Intra-Service Rivalries," pp. 902–04.

[119]   This term refers to a subordinate nominally going along with orders, but in practice finding ways to circumvent their intent; it was coined by the late Richard Holmes and was popularized in the 1980s at the Royal Military Academy Sandhurst. I am grateful to Professor Gary Sheffield for this information. This was by no means the only example of "consent and evade" to be found in the bombing campaign; Gray applies the term to the Pointblank directive of 1943, Gray, "Strategic Leadership and Direction of the Royal Air Force Strategic Air Offensive," pp. 228–30.

[120]   Air Vice Marshal N. H. Bottomley (Deputy Chief of the Air Staff) to Air Marshal Sir Richard Peirse, 9 July 1941, in Webster and Frankland, Vol. IV, Appendix 8, p. xvi.

expressions of intent as his attention shifted elsewhere, so even the grudging and partial shift of effort that the RAF was prepared to concede was soon reversed. In this case, as so often, Churchill proved unwilling or unable to resist the seductively ambitious claims of the bomber barons.

This directive was by no means the only instance of apparent Prime Ministerial reverses of course. In October 1940, Churchill described the disabling of *Bismarck* and *Tirpitz* as the "greatest prize open to Bomber Command."[121] In December 1940, he conferred on Coastal Command "supreme priority. The bombing of Germany took second place. All suitable machines, pilots, and material must be concentrated upon our counter-offensive."[122] Yet by July 1941 he was deploring "the fact that the Liberators received from America had been allocated to Coastal Command; now was the time for every heavy bomber to concentrate on Germany."[123] At the beginning of September 1941, he determined that greater efforts should be devoted to the production of heavy and medium bombers and ordered that the RAF expansion plan should be revised accordingly, accepting that to achieve this it "may be necessary to slow up the Admiralty programme or to reduce the flow of equipment to the Army."[124] Yet later that same month, a visit to the carrier HMS *Indomitable* prompted him to instruct the Chiefs of Staff "that only the finest aeroplanes that can do the work go into all aircraft carriers. . ... The aircraft carriers should have supreme priority in the quality and character of suitable types," and in December the Defence Committee (Supply) that he chaired agreed the highest priority should go to fighters for armored carriers, after a complaint from the First Lord that the Fleet Air Arm was still equipped with obsolescent aircraft types.[125] Later that month, he stressed the importance of carriers for the Allied campaign in the Pacific, and maintained that they should have priority even though this "will involve a retardation in the full-scale bombing offensive against Germany. . ... Our joint programme may be late, but it will all come along. And meanwhile, the German cities and other targets will not disappear. While every effort must be made to speed up the rate of bomb discharge upon Germany until the great scales prescribed for 1943 and 1944 are reached, nevertheless we may be forced by other

---

[121]   Prime Minister to General Ismay, 13 October 1940, Churchill, *The Second World War*, Vol. II, pp. 443–46.

[122]   Ibid., pp. 536–37.

[123]   CAB 69/2, DO(41)52nd Meeting, 21 July 1941.

[124]   Prime Minister to Lord President of the Council, 7 September 1941, Churchill, *The Second World War*, Vol. III, pp. 450–51; reflecting on this memorandum, he commented that "Coastal Command was particularly hard hit by the cuts which we were forced to make in its expected scale of expansion."

[125]   CAB 69/4, DO(42)49, First Lord, "Fleet Air Arm Fighters," 16 June 1942.

needs to face a retardation in our schedules."[126] January 1942 saw him put strategic bombing behind aircraft for carriers: "Having regard to the fact that the bombing offensive is necessarily a matter of degree and that the targets cannot be moved away, it would be right to assign priority to the fighter and torpedo-carrying aircraft required for the numerous carriers and improvised carriers which are available or must be brought into existence."[127] Yet in late 1942, the Fleet Air Arm was still equipped with insufficient numbers of poor-performance fighters and the Admiralty believed that the Fleet Air Arm had been "crowded out by Bomber and other RAF requirements . . . there is no doubt that priority has NOT been given to the production of up-to-date aircraft, either for Coastal Command or Fleet Air Arm, and consequently neither of these forces is properly equipped."[128] Which had the higher priority, bombers for the strategic offensive or fighters for the Fleet Air Arm? A Prime Ministerial memorandum in December 1942 explained the situation: "The bombing offensive over Germany and Italy must be regarded as our prime effort in the Air," while providing the Fleet Air Arm with "highest grade fighter aircraft . . . remains the paramount object, and the highest priority should continue to be given to the supply of the best fighter types to the carriers."[129] So, the one is the "prime effort" while the other is the "paramount object . . . the highest priority." In his own account of the war, Churchill resonantly declared, "The Battle of the Atlantic was the dominating factor all through the war. Never for one moment could we forget that everything happening elsewhere, on land, at sea, or in the air, depended on its outcome."[130] Yet his actual policy and his dizzying inconsistency on the issue suggests that often during the war he did forget this reality just as the Air Staff did.

Brooke, his closest collaborator, was well aware of this feature of Churchill's personality. In May 1943, the long suffering CIGS wrote that Churchill: "Thinks one thing at one moment and then another at another moment. At times the war may be won by bombing and all sacrificed to it," while at other times he favored fighting on the continent, or in the Mediterranean, Italy, the Balkans, or Norway; "But more often than all he wants to carry out ALL operations simultaneously irrespective of shortages of shipping!"[131] Perhaps the most memorable description of

---

[126]   CAB 69/4, DO(42)6, Note by the Prime Minister, "Memorandum on the Future Conduct of the War, Part IV, Notes on the Pacific," 22 January 1942.

[127]   Ibid., Part III, para. 8.

[128]   ADM 205/18, Note by ACNS(F) and ACNS(H) on Question by Lord Cork in House of Lords, 23 November 1942, emphasis original.

[129]   CAB 66/32, WP(42)580, Prime Minister, "Air Policy," 16 December 1942.

[130]   Winston S. Churchill, *The Second World War*, Vol. V, *Closing the Ring* (London: Cassell, 1952), p. 6.

[131]   Danchev and Todman, *Alanbrooke: War Diaries*, pp. 409–10, emphasis original.

Churchill in Brooke's diaries appears in January 1944: "In all his plans he lives from hand to mouth. He can never grasp a whole plan, either in its width (i.e. all fronts) or its depth (long term projects). His method is entirely opportunist, gathering one flower here another there!" This depicts accurately the way in which he would leap from one project to another, throwing around priority labels repeatedly, even incontinently. One field of endeavor would be lifted to the heights of importance only for another to follow it—or should that be, to top it?—with the same, or even worse, a different label. His restless creativity was not matched by a facility for thinking things through and balancing them against each other, and while he sometimes delved down into topics of extraordinarily narrow detail,[132] he frequently lacked attention to detail.

At various times in the war, Churchill and his government adorned assorted air and naval air projects and campaigns—to say nothing of other matters such as land campaigns—with priority, high priority, highest priority, very highest priority, absolute priority, over-riding priority, first priority, A1 priority (and also 1A priority), extreme priority, and supreme priority. What were the service chiefs to make of this terminological mayhem? Are two programs with "supreme" priority equal in importance, or does the one awarded this status most recently have the edge? Is this supreme priority lower than, equal to, or higher than "absolute" priority?[133] Well might the First Lord of the Admiralty write to Churchill that "Specific priorities given in one direction are nullified by subsequent priorities granted in another."[134] This confusion, of course, was added to that surrounding the definition of what precisely was meant by the "minimum" resources that should be devoted to those programs that were not priorities of one form or another. Small wonder that the service Chiefs could not decide where the priority for British strategy should lie. Pound was quite right that the priorities were "unintelligently interpreted," yet they were anything but "hard and fast."

---

[132]   See Churchill, *The Second World War,* all volumes, passim. Two particularly fine examples stand out: interrogating the Foreign Office as to the reasons for Siam calling itself "Thailand" and asking for "the historic merits of these two names," 27 August 1941, Churchill, *The Second World War,* Vol. III, p. 728; and admonishing the Admiralty for not having secured the permission of the Cabinet for a bicycle shed erected on Horse Guards' Parade, Prime Minister to First Lord, 6 July 1942, Winston S. Churchill, *The Second World War,* Vol. IV, *The Hinge of Fate* (London: Cassell, 1951), p. 779. These two examples, it should be noted, are from his own memoirs.

[133]   One exception where the decision was clear, albeit temporary for three and a half months, was when Churchill ordered that expanding Bomber Command to fifty operational squadrons should enjoy "priority over every other competing claim." CAB 66/30/11, Prime Minister to Secretary of State for Air and CAS, 17 September 1942.

[134]   ADM 205/15, First Lord to Prime Minister, 25 October 1942, p. 7.

Conclusion

The period from 1940 to early 1943 saw bitter disputes between the Admiralty and the Air Ministry over the provision of air support for the Battle of the Atlantic. The Admiralty had by now embraced the modern reality that sea power could only be adequately exercised by a combination of naval and air power and repeatedly sought the air support that they required. The Air Ministry, however, repeatedly refused to concede that the needs of the Battle of the Atlantic were sufficiently pressing to justify any reduction in the scale of the strategic air offensive. They genuinely believed that it could either win the war or leave the land forces with a task little harder than occupation, and hence, naturally pushed it hard. The dispute between the two was not resolved by a compromise reached by the participants or an allocation imposed by the government; rather it was submerged by the rising tide of Allied materiel.

This chapter has argued that the Air Ministry were in the wrong in this long drawn-out debate. This was in large part due to a contradiction in RAF philosophy: the insistence that all air power should be unified under the central control of a single service works only to the extent that the requirements of the other services are, if not fully met, then at least reasonably addressed. The superimposition of a narrow and dogmatic fixation on strategic bombing as the way to win the war meant that the Air Staff was in effect declining to provide the air power that the other services freely acknowledged they needed, on the grounds that the RAF had better things to do with it. The RAF maintained that the other services would not be able to operate without air power, insisted that they should be its only provider, and then refused to meet this responsibility. Small wonder that the Navy and the Army found this unsatisfactory and periodically sought to bring a proportion of British air power under their own control. In the case of the Battle of the Atlantic, the Air Staff—driven by a brash, young ideology—refused to concede the evident, desperate needs of a campaign that was essential for Britain's survival and for any other military operations, and focused instead on their favored theory that was, at the time, not only unproven, but contradicted by all the available evidence. What was at issue was not—despite the hysterical reaction of the bomber barons—an end to or even a significant reduction in the bomber offensive, but rather a relatively small reallocation of resources. This case applied in particular to very-long-range aircraft where, as was pointed out at the time, the losses of one night could have had a decisive effect on the campaign against the U-boats.[135]

The strategic bombing campaign did make a significant contribution to the Allied victory. However, this was very much less than had been promised and was

---

[135]   According to Milner, "In the end about 40–50 Liberators were needed to close the air gap—permanently: the same number of Liberators lost from the first Ploesti raid alone." Milner, "The Battle of the Atlantic," p. 59. Overy writes that in total during the war, Britain and the U.S. between them lost 21,000 bombers, Overy, *Why the Allies Won*, p. 128.

merely a consolation prize for the bomber barons and for the air theorists, who believed it could win the war on its own, and who translated this blind faith into policy, resisting any deviation from it. Moreover, this impact came at an enormous cost in resources and manpower. Once it became clear that strategic bombing would not and could not win the war alone, let alone quickly, then it became one line of operation among several. It thereby lost its claim to automatic first and overriding priority, and its requirements would have to be balanced against those of other campaigns and operations. Some proportion of the resources devoted to the strategic bombing of Germany, which had distinctly modest results during the years in question, would have been better allocated to an increased provision of long-range reconnaissance aircraft, fighters, and torpedo bombers to Coastal Command. In this way, the enormous contribution of air power to the Allied victory could have been still greater.

Even those who are not persuaded by this argument might acknowledge two other conclusions that emerge. First, just as earlier quarrels had paved the way for them, the prolonged and bitter disputes of the wartime years left a legacy of mistrust and suspicion that carried over into the postwar years. This continuity did not apply only to a general and mutual prickliness between the Admiralty and the Air Ministry; the specific issues that were the subject of the on-going disputes were remarkably similar to those of the war, including the extent to which British strategy could and should rely on strategic bombing versus the need to protect sea communications, and the strength and (to a far greater extent than during the war) the control of Coastal Command. The similarity of the issues dividing the Navy and the RAF in the early 1940s and in the early 1950s was truly remarkable. Even such an enormously significant technological innovation as the introduction of atomic weapons had a strangely minor effect on the relationship, becoming simply one more element in an ongoing debate rather than igniting a whole new one.[136]

Second, the intensity and longevity of the disagreements between the two services, from the 1920s to the 1960s and beyond, suggest that they rested on basic and fundamental differences over the nature of warfare and the conduct of strategy. Dismissing these issues as "inter-service squabbling" is inadequate, implying as it does that they were no more than partisan bickering, classic exercises in noisy bureaucratic politics to seek the greatest possible share of limited resources. While this was no doubt one element of the explanation, it is not sufficient by itself. There was more substance to the controversy than this depiction suggests and it is hardly surprising that the disagreements would continue into peacetime.

---

[136] For an account of these disputes, see Tim Benbow, "British Naval Aviation and the 'Radical Review,' 1953–1955," in Tim Benbow, ed., *British Naval Aviation: The First 100 Years* (Farnham: Ashgate, 2011). Churchill, of course, would reprise his role at the center of these disputes, see Bell, *Churchill and Sea Power,* chapter 11.

5

The Fleet Air Arm and Trade Defense, 1939–1944

Ben Jones

This chapter consists of an examination of the role of the Fleet Air Arm (FAA) in trade defense in the Atlantic and the Arctic during the Second World War. It addresses the threats posed to Allied trade by enemy surface raiders, aircraft, and U-boats, the extent to which the FAA's resources were employed to combat them, and the success which the FAA's carriers and their squadrons achieved. The first section focuses on the perceived threat posed by surface raiders, a concern which dominated the Royal Navy's (RN) thinking in terms of pre-war doctrine, and the limited employment of carriers in trade defense roles between 1939 and 1941. This is followed by an assessment of early British efforts to deter long-range Focke-Wulf Fw 200 Condor attacks on Allied shipping by deploying fighters at sea, and the various options that were considered during the course of 1942, once the full extent of the U-boat threat became apparent, for deploying as many aircraft as possible to cover convoys. The final section of this chapter consists of an analysis of the heated debates within the Admiralty itself, as well as between the British and the Americans, over the Royal Navy's priorities for the employment of its escort carriers (CVE).[1] This section ends with an examination of the performance of the FAA in trade defense, primarily in the anti-submarine role, during 1943 and 1944.

Pre-war Doctrine

The overwhelming view within the Admiralty in the late 1930s was that the limited U-boat threat—there were thirty-nine operational U-boats in 1939, of which only twenty-five were ocean-going—would be dealt with by escorts equipped with a combination of Asdic and depth charges. The Naval Staff declared in 1937 that "the submarine would never again be able to present us with the problem we were faced with in 1917."[2] Admiral of the Fleet Sir Ernle Chatfield, the First Sea Lord between

---

[1] Such ships were initially referred to as auxiliary carriers (ACV), but their title was changed to escort carriers (CVE) in early 1943.

[2] Donald Macintyre, *The Battle of the Atlantic* (London: BT Batsford, 1961), p. 24.

1933 and 1938, rated the effectiveness of the Navy's anti-submarine methods in 1936 as being eighty percent.[3] Furthermore, U-boats would be unable to interfere with cross-Channel traffic due to the Dover Barrage, which was scheduled to be completed by October 1939. Unfortunately, the anti-submarine exercises which the Navy conducted were infrequent and under favorable conditions, while no proper trials had been carried out to ascertain the effectiveness of depth charges against submarine hulls.[4] Therefore, the major perceived threat to British trade would be, as was the case prior to the First World War, from surface raiders. Admiral of the Fleet Sir Dudley Pound, the First Sea Lord between 1939 and 1943, wrote shortly before the outbreak of war that "Nothing would paralyse our supply system and seaborne trade so successfully as attack by surface raiders."[5] This misdiagnosis of the success of the methods of dealing with the U-boats had serious repercussions, not only for the Navy in operational terms, but also for its reputation with Prime Minister Winston Churchill, who complained in November 1941 to Admiral Pound and A. V. Alexander, the First Lord of the Admiralty, about "the failure of our methods [Asdic], about which so much was proclaimed by the Admiralty before the war."[6]

When the Admiralty, in 1936, was considering its priorities for a new generation of carriers, the decision to build vessels with armored flight decks, at the behest of Controller of the Navy Admiral Reginald Henderson, and a lack of shipbuilding capacity worked together to ensure that the building of smaller carriers purely for trade defense would have to take a back seat until the fleet's needs were met. As Deputy Chief of the Naval Staff (DCNS) Vice Admiral William James put it: "important as is the protection of our trade, the provision of adequate carrier strength to the main fleets must come first."[7] The eight new fleet carriers then envisaged would not be ready until 1942 at the earliest.[8] In the meantime, the available carriers would have to operate in both roles. At a meeting held by the Assistant Chief of the Naval Staff (ACNS) in April 1936, it was recommended that in light of this decision the terms Fleet Carrier and Trade Protection Carrier should be discontinued.[9]

---

[3]   Stephen Roskill, *Naval Policy Between the Wars*, Vol. II, *The Period of Reluctant Rearmament, 1930–1939* (London: Collins, 1976), p. 227 and Marc Milner, *Battle of the Atlantic* (Stroud: Tempus, 2005), p. 13.

[4]   Milner, *Battle of the Atlantic*, p. 13.

[5]   Stephen Roskill, *The Navy at War, 1939–1945* (Ware: Wordsworth, 1998), p. 34.

[6]   Stephen Roskill, *Churchill and the Admirals* (Barnsley: Pen & Sword, 2004), p. 135.

[7]   The National Archives, London (hereinafter TNA), Admiralty records (hereinafter ADM) 1/11971, Minute by DCNS, 15 June 1936.

[8]   In fact, the first six fleet carriers – *Illustrious, Victorious, Formidable, Indomitable, Indefatigable,* and *Implacable* – were not in service until August 1944.

[9]   ADM 1/11971, Minute by ACNS, 11 May 1936.

While there was agreement that hunting for surface raiders was a carrier's primary trade defense role, there was debate over whether both reconnaissance and strike aircraft were necessary. Vice Admiral James recommended that since a carrier would be operating with a striking force of cruisers and taking into account improvements in anti-aircraft guns, "the balance tips against carrying a striking force as well as reconnaissance machines."[10] On the other hand, Henderson argued that it was essential for carriers on trade routes to possess sufficient aircraft to fly off a striking force once an enemy raider had been located.[11] Given the overall shortage of carriers, it was decided to concentrate a few large carriers, which could also operate with the fleet if necessary, at key focal points on trade routes. Four ships carrying a total of 100 aircraft was deemed necessary for this task. Some thought was also given to utilizing mercantile conversions as auxiliary carriers and designs were drawn up for the liners *Winchester Castle* and *Waipawa*. However, the procurement of key items such as aircraft lifts had a low priority and such plans were abandoned in January 1939.[12] The idea of using converted merchant ships or small carriers to provide air cover for trade protection was to resurface in 1940.

Early Setbacks—Anti-submarine Hunting Groups

While orders were given for the operation of convoys as soon as war broke out, it took two months before the convoy system could be fully instituted. In the meantime, anti-submarine hunting forces, some operating with carriers, were employed to defend independently routed shipping.[13] What quickly became apparent was that the use of carriers in anti-U-boat operations was an extremely hazardous enterprise. Aircraft flying at 1,500 feet could spot a surfaced U-boat from six miles away, comparing favorably to the one-mile range of Asdic, but the submarine's lookouts would have similar warning.[14] Pre-war views on the threat posed by submarines to carriers were mixed. Captain Cosmo Graham, the Director of the Naval Air Division (DNAD), argued in 1938 that "Torpedo aircraft may be a greater menace to Carriers than submarines against which, incidentally, our own aircraft

---

[10]   ADM 1/11971, Minute by DCNS, 15 June 1936.

[11]   ADM 1/11971, Minute by Controller, 18 May 1936.

[12]   TNA, Cabinet Office records (hereinafter CAB) 102/536, "Requirements for new naval construction, 1939–1941, Part II, Requirements, Outbreak of War to Dunkirk," and David Hobbs, *Royal Navy Escort Carriers* (Liskeard: Maritime Books, 2003), p. 7.

[13]   Malcolm Llewellyn-Jones, *The Royal Navy and Anti-Submarine Warfare, 1917–49* (London: Routledge, 2006), p. 17.

[14]   ADM 199/124, Tactical Division memorandum, "Anti-Submarine Striking Forces," September 1939; Norman Friedman, *British Carrier Aviation: The Evolution of the Ships and Their Aircraft* (London: Conway, 1988), pp. 178–79.

provide a considerable defence,"[15] while Captain Douglas Adams Budgen, the Director of the Tactical Division, emphasized "an aircraft carrier is so valuable a unit that a special escort against submarine and heavy air attack must be employed whenever there is a chance of her being so attacked."[16]

Carriers were employed as part of hunting groups in the South-Western and North-Western Approaches, but they quickly became the hunted. *U-39* narrowly missed HMS *Ark Royal*, the Royal Navy's most modern carrier, with two torpedoes on 14 September before being sunk by her escorting destroyers. On the same day, two Blackburn Skuas from *Ark Royal* unsuccessfully attacked *U-30* and were brought down during the attack by their own malfunctioning 100-pound anti-submarine bombs, the pilots subsequently being captured by the U-boat crew.[17] As Marc Milner observed, "British attempts to find and sink U-boats with hunting groups and aircraft were tragically futile."[18] Tragedy struck at 19.58 on 17 September when HMS *Courageous* was hit by two torpedoes fired by *U-29* while patrolling in the Western Approaches. The explosions severed the ring main and caused the ship to be plunged into darkness. Many of her watertight doors were open and she sank nineteen minutes later. She was being escorted at the time by only two destroyers, HMS *Ivanhoe* and HMS *Impulsive*, the other two destroyers having been detached at 16.00. No aircraft were on patrol at the time of the attack and the Board of Inquiry observed that "With an inadequate escort it seems imperative to employ all means available for the detection of submarines."[19] Given the ships were steaming westward at 26½ knots at the time of the attack, any detection using Asdic would have been impossible. This attack had far-reaching consequences, highlighting as it did the vulnerability of major surface units to submarine attack, especially if they did not have an adequate surface escort. This vulnerability was also apparent while HMS *Hermes* was conducting anti-submarine operations in the Western Approaches on 14–18 September. Three of her nine aircraft were in the air throughout daylight hours and one U-boat was sighted, but it was nearly dusk and too far away for the escorts to mount any attacks. Destroyers dropped depth charges after good contacts on three occasions, but no success was achieved. According to Captain Charles Larcom, DNAD, the protection afforded by aircraft should not be considered as a substitute for destroyers on screening duties, and he issued a stark warning: "There were times during this operation when HERMES' chance of destroying a S/M [submarine] were [sic] probably less than the chance

---

[15]   ADM 1/10120, Minute by DNAD, March 1938.

[16]   ADM 1/10120, Minute by Director of Tactical Division, 23 June 1938.

[17]   ADM 199/393, Despatch from Commander-in-Chief, Home Fleet to Secretary of the Admiralty, 15 April 1940.

[18]   Milner, *Battle of the Atlantic*, p. 20.

[19]   ADM 156/195, Report from Board of Inquiry into loss of HMS *Courageous* to Commander-in-Chief, Western Approaches, 4 October 1939.

of her being successfully attacked. In the normal course of nature, a continuance of that condition could only be expected to have resulted in disaster. . . ."[20]

Vice Admiral Lionel Wells, Vice Admiral, Aircraft Carriers, aboard HMS *Ark Royal*, concluded that the equipment of the Swordfish aircraft was not up to the task. When U-boats were spotted, the available Mark I and II aluminum sea markers were unable to mark its position for any length of time unless in a calm sea. Worse still, the experience of *Ark Royal's* aircraft had shown that the 100-pound anti-submarine bomb with which they were equipped was not powerful enough to destroy a U-boat and also had a tendency to malfunction, as demonstrated in the loss of the Skuas on 14 September. Wells duly noted, "Experience to date shows that the unit which first FINDS the submarine must be able to DESTROY it," and, therefore, aircraft needed to be equipped with depth charges to carry out attacks without delay.[21]

As a result of these incidents and the loss of *Courageous*, Admiral Pound issued instructions on 23 November 1939 for the use of aircraft carriers and destroyers in anti-submarine operations. Eight destroyers would be deployed with a carrier and the latter's reconnaissance aircraft would be used primarily to search within a radius of thirty miles of the ship, an area in which the escorts could be brought to bear. The remaining reconnaissance aircraft would search the maximum area practicable. The objective was to "force them [the U-boats] to dive and use their battery power; and generally restrict their activities."[22] Four of the escorts were to be utilized as a hunting group while the remainder were to remain in close proximity to the carrier. Captain Budgen, by this date the Director of Anti-Submarine Warfare, observed that the "combination of air and surface forces has great possibilities," but in terms of the cooperation between naval aircraft and surface forces it would be 1941 before this combination was practically demonstrated against the U-boat.[23]

Hunting for Surface Raiders

As the requirement for offensive anti-submarine sweeps declined with the advent of the convoy system, the carrier force resorted to its pre-war trade role of searching for surface raiders. Captain Charles Daniel, the Director of Plans, estimated in January 1940 that in normal weather conditions a carrier with twenty-four aircraft could search an area equivalent to that by twenty-five surface ships, which

---

[20]   ADM 199/137, Minute by DNAD, 9 October 1939.

[21]   ADM 199/124, Letter from Vice Admiral, Aircraft Carriers, HMS *Ark Royal* to C-in-C Home Fleet, 2 October 1939.

[22]   ADM 199/124, Minute by First Sea Lord, 23 November 1939.

[23]   ADM 199/135, Minute by Director of Anti-Submarine Warfare, 17 October 1939.

represented very good value for money given that one carrier cost the same as three 8,000-ton cruisers. A force of one carrier and three cruisers would represent a potent force against enemy raiders, and he estimated that six carriers were necessary to cover trade route requirements. Up to the start of 1940, the whole of the carrier force, with the exception of the training carrier *Argus,* had been utilized with hunting groups on trade routes. While they had little to show for their efforts, it was believed that their presence in important focal areas had forced enemy raiders to operate where they posed less danger to Allied shipping.[24] Daniel acknowledged that in the North Atlantic the prospective German aircraft carrier *Graf Zeppelin* was "our most disagreeable problem" because her aircraft would be able to reconnoiter about 20,000 square miles per day, locating both convoys and the Allied hunting groups searching for the raiders. Should the enemy be located, carrier strike aircraft would have the job of reducing the enemy's speed in order to allow heavy British ships such as the battleships *Nelson* or *Rodney* to engage them.[25]

Captain Larcom complained on 2 February that the carriers being employed in trade defense were hampered because they did not have enough aircraft. Whereas carrier aircraft had searched 8,000,000 square miles by mid-January 1940, he argued that 40,000,000 square miles could have been searched in the same time period if the carriers had been in possession of their full aircraft complements.[26] Furthermore, he believed that the value of a carrier's aircraft in terms of anti-submarine protection while away from the fleet "is inherently unreliable, and should not be counted on when assessing the risk from submarines in such operations."[27] Captain R. H. Bevan, the Director of the Operations Division (Foreign), supported the increase in aircraft complements by arguing that the full value of a carrier could not be attained unless sufficient strike aircraft were available to follow up a sighting of an enemy raider.[28]

When the three cruisers – *Exeter, Ajax,* and *Achilles* – engaged the German pocket battleship *Admiral Graf Spee* off the River Plate on 13 December 1939, they had no carrier support for reconnaissance or strike purposes and relied upon their floatplanes. *Exeter's* two aircraft were put out of action by splinters before they could take off and only *Ajax's* Seafox was able to take part. Admiral Reginald Plunkett-Ernle-Erle-Drax, Commander-in-Chief (C-in-C) The Nore, recommended that cruisers should not join an action until their aircraft had been flown off to bomb or strafe the raider, conduct spotting for fall of shot, or engage any enemy

[24]   ADM 1/11971, Director of Plans memorandum, "Aircraft Carrier Requirements," 24 January 1940.

[25]   ADM 1/10617, Minute by Director of Plans, 29 January 1940.

[26]   ADM 1/11971, Minute by DNAD, 2 February 1940.

[27]   Ibid.

[28]   ADM 1/11971, Minute by Director of Operations Division (Foreign), 8 February 1940.

reconnaissance aircraft. "Naval forces which can arrange effective co-operation with aircraft will have a great advantage over those which do not."[29]

The fear of German surface raiders operating in the Atlantic was one that remained at the forefront of Churchill's and the Admiralty's minds. The most successful foray of these raiders involved the battlecruisers *Scharnhorst* and *Gneisenau,* which sailed from Kiel at the beginning of February 1941 and between then and their arrival at Brest on 22 March sank 115,622 tons of shipping.[30] However, it was against the battleships *Bismarck* and *Tirpitz* that the FAA played its most substantial role. *Bismarck* made her single famous North Atlantic foray in the company of the heavy cruiser *Prinz Eugen* in May 1941. At the time, all of the Home Fleet's carriers were being utilized to ferry aircraft to Gibraltar[31] and the only available aircraft were nine Swordfish of 800 Squadron on the newly-commissioned HMS *Victorious.* Despite the fact that the Squadron was not properly worked up, they mounted a gallant attack on *Bismarck* on 24–25 May, scoring one hit on the battleship's fuel tanks. Admiral Sir John Tovey, the C-in-C of the Home Fleet, remarked that the strike was "magnificently carried out and reflects the greatest credit on all concerned and attested that the damage caused played a key role in the eventual outcome."[32] It was two days later when *Ark Royal,* lately serving with Force "H" at Gibraltar, launched the single most important air strike by naval aircraft in the Battle of the Atlantic: fifteen Swordfish from 810, 818, and 820 Squadrons mounted a textbook attack on *Bismarck* scoring two hits, one of which jammed the battleship's rudder, and condemning her to destruction at the hands of the capital ships of the Home Fleet.[33]

The threat of *Tirpitz* remained, and the fear that she was at sea caused Pound to order Arctic convoy PQ-17 to scatter on 4 July 1942 with disastrous consequences.[34] Churchill informed Pound in early 1942 that the crippling of *Tirpitz* would be worth the loss of up to 100 aircraft and 500 airmen.[35] An opportunity arose to cripple *Tirpitz* when she sortied against an Arctic convoy, PQ-12, in March 1942 and was attacked by Albacore torpedo-bombers of 817 and 832 Squadrons

[29] ADM 199/847, Letter from Commander-in-Chief, The Nore to Secretary of the Admiralty, 9 September 1940.

[30] Macintyre, *Battle of the Atlantic,* pp. 74–75.

[31] Doc. 143 in Ben Jones, ed., *The Fleet Air Arm in the Second World War,* Vol. I, *1939–1941, Norway, the Mediterranean and the Bismarck* (Farnham: Ashgate/Navy Records Society, 2012), p. 473.

[32] Doc. 157a in ibid., pp. 503–05.

[33] Doc. 127 in ibid., pp. 421–24.

[34] For an account of PQ-17, see Correlli Barnett, *Engage the Enemy More Closely: The Royal Navy in the Second World War* (London: Penguin, 2001), pp. 710–22.

[35] Roskill, *Churchill and the Admirals,* p. 131.

from HMS *Victorious*. Captain Henry Bovell, *Victorious'* Commanding Officer, noted that while both Squadron Commanders had been replaced shortly before the engagement, the conditions for the attack were ideal with the battleship being escorted by only a single destroyer. He identified an "accumulation of elementary mistakes in conduct of attack," with the Albacores coming out of the clouds astern and leeward of *Tirpitz* and both leading sub-flights making their attacks from the port side which allowed the battleship to turn to port under full wheel to comb the torpedo tracks. The other two flights attacked from the starboard side allowing the ship to carry out a similar maneuver. Many pilots, deceived by *Tirpitz's* size, tended to underestimate it and dropped their torpedoes 1,000 yards farther away than they intended. The sense of huge disappointment is clear from Bovell's concluding remarks: "The gravity of the failure to take full advantage of this opportunity (which may never recur) and its far reaching implications are fully realized. No one is more disappointed than the crews of the aircraft who took part in the attack: it was the chance they had dreamed of and prayed for."[36]

Admiral Tovey recognized that torpedo attacks required long and specialized training which had not been undertaken prior to this operation, an oversight that contributed to the failure of the attack.[37]

The impact of this action was felt both by the Royal Navy and the *Kriegsmarine*. Firstly, it infuriated Churchill, who demanded to know "how it was that 12 of our machines managed to get no hits as compared with the extraordinary efficiency of the Japanese attack on PRINCE OF WALES and REPULSE."[38] Pound pointed out that an attack by twelve aircraft would likely achieve one or possibly two hits, but that a number of the hits on *Prince of Wales* had occurred when she had stopped and many of her guns were inoperable.[39] Secondly, and by far more significantly, following what the Germans perceived to have been *Tirpitz's* narrow escape, the Commander-in-Chief of the *Kriegsmarine*, Grand Admiral Erich Raeder, downplayed the chances of success of his surface raiders. In the future, Raeder would only authorize an attack on a convoy if he knew the exact position and strength of the escort and if the *Luftwaffe* could guarantee him air support.[40] He ordered that German capital ships were not to be risked if intelligence indicated that the convoy escort or covering force included an aircraft carrier. The major threats to convoys would henceforth be posed by U-boats or aircraft.

---

[36]   ADM 199/167, Report from Commanding Officer, HMS *Victorious* to C-in-C, Home Fleet, 15 March 1942.

[37]   ADM 199/167, Letter from C-in-C Home Fleet to Admiralty, 11 April 1942.

[38]   ADM 205/13, Minute from Prime Minister to First Sea Lord, 13 March 1942.

[39]   ADM 205/13, Minute from First Sea Lord to Prime Minister, 15 March 1942.

[40]   Keith W. Bird, *Erich Raeder: Admiral of the Third Reich* (Annapolis: Naval Institute Press, 2006), p. 187.

Air Cover—Early Solutions

As far as air cover for convoys was concerned, a pressing need arose to deter long-range Fw 200 Condor aircraft flying from their base at Bordeaux-Merignac. These aircraft sank twenty ships totaling 78,517 tons in January 1941 and twenty-seven ships totaling 89,305 tons in February.[41] By March there were thirty-six Condors in operation. The initial solution was for the old seaplane carrier *Pegasus* to be equipped with fighters which could be launched by her catapult. In addition, four Auxiliary Fighter Catapult ships—*Ariguani, Springbank, Maplin,* and *Patia*—were commissioned into the Royal Navy in April 1941. They achieved limited success, the first being in August 1941 when *Maplin's* Hurricane shot down a Condor 400 miles out in the Atlantic. However, *Patia* was sunk by air attack while on trials on 27 April 1941 and both *Springbank* and *Ariguani* were later torpedoed while on operations, the latter being sunk. Twenty-nine merchant ships were designated to operate as Catapult Armed Merchantmen (CAM ships) and the first of these was completed in May 1941. Since they were equipped with a single catapult-launched fighter aircraft with no means of recovery, in a similar manner to Auxiliary Fighter Catapult ships, they also had a limited impact. In 170 voyages, CAM ships launched aircraft on only eight occasions, shooting down seven enemy aircraft and damaging three more.[42]

A more operationally efficient and flexible solution was required, but as late as December 1940 the estimate of the Royal Navy's overall carrier requirements for both fleet operations and trade defense had remained at fourteen operational ships plus one for training, a level that had altered little since 1937.[43] It was in that month that Captain Matthew Slattery, the Director of Air Matériel, suggested the need for what he termed an Auxiliary Fighter Carrier, a simple merchant ship conversion carrying six fighters. Slattery's idea materialized in mid-1941 in the form of HMS *Audacity*.[44] However, more capable ships of some 10,000 tons and carrying a dozen aircraft were needed, the vast majority of which would be built in the United States under Lend-Lease.[45] A memorandum from Alexander to Churchill on 21 November 1941 identified a requirement for twenty-two auxiliary carriers, fifteen American

---

[41] Stephen Roskill, *The War at Sea, 1939–1945*, Vol. I, *The Defensive* (London: HMSO, 1954), pp. 362–63.

[42] For details of Auxiliary Fighter Catapult Ships and Armed Merchantmen, see Arnold Hague, *The Allied Convoy System, 1939–1945: Its Organization, Defence and Operation* (London: Chatham Publishing, 2000), pp. 77–82.

[43] ADM 1/11971, Minute by Director of Plans, 1 December 1940, and CAB 16/132, Memorandum, "A New Standard of Naval Strength," from First Lord of the Admiralty to Committee of Imperial Defence, Defence Plans (Policy) Sub-Committee, 29 April 1937.

[44] Friedman, *British Carrier Aviation,* pp. 181–82.

[45] CAB 102/536, Requirements for new naval construction, 1939–1941, Part I, The strategic and production background.

and seven British, including *Audacity*. Each of the American ships would carry six fighters plus nine Torpedo Spotter and Reconnaissance (TSR) planes for anti-submarine work, while the usual complement of British Auxiliary Carriers would be only six TSRs.[46] As early as July 1941, Rear Admiral Lumley Lyster, the Fifth Sea Lord, noted that the additional aircraft requirements for catapult ships and auxiliary carriers had "placed a heavy burden on the resources of the Navy and additional sources of supply of aircraft had to be sought."[47]

The utility of the auxiliary carrier was proven by the role played by HMS *Audacity* in escorting the convoys OG-74/NG-74 and OG-76/HG-76 on the Gibraltar route from September to December 1941. Her Martlet fighter aircraft shot down five Condors during these operations and damaged three more.[48] She played a particularly important role in the escort of convoy HG-76 from Gibraltar between 14 and 21 December 1941, when her aircraft were frequently in action.[49] One of her Martlets also spotted *U-131* on the surface at 09.25 on 17 December. The U-boat was engaged subsequently by five escort vessels and sunk. Admiral Dönitz, in his memoirs, recalled that only two merchant ships were lost by this convoy in comparison to five U-boats, including that of Lieutenant Commander Andres, one of his most experienced commanders. He attributed many of the difficulties faced by his crews to the presence of *Audacity*. Despite the U-boats' best efforts, he remarked that "the results were very disheartening."[50] *Audacity's* fledgling career was abruptly cut short when she was torpedoed and sunk by *U-751* on the evening of 21 December. The Board of Enquiry vindicated her Captain's decision to leave the security of the convoy, but noted that being only ten miles away meant she would have been well-illuminated by the snowflake flares fired by the convoy, which undoubtedly assisted the U-boat attack.[51]

1942—The Fleet Air Arm's Options for Trade Defense

In the view of the Director of Anti-Submarine Warfare, Captain George Creasy, the experience of *Audacity* and HG-76 proved the point made in the report of the Committee on the Winter Anti-Submarine Campaign, 1941–42, that the

---

[46]   ADM 1/11851, Minute by DNAD, 30 November 1941.

[47]   ADM 1/12126, Minute from Fifth Sea Lord to First Lord of Admiralty, 10 July 1941.

[48]   David Hobbs, *Aircraft Carriers of the Royal and Commonwealth Navies: The Complete Illustrated Encyclopedia from World War I to the Present* (London: Greenhill Books, 1996), p. 55.

[49]   Doc. no. 171 in Jones, *Fleet Air Arm*, Vol. I, pp. 544–52.

[50]   Karl Doenitz, *Memoirs: Ten Years and Twenty Days* (London: Cassell, 2000), pp. 180–81.

[51]   ADM 1/11895, Minutes of Board of Enquiry on the circumstances of the sinking of HMS *Audacity*, 30 December 1941.

anti-submarine protection of a convoy would never be complete until the convoy had available its own ship-borne aircraft. Creasy noted that "On the only occasion on which an Auxiliary Aircraft Carrier has been in company with a convoy beset by U-boat . . . we inflicted the most outstanding U-boat defeat of the war on the enemy."[52]

The beginning of 1942 also marked a seminal change in the way in which the requirement for auxiliary carriers was calculated. According to Captain Edward Bellars, the Director of Plans, and Captain Arthur Bridge, the Director of the Naval Air Division, the number of carriers allocated for work on trade routes had previously been "arbitrary," a situation that was no longer acceptable given the increased danger of heavy attack from submarines and aircraft.[53] They argued that, in the future, every convoy in danger of submarine or air attack needed its own aircraft protection. The number of carriers for trade protection would be dictated by the number of convoys and not, as was the case for fleet duties, by the number of aircraft required. Twenty-one carriers were needed in the North Atlantic, fourteen for the route to Halifax, two to Gibraltar, and five to Freetown. South Atlantic hunting groups required two ships, while anti-submarine operations in the Indian Ocean required another four. With a further thirteen ships in refit or under repair, this brought the overall total of auxiliary carriers to forty-one. Any auxiliary carriers needed to afford fighter protection to combined operations would be additional.[54] The British Admiralty Delegation in Washington reported in mid-April 1942 that thirty-two American-built auxiliary carriers had been allocated for the Royal Navy thus far, twenty-eight for operations, one for training, and three as spares or in refit. Rather optimistically, it forecast that eighteen vessels would be in service by the end of 1942 with the remainder entering service by the end of 1943.[55]

The construction of auxiliary carriers provided the most orthodox solution to the issue of providing indigenous air support for convoys, but given the extent of the U-boat threat in 1942, when 5.4 million tons of shipping were sunk in the North Atlantic alone, a number of options were evaluated to get as many aircraft to sea by whatever means were considered practicable.[56] These were laid out by Creasy at the end of May 1942. At the top of the list was the conversion of mercantile hulls into auxiliary carriers. The first auxiliary carriers were just then coming

---

[52]   ADM 1/11848, Minute by Director of Anti-Submarine Warfare, 30 May 1942.

[53]   ADM 1/11971, Minute by Director of Plans and DNAD, 17 January 1942.

[54]   ADM 1/11971, Paper, "Review of Aircraft Carrier Requirements," by Director of Plans and DNAD, 17 January 1942.

[55]   ADM 1/11939, Message from British Admiralty Delegation, Washington to the Admiralty, 16 April 1942.

[56]   Stephen Roskill, *The War at Sea, 1939–1945*, Vol. III, *The Offensive*, Part II, *June 1944 – August 1945* (London: HMSO, 1961), Appendix ZZ, p. 479.

into service, and Creasy appreciated that the lack of fleet carriers was likely to see them being used for operations other than trade protection or, possibly, escorting Arctic convoys rather than those in the Atlantic. In addition, there were plans for a more basic auxiliary carrier, one capable of still operating as a merchant ship, which eventually manifested itself as the Merchant Aircraft Carrier (MAC ship). Future options included the development of auto-gyro aircraft and helicopters, which were being developed in the United States, but these were unlikely to be in service for at least eighteen months. The final option was for the employment of low-performance light aircraft capable of landing on a platform, as opposed to a flight deck, on merchant ships.[57]

Captain Bridge had always been of the opinion that the more "air" utilized in trade defense the better. Consequently, he was involved with the Ministry of Aircraft Production in investigating the utility of the Taylorcraft light aircraft project, trials of which took place on HMS *Avenger*.[58] A light aircraft which could patrol a radius of between ten and twenty miles around a convoy would most likely cause a U-boat to dive to avoid attack, and promising trials with a light hollow-charge anti-submarine bomb, weighing not more than thirty pounds, were ongoing.[59] The trials of the Taylorcraft in June 1942 demonstrated the aircraft's ability to take off from an Auxiliary Carrier in 130 feet in a 14½ knot wind and to land on the carrier at the same speed in 100 feet. However, the aircraft was affected by the air flow astern of the ship and it was feared this would be far worse if operating from a merchant ship platform rather than a carrier deck.[60] Captain Casper John, the Director General of Naval Development and Production at the Ministry of Aircraft Production, judged that "no known form of fixed wing aeroplane would prove operationally practicable from a merchant vessel's platform."[61] The take-off and landing requirements of a light aircraft with a very low wing loading was such that the aircraft would be uncontrollable except in steady and low wind conditions, which would rarely present themselves on a pitching and rolling merchant ship. While the helicopter looked more promising than the auto-gyro, both of these types were also likely to be affected by variable wind conditions. John's view was that the quickest method to provide more air support for convoys was the adoption of the MAC ship. Captain Creasy admitted that the Taylorcraft light aircraft was a failure and that, while the auto-gyro and the helicopter showed promise,

---

[57]   ADM 1/11848, Minute by Director of Anti-Submarine Warfare, 30 May 1942.

[58]   ADM 1/11848, Minute by DNAD, 6 June 1942.

[59]   ADM 1/11848, Minute by Naval Assistant to First Sea Lord on U-Boat Warfare, 22 May 1942.

[60]   ADM 1/11848, Minute by DNAD, 23 June 1942.

[61]   ADM 1/11848, Minute by Director General of Naval Development and Production, Ministry of Aircraft Production, 26 June 1942.

neither of them were likely to be in production for a long time.[62] He, therefore, also gave his strong backing for the construction of MAC ships.[63]

The meeting of the Anti-U-Boat Warfare Committee on 25 November 1942 heard that twelve MAC ships were to be converted in the United Kingdom with the first due to enter service in April 1943 and the remainder by the end of the summer. The United States had been asked to convert thirty MAC ships by July 1943, but in case these did not materialize, the conversion of an additional six tankers in the UK was recommended.[64] If convoys on the Freetown-Cape route were undertaken on a fourteen-day cycle, then a further six MAC ships would be needed.[65]

Fleet Air Arm Priorities and the Battle of the Atlantic

1943 proved to be the decisive year in turning the tide in the Battle of the Atlantic, and yet the FAA was to play a relatively minor role in achieving this. As Alexander wrote on 5 January, "It is our intention in 1943 to take the offensive against the Axis Powers to the greatest extent possible . . . under modern conditions aircraft, either from shore bases or carriers, are as much a part of the escorting force as surface vessels. Without aircraft the convoys could only be safeguarded by increasing the strength of the surface escorts to a scale which cannot possibly be met."[66] The Admiralty's formula was three escorts per convoy plus one escort for every ten ships in the convoy, but without air escort this would be totally inadequate against U-boats deployed in wolf packs.

The nineteen MAC ships, six grain carriers, and thirteen tankers which were due to be completed in the United Kingdom between April 1943, when *Empire MacAlpine* would enter service, and May 1944 were earmarked for purely convoy escort duty.[67] The grain ships had a speed of twelve knots, an endurance of fifty-six days, and carried four Swordfish aircraft which could be stowed in the hangar. The tanker conversions had a speed of only 10½ knots, an endurance of forty days, and carried three or four Swordfish which had to remain on the flight deck as no hangar was provided. They were to be primarily employed on routes between the

---

[62]   ADM 1/11848, Minute by Director of Anti-Submarine Warfare, 27 June 1942.

[63]   ADM 1/11848, Minute by Director of Anti-Submarine Warfare, 7 July 1942.

[64]   ADM 1/12101, Extract from minutes of Anti-U-Boat Warfare Committee (42) 4th meeting, 25 November 1942.

[65]   ADM 1/12101, Report, "Measures required to meet U-boat threat in South Atlantic," to War Cabinet in accordance with A.U.(42) 2nd meeting, 7 December 1942.

[66]   ADM 1/14793, Annex I to memorandum, "A/S Warfare in Relation to Future Strategy," from First Lord of the Admiralty to Anti-U-Boat Warfare Committee, 5 January 1943.

[67]   Note that the tankers *Ancylus* and *Gadila* operated under the Dutch ensign.

United Kingdom and Halifax and New York under the operational control of the C-in-C, Western Approaches.[68] MAC ships would fly the Red Ensign and were not to be used for offensive purposes or to make ocean passages independently. Three crew members per aircraft and seventeen maintenance personnel, nineteen of the latter for four aircraft, would be embarked. New ships were to spend three weeks working up in the Clyde or another suitable area.[69] It was planned that the air units on MAC ships would be provided from squadrons formed for use in CVEs and not from any special organization.[70] However, 836 Squadron was designated as the MAC ship air unit and included the remnants of 833 and 834 Squadrons plus personnel from 838 and 840 Squadrons when they disbanded.[71] 860 Squadron, Royal Netherlands Navy, was formed in June 1943 to provide flights for Dutch MAC ships *Ancylus* and *Gadila*.

There was much debate within the Admiralty about whether to get the escort carriers, as the auxiliary carriers were now known, into service as quickly as possible in the Atlantic or to take the time needed to ensure that they were equipped to carry out all the roles that might be demanded of them. Christopher Bell has criticized the failure of the Royal Navy to employ the first four American-built auxiliary carriers, *Avenger, Archer, Biter,* and *Dasher,* on Atlantic convoy duty in 1942 when the losses were most severe.[72] *Archer* had arrived in Britain in March 1942, followed by *Avenger* in May, *Biter* in June, and *Dasher* in September. Rather than being allocated to the Atlantic in the light of *Audacity's* success, they were taken in hand for modifications. *Archer's* short career was blighted by a series of machinery breakdowns, but she was taken in hand for the lengthening of her flight deck in Liverpool between December 1942 and February 1943. Similar work was undertaken to *Avenger* on the Clyde between May and July 1942.[73] *Avenger's* Commanding Officer had made strong representations for such work to be carried out, but no such requests had been made from the other three ships.[74] In a clear demonstration of the Admiralty's priorities, *Avenger, Biter,* and *Dasher* were subsequently allocated to Operation Torch, rather than Atlantic convoys, and it was during this operation that *Avenger* was sunk.

---

[68]   ADM 1/13087, Minute by Director of Trade Division, 10 January 1943.

[69]   ADM 1/16492, Letter from Admiralty to Commanders-in-Chief, 7 April 1943.

[70]   ADM 1/13523, Minute by Director of Naval Air Organisation, 5 February 1943.

[71]   ADM 1/13523, Message from Admiralty (Director of Naval Air Organisation) to Flag Officer Naval Air Stations, 13 August 1943.

[72]   Christopher M. Bell, "Air Power and the Battle of the Atlantic: Very Long Range Aircraft and the Delay in Closing the Atlantic 'Air Gap,'" *The Journal of Military History* 79:3 (July 2015), pp. 691–719.

[73]   Hobbs, *Aircraft Carriers of the Royal and Commonwealth Navies,* pp. 38–39, 56.

[74]   ADM 1/14842, Minute by Director of Air Matériel, 17 February 1943.

The evidence shows that there was some dissension within the Admiralty from the more widespread view that the modifications were necessary, but this difference of opinion had little impact on overall policy. Captain John Eccles, the Director of Operations Division (Home), commented on 18 January 1943 that the prospect of another new CVE, *Battler,* being taken in hand in Liverpool for ten weeks of modifications before working up commenced was "so serious that it merits further investigation." He argued that more ships could be employed in the Atlantic more quickly if modifications, such as the installation of equipment for fighter direction, were omitted.[75] As Bell comments, Eccles referred to such arrangements as "Rolls Royce." In addition, Captain B. L. Huskisson, the Director of Air Matériel, observed that "1943 is certain to be critical year as far as U-Boat warfare is concerned and D. A. M. does not feel justified in laying up vitally needed new Escort Carriers for periods of at least two months if it can be avoided."[76] Huskisson contended that the only really essential modification was enhanced bomb room protection. However, such views met with strong opposition from other Admiralty departments, with Captain John Wright, the Director of Air Warfare and Flying Training, claiming "all the major alterations including the lengthening of the flight deck are essential if these carriers are to be general purpose vessels. To restrict their employment may be a great operational disadvantage."[77] Indeed, less than two months after his comments on "Rolls Royce" modifications, Captain Eccles cautioned that, while there was an urgent need for carriers on trade routes, ships equipped for a single role represented an operational handicap.[78] The three main priorities identified for these ships at the beginning of 1943 were for convoy escort in the North Atlantic and the Arctic, where fighters were definitely required, plus combined operations. Given the pressure on refitting and repair facilities, Vice Admiral Sir Cecil Talbot, the Director of Dockyards, was in favor of reducing alterations to a minimum, but pointed out that undertaking fewer alterations would not appreciably shorten the time in dockyard hands.[79] Work on the bomb room took about five weeks with that on the flight deck and fighter direction facilities six or seven.[80]

The Royal Navy's insistence on carrying out modifications to its American-built CVEs was controversial because it delayed their introduction into service, but

---

[75]   ADM 1/14842, Minute by Director of Operations (Home), 18 January 1943.

[76]   ADM 1/14842, Minute by Director of Air Matériel, 17 February 1943.

[77]   ADM 1/14842, Minute by Director of Air Warfare and Flying Training, 5 February 1943.

[78]   ADM 1/14806, Minute by Director of Operations Division (Home), 2 March 1943.

[79]   ADM 1/14842, Minute by Director of Dockyards, 23 January 1943.

[80]   ADM 1/14806, Minutes of meeting, "Escort Carriers—Allocation and Employment," held by ACNS (Air), 24 February 1943.

some of these changes were essential. Basic modifications included adding further protection to the bomb room in the light of the loss of HMS *Avenger,* torpedoed on 15 November 1942 in the aftermath of Operation Torch. *Avenger* was struck by a single torpedo fired by *U-155* at frame 75, abreast of the bomb room, resulting in a massive explosion. *Ulster Monarch* passed over *Avenger's* position within three minutes and the carrier had entirely disappeared. There was not a single survivor from the forward 336 feet of the ship's overall length of 465 feet and only twelve survivors in total.[81] The other essential piece of work, improvements to the petrol system, arose following the loss of HMS *Dasher* in the Clyde on 27 March 1943 after petrol in the main storage compartment, which was located next to the after depth charge magazine, ignited.[82] The ship was destroyed in a massive explosion with only 149 survivors out of a crew of 550.[83] Rear Admiral Charles Simeon, the Deputy Controller, concluded that "safeguards against accidents of this nature are, by our standards, practically non-existent in the petrol arrangements and hangars of these American-built escort ships."[84]

It was the alterations to enable the ships to operate as fighter carriers for combined operations, namely the lengthening of the flight deck and the installation of fighter direction facilities, which were the most controversial. At a meeting chaired by Rear Admiral Reginald Portal, the Assistant Chief of the Naval Staff (Air), on 17 February 1943, Arctic convoys, and not those in the Atlantic, were given the first call on resources and two carriers were deemed necessary per convoy. In the light of these conclusions, *Dasher* and *Battler* were allocated to these duties with *Biter* as a spare. Of the remaining CVEs, *Archer* was allocated to the North Atlantic while *Attacker, Fencer, Hunter, Stalker,* and *Tracker* could be accepted into service with a minimum of modification, the bomb room only, unless required for combined operations. If four CVEs were required for combined operations, then *Attacker, Hunter,* and *Stalker* would be taken in hand for more extensive modifications and not made available for trade protection duties.[85] The American-built *Tracker*-class ships were steam-driven, capable of eighteen knots, and their flight decks could be lengthened for Seafire operations. *Biter* and *Dasher* were smaller and less reliable diesel-driven ships. At the beginning of March, Rear Admiral Patrick Brind, the Assistant Chief of the Naval Staff (Home), insisted that three carriers plus one spare must go to North Atlantic support groups before any were sent on combined

[81]   ADM 1/12605, Report of Enquiry into loss of HMS *Avenger* by Director of Naval Construction, 4 October 1943.

[82]   ADM 1/15072, Report of Board of Enquiry into the loss of HMS *Dasher,* 31 March 1943.

[83]   Hobbs, *Aircraft Carriers of the Royal and Commonwealth Navies,* pp. 78–79.

[84]   ADM 1/15072, Minute by Deputy Controller, 30 April 1943.

[85]   ADM 1/14806, Minutes of meeting, "Escort Carriers—Allocation and Employment," held by ACNS (A), 17 February 1943.

operations, while a single carrier would be acceptable for Arctic convoys in light of the strength of the *Luftwaffe*.[86]

Captain B. L. Moore, the Assistant Director of Plans (Air), updated the allocation of CVEs on 13 May, midway through the month which signified the turning point in the Battle of the Atlantic. At this point, the Royal Navy had only three CVEs—*Archer, Biter,* and *Battler*—in the North Atlantic, while *Activity* was on deck landing training duty. *Biter* scored the first success for a British CVE when her aircraft, in conjunction with HMS *Pathfinder,* sank *U-203* on 25 April. She also contributed to the destruction of *U-89* on 11 May. A Swordfish from 819 Squadron on board *Archer* sank *U-752* using rocket projectiles on 23 May.[87] Of the remainder, *Attacker, Hunter,* and *Stalker* were due to commence combined operations at the end of July, being reinforced by *Tracker, Fencer,* and *Chaser* (as a spare) at the end of September. It was not until mid-October 1943 that the Admiralty intended to allocate any further CVEs, in the form of *Searcher, Striker,* and *Ravager,* to the North Atlantic. The American petrol system in *Archer, Biter,* and *Battler* was unmodified and, therefore, they were deemed unsuitable for combined operations, although *Battler* was used for Operation Avalanche off Salerno. All other American-built carriers would be partially modified in the United Kingdom.[88] Rear Admiral Portal judged that, should it be necessary to withdraw ships from trade protection duties for combined operations, this must happen two months before the combined operation in order to allow sufficient time for the squadrons to practice with the ship and for the carrier to work up and reach the operational area.[89]

By the end of August 1943, the policy of modifications and inherent delays was resulting in what the British Admiralty Delegation in Washington reported as "strong and increasing criticism by certain U.S. Naval Officers of length of time that elapsed between our CVE being handed over to us and our getting them into action[,] this being in some cases between 6 and 8 months."[90] The Allied Anti-Submarine Survey Board, chaired by Rear Admiral J. M. Mansfield, RN, and Rear Admiral J. L. Kauffman, USN, concluded on 27 August that the delays in getting the next seven CVEs for delivery to the Royal Navy over the next three months were "At the present stage of the war . . . not considered acceptable."[91] The Board noted

---

[86]   ADM 1/14806, Minute by ACNS (Home), 3 March 1943.

[87]   David Brown, *Carrier Operations in World War II,* Vol. I, *The Royal Navy* (London: Ian Allan, 1976), p. 49.

[88]   ADM 1/14806, Minute by Assistant Director of Plans (Air), 13 May 1943.

[89]   ADM 1/14806, Minute by ACNS (Air), 27 May 1943.

[90]   ADM 1/12857, Message from British Admiralty Delegation, Washington to Admiralty, 25 August 1943.

[91]   ADM 1/12730, Report, "Employment of CVEs in offensive action against U-boats," from Allied Anti-Submarine Survey Board to Commander-in-Chief, United States Fleet, 27 August 1943.

that these ships could all be in service by January 1944, three months before the Royal Navy's estimate, if they were allocated instead to the United States Navy. Unsurprisingly, the Board's priority was to get as many ships into action in anti-submarine duties as soon as possible.[92] The Board was supported in this assessment by United States Chief of Naval Operations Admiral Ernest J. King.[93] The Board's criticism was supported by the fact that all five CVEs in the anti-submarine role in the North Atlantic at the end of August 1943 were U.S. Navy ships. The Royal Navy had allocated six CVEs for operations. Of these, four were employed in the Mediterranean, one was refitting, and *Archer* had serious operational defects. Of the remaining seven CVEs, two were working up, four were undergoing modifications, and one was assigned for deck landing training.

The Admiralty's response was that, in addition to Atlantic operations, it required CVEs for a wide range of duties. These included air cover for combined operations, aircraft ferrying, offensive operations in the Bay of Biscay, and covering revived Arctic convoys. Given the lack of sufficient Fleet and Light Fleet Carriers in comparison with the U.S. Navy, the Royal Navy was forced to rely upon CVEs to a far greater degree for fighter operations and, crucially, the Admiralty also pointed out the decrease in U-boat activity on Atlantic convoy routes.[94] Furthermore, the Admiralty could not put ships into service more quickly due to manpower shortages, regardless of the time taken for modifications. Put simply, the Admiralty did not want unmodified carriers because of the operational restrictions this imposed.[95] Captain C. P. Clarke, the Director of the Anti-U-Boat Division, had no objection if the seven ships were reallocated to the U.S. Navy and thereby would be in action against the U-boats more rapidly.[96] The irony was that, when the Allied Anti-Submarine Survey Board offered the ships to the Americans, they had to decline because they could not man them either.[97]

Furthermore, the FAA's aircraft requirements in the Far East were rapidly increasing, the existing shipments from America were inadequate, and the RN came second best to the RAF in terms of shipping space for aircraft coming from Britain. This led Captain Moore to propose allocating not only the CVEs *Searcher, Empress, Patroller,* and *Ranee* to this task, but also the Fleet Carrier *Formidable* and the aircraft transport ships *Athene* and *Engadine*.[98] Despite obvious concerns

---

[92]   Ibid.

[93]   ADM 1/12730, Memorandum from C-in-C, United States Fleet to Secretariat, Combined Chiefs of Staff, 3 September 1943.

[94]   ADM 1/12857, Letter from Secretary of Admiralty to Deputy Secretary, British Admiralty Delegation, Washington, 7 September 1943.

[95]   ADM 1/12857, Minute by Assistant Director of Plans (Air), 1 September 1943.

[96]   ADM 1/12730, Minute by Director of Anti-U-Boat Division, 9 September 1943.

[97]   ADM 1/12730, Minute by Assistant Director of Plans (Air), 30 September 1943.

[98]   ADM 1/13752, Minute by Director of Plans, 3 October 1943.

within the Anti-U-Boat Division over the allocation of resources, with Clarke commenting that "Both the numbers and names of C.V.E.s [sic] allocated to A. U. [Anti-U-boat] operations change every time the bell strikes,"[99] Rear Admiral Brind reasserted that "The policy is deliberate and considered, having regard to the state of the U-boat war."[100] Brind reasoned that if the U-boat war could be brought to a swift end by reallocation of extensive resources to it, then it would be worth doing, but since this was not the case, then such a move would hamper the war effort elsewhere. Atlantic convoys were also now benefiting from the cover provided from MAC ships. Brind was writing in October 1943 when the Allies no longer faced the prospect of losing the Battle of the Atlantic; while 5.4 million tons of Allied shipping was sunk in the North Atlantic in 1942, this dropped to only 1.6 million tons in 1943.[101] In the autumn of 1942, the Admiralty judged that Operation Torch had the priority for the employment of CVEs, and by the autumn of 1943, the Battle of the Atlantic did not warrant the allocation of a large number of CVEs in addition to MAC ships, as this would hinder progress elsewhere. The CVEs which were modified for fighter operations played an important role in covering the landing at Salerno in September 1943. It was also striking that the RN was prepared to hand over a number of carriers to the USN rather than operate them in unmodified condition.

1943–1944: The Effectiveness of the Fleet Air Arm in Trade Defense

While there was much debate within the Admiralty and elsewhere as to the employment of the RN's smaller carriers, this should not obscure the role played by the FAA in defense of trade. As far as trans-Atlantic and Gibraltar convoys are concerned, FAA aircraft flying from CVEs were directly responsible for the destruction of two U-boats, and they participated in the destruction of a further four in conjunction with surface vessels during 1943 and 1944.[102] The attack by a Mk II Swordfish from 825 Squadron flying from HMS *Vindex* against *U-765* on 6 May 1944 was conducted in very poor visibility and through the fire of three frigates; *U-765* was spotted at the range of one mile and the Swordfish dropped its two depth charges at seventy-five feet while flying at 120 knots. The U-boat was

---

[99]   ADM 1/13752, Minute by Director of Anti-U-Boat Division, 15 October 1943.

[100]   ADM 1/12730, Minute by ACNS (Home), 19 October 1943.

[101]   Roskill, *The War at Sea, 1939–1945*, Vol. III, *The Offensive*, Part II, Appendix ZZ, p. 479.

[102]   FAA kills: *U-752* (HMS *Archer*, 23 May 1943); *U-666* (HMS *Fencer*, 10 February 1944). Shared kills with escorts: *U-203* (HMS *Biter*, 25 April 1943); *U-89* (HMS *Biter*, 11 May 1943); *U-653* (HMS *Vindex*, 15 March 1944); *U-765* (HMS *Vindex*, 6 May 1944). Sources: Brown, *Carrier Operations in WWII*, pp. 49–50 and Hobbs, *Aircraft Carriers of the Royal and Commonwealth Navies*, pp. 39, 60, 89, and 202.

seen to break in two within forty-five seconds of the explosions.[103] As the war progressed, targets in the Atlantic became fewer; for example, HMS *Striker's* escort of four convoys between 16 December 1943 and 17 January 1944 resulted in the ship's aircraft making only a single submarine contact on 26 December and one fighter interception on 9 January. This was despite being in range of Bay of Biscay air bases for several days in favorable weather. The role of air operations by shore-based and U.S. carrier aircraft was deemed to be significant in greatly reducing the threat to convoys.[104] HMS *Campania* escorted convoys OS-79/KMS-153 and SL-160/MK-551 on the UK-to-Gibraltar route 3–20 June 1944 and, despite flying Swordfish patrols from dawn to dusk, her Captain reported that "We were all disappointed in not encountering the enemy on our maiden trip."[105]

In comparison, eight U-boats were sunk by the FAA in five Arctic convoy operations between February and August 1944, while surface escorts combined with the FAA to account for three more.[106] Three of the kills—*U-277, U-674,* and *U-959*—were achieved by 842 Squadron's Swordfish flying from HMS *Fencer* during convoy RA-59 in May 1944.[107] The cold waters in the Arctic rendered Asdic far less effective than elsewhere with the result that the FAA had a proportionally more important role to play; during RA-57 in March 1944 *Chaser's* Swordfish sank two U-boats and took part in the destruction of another over a three-day period, having expended fewer than 100 rocket projectiles as compared to over 1,000 anti-submarine munitions expended by the escorts with no success.[108]

As far as the MAC ships were concerned, their aircraft flew around 4,000 sorties and conducted a dozen attacks against U-boats, albeit without success.[109] The first attack by MAC ship Swordfish occurred on 22 September 1943 when two

---

[103]   ADM 217/104, Report from Commanding Officer, HMS *Vindex* to C-in-C, Western Approaches, 20 June 1944.

[104]   ADM 217/375, Report from Commanding Officer, HMS *Striker* to C-in-C, Western Approaches, 24 January 1944.

[105]   ADM 217/528, Report from Commanding Officer, HMS *Campania* to C-in-C, Western Approaches, 22 June 1944.

[106]   FAA kills: *U-366* (HMS *Chaser,* 5 March 1944); *U-973* (HMS *Chaser,* 6 March 1944); *U-288* (HMS *Activity* and *Tracker,* 3 April 1944); *U-277* (HMS *Fencer,* 1 May 1944); *U-674* and *U-959* (HMS *Fencer,* 2 May 1944); *U-344* (HMS *Vindex,* 22 August 1944); *U-921* (HMS *Campania,* 30 September 1944). Shared kills with escorts: *U-472* (HMS *Chaser,* 4 March 1944); *U-355* (HMS *Tracker,* 1 April 1944); *U-394* (HMS *Vindex,* 2 September 1944). Sources: Brown, *Carrier Operations in WWII,* pp. 40–44 and Hobbs, *Aircraft Carriers of the Royal and Commonwealth Navies,* pp. 32, 69, 74, 89, 174, 182, 202.

[107]   ADM 217/103, Report from Commanding Officer, HMS *Fencer* to Secretary of Admiralty, 5 May 1944.

[108]   Brown, *Carrier Operations in WWII,* p. 44.

[109]   Ibid., pp. 51–52.

aircraft from *Empire MacAlpine* sighted a U-boat while escorting convoys ONS-18 and ON-202. Between 18 and 23 September, six merchantmen, three escorts, and three U-boats were sunk during intense engagements that saw the debut of the *Kriegsmarine's* acoustic torpedo.[110] However, for the majority of the 323 convoys which MAC ships escorted across the Atlantic, there was far less action in which the role of the aircraft patrols was primarily that of a deterrent, reflecting the reduced U-boat threat in the later stages of the war. *Amastra's* experience, making six round trips from the Clyde to Halifax between 5 November 1943 and 30 July 1944, was typical, with no sightings of the enemy during forty-eight Swordfish patrols lasting a combined 114 hours and 35 minutes.[111] A report on the operations of *Empire MacAlpine* in June 1943 also highlighted its positive psychological effect on the convoy: "Co-operation with Master and crew of EMPIRE MACALPINE excellent. Master reports presence of ship had a most heartening effect on the general morale and was much appreciated by the rest of the convoy."[112] In addition to convoy escort duties, MAC ships made eleven trips ferrying aircraft from America to Britain in the spring of 1944.

Captain Clarke of the Anti-U-Boat Division claimed that there were a number of key advantages of utilizing carrier aircraft in the anti-submarine role. Aircraft from carriers were capable of delivering attacks by several aircraft in succession and sending reinforcements more rapidly than from shore bases. In July-August 1943, Allied carrier aircraft sank thirty percent of the U-boats they located and USS *Bogue* sank a U-boat with ten aircraft attacks. U-boats sighted by aircraft patrols within a radius of about thirty miles of the convoy were then engaged by surface striking forces, which by this stage in the war had a fifty percent chance of achieving a kill. Experience of the coordination between shore-based aircraft and ships in other theaters demonstrated that escorts were seldom able to follow up a sighting in an effective time.[113]

However, it was soon apparent that British CVEs suffered from a number of disadvantages compared with their American counterparts, as Admiral Max Horton, C-in-C Western Approaches, highlighted in November 1943.[114] Because of a

---

[110]   Kenneth Poolman, *Escort Carrier, 1941–1945: An Account of British Escort Carriers in Trade Protection* (London: Ian Allan, 1972), pp. 95–96.

[111]   ADM 217/300–305, Reports of voyages 1–6 by MAC *Amastra* from Captain DEMS, West Coast of Scotland (1–2) and Lieutenant Commander E Flight, 836 Squadron (3–6) to C-in-C, Western Approaches, 28 December 1943—3 September 1944.

[112]   ADM 1/15553, Message from C-in-C C. N. A. to Admiralty, 14 June 1943.

[113]   ADM 1/12731, Appreciation, "Anti-U-Boat Escort Carrier Requirements," by Director of Anti-U-Boat Division, 23 September 1943.

[114]   ADM 1/12865, Report, "Employment of British and American Escort Carriers in Anti-U-Boat Warfare," from C-in-C, Western Approaches to Secretary of Admiralty, 7 November 1943.

shortage of manpower, British ships carried only ten percent reserve aircrews as compared to the American fifty percent, and the American ships' crews for operations, aircraft direction, maintenance, and deck handling parties were sufficiently large to ensure continual operations over longer periods. As a consequence, on average, U.S. CVEs operated continuously for 33–40 days while those of the RN did so for only 16–18 days. The commanding officers of American squadrons were free of organizational, clerical, and maintenance responsibilities, allowing them to focus on operational matters. The main strike aircraft employed on British CVEs was the venerable Fairey Swordfish—capable of 4½ hours endurance at ninety knots—as opposed to the American Grumman Avenger's six hours at a cruising speed of 150 knots. Furthermore, ninety percent of take-offs aboard U.S. ships were catapult-assisted, thereby increasing operational flexibility, whereas British-designed aircraft were not compatible with U.S. catapults. In light of this serious handicap, MK III Swordfish were later fitted with Rocket-Assisted Take-Off Gear (RATOG), which Captain Short of HMS *Campania* described in August 1944 as "a godsend."[115]

While CVEs from both navies achieved their first successes against U-boats in April 1943, the U.S. carriers were moved south to the Azores area soon afterwards, where they could take advantage of better flying weather and could refuel their escorts more easily. The commanding officers of American CVEs were afforded discretion to select their area of operations, guided by intelligence, and therefore were able to pay particular attention to U-boat refueling areas. By comparison, British CVEs spent most of their time as convoy escorts. Horton's solutions included the unpalatable prospect of reducing the number of CVEs in service in order to ensure that the remainder were adequately manned, increasing the aircraft complement to twelve strike and 8–9 fighter aircraft, and replacing the Swordfish with the Tarpon, as the Avenger was referred to by the British at the time.

Horton's assertions were supported in a report by the Directorate of Naval Operational Research (DNOR) in February 1944 which analyzed the achievements of British and U.S. CVEs in anti-submarine operations in the first ten months of 1943. On average, thirty hours per day were flown from American CVEs with their larger aircraft complement as compared to only eight from their British counterparts. In addition, British aircraft flew on only sixty percent of days at sea compared with seventy-four percent for American aircraft. While British CVEs operated farther north in worse weather conditions and more than half of U.S. attacks were carried out south of 40°N, whereas no British attack was made south of that line of latitude, the effect of the weather on British operations was not particularly pronounced. Even when conditions were good, it was rare for more than ten sorties per day to be flown while U.S. carriers could operate more than

---

[115]   ADM 217/530, Report of Proceedings from Commanding Officer, HMS *Campania* to C-in-C, Western Approaches, 23 August 1944.

twenty-five. *Attacker, Battler, Fencer,* and *Striker* escorted OS, SL, KMS, MKS, XK, and UC convoys, and flying took place on sixty-four of ninety-five days mounting 403 sorties, even though in comparatively southern latitudes. It should be taken into account, however, that British CVEs spent a greater percentage of their time in range of shore-based air cover, periods during which no carrier sorties were required.[116]

The average number of hours flown per sighting was 170 for the Americans and only 105 for the British. More tellingly, however, of the sixty U-boats sighted by U.S. aircraft, twenty-three—thirty-eight percent—were judged to be sunk or probably sunk, while of eighteen U-boats sighted by British aircraft, only three—sixteen percent—were judged to have been destroyed. A key factor in this difference was the number of aircraft the Americans were able to deploy. In only two British attacks did more than one plane take part, while in half of the U.S. attacks at least two planes participated, sometimes as many as eight. British depth charges were about twice as efficient, but the Avengers used a homing torpedo, the Mk24 mine, on a dozen occasions whereas the British carrier aircraft used it only once. American carriers suffered less from aircraft wastage with only fourteen aircraft lost or damaged in 1,420 sorties against sixty-five aircraft in 880 sorties aboard British escort carriers. The high deck landing accident rate for the Swordfish—3.9 per 100 sorties—was attributed to weakness in its undercarriage. This could not be attributed to the sea state or weather conditions, as wastage rates were as high on voyages in southern latitudes as in northern ones. At times, the lower level of serviceability on the Royal Navy's CVEs led some captains to withhold serviceable planes from flying to "conserve their strength" for times of emergency.[117]

Of the 179 operations in which British CVEs participated in 1944, eighty-one, or forty-five percent of the total effort, involved trade defense; sixty-four were used as convoy escorts and seventeen as part of anti-submarine hunting groups.[118] Details for seventy-five of these eighty-one trade defense operations indicate a total of 4,243 sorties were flown, at an average of 8.2 sorties per carrier per day.[119] During the sixty-four convoy escort operations, 3,237 sorties took place at an average of 7.3 per carrier per day; of these, thirty were Arctic convoys, twenty were Gibraltar convoys, and the remainder were either escort duties elsewhere or in anti-submarine hunting groups. Twenty-six convoys had a single CVE in support,

---

[116]   ADM 219/95, Report no. 9/44, "Achievements of British and U.S. Escort Carriers, 1943," by Directorate of Naval Operational Research, 12 February 1944.

[117]   Ibid.

[118]   Of the remaining operations, forty-two were ferrying aircraft, twenty-three in support of land operations, twenty for anti-shipping strikes, twelve for minelaying strikes, and one searching for a blockade runner.

[119]   ADM 219/494, Memorandum no. 132, "Operational Employment and Flying Performance of Escort Carriers in 1944," by Directorate of Naval Operational Research, 1954.

while thirty-two had two, and six no fewer than three. On completion of operations, half of the CVEs had an aircraft serviceability rate of between 90–100 percent and one-third maintained this throughout the entire operational period. The highest flying effort recorded by a British CVE was by HMS *Striker* on Arctic convoys JW-59/RA-59A in August-September 1944. With a complement of twenty-two aircraft, *Striker* flew off 133 sorties with an average of 16.6 sorties per day on the outward voyage and 15.6 sorties on the return trip. The effort peaked at twenty-six and twenty-seven sorties on two consecutive days.[120] A further DNOR report in 1954 concluded that "these carriers maintained a reasonable sustained flying effort under such diverse operating conditions as those on Gibraltar and Russian convoy routes and on convoy routes and patrol areas in the North Atlantic."[121] A major improvement in the future was foreseen with the use of larger light fleet carriers in the trade defense role.

Conclusion

The Admiralty may have got it wrong when it identified surface raiders as the main threat to British trade, but the threat did exist, and the crippling of *Bismarck* and near-miss of *Tirpitz* made the Germans far more cautious in the use of their heavy ships. The Admiralty recognized that the possession of a carrier on the part of the Germans would have transformed the capabilities of their surface forces. Having hurriedly abandoned the use of fleet carriers in anti-submarine hunting groups in 1939, it was another four years before a number of capable aircraft-carrying ships were deployed by the Royal Navy in trade defense, stopgaps such as the Catapult Armed Merchantman having very limited capability. The Admiralty's priorities over the use of CVEs was clearly demonstrated at the height of the Battle of the Atlantic in the autumn of 1942 when three of four ships were sent to cover Operation Torch. A limited number of fleet carriers and no prospect of light fleet carriers until 1945 was the stark reality which confronted the Admiralty. When large numbers of CVEs were available in mid-1943, significant tasks other than trade defense, such as combined operations and aircraft ferrying, demanded their attention. The Admiralty was unwilling to accept unmodified ships, thereby limiting their operational flexibility. The fact that the Battle of the Atlantic was past its peak made the diversion of such vessels elsewhere easier for the Admiralty to justify against mounting American pressure, as did the entry of the MAC ships into service.

---

[120]   ADM 219/343, Report, "Escort carriers: flying effort and aircraft serviceability," by Directorate of Naval Operational Research, 2 March 1949; ADM 219/341, Report no. 5/49, "Trade Defence Carriers, Past and Future," by Directorate of Naval Operational Research, 1949.

[121]   ADM 219/494, Memorandum no. 132, "Operational Employment and Flying Performance of Escort Carriers in 1944," by Directorate of Naval Operational Research, 1954.

All MAC ships and the vast majority of the Royal Navy's trade defense operations with CVEs were involved in convoy escort, the key objective of which, as David Hobbs pointed out, was that the convoy reached its destination with minimal loss.[122] This is a key yardstick by which the FAA's success can be measured, the number of U-boat kills to which the FAA contributed in the Atlantic being relatively few compared with those of the CVEs of the United States Navy. A few factors stand out in explaining the discrepancy between the successes of the two nations. Strategically, the American CVEs operated largely as hunting groups in areas of their choosing and not as convoy escorts. Operationally, the American vessels carried a larger number of aircraft which, in the case of the Avenger, were more capable than the Swordfish, and the larger American crews, both aircrew and those on the ships supporting air operations, resulted in more intensive flying being carried out over a longer period. Greater success was achieved by the FAA squadrons operating in the convoy escort role in the Arctic in 1944, where targets were more plentiful. The FAA augmented the operations conducted by escort vessels and shore-based aircraft in terms of providing effective defense of the Atlantic and Arctic convoys upon which Allied victory in the Second World War was so dependent. The overall lack of carriers forced the Admiralty to make difficult choices as to the proportion of the FAA's resources to be employed in the defense of trade at the height of the Battle of the Atlantic in 1942–43, and such decisions remain controversial.

---

[122]   Hobbs, *Royal Navy Escort Carriers*, p. 12.

6

All Should be "A" Teams

The Development of Group Anti-Submarine
Escort Training in the British and Canadian
Navies during the Atlantic Campaign

James Goldrick

The creation of permanent escort groups incorporating different types of ship was an innovation for the Royal Navy as a result of the largely unforeseen oceanic circumstances of the U-boat campaign in the Atlantic. Recent historical research has created a much more balanced picture of pre-war anti-submarine development in the Royal Navy and dispelled some of the myths as to an alleged lack of preparation for and understanding of the operational requirement.[1] In 1939, despite overconfidence, anti-submarine doctrine was in fact relatively sophisticated at the procedural level in terms of responses and actions on gaining contact. Much certainly needed to be done in relation to understanding the effects of water conditions, on improving weaponry, and in finding solutions to the challenges posed by submarines operating on the surface at night. Yet it is arguable that the key deficiency lay in the longer term conduct of battle in the context of the protracted defense of an ocean convoy over its entire voyage. That such a requirement should not have been predicted was in some measure due to the fact that the French surrender and the opening of their Atlantic ports to the U-boats created a very different problem than that which applied before June 1940. The deep water campaign that effectively began in the second half of the year brought requirements for the organization and the direction of the Anti-Submarine Warfare (ASW) war that demanded new responses.

This chapter examines the formation of the mixed-type escort groups which proved to be the primary tactical formation for the close defense of the merchant ship convoys in the Atlantic and, in a modified form, the method of reinforcement of convoys under threat, as well as for more specialist ASW work such as the inshore operations in the English Channel and Canadian coast in 1944–45.

---

[1]   See George Franklin, *Britain's Anti-Submarine Capability, 1919–1939* (London: Frank Cass, 2003) and Malcolm Llewellyn-Jones, *The Royal Navy and Anti-Submarine Warfare, 1917–49* (London: Routledge, 2006).

Focusing on the Royal Navy (RN) and the Royal Canadian Navy (RCN), this study assesses their training and its relationship with, and dependence upon, a whole range of other factors, such as unit availability, collective experience levels, doctrine, and technology. In particular, it argues that there were two elements that had to work together. The first was that the leadership of the individual group commanders was critical to the performance of their units at every stage of the campaign, most notably in its early years when tactical doctrine had still to be defined and individual and collective experience levels were very low indeed, but also at its end. The second, conversely, was that the increasing challenges of the conflict demanded ever more sophisticated and comprehensive organizational effort and an effective continuum of operational research and analysis, technical development and manufacture, accompanied by continuing doctrinal innovation and constant training, if escort groups were to be equal to their mission.

The Organization of the Formations

The initial organization for the trans-Atlantic convoy anti-submarine protection was based on thirty-two destroyers organized into four escort flotillas.[2] This arrangement reflected the Royal Navy's historical disposition of its seagoing units into single-type (or as near single-type as possible) formations, providing tactical compatibility, as well as the application and maintenance of consistent unit and group standards by a "leader" ship which had a senior officer and a larger and more experienced staff than the private units within the formation. In the case of minor war vessels, where size inherently limited the capacity of the senior ship to exercise the full range of such supervision, a depot ship or shore base provided the majority of the staff functions involved.

Such arrangements were effective when operations (such as by submarines) were normally conducted by individual units, or, as had been the case for escorts in the 1914–18 conflict, relatively close to the coast and for limited periods. This was not the case in the Battle of the Atlantic, whose oceanic conditions created new challenges that became steadily clearer as 1940 drew on. The nature of the operational requirement dictated a different approach to the type formation in particular. The new Flower-class corvettes began to emerge in numbers from April 1940 and it became increasingly obvious that these ships would have to bear the brunt of the ocean escort work for at least the next eighteen months, before more capable platforms could be produced. With their small crews, very basic equipment and, above all, lack of speed, the Flowers were manifestly inadequate for the task of senior ship of an ocean convoy escort, however experienced their

---

2   Peter Elliott, *Allied Escort Ships of World War II: A Complete Survey* (London: Macdonald & Jane's, 1977), p. 59.

commanding officers.[3] Although a comprehensive basic training regime was being organized in the UK through a new work-up organization based at Tobermory[4] in the Western Isles, the corvettes would need other support.

The failures of the defense of Convoys HX 79 and S67 led to a series of decisions in October 1940 which recognized that the anti-submarine war was no longer being fought in the narrow seas. One measure was to leaven the corvettes with destroyers (and, when available, sloops), whose larger (and, at this stage, more experienced) crews, better communications, and higher speed would provide both more effective command platforms and a measure of tactical offensive capability, and to do so by creating new, at least semi-permanent "escort groups." Despite some opposition,[5] the creation of such formations was approved under the umbrella of the various Captains(D) who were being located at the major convoy ports and whose staff would provide the administrative and maintenance coverage which the group leaders could not.

Making the Escort Groups Work

Permanent groups with their associated stability were, however, always to represent as much of an ideal as a consistent achievement, especially in the early years of the war. As one authority complained, "With such a loosely woven, extended force, it was of vital importance that it should have trained as a team and that each commanding officer should know what was required of him without the necessity for signalled instructions. Lack of these conditions time and again led to unnecessary defeats at the hands of the U-Boats."[6]

Furthermore, although the arrangements for unit work-up training were soon operating well for the RN, the escorts at sea had yet to learn their job in full and it was recognized that Tobermory itself was not enough. Relatively few escort personnel had been part of the full-time pre-war Navy and the collective experience levels were dropping as the crews of the ships in service were diluted to man new construction. This was always a greater problem for the RCN than it was for the RN, whose expansion was relatively much smaller, but it affected both services. In 1941, it was estimated in the RN that at least ten days more concentrated training

---

[3]   There were isolated examples of Flower-class corvettes acting as senior officers of groups in later years.

[4]   James Goldrick, "Work-Up," in Stephen Howarth and Derek Law, eds., *The Battle of the Atlantic, 1939–1945: The Fiftieth Anniversary International Naval Conference* (London: Greenhill, 1994), pp. 221–22.

[5]   S. W. Roskill, *The War at Sea, 1939–1945,* 3 vols. (London: HMSO, 1954), Vol. I, pp. 358–59.

[6]   Donald Macintyre, *U-Boat Killer: Fighting the U-Boats in the Battle of the Atlantic* (London: Rigel, 2004), p. 25.

following Tobermory were required to achieve operational status for a newly-commissioned escort.[7]

For Canada, a key issue by comparison with the Royal Navy was the lack of a sufficient leaven of qualified long-service personnel at sea. Even when experienced merchant mariners could be brought onto the strength of the RCN Reserve and despatched to the new corvettes as commanding officers, they lacked the peace time training in naval units which their British equivalents had undertaken as part of their Reserve progression and there was often no one else in their ships who knew much more.[8] This created an unfamiliarity with basic naval routines and procedures which made it extremely difficult to achieve the internal efficiency which was the foundation for effective interaction with other units. Furthermore, although the consolidated work-up package at Tobermory became an integral part of British escorts' progression from build to operations, the RCN's attempts to organize equivalent training were consistently hamstrung by the effects of the over-commitment of Canada to the escort task, the scale of the Navy's expansion, and the lack of training facilities and assets such as submarines and expert staff—as well as being generally well behind the RN in the acquisition and fitting of new sensors and weapons.[9]

People did their best and the waterfront authorities in Canada rarely under-estimated the actual training requirement, the RCN's assessment being that eight weeks of focused effort were required to bring an escort from commissioning to a

---

[7]   Estimate by Captain(D) Greenock, October 1941. W. A. B. Douglas, Roger Sarty, Michael Whitby, et al., *No Higher Purpose: The Official Operational History of the Royal Canadian Navy in the Second World War, 1939–1943,* Vol. II, Part 1 (St. Catharines: Vanwell, 2002), p. 167.

[8]   See Mac Johnston, *Corvettes Canada: Convoy Veterans of WWII Tell Their True Stories* (Toronto: McGraw-Hill Ryerson, 1994), pp. 15–17. These comments may be subject to the exaggerations and "red shift" of receding memory, but they give a good idea of how the very inexperienced crews saw themselves.

[9]   There has been a remarkable historiographical effort in Canada to understand the problems and achievements of the RCN in the Battle of the Atlantic. Early monographs which provided new perspectives include Marc Milner, *North Atlantic Run: The Royal Canadian Navy and the Battle for the Convoys* (Annapolis: Naval Institute Press, 1985) and David Zimmerman, *The Great Naval Battle of Ottawa* (Toronto: University of Toronto Press, 1989). Most recently, the two volumes of the new official operational history have been published after much work by the Directorate of History and Heritage of the Canadian Armed Forces. These are: W. A. B. Douglas, Roger Sarty, Michael Whitby, et al., *No Higher Purpose: The Official Operational History of the Royal Canadian Navy in the Second World War, 1939–1943,* Vol. II, Part 1, and *A Blue Water Navy: The Official History of the Royal Canadian Navy in the Second World War, 1943–1945,* Vol. II, Part 2 (St. Catharines: Vanwell, 2002 and 2007). They provide considerable insights into the British effort as well as that of Canada and show just how official history can and should be done.

reasonable level of efficiency, followed by a period "running in" on local operations. Nevertheless, even as their own experience and manning levels improved from 1941 onwards,[10] the work-up units at Halifax and (later) at St. John's struggled to keep up with the demand. Even in early 1942, the package averaged only four days harbor training and sixteen to twenty-two days sea work.[11] Given the continuing pressure on manpower and the consequent limits of collective expertise in the crews involved, this was not sufficient. In addition, while winter in Britain's Western Isles could be challenging enough for the work-up programs there, conditions on the Canadian coast were much more severe and certainly limited the progress which could be achieved in that season. Although some training was provided to the RCN in Tobermory and at the lately-formed RN training facility in Bermuda, it was arguably not until the commissioning of HMCS *Somers Isles* on the same island in August 1944 that the Canadian problem of individual ship training was properly solved.[12]

The Problems of Command and Tactics

The convoy escort commander's job represented a combination of challenges arguably unparalleled in maritime warfare. For long periods, which could extend to weeks, a relatively junior officer had responsibility for the protection of dozens of merchant ships with, for the early years of the war, an escort force insufficient to maintain a reasonable probability that the adversary could be detected before he made his attack. He had to exercise command over a formation that was, in poor weather or at night, often largely invisible to him and in which communications could be tenuous. As Admiral Sir Max Horton (C-in-C Western Approaches, 1942–1945) declared, this demanded "the highest standards of decision, resource and initiative in the most rigorous conditions."[13] He himself was never in doubt as to the requirement for such leadership. Horton was not only ruthless in removing officers who he did not think had made the grade,[14] but also careful to nurture those who he thought were up to the task.[15] Notwithstanding later comments (largely made by the officers involved) about convoy escort work being unglamorous and the A/S

---

[10]   Douglas, *No Higher Purpose,* p. 229.

[11]   Douglas, *A Blue Water Navy,* p. 580.

[12]   Ibid., p. 584.

[13]   Rear Admiral W. S. Chalmers, *Max Horton and the Western Approaches* (London: Hodder & Stoughton, 1954), p. 158.

[14]   Captain G. N. Brewer, "The Melody Lingers On—IV," *The Naval Review* LXII:3 (July 1974), pp. 228–29.

[15]   See D. A. Rayner, *Escort: The Battle of the Atlantic* (London: Futura, 1974), pp. 208–09 and 224–25, and Terence Robertson, *Walker, RN* (London: Evans, 1958), pp. 173–74.

sub-specialization in particular being a "Cinderella" branch, the quality seems to have been very high. Many were promoted and a good number went on to flag rank after the war.[16]

Matters were not helped by the shortages of the early years of the campaign which repeatedly forced a mix-and-match approach in the escort groups by the operational authorities, something that continued to happen in the RCN almost to the end of the war. Even when numbers had permitted allocation of the necessary additional units to provide a margin for refit and repair, weather, the action of the enemy, and unexpected defects forced short notice reassignments, often of ships which had only just completed a convoy. These experienced a "terrible depression which gripped everyone on board at receiving a signal, on arrival in harbour at long last after a tough crossing, to 'fuel, water and store with all dispatch,' in order to catch up with some outward-bound group sailing short-handed."[17] The escort commander, therefore, sometimes not only had to cope with units which were new to his group, but which could well be at low levels of efficiency and morale.

To be fair, the requirement for a collective training period for the group under the supervision of its commander before it embarked on a convoy operation was recognized very early and programmed where possible, but, in 1941 and 1942, particularly for the trans-Atlantic run, such exercises seem to have been more honored in the breach than the observance. As Nicholas Monsarrat noted, "No wonder the senior officers of escort-groups are men of half-humorous despair."[18]

---

[16]   Amongst A/S specialists, Howard-Johnston and P. W. Burnett both became rear admirals, as did the former submariner B. W. Taylor. Amongst the non-specialists, Gretton retired from ill health as a still very young vice admiral (he might well otherwise have gone on to become First Sea Lord) and Edmund Currey retired as a rear admiral. Other early group commanders included Walter Couchman, who later became a full admiral, as did Gerald Gladstone. Baker-Cresswell, Macintyre, Brewer, Evans, Hart, and several others achieved captain's rank in a competitive environment during and after the war. The perspective of the treatment given to the A/S branch and to escort ship captains may have been distorted by post-war popular histories, particularly those relating to F. J. Walker. Notwithstanding his later being passed over, Walker's appointment as XO of a battleship showed that he was once considered to be in the front rank of his contemporaries. As to the "Cinderella" label for the branch as a whole, this was true to an extent, but, if the analogy can be extended, Cinderella was young, beautiful, and intelligent, and ready for a change. If Prince Charming had not appeared, it is likely that she would soon have poisoned her stepmother and ugly step-sisters and run off with someone else. The A/S sub-specialization had been around long enough that, by 1939, it was arguably on the brink of coming into its own as its members started to reach the higher ranks, even if in small numbers.

[17]   James B. Lamb, *The Corvette Navy: True Stories from Canada's Atlantic War* (Toronto: Macmillan, 1977), p. 53.

[18]   Nicholas Monsarrat, *Three Corvettes* (London: Cassell, 1953), p. 35.

Then, too, so much involved in the operational art of oceanic convoy ASW defense was still new and evolving and could only be learned through hard-won experience at sea. It was only after many months of the war that sufficient expertise—in both individuals and within the navies as organizations—had accumulated to provide a basis for assessment, analysis, and doctrinal development. Admittedly, this process happened quickly and continued to evolve. As an example, the Admiralty *Monthly Anti-Submarine Reports* for the first half of 1941 provide much more sophisticated—and useful—tactical guidance than those of 1940.[19] Notably, the use of RDF (radar) was not only discussed at length, but specific anti-U-boat tactics proposed—an open airing of the capability which was contrary to much of the secrecy that surrounded it in other domains. Unfortunately, the evidence is mixed as to whether units actively assessed the knowledge that was made available to them in this way[20] and it was this that made the individual performance and leadership of the group commander all the more critical.

The initial absence of the higher level of tactical doctrine from the existing confidential books and other references forced the early group commanders, particularly the more expert anti-submarine sub-specialists, to devise their own tactics, procedures, and associated signals and code words, with varying degrees of effectiveness and coherence. That this was expected was not only implied, but stated outright.[21] In the main, based as they were on the emerging guidance (as well as hard won personal experience), the various plans were remarkably similar, but their differences in execution could create significant problems for a newly-joined ship. D. A. Rayner, an early RNVR corvette captain, noted, "in January 1941

---

[19]   The *Monthly Anti-Submarine Reports* for 1939, 1940, and the first half of 1941 are now available in facsimile reprint from UK publishers MLRS Books. They were published in 2011 with the cooperation of the RN Historical Branch. Extracts for the period 1940–45 have been published in a series subtitled "annotated extracts from secret British wartime anti-submarine reports" under the editorship of Jak P. Mallmann Showell and include *Countermeasures against U-Boats, The U-Boat Offensive, Weapons used against U-Boats during World War Two,* and *What Britain Knew and Wanted to Know about U-Boats* (Milton Keynes: Military Press; Altenbruch: U-Boot-Archiv, 2001–2003).

[20]   See Commander F. M. Osborne CMG, DSC*, RANVR, "Recollections," in G. R. Worledge, ed., *Contact! HMAS Rushcutter and Australia's Submarine Hunters, 1939–1946* (Sydney: Anti-Submarine Officers Association, 1994), p. 335. Osborne was CO of HMS *Gentian,* which received Type 271 radar in mid-1941.

[21]   ASW Division Admiralty Naval Staff, *Monthly Anti-Submarine Report: February 1941,* p. 10. See also Malcolm Llewellyn-Jones, "The Pursuit of Realism: British Anti-Submarine Tactics and Training to Counter the Fast Submarine, 1944–52," in John Reeve and David Stevens, eds., *The Face of Naval Battle: The Human Experience of War at Sea* (Crows Nest: Allen & Unwin, 2003), pp. 220–21.

to be attached to a strange group was to find oneself submerged by a flood of code words which meant just nothing to you."[22]

There was another issue, the overall approach to be taken in defense of the convoy by its escort commander. The problem, although not its solution, was stated by the committee which examined the prospective "winter campaign" of 1941–42. This found it "impossible to divorce the tactical problems involved from the strategical [sic] background. Tactics must depend to some extent on the number of escort ships and aircraft available with each convoy and this is dependent on strategy."[23] In more modern terms, this was a problem not only of strategy, but of operational art. The key division lay between those who focused on the "safe and timely" arrival of the convoy as the operational aim and those who believed that risks had to be taken in order to prosecute contacts to destruction. The first school was represented by Commander C. D. Howard-Johnston (although he partly changed his view in old age,[24] and on at least one occasion left his own convoy to prosecute a contact to destruction), the latter by Commander F. J. Walker. It was the fact that the arguments on both sides had their merits which made alignment so difficult. The problem could only be solved by the provision of sufficient resources to maintain the overall defense of the convoy while allowing prosecution of individual contacts to the end. As more ships became available, a solution which maintained the appropriate focus on the convoys themselves came with the creation of the support groups, a concept suggested as early as 1941[25]—that focus being emphasized by the fact that their formal designation, as opposed to their popular label, being "Escort Groups," not "Support Groups."[26] Furthermore, notwithstanding rank and seniority, it was the Senior Officer of the close escort who remained in

---

[22]   Rayner, *Escort*, p. 79.

[23]   "Battle of the Atlantic: (a) Report of the Committee on the Winter Campaign of 1941–42," ASW Division, *Monthly Anti-Submarine Report: April 1941*, CB 04050/41(4), p. 6.

[24]   Rear Admiral C. D. Howard-Johnston to Vice Admiral Sir Peter Gretton, 18 March 1975, National Maritime Museum, Greenwich (hereinafter NMM), Gretton Papers, GTN7/2(3b).

[25]   Douglas, *No Higher Purpose*, p. 285. The concept was suggested by Commander A. Baker-Cresswell, who sank *U-110* and recovered her Enigma rotors. He was to be a key player in the campaign in the years ahead.

[26]   Anecdotal evidence from discussions with RANR and RANVR veterans of the Atlantic suggests that there was some bitterness over the attention given the "Support Groups" and their assumption (which was certainly done by Walker at every opportunity) of the designation, rather than their formal title of "Escort Groups." Captain Stanley Darling OBE, DSC**, RANVR, who commanded *Loch Killin* in 1944–45, was aware of and sensitive to this and always talked of having operated in the "Second Escort Group." See Darling, "Recollections," in Worledge, *Contact!*, p. 206. Confirmed in personal conversations with the author, 1992–93.

tactical command of the operation at all times, thus indicating that the aim was still protection of the convoy.[27]

The RCN's position on this matter was never fully defined. Although the Canadian escorts operating in the Western Approaches were generally operating as close escorts under the "safe and timely" arrival construct, the influence of Commander (later Captain) J. D. Prentice seems to have been critical in the approach around Canada's coasts. Prentice himself was a driving force in the Canadian efforts to achieve higher training standards and a pioneer within the RCN's group training program, and he insisted on the benefits of the "prosecute to destruction" approach in the guidance that he issued to RCN units as "Hints on Escort Work" in March 1943.[28]

In the early years, such absence of agreed service-wide doctrine and the limitations of numbers and equipment, particularly in communications, made it all the more essential that each of the ships' captains knew exactly what their senior officer wanted, no matter what the contingency. This worked in the other direction; time in company allowed the senior officer to develop an understanding of the personalities of the ships' captains and their strengths and weaknesses, as well as those of their crews, all of which was critical in assigning tasks and in assessing the quality and reliability of their reports and recommendations. Howard-Johnston ran his own "tactical floors" in his day cabin in harbor.[29] This allowed him to inculcate his own approach within the group,[30] but also had the benefit of drawing out good ideas and individual insights. And, at times, group commanders had to seek the replacement of those they viewed as inadequate, and they were in a much better position to judge this than either the administrative authorities or the operational analysis teams ashore—although the assessments of Tobermory also helped.[31] Conversely, the more experienced ship commanders formed their own

---

[27]   See the discussion of this issue in Llewellyn-Jones, *The Royal Navy and Anti-Submarine Warfare*, pp. 42–44. Notably, the concept received clear endorsement from Captain J. A. McCoy DSO, RN in the wake of ONS 5. Senior Officer Third Escort Group, "Summary of the Experiences of the Third Escort Group and Summary of the Recommendations Arising Therefrom," Report to the C-in-C Western Approaches, 6 June 1943. Provided to the author by Commander J. A. A. McCoy, RN (son of Captain McCoy).

[28]   Milner, *North Atlantic Run*, p. 246. See also Marc Milner, "Inshore ASW: The Canadian Experience in Home Waters," in W.A.B Douglas, ed., *The RCN in Transition, 1910–1985* (Vancouver: University of British Columbia Press, 1988), p. 148.

[29]   Llewellyn-Jones, "The Pursuit of Realism," p. 221.

[30]   Rayner is unequivocal in his endorsement of Howard-Johnston as a commander—and of his tactical expertise. *Escort*, p. 88.

[31]   Captain G. N. Brewer, "The Melody Lingers On—V," *The Naval Review* LXII:4 (October 1974), p. 336.

views as to the qualities of the group senior officers and could—and did—seek not to serve at sea with them.[32]

At a lower level, if the ships within a group were used to working with each other, there was a much greater chance that their cooperation would be effective in a particular engagement. In Rayner's words, they could "speak the same language,"[33] and this was all the more important in the early years of the war before guidance for complex tactics had been evolved and made available. Some groups were better off than others. The Gibraltar convoy cycle provided more opportunities than the trans-Atlantic run for group training, something of which Walker took full advantage during his command of the 36th Escort Group in 1941–42.[34] The necessary cooperation involved not only the commanding officers, but their officers of the watch, signalmen, asdic and radar teams, and weapons crews. Walker himself emphasized inter-ship drills in his groups, using the competitive instinct to improve skills in key areas such as depth charge handling and launching, the smooth operation of which were integral to successful multi-ship prosecutions.[35] Above all, effective inter-ship communications were vital. Peter Gretton went so far as to assert that assembling the signalmen and wireless ratings to make it clear what was wanted "was even more important" than explaining his approach to his captains.[36] Gretton had a point, because effective working relations between the various units of the group, as well as with their commander, were key to its success and much of this depended upon the effective interaction of the communications staffs. Lieutenant Commander E. C. Hulton of *Leith* assembled his group's officers of the watch to impress upon them the importance of knowing what was in the signal book.[37] The same observations were made by RCN personnel who experienced the reality of the signalling deficiencies of a "recently . . . formed" escort group in late 1941.[38] Nicholas Monsarrat detailed the guidance of his group commander in 1943, much of which was focused on the need to communicate effectively—both between each ship and with himself.[39] Howard-Johnston,

---

[32]   Captain Reginald Whinney, *The U-Boat Peril: An Anti-Submarine Commander's War* (London: Arrow, 1989), p. 147.

[33]   Rayner, *Escort,* p. 87.

[34]   Brewer, "The Melody Lingers On—IV," p. 223.

[35]   D. E. G. Wemyss, *Relentless Pursuit: The Story of Captain F. J. Walker* (Barton-under-Needwood: Wren's Park, 2003), p. 20.

[36]   Vice Admiral Sir Peter Gretton, *Convoy Escort Commander* (London: Cassell, 1964), p. 102.

[37]   Lieutenant Max Shean DSO*, RANVR, *Corvette and Submarine* (Claremont: privately published, 1992), p. 52.

[38]   Douglas, *No Higher Purpose,* p. 258.

[39]   Nicholas Monsarrat, *H. M. Frigate* (London: Cassell, 1946), pp. 24–25.

nevertheless, also emphasized the constant practice of tactics as well, so that "when the blasted R/T didn't work everyone knew more or less what to do."[40]

As the war progressed, the identities of the longer-established groups became more prominent. For the RN, the most well-known was Walker's Second Escort Group, but some of the Canadian units developed their own, very effective personae, including the "Barber-Pole Brigade" with its distinct funnel marking.[41] In creating and encouraging such a group identity, the group commander needed to generate and sustain a balance between healthy inter-ship rivalry, which led personnel to do their best for their own ship, and a collective approach which recognized the contribution of every unit. The more time in company, on operations, working up or in harbor, the greater the opportunities for the development of such a group spirit, but there were also opportunities for individual rivalries and animosities to develop and these had to be watched for carefully.

Ship Commander or Embarked Senior Officer

This approach bore on another issue which had training implications. Most, if not all, group commanders in the RN and RCN preferred to command their own ships rather than ride another unit as their flagship. This is certainly a consistent judgement from the memoirs. There were obvious issues of space and personality, as were the possibilities of confusion between the tactical direction of the group as a whole and of the flagship itself. HMCS Chebogue's torpedoing in October 1944 was arguably—although only in part—the result of such misunderstanding.[42] Yet there was a more subtle element as well. A senior officer with his own ship was in a better position to insist on his crew—who usually included some of the most senior and experienced personnel in the group—leading the way in terms of performance and operational standards.[43] Furthermore, staff officers who also had ship responsibilities were regarded as much more credible by the remainder of the group if their department or sub-department really did set a standard for others. There was another side to this coin, as Gretton himself admitted, when he found that not having his own ship allowed him to spend more time with the other units,[44] but the

---

[40]   Howard-Johnston to Gretton, 12 July 1980, Gretton Papers, GTN7/2(4b).

[41]   Lamb, *The Corvette Navy*, p. 60. Although it has to be noted that the "barber pole" was devised by one Canadian group and then adopted by another.

[42]   Douglas, *A Blue Water Navy*, pp. 381–82.

[43]   This was clearly an approach of Walker's. His A/S officer in *Stork*, M. E. Impey, after a short period of CO of *Philante* in its group training role, came as First Lieutenant (and effectively group A/S officer) in *Starling*. Exceptionally, he was awarded a DSO in 1943 to supplement his DSC and bar of 1942.

[44]   Vice Admiral Sir Peter Gretton, *Crisis Convoy: The Story of HX231* (Annapolis: Naval Institute Press, 1974), p. 37.

balance generally lay with the senior officer having his own command—if only because in the end, "the ships themselves were not big enough to house the two in comfort."[45] It is significant that, in commenting on an occasion in the RCN in which the relationship with the embarked group commander worked well, the ship's captain should remark on his senior's "reticence . . . [and] fine sense of propriety,"[46] while for his part, the (RN) group commander concerned had been well aware of his own tendency to interfere and the need to guard against it.[47]

The strain on the group commanders was and remained great, even to the end of the war. Nevertheless, it was also true that the combination of agreed (and effective) doctrine, an effective training system ashore and afloat, and the increasing levels of collective experience and understanding in the ships themselves, notwithstanding continuing expansion, did mean that much more in later years could be assumed with new joining units and much less had to be explained or taught from scratch. Monsarrat recognized this reality in a rueful comment about his own transition from unqualified corvette watchkeeper to frigate captain within just a few years.[48] The RCN remained somewhat further behind this curve than the RN, largely because it could never accumulate the same reserves of both experience and materiel, but it too was able to achieve progressively higher standards across the seagoing fleet. Notwithstanding the problems encountered by RCN groups during their operations in the complex and difficult oceanographic environment of the Canadian Atlantic coast in 1944–45, their performance was a quantum improvement on that which would have been possible in 1941–42.[49]

Training Support—Ashore and Afloat

Permanently formed escort groups could never be the whole answer, even when they had adequate numbers of ships allocated to them and a degree of stability was achieved in their composition. What was also needed was the stimulation that could only be achieved by a formal training effort. This also provided a vital element of auditing. As Gretton commented, "long periods of operating, often with no incidents except bad weather, resulted in more need for training—ships got into bad habits."[50] The development of a supporting infrastructure in and around the

---

[45]   Rayner, *Escort*, p. 213.

[46]   D. M. McLean, "The Last Cruel Winter: RCN Support Groups and the U-Boat Schnorkel Offensive," unpublished Master of War Studies thesis, Royal Military College of Canada, Kingston, Ontario, 1992, p. 85.

[47]   Douglas, *A Blue Water Navy*, p. 382.

[48]   Monsarrat, *H. M. Frigate*, p. 16.

[49]   See McLean, "The Last Cruel Winter," for a comprehensive analysis. His judgements are generally endorsed by Douglas, *A Blue Water Navy*, pp. 409–52.

[50]   Vice Admiral Sir Peter Gretton, "Foreword," Milner, *North Atlantic Run*, p. x.

base ports formed an important part of the solution because most training activities required much more than the groups could do by themselves.

What was fundamental to the effectiveness of these systems was coherent doctrine, and at a higher level than had been achieved prior to the war. It was the "industrialisation" of tactical development, the introduction of operational research, and the creation of an effective chain of analysis, innovation, test, and publication that finally allowed the enforcement of systematic, navy-wide procedures. This in turn made both shore and sea training on the large scale practicable, since it provided formulae and processes with which to work (and which did work), and valid standards to aim at. But it could not be properly achieved until sufficient basis of operational knowledge had been established. This was not a straightforward issue. *Western Approaches Convoy Instructions* were promulgated in April 1941, but they initially focused more on the general management of the convoys, rather than tactics, while references such as CB 4097, *The Conduct of Anti-U-Boat Operations,* tended to concentrate on detailed ship procedures.

As was to become clear when a new system of coherent tactical development was implemented with the formation of the Western Approaches Tactical Unit (WATU) in January 1942, even the most experienced group commanders could devise tactics based on false assumptions. Furthermore, well on into the war, the lack of standardized procedures for attack and search plans still made life very difficult for units assigned at short notice to a different group. Notwithstanding the early impact of WATU through its promulgation of group search and attack plans from early 1942 onwards, and the establishment of additional units,[51] even its supporters amongst the group commanders (such as Gretton) were being criticized for the continuing existence of "private" close escort group signals as late as June 1943.[52]

Furthermore, not all commanders fully supported WATU. Baker-Cresswell "was never in favour,"[53] while Walker refused to attend any of its courses and maintained his own tactics (such as the slow speed "creeping attack") despite criticism.[54] To be fair, this may have been as much a matter of the interaction of strong personalities as one of fundamental disagreement between Walker and the director of WATU, Captain Gilbert Roberts, since Walker proved extremely receptive to the

---

[51]   The National Archives, London (hereinafter TNA), Admiralty Records (hereinafter ADM) 239/248, CB 3212D, *Anti-Submarine Warfare,* Vol. IV, *A/S Training,* p. 20.

[52]   Senior Officer Third Escort Group, "Summary of the Experiences of the Third Escort Group and Summary of the Recommendations Arising Therefrom," report to the C-in-C Western Approaches, 6 June 1943.

[53]   Captain A. J. Baker-Cresswell to Gretton, 5 October 1981, Gretton Papers.

[54]   Osborne, "Recollections," pp. 339–40. Osborne was on the staff of WATU after commanding *Gentian.* Such criticism was included in *Monthly Anti-Submarine Report: February 1944,* p. 5.

capabilities of the new Squid ASW weapon in 1944 and gave the captains of ships so fitted a free hand to display its worth.[55]

Nevertheless, whatever the hiccups and delays, the vital role of the tactical floor system in developing the operational art of convoy defense and ASW tactics cannot be discounted. It allowed a level of conceptual analysis and debate which was simply impossible either during the most realistic "real time" training, whether live or simulated, or during operations themselves. It forced group commanders, captains, and their officers to work through problems and achieve solutions together, creating not only the potential for improved cooperation within individual escort groups, but between the groups themselves, and other elements such as maritime patrol aircraft.

Providing the Training Assets

The creation of a second line of training units and formations to provide targets and facilities was also vital to the achievement of better escort efficiency, but took time, particularly as the operational formations always had priority. The need, as with many others, was in fact recognized early; the difficulty came in meeting it, particularly with "live" targets, although there were ingenious (if makeshift) substitutes, such as a replica U-boat conning tower on an old lifeboat for radar training at Holyhead in 1941.[56] The 7th Submarine Flotilla was formed in July 1940 with the dual role of submarine and anti-submarine training. Based at Rothesay at the entrance to the Clyde, it was well located to support Tobermory and locally-based escorts, such as those working out of Greenock. Certainly, Clyde-based group senior officers such as Baker-Cresswell were quick to take advantage of its presence. By September 1940, there were thirteen boats in the flotilla.[57]

This was not enough, particularly for the other side of the Atlantic. Canada's desperate need for live A/S targets was not met until May 1941,[58] and then only with a single boat. The real scale of the overall requirement of the RN and RCN is best demonstrated by the allocation of submarines for ASW training alone in April 1945—no less than seventeen in the Clyde, four in Nova Scotia, three in Bermuda, one at Gibraltar, four in the East Indies, and three in the British Pacific Fleet.[59] This was in addition to a number of other boats at various bases listed as being "operational and

---

[55] Darling, "Recollections," p. 206.

[56] Admiralty Naval Staff ASW Division, *Monthly Anti-Submarine Report: March 1941*, p. 36.

[57] Admiralty Historical Section, *Naval Staff History, Second World War: Submarines*, Vol. 1, *Operations in Home, Northern and Atlantic Waters (Including the Operations of Allied Submarines)* (London: Admiralty, 1953), pp. 54–55.

[58] Douglas, *No Higher Purpose*, p. 166.

[59] *Naval Staff History: Submarines*, pp. 226–27.

training" and likely to be available for some use as ASW targets, as well as a program to sink obsolete hulls as bottom targets.[60] The great advance had come in 1943, with thirty-one boats allocated to ASW training in September in comparison to only fifteen the previous year.[61] This total was assisted by the decision to include fourteen days ASW training in the programs of all new construction and newly-refitted submarines, a measure intended to assist both submariners (in familiarizing them with ASW tactics) and the escorts.[62] In fact, even to the end of the war, providing sufficient boats required significant planning effort.[63] For Canada there were arguably never enough, and the demands of the escort groups on the three or four boats maintained in Canadian waters, if met, would have cut into the time available for the basic training of RCN ratings and officers.[64] Even in the later stages of the war, some Canadian groups were going without such in-contact training at all.[65]

Matters were improved in the United Kingdom with the introduction of much more sophisticated pre-deployment training in the form of multi-threat exercises in local areas, supervised by the staff of the Captain(D) concerned, although this externally-supported activity took time to organize. It was taken an important step further with the inauguration of a tactical training organization led by an experienced commander (the now-Captain Baker-Cresswell) at the end of 1942. This reflected the newly-arrived C-in-C Admiral Sir Max Horton's experience of submarine command qualification, and his insistence that the efficiency of the escort groups depended upon the quality of their training.[66] The sea training group adopted a deliberately practical and realistic approach not only to ASW, but to other threats through the provision of a staged program that started with twenty-four hours to shake down after the period in harbor and culminated with up to forty-eight hours on a "racetrack" around the Irish Sea in which a variety of encounters with submarines, surface vessels, and aircraft were staged within the scenario of the passage of a convoy based around the armed yacht *Philante*. It was of this activity that Gretton later noted that the training sometimes proved more arduous than the convoy operation which followed.[67] Monsarrat also commented on the relief of being able to "go off to sea for a rest."[68]

---

[60]   Ibid., p. 215.

[61]   Ibid., p. 150.

[62]   Admiralty Naval Staff ASW Division, *Monthly Anti-Submarine Report: April 1943*, CB 04050/43(4).

[63]   See the material on this subject in ADM 199/1732.

[64]   Professor Marc Milner letter to the author, 24 March 1993.

[65]   McLean, "The Last Cruel Winter," p. 47.

[66]   Rear Admiral W. S. Chalmers, *Max Horton and the Western Approaches* (London: Hodder & Stoughton, 1954), p. 158.

[67]   Gretton, *Convoy Escort Commander*, p. 132.

[68]   Monsarrat, *H. M. Frigate*, p. 21.

The air side also required attention. This was not only a matter of higher train-ing standards for the aircraft themselves, but practice for both aircrew and escort ship personnel in cooperation. There was more to this than achieving good com-munications; it also involved developing a mutual understanding of how units could be best employed to achieve the greatest joint effect. The need for such coop-eration was recognized with the formation of the Joint Anti-U-Boat School in Northern Ireland in April 1943[69] after a successful trial for one of the early escort carrier air groups. Located close to the second tactical unit at Londonderry and operating in conjunction with the *Philante* group, this school became an impor-tant component of the composite training effort at sea.[70]

There were always limits to such a "live" effort. It was extremely resource inten-sive. Not all ships were able to take advantage of the program and the priority seems to have been given to the escort groups designated as support units. This had its logic, since the support groups were intended to be despatched where the threat was greatest, but there was always the danger that the close escort groups could become a "second eleven" in the campaign. The Canadian Navy, despite repeated attempts by key personnel such as J. D. Prentice to put group training on a consistent basis,[71] never really achieved the goal, not only because of the rela-tive lack of resources, but the repeated reallocation of escorts to operations—frequently in response to British requests for such support.[72] The Canadian units sent to the eastern Atlantic which were able to undertake the training quickly appreciated—and demonstrated—its benefits.[73]

What does seem to have provided remarkable value for money was the devel-opment of simulators ashore to create the experience of various components of the ASW effort. Sonar and plotting trainers were in the vanguard of this initiative, but a whole range of such facilities was eventually brought into being, including bridge and signalling simulators, which even included the odd bucket of cold water to reproduce the realities of open bridges in the Atlantic, as well as depth charge load-ing and other weapon trainers. Canada led the way in some of this activity with Commander J. C. Hibbard's Night Attack Teacher in September 1942.[74] All of it,

---

69   ADM 239/248, CB 3212D, Vol. IV, *A/S Training*, p. 22.

70   Llewellyn-Jones, "The Pursuit of Realism," p. 223.

71   Douglas, *No Higher Purpose*, p. 583.

72   Ibid., p. 446.

73   Lieutenant Barry O'Brien, CO of HMCS *Snowberry*, recalling the experience of EG-5 in 1943. Cited in Johnston, *Corvettes Canada*, pp. 206–07. See also Marc Milner, "Royal Cana-dian Navy Participation in the Battle of the Atlantic Crisis of 1943," in James A. Boutilier, ed., *The RCN in Retrospect, 1910–1968* (Vancouver: University of British Columbia Press, 1982), pp. 170–71.

74   Douglas, *No Higher Purpose*, p. 582.

however, depended upon the development of a real understanding of what was required to be simulated and how—as well as why. For example, it took the capture of *U-570* to identify the need for escort boarding parties to have sufficient knowledge of submarine construction and operation to prevent or reverse their scuttling, and the creation of mock up trainers for this purpose at Liverpool, Greenock, and Londonderry.[75]

Apart from the relatively limited cost of these systems, they could be utilized while maintenance was conducted on the ships involved, thus avoiding a conflict between the needs of repair and training. They also provided a vital foundation of group efficiency because they could reproduce many of the external inputs to the ships, such as sonar and radar contacts, radio messages, Talk Between Ships, and light signals, upon which unit cooperation depended. This practice allowed ships to proceed to sea ready to derive full benefit from the much more resource intensive live training effort. They and the training schools which supported them eventually formed what Monsarrat described as a "complete curriculum" for the escort ships.[76]

The Shallow Water Challenge

It is arguable that the mechanisms for analysis, tactical development, and training proved themselves, at least in British waters, in the relatively prompt and largely successful response to the Germans' adoption of the *Schnorkel* and deployment into shallow, coastal waters, a challenge which coincided with the preparations for the invasion of Europe and the massive effort that would be required to protect shipping for the assault and the reinforcement and supply that would follow. This environment presented very different problems to the open sea and called for the employment of new techniques of search, detection, classification, and attack. The eastern Atlantic groups were generally able to receive training that equipped them very well to meet these new requirements, and their performance in the difficult environment of the English Channel in 1944–45 reflected as much.[77]

Two points are notable. Firstly, WATU and its associated units played a significant role in assessing the operational and tactical issues that would be involved in protecting the invasion of Europe, and developed tactical courses, which acted as a foundation for the live multi-threat training that was provided to the ships which

---

[75]   *Naval Staff History: Submarines*, Vol. 1, p. 107.

[76]   Monsarrat, *H. M. Frigate*, p. 21.

[77]   The best modern survey of events is Douglas, *A Blue Water Navy*, in the chapter "The Inshore Antisubmarine Campaign in European Waters, June 1944–May 1945," pp. 349–408.

would be assigned to the operation.[78] The second was, as noted earlier, that collective efficiency levels had reached a point at which new, sometimes temporary escort groups could be formed and despatched with confidence that this training would be enough to allow them to work together effectively.[79] This was only possible because of the much greater base of experience within the escorts' crews after nearly five years of war. Despite the much younger average age of the personnel concerned than in 1939, by 1943 their "collective experience . . . was impressive,"[80] and this was, despite some of the cultural changes which also took place in the seemingly ever younger ships' companies,[81] even more the case in 1944–45.

Conclusion

The creation of a sophisticated learning and training system to prepare ships and men for the ASW war is one of the most significant but under-recognized elements of the Atlantic campaign. It was central to the effectiveness of the escort units of the RN and RCN. This is a story of professionalization, not only of the "hostilities only" personnel, but of the permanent cadres, who in later years would find themselves, in facing a new undersea threat, utilizing many of the lessons and organizational methods that they had learned between 1939 and 1945. The development of these programs took place in the context of two services being forced to adapt rapidly to profound changes in their operational environments and the strategic challenges that they faced. That development faced many challenges, not only from a scarcity of resources, but from the necessity to develop sufficient understanding for the totality of the problem within the responsible authorities. The "master-apprentice" culture of professionalization managed through long service, sometimes characterized as "osmostic training," had been central to the Royal Navy's system in the past. Under the pressures of the oceanic small-ship war, it would not serve—and it could never serve for the much more rapidly expanding Canadian Navy. The effort had to be systematized and industrialized. Effective group training, and thus acceptable levels of collective efficiency, only became possible when the right equipment and training assets, sufficiently—even if barely—experienced personnel, and proven tactical doctrine could be brought together to provide the necessary fidelity within the training experience. From the outset, this

---

78   The development of the campaign is detailed in Llewellyn-Jones, *The Royal Navy and Anti-Submarine Warfare, 1917–49*, pp. 46–58. See also Mark Williams, *Captain Gilbert Roberts R. N. and the Anti-U-boat School* (London: Cassell, 1979), pp. 136–39; Osborne, "Recollections," pp. 341–42.

79   Whinney, *The U-Boat Peril*, pp. 176–78.

80   Monsarrat, *H. M. Frigate*, p. 12.

81   See Rayner, *Escort*, pp. 211–13 for a lament on the changes between 1939 and 1944.

would always be a much more complex and resource intensive operation than the straightforward working up of individual units which Tobermory and the other basic training bases did so well. It is perhaps unsurprising that it took so long to mature. In the interim, it made the leadership and professionalism of the escort group commanders all the more vital as they took their own measures to improve the efficiency of their ships. They themselves, however, always appreciated that their own efforts could never be enough, and to the senior officers of the groups between 1940 and 1943, much is owed for the burden they bore.

7

"A Most Disagreeable Problem"

British Perceptions of the *Kriegsmarine's* Aircraft Carrier Capability

Marcus Faulkner

The German attack on Allied maritime communications in the Atlantic theater during the Second World War is first and foremost seen as a campaign waged by U-boats. This is a logical conclusion to draw, given that U-boats accounted for between sixty and seventy percent of Allied and neutral merchant shipping losses throughout the war.[1] The fact that most of this shipping was sunk in the North Atlantic has reinforced the notion that the Battle of the Atlantic was one of U-boats versus convoys and their escorts. This masks the fact that the campaign was geographically more diverse and strategically and operationally more challenging. The German ability to prosecute the attack along multiple vectors substantially complicated the defense of maritime communications as different methods required different countermeasures. From a British perspective, combined German surface, subsurface, and air operations represented the worst-case scenario. The Admiralty's longstanding concern that just such a campaign might be waged on a sustained basis is often underestimated because ultimately the Germans only rarely succeeded in coordinating operations. The annihilation of convoy PQ17 in early July 1942 stands out as the prime example of the destructive potential a combined attack could have on Allied convoys.

Within the historiography of the Battle of the Atlantic, operations by U-boats, aircraft, warships, small combatants, and auxiliary cruisers operating in distant waters have tended to be dealt with as linked, yet distinct, components of the German attack, when in fact the Admiralty perceived it as a single campaign. More recently, the interaction between the various elements has received more attention

---

[1] A precise figure is hard to ascertain given the different figures and methodologies employed, see The National Archives, London (hereinafter TNA), Admiralty File (hereinafter ADM) 234/579, "Losses by Enemy Action of British, Allied & Neutral Merchant Ships—Analysis according to Cause for the years 1940 to 1944" in Defeat of the Enemy Attack on Shipping 1939–1945; ADM 186/804, Volume 1B, Table 4 in BR1337 British and Foreign Merchant Vessels Lost or Damaged by Enemy Action During the Second World War.

and the campaign itself is being examined in the wider context of British strategy. One aspect has, however, never been addressed in terms of Admiralty thinking and the implications for British strategy—the potential threat that German carriers posed to Allied naval operations and the passage of maritime traffic in the North Atlantic and Arctic Oceans. Simply because no German carrier came close to being deployed against the Royal Navy or Allied merchant shipping, nor was even completed, does not mean this potential threat was not taken seriously. It will be argued that in fact the Admiralty was, until the late summer of 1943, concerned that the *Kriegsmarine* might deploy a carrier group, centered on *Graf Zeppelin*, against Allied maritime communications.[2]

This chapter seeks to address two issues. First, what did the British know about the *Kriegsmarine's* efforts to develop aircraft carriers and how did they know it? Understanding the nature and quantity of intelligence gathered is of vital importance in examining any assessment process, yet often this aspect is ignored. Secondly, how did the Admiralty perceive German efforts both before and during the war, and what implications did this have on British strategy, naval planning, and fleet deployments? In covering these aspects, this chapter fills an existing gap concerning the Admiralty's view of German aircraft carriers and contributes to understanding the complexity of the maritime threat Britain faced during the war. It also illustrates the problems involved in evaluating enemy military capabilities and intentions when set against a spartan intelligence picture. This in turn helps to explain why the Admiralty remained so apprehensive of the *Kriegsmarine's* surface fleet until 1943.

Before examining these questions, it is necessary to outline why so little attention was devoted to the development of German aircraft carriers from the British perspective in the post-war history dealing with both Anglo-German naval relations prior to 1939 and the naval war between 1939 and 1945. Carriers and *Graf Zeppelin* are noticeably absent from the Admiralty assessments and mainstream histories that emerged in the decades following the end of the war.[3] The reasons for this lay in a combination of factors. The Royal Navy as a leading developer of carrier aviation had little to learn from a failed project, and there was no reason to study German developments. Within days of the cessation of hostilities in May 1945, the bulk of the remaining German surface fleet had fallen into British hands, allowing for the first inspection and assessment of the technology that had gone into its construction. It quickly became apparent that wartime concerns regarding

---

[2]   On *Graf Zeppelin's* development, see Marcus Faulkner, "The Kriegsmarine and the Aircraft Carrier: The Design and Operational Purpose of the *Graf Zeppelin*, 1933–1940," *War in History* 19:4 (2012), pp. 492–516.

[3]   For example, W. M. James, *The British Navies in the Second World War* (London: Longmans, 1946); John Creswell, *Sea Warfare, 1939–1945* (London: Longmans, 1950); P. K. Kemp, *Victory at Sea* (London: Frederick Muller, 1957).

the qualitative superiority of German material were overstated and that design and construction methods utilized harbored serious problems in terms of the propulsion engineering and habitability of warships.[4] In due course, further analysis would underline this first impression and show how machinery defects had severely limited the availability of the surface fleet and reduced the German potential to interdict Allied maritime communications.[5]

At the end of the war, *Graf Zeppelin* lay abandoned and moored off a small island to the east of Stettin harbor in what was to become the Soviet sector of occupied Germany. In its final wartime reference to the carrier, the Naval Intelligence Division (NID) had noted her as "Under construction. Damage yet undetermined."[6] The Admiralty was still interested in ascertaining her condition and whether the Soviets were making salvage plans.[7] As part of the work of the Tripartite Naval Commission, Admiralty inspectors were able to access her in August but found little of value and classified the hull as internally smashed.[8] In the final settlement on the division of German naval assets, the Soviets were given the responsibility to dispose of *Graf Zeppelin* and, as far as the British were concerned, the matter was closed.[9] Admiralty interest lay primarily in obtaining information on the new generation of U-boats and their associated technology as the resurgent efficacy of the U-boat arm during the inshore campaign of late 1944 and 1945 had presented tactical and operational problems that had diminished Allied Anti-Submarine Warfare (ASW) capabilities.[10] Understanding both German U-boat development and operational employment continued to drive Admiralty interest in the *Kriegsmarine* into the Cold War era.[11]

---

[4]   ADM 1/18255, German Cruiser PRINZ EUGEN: Reports of preliminary inspection of engineering and medical departments carried out by officers of H.M.S. DIDO (1945).

[5]   ADM 234/372, "Disposition of German Battleships and Cruisers from 9th April 1940 to 6th December 1941" in BR1736 Home Waters and the Atlantic, Vol. II; D. K. Brown, *Nelson to Vanguard: Warship Design and Development, 1923–1945* (London: Chatham, 2006), p. 102.

[6]   ADM 228/19 Part I, No.A.504, 27th August 1945.

[7]   ADM 228/19 Part I, Directive to the Tripartite Naval Commission, 13th August 1945.

[8]   Chris Madsen, *The Royal Navy and German Naval Disarmament, 1942–1947* (London: Frank Cass, 1998), p. 114. By this stage, the Admiralty had information on some of the specialist equipment installed or designed for *Graf Zeppelin* from an extensive report produced by the Italian Navy stemming from a mission sent to inspect the carrier in December 1942, translation in ADM 1/19137, German Aircraft Carrier Graf Zeppelin.

[9]   ADM 116/5565, British Minutes of the 27th Tripartite Naval Commission Meeting, 6 December 1945.

[10]   Malcolm Llewellyn-Jones, *The Royal Navy and Anti-Submarine Warfare, 1917–49* (London: Routledge, 2006).

[11]   See, for example, ADM 186/802, The U-boat War in the North Atlantic, Vol. 1, 1939–1941.

As *Graf Zeppelin* had never taken part in actual operations, there was little reason for her to feature in the narrative histories of the war at sea. This is hardly surprising given that histories of events that do not happen tend not to be written. Her treatment in two key works, Winston Churchill's history of the Second World War and Stephen Roskill's official history of the war at sea, is illustrative. Churchill's extensive narrative only mentions *Graf Zeppelin* once, and then only in a letter to President Roosevelt from December 1942 concerning the deployment of British carriers to support the U.S. Pacific Fleet. The content offers a first clue that there was more to the issue: "In view of the vital importance of the Atlantic communications, the necessity of supporting North Russian convoys, the possible appearance of *Graf Zeppelin* at the end of the year, and the present condition of *Indomitable* and *Formidable,* we could not release both *Victorious* and *Illustrious* without the addition of *Ranger* to the Home Fleet. . . ."[12] Roskill refers to *Graf Zeppelin* only as part of his initial outline of the *Kriegsmarine's* order of battle. There is no further discussion of the carrier and no indication as to how the Admiralty assessed the threat or what impact, if any, it had on British strategy and operations.[13]

While the publication of memoirs and progressive opening of archival records enabled the history of the Atlantic campaign to be explored further, the focus tended to remain on certain aspects. As far as the German surface threat was concerned, the events surrounding *Unternehmen Rheinübung* remain the most written about individual episode of the Atlantic campaign. Beyond the hunt for *Bismarck,* the sinking of *Scharnhorst* in the Battle of the North Cape and the destruction of *Graf Spee* in the South Atlantic have become well-covered episodes. This focus is understandable given that the presence of one of the most powerful warships astride Britain's most important maritime artery at that time in the war was a decisive moment. The Admiralty's post-war analysis could not help but note that "this drama of the *Bismarck* was one of the most striking events of the war and will take its place with the many striking events recorded in British naval history."[14] From an operational and strategic perspective there was much to study, but it was the destruction of the Royal Navy's largest warship, HMS *Hood,* that imprinted the events on successive generations.[15] The sinking of *Bismarck* is often seen today as the end of the surface threat phase of the Atlantic campaign when at the time the Admiralty was concerned that an intensification of surface operations and new

---

[12]   Winston S. Churchill, *The Second World War,* Vol. V (London: Penguin, 1985 edition), p. 18.

[13]   S. W. Roskill, *The War at Sea, 1939–1945,* Vol. I (London: HMSO, 1954), p. 57 and p. 368.

[14]   ADM 234/322, BR1736 (3/50) Battle Summary No. 5, The Chase and Sinking of the "Bismarck," pp. 36–37.

[15]   Ludovic Kennedy, *Pursuit: The Sinking of the Bismarck* (London: Cassell, 2004), pp. 91–92; Ralph Harrington, "'The Mighty Hood': Navy, Empire, War at Sea and the British National Imagination, 1920–60," *Journal of Contemporary History* 38:2 (2003), pp. 171–85.

warships—including *Graf Zeppelin*—might push British defenses to a breaking point.

The *Bismarck* episode raised another issue that went to the core of debates surrounding British appeasement policy in the 1930s. The battleship sunk in May 1941 was a different ship to what the Admiralty had previously considered her to be. The substantially larger displacement translated into a much more robust vessel that had proven to be very resilient in its final engagement despite British numerical superiority. In the operation's immediate aftermath, the Admiralty was forced to reassess its appreciation of the *Kriegsmarine's* material and this was a major factor in the continued concern regarding the German surface fleet. After the war, the Admiralty's view of German naval rearmament came under scrutiny with a view to assessing whether the Navy had been sufficiently prepared materially to face the German fleet. Vice Admiral John Godfrey, the Director of Naval Intelligence (DNI) 1939–42, was particularly vocal in his criticism of decisions taken before the war.[16] The question of what intelligence had been available and how it had been interpreted has since become a focus of historians examining British reactions to German naval rearmament. Case studies have addressed *Panzerschiffe*, battleships, and U-boats, but *Graf Zeppelin* was never examined from this perspective.[17] She does offer additional insights into the pre-war assessment of German naval capability and intentions.

Graf Zeppelin has received mention in two other contexts. The earliest may be found in Wing Commander Guy Gibson's account of his wartime operational service in which he outlines a raid against Gdynia on 27 August 1942 targeting *Graf Zeppelin*.[18] The raid by No. 106 Squadron, then Bomber Command's test-bed unit for special missions, involved one of the longest-range missions of the war and employed a new bomb type. As a result, this very uncharacteristic mission for the

---

[16]   National Maritime Museum, Greenwich, London (hereinafter NMM), Godfrey Papers (hereinafter GOD) 171, Memoirs, Vol. 5, Part II. Godfrey's account was compiled with the assistance of others involved with pre-war intelligence and construction. It was published as part of Donald McLachlan's influential book on NID's wartime work: Donald McLachlan, *Room 39: Naval Intelligence in Action, 1939–45* (London: Weidenfeld & Nicolson, 1968), pp. 135–42.

[17]   Wesley K. Wark, "Baltic Myths and Submarine Bogeys: British Naval Intelligence and Nazi Germany, 1933–1939," *The Journal of Strategic Studies* 6:1 (1983), pp. 66–81, and *The Ultimate Enemy: British Intelligence and Nazi Germany, 1933–1939* (Oxford: Oxford University Press, 1986), pp. 125–54; Andrew Lambert, "Seapower 1939–1940: Churchill and the Strategic Origins of the Battle of the Atlantic," *The Journal of Strategic Studies* 17:1 (1994), pp. 86–107; Joseph A. Maiolo, *The Royal Navy and Nazi Germany, 1933–39* (Basingstoke: Palgrave Macmillan, 1998).

[18]   Guy Gibson, *Enemy Coast Ahead* (London: Michael Joseph, 1946), pp. 199–204.

time is often mentioned, but the context in which it took place is never addressed.[19] The second more important reference may be found in the official British intelligence history of the war. In an otherwise functionally footnoted study, an extensive reference listing intelligence relating to the carrier in 1942–43 stands out as an anomaly.[20] That Churchill was given specific intelligence on the carrier's status for the Casablanca conference (which took place approximately a month after the letter quoted above) suggests the matter did in fact feature heavily in Admiralty thinking. Despite such clues, no examination of the available intelligence or its impact has been attempted to date.[21]

The Intelligence on *Graf Zeppelin*

The first consideration of German aircraft carriers within the Admiralty may be traced back to the summer of 1934 as part of a wider assessment of German naval rearmament efforts and the implications this had for British strategy.[22] Resurgent German naval ambitions were taken seriously and, to control the scale and scope of rearmament, the Admiralty wanted to lock the Germans into the existing international naval agreement framework. In doing so, it would not be possible to bar Germany from acquiring warship types other navies had, and this also implied that the ban on possessing an air force as laid out in the Treaty of Versailles would need revision. Consequently, the Admiralty was prepared to allow the construction of one carrier to maximum permissible size as laid down under the 1922 Washington Treaty.[23] It is highly likely that the Admiralty also wanted to forestall the Germans from laying down any cruiser-carrier hybrids that, similar to the *Panzerschiff* design, straddled multiple warship categories and complicated the regulatory framework the British were seeking to establish. Such hybrids were, at the time, still considered as a type with potential in international naval circles for,

---

[19] Martin Middlebrook and Chris Everitt, *The Bomber Command War Diaries: An Operational Reference Book, 1939–1945* (London: Viking, 1985), 27/28 August 1942; Leo McKinstry, *Lancaster: The Second World War's Greatest Bomber* (London: John Murray, 2009), pp. 106–07.

[20] F. H. Hinsley et al., *British Intelligence in the Second World War,* Vol. 2 (London: HMSO, 1991), p. 530.

[21] It should be noted that some more recent studies do mention *Graf Zeppelin* although provide no further consideration, see James P. Levy, *The Royal Navy's Home Fleet in World War II* (Basingstoke: Macmillan, 2003); Christopher Mann, *British Policy and Strategy Towards Norway, 1941–45* (Basingstoke: Macmillan, 2012).

[22] Maiolo, *The Royal Navy,* pp. 11–37; Christopher M. Bell, *The Royal Navy, Seapower and Strategy Between the Wars* (Basingstoke: Palgrave Macmillan, 1998), pp. 99–116.

[23] ADM 116/3373, PD04586/34, Limitation of German Naval Armaments, 29.6.34.

on paper, they combined the firepower of a cruiser with the capabilities of a small air group.[24]

Captain Edward King, the Director of Plans (DoP), addressed the implications that December. German carriers, from the outset assumed to be bigger and more capable than existing British ones, would limit the number of carriers the Royal Navy could deploy to the Mediterranean or Far East. Gauging the threat was difficult in the absence of any details. Rear Admiral Gerald Dickens, the DNI, thought that the Germans would want two carriers and would be able to construct them within three years—one to be completed in 1939, the other in 1942.[25] Captain Gerard Muirhead-Gould, the naval attaché in Berlin, reported in February 1935 that it was evident that the Germans had been studying foreign carrier developments with great interest. Although there was no specific evidence, there seemed to be a preference for a medium-sized vessel and two seaplane-carrying cruisers rather than a larger 22,000 tons carrier.[26] As Germany might be afforded a construction quota of up to thirty-three percent of British tonnage under a treaty arrangement, this would give it an allocation of 42,000 tons for carriers. In view of the preference for medium-sized vessels, this would in turn equate to at least three vessels. A few weeks later, Muirhead-Gould reported that a conversation with Commander Leopold Bürkner of the *Marineleitung* had revealed that carriers were at that time a secondary consideration.[27]

During the Anglo-German discussions concerning a naval agreement conducted throughout the late spring of 1935, the Admiralty made no particular provision for German carriers or maritime aviation. The issue of the legality of German air armaments had been rendered mute by Hermann Göring's public announcement of the existence of the *Luftwaffe* on 10 March. The Anglo-German Naval Agreement signed on 18 June set German naval construction at thirty-five percent of British tonnage and allowed for warship types hitherto banned under the Treaty of Versailles—U-boats and aircraft carriers. Shortly thereafter, the Germans presented their building program through to 1942 that included 44,000 tons earmarked for carriers.[28] How this allocation would be employed remained open. The first actual details came courtesy of the Germans themselves in October 1936

---

[24]   R. D. Layman, *The Hybrid Warship: The Amalgamation of Big Guns and Aircraft* (London: Conway, 1991).

[25]   ADM 116/3373, PD04754/34, 12.12.1934, Germany's Naval Forces—1939 and 1942.

[26]   TNA, Foreign Office File (hereinafter FO) 371/18860, C1536/206/8, 26 February 1935, MG to Phipps.

[27]   FO 371/18860, No. 294 (96/14/35).

[28]   J. A. Maiolo, "The Admiralty and the Anglo-German Naval Agreement of 18 June 1935," *Diplomacy and Statecraft* X (1999), pp. 87–126; Stephen Roskill, *Naval Policy Between the Wars,* Vol. II (Barnsley: Seaforth, 2016/1968), pp. 305–06.

when Captain Erwin Waßner, the German naval attaché in London, provided the necessary particulars in accordance with reciprocal exchange of information under the terms of the 1930 London Naval Treaty to which the Germans were now subject. This was very limited information and merely outlined that on 1 October, aircraft carrier B of 19,250 tons standard displacement and with a length of 250m, beam of 27m, and mean draught of 5.6m at standard displacement, had been laid down. The ship would carry guns of up to 15cm and the date of completion remained unknown.[29]

From the British perspective this was a surprisingly long and narrow vessel and S. V. Goodall, the Director of Naval Construction (DNC), speculated that either the Germans were not dividing the deck into separate flying-off and landing spaces or that they were emphasizing speed with the design capable of 32kts.[30] It was now clear that a large platform was being pursued and inevitably there was confusion as to what had happened to carrier A.[31] In November, Captain Thomas Troubridge, Muirhead-Gould's replacement in Berlin, offered an explanation that it seemed two designs had been prepared, but for "technical reasons" it had been found more convenient to start work on B and that A would be laid down when possible.[32] At this stage, it was not even known where the carrier was under construction. In mid-December, the Germans informed the British that A, identical in all respects, had been laid down on 1 December.[33]

Further details came a year later in December 1937 when the Germans provided more information under the provisions of the Anglo-German Naval Agreement of July 1937. The dimensions of the carriers had not changed, but their turbines were given as being capable of developing 110,000 SHP/PS, 32kts, mounting sixteen 15cm guns, ten 10.5cm, and lighter anti-aircraft (AA) armament, and capable of embarking forty aircraft.[34] This confirmed Goodall's earlier assumption that these were to be fast vessels and ones equipped with a very heavy AA battery by British standards. No more information appears to have been obtained and the DNC never conducted further analysis as was undertaken for other German warships.[35]

On 8 December 1938, *Graf Zeppelin* was launched in Kiel with most of the Third Reich's senior military-political leadership in attendance. The launch was reported in the German and international press, but what exactly the Admiralty

---

29   ADM 116/3368, Mar.No. 847/36, 8th October 1936.

30   ADM 116/3368, DNC comments, 26.10.1936.

31   ADM 116/3368, see DofP and DNI comments on the jacket of M05271/36.

32   ADM 116/3368, Reference Sheet G. 196/36, 19th November 1936.

33   ADM 116/3368, Mar.No. ?/36, 16.12.1936.

34   ADM 116/3368, Mprar.Nr 143 g, 4 December 1937.

35   ADM 229/19, Legend of Particulars Scharnhorst & Gneisenau (1938).

knew and when is unclear. *The Illustrated London News* published a short story complete with a large, impressive bow-on photograph of the carrier shortly before launch. It is fair to assume the NID provided the British press with the known details of the carrier as the technical information printed matched that given above. It would be speculation to assume that the Admiralty also gave its views to the British press, but nonetheless, in the absence of any official record, the assessment printed by *The Illustrated London News* is noteworthy: "Although it was expected that these aircraft-carriers would be of revolutionary design, the "Graf Zeppelin" is similar to our own ships of these type and not quite so large as the 22,000-ton "Ark Royal" which is just going into service."[36] The 1939 edition of *Jane's Fighting Ships* added a press agency picture of *Graf Zeppelin* shortly after launch to the carrier's entry, and a second was added for the 1940 edition.[37] These photographs were oblique shots from which little assessment could be made concerning the validity of the dimensions the Germans had provided.

That the launch represented a milestone in the German effort and that this raised concerns in the Admiralty may be inferred from the fact that a month later, Rear Admiral James Troup, Dickens' successor as DNI, wrote to Troubridge in Berlin with the request to obtain details on German maritime aviation. Specifically of interest was information concerning what types of carrier aircraft existed and whether carrier squadrons had been formed.[38] While neither Troubridge nor NID had any information on German maritime aviation, the Air Ministry was able to supply an overview of its development and organization. It had been rightly identified that *186 Gruppe* was intended as the carrier air unit and that its squadrons would be equipped with wheeled variants of the floatplanes then in use.[39] This was a reasonably accurate assessment for the time and, although the Germans would go on to employ navalized versions of the Me109 fighter and Ju87 dive-bomber, this decision had only recently been taken.

The bulk of British information stemmed from the exchanges, and what little information was obtained beyond this came from press photographs, observations in foreign ports, or port visits in Germany. The latter were rare in the case of new launches, and while the British vice consul in Hamburg did get a look at *Bismarck* shortly after launch, there is no indication that any British official or informant visited Kiel at the time. There were few clandestine sources to inform naval intelligence. Throughout the interwar years, the best sources on German naval

---

[36]   "The German Navy's First Aircraft-Carrier," *The Illustrated London News,* 17 December 1938.

[37]   *Jane's Fighting Ships of World War II* (London: Studio Editions 1992 reprint of 1946/47 original), p. 146.

[38]   TNA, Air Ministry File (hereinafter AIR) 2/9376, Troup to Troubridge, 30th January 1939.

[39]   AIR 2/9376, S.49707/A.I.1, 4th February 1939.

armaments were the renowned naval correspondent, Hector Bywater, and Dr. Karl Krueger, a German naval engineer and British spy. Bywater's naval expertise and links with the Admiralty stretched back decades, and he had been the first foreign correspondent to report the true specifications of the first *Panzerschiff*. By the 1930s, these links had broken and the focus of his investigative journalism had shifted to the Imperial Japanese Navy.[40] Krueger had worked for the Secret Intelligence Service (SIS) since late 1914 and provided regular and accurate information from German shipyards throughout the First World War, resuming his role in the 1930s.[41] While his information was instrumental in establishing that Germany was preparing to construct U-boats, there is no evidence that either Krueger or Bywater, or any similar source, provided technical information on the carriers. Thus, Admiralty intelligence on the German surface fleet remained limited and would continue to be so in the opening stages of the war.[42]

The first wartime sighting of *Graf Zeppelin* reportedly occurred in October 1939 when she was photographed at Kiel and, based on this, her completion was expected by February or March 1940.[43] The so-called Oslo Letter, written by Hans Ferdinand Mayer and handed over in November 1939, contained on its first page a short reference to a carrier lying at anchor in Kiel and slated for completion in April 1940.[44] Mayer did however wrongly identify the name as *Franken*—quite likely adding to the confusion about whether two German carriers existed.[45] Despite the

---

[40]   William H. Honan, *Bywater: The Man Who Invented the Pacific War* (London: Futura, 1991).

[41]   Keith Jeffery, *MI6: The History of the Secret Intelligence Service, 1909–1949* (London: Bloomsbury, 2010), pp. 297–300.

[42]   F. H. Hinsley et al., *British Intelligence in the Second World War: Its Influence on Strategy and Operations,* Vol. I (London: HMSO, 1979), pp. 505–07.

[43]   TNA, Cabinet Office File (hereinafter CAB) 66/11/42, W. P. (40) 362, 4 September 1940. The source is unclear. At this early stage in the war, the activities of Sydney Cotton's "Heston" Flight activities are too nebulous to precisely reconstruct. According to Norman Denning, involved in the establishment of the OIC, the first useful aerial photographs were taken by a Beaufort from Bomber Command's photo-reconnaissance flight on 4.11.39 over Wilhelmshaven. As Beauforts were not yet in service, he presumably meant a Blenheim. See Sir Norman Denning, "Erfolge und Misserfolge bei der Nutzung von Aufklärungserkenntnissen," in Jürgen Rohwer and Eberhard Jäckel, eds., *Die Funkaufklärung und ihre Rolle im Zweiten Weltkrieg* (Stuttgart: Motorbuch, 1979), p. 275. If the intelligence came from ground-based observation, there is no indication in the existing history as to the potential source.

[44]   AIR 40/2572, Oslo Letter; R. V. Jones, *Most Secret War* (London: Hamish Hamilton, 1978), pp. 67–71.

[45]   The 1939 edition of *Jane's Fighting Ships* reported the German carriers' names as *Graf Zeppelin* and *B,* while for unknown reasons in the 1940 edition (issued in January 1941) they were designated as *Graf Zeppelin* and *Deutschland.* Why a carrier should have been given the name previously assigned to one of the *Panzerschiffe* is unclear.

paucity of information and the misnaming of the carrier, this seems to have caught the interest of British intelligence. At the end of November, when air intelligence interrogated the sole survivor of a Ju88 bomber that had been shot down in mid-October, he was asked about aircraft carriers. The chance of a *Luftwaffe* non-commissioned officer knowing anything about the progress of naval construction was remote, and all he reported was that *Graf Zeppelin* was not yet ready.[46]

A number of months would again pass before further information was obtained and, in the meantime, the Admiralty continued to assume that the carrier had commenced trials and would reach completion in April or May.[47] The first operational sortie of the longer-range Spitfire PR1C variant over northern Germany on 7 April photographed the Kiel area for the first time, sighting the carrier in the harbor.[48] In the Joint Intelligence Committee (JIC) appreciation of German naval forces available for an attack on the British Isles at the beginning of June 1940, *Graf Zeppelin* was considered as part of the German frontline strength.[49] Kiel seems not to have been covered by another Photo Reconnaissance (PR) flight until the end of June, followed by another in early July.[50] By August, air reconnaissance had lost *Graf Zeppelin,* nor was she relocated in the following weeks, yet it was assumed she was serviceable.[51] On 1 July the RAF had bombed Kiel, and while the raid had caused little material damage, it prompted the *Kriegsmarine* to disperse the large concentration of warships that had accumulated in the port, and the carrier was moved to the safety of the eastern Baltic. At the beginning of September, the British believed that the *Kriegsmarine* was undertaking trials on a carrier believed to be *Graf Zeppelin.* What was less clear was whether the second carrier existed. For the first time it dawned upon the analysts that both carriers had "never been located simultaneously and it is possible that in fact only one exists; progress on the second having been suspended on or before the start of the war."[52] This is what had in fact happened. Intelligence arriving in London had still erroneously differentiated between carrier A and B.

---

[46]   AIR 40/2394, K. G. 25. Ju. 88: Interrogation of Survivor, 30th November 1939.

[47]   ADM 1/10617, Methods of Attack on German Ships Bismarck and Graf Zeppelin (27.03.1940).

[48]   On the background, see Alfred Price, *Targeting the Reich: Allied Photographic Reconnaissance over Europe, 1939–45* (London: Greenhill, 2013), p. 13; AIR 34/243, Evidence in Camera, p. 4.

[49]   CAB 66/9/35, C. O. S. (40) 432 (J.I.C), 6 June 1940. Interpretations varied, only a week earlier an Admiralty assessment of the German frontline strength stated, "Undergoing trials; may be available for active service now," ADM 223/7484, 29.5.40, Appendix I.

[50]   AIR 40/1637. This is an estimate based on daily intelligence overviews.

[51]   CAB 66/10/48, W. P. (40) 317, 16 August 1940; CAB 66/11/14, W. P. (40) 334, 23 August 1940.

[52]   CAB 66/11/42, W. P. (40) 362, 4 September 1940.

For nearly a year, there is no record of any new intelligence having been obtained and *Graf Zeppelin* remained an unknown factor. The ongoing appreciation of German naval strength continued to credit the *Kriegsmarine* with an operational carrier by August 1941 and, presumably to err on the safe side, with a second by August 1942.[53] The destruction of *Bismarck* in May had numerous implications. The pivotal role carriers played in conducting operations beyond the reach of land-based airpower became clear to both sides. From the British perspective, it also became apparent that the German warships were most likely larger than thought, as the interrogation of the surviving crew offered evidence that pre-war German official data did not conform to the correct methodology. The interrogations provided a first indication of *Graf Zeppelin's* status as most prisoners confirmed that she was lying in Gdynia, was not being worked on, and had had her guns removed.[54]

The period from the autumn of 1940 through to the autumn of 1941 also saw a reorganization and expansion of the British intelligence community in response to the failures during the German offensives in the west, the invasion threat, and the developing Atlantic campaign. This was important in relation to the understanding of German naval strength and the operational availability of major combatants. The lack of human intelligence would become a key weakness in assessing the activity within German yards. By contrast, during the First World War Krueger and others had provided such information that had been important in assessing the status of the High Seas Fleet following the Battle of Jutland and its post-1916 decline.[55] Signals intelligence proved to be a far less useful source when it came to charting German naval construction as there was very little radio traffic associated with the process. Although, as will be shown, a very small number of Enigma decrypts were pivotal in influencing the Admiralty's perception in 1942–43.

The key to monitoring the development of the *Kriegsmarine's* operational strength lay in the expansion and development of the RAF's PR capability. A full treatment of this is beyond the scope of this chapter, but it is important to note that, from a minimal capability in the first year of the war, rapid improvements were being made across the board with more and better aircraft, cameras, and photographic techniques.[56] The RAF continued to incrementally increase the depth of its flights as more PR1D Spitfires and then, from September 1941, a small number of Mosquitoes became available. While Stettin had been first photographed in late October 1940, none of the ports and yards at the eastern end of the Baltic—Königsberg, Gdynia, and Danzig—were until August 1941 because they remained out of range. However,

---

[53]   ADM 1/11317, Appendix I, German Fleet as estimated at 31.3.41.

[54]   ADM 186/803, BR1907(24), Bismarck Interrogation of Survivors.

[55]   Jeffery, *MI6*, pp. 83–85.

[56]   Hinsley, *British Intelligence*, Vol. 2, p. 3; Price, *Targeting*, p. 101; Roy M. Stanley II, *World War II Photo Intelligence* (London: Sidgwick & Jackson, 1982), pp. 107–11.

the focus of PR work in 1941 remained on ports in the Low Countries and France in view of German surface operations in the Atlantic and the latent threat of invasion. It was not until 1942 that regular flights over Baltic ports were possible and the introduction of higher resolution and oblique cameras improved the product. Alongside the ability to penetrate farther into the Reich and take better photographs of targets, their interpretation was put on a more systematic footing. In November 1940, the staff for the interpretation of naval imagery numbered two and this was progressively expanded as the Combined Interpretation Unit moved to RAF Medmenham in April 1941. By the end of 1941, the naval "A" Section numbered seven, and by the end of 1942 it had increased to eleven.[57] From mid-1941, aerial photography had been developed sufficiently to provide reasonable estimates on the state of completion of a warship.[58]

The first actual sighting of *Graf Zeppelin* since the summer of 1940 occurred in September 1941 when she was observed lying off Stettin.[59] The carrier's wartime movements may be surmised as follows. After being moved from Kiel to Gdynia in July 1940, she remained there until being moved back west to Stettin in June 1941 to take her out of range of potential Soviet air attacks. In November, she was moved back to Gdynia where she remained until early December 1942. She was then brought back to Kiel for completion, but only two months into the works, on 2 February 1943, the project was abandoned. In April, she was towed back to Stettin and moored in her final wartime resting place with only a small caretaker crew.[60]

As RAF PR flights over the Eastern Baltic increased throughout 1942, so too did the sightings of *Graf Zeppelin*.[61] In April 1942, the JIC assessment was that she might be in service by September and, given that the Germans were concentrating on U-boat and small craft construction, she would be the last major reinforcement to the fleet.[62] One factor that been taken out of the equation was that it was clear that work on the French carrier *Joffre* had halted and that the Germans were making no effort to complete the vessel.[63] A complete break-down of each sighting is

57   AIR 34/85, ACIU Historical Record of "A" Section.

58   ADM 229/25, N. I. D. 0068, German Naval Building in German Yards and in Occupied Territory, 12.8.41; Stanley, *World War II,* pp. 271–79.

59   AIR 15/359, AOC-in-C's Coastal Command Daily Conference, 9.9.41. The move back to Gdynia was also noted in mid-November, AIR 15/359, AOC-in-C's Coastal Command Daily Conference, 17.11.41.

60   Ulrich H. J. Israel, *Einziger deutscher Flugzeugträger Graf Zeppelin* (Herford: Koehlers, 1994), pp. 154–62.

61   AIR 29/255, Interpretation Report 4196, 5.10.1942.

62   FO 371/30895, J. I. C. (42) 113, 10 April 1942, Axis Strength and Policy, 1942; see also ADM 1/12126, DoP to FSL, Aircraft Requirements, 13 March 1942.

63   ADM 229/25, NID 0068 (1941); AIR 29/256, Interpretation Report NOS5, 21.10.42.

neither possible, owing to the gaps in the records of flights in 1941 until the autumn of 1942, nor necessary, as many sightings yielded little more than that she was in her berth in the naval port at Gdynia. It is unclear how regularly PR flights to the area would occur at this stage, but every one or two weeks is a reasonable assumption. This, however, does not mean individual targets would be seen on each flight as cloud cover could obscure the target and the altitude from which the photographs were taken affected the amount of detail that could be picked out.[64]

The imagery obtained in the summer offered differing views as to the status of *Graf Zeppelin*. Interpretation at Medmenham concluded that although she looked complete, there was little active work going on and she seemed to be berthed in a less active part of the harbor.[65] At the War Cabinet level it was only reported that she was "to outward appearance complete."[66] Similarly, in early August it was understood that her main and secondary armament were installed and thus she should be nearing completion.[67] This was incorrect or a misunderstanding. From August onwards, increasing German efforts to camouflage her appearance were noted and it appeared that work was in progress. The addition of a superstructure around parts of the hull suggested that her heavy AA battery was being fitted and this could be taken as a barometer of the carrier's readiness. There does not, though, ever seem to have been direct photographic evidence of heavy AA guns being installed. Understanding what work could be carried out at Gdynia was an issue itself as this was a new naval base and little was known about its facilities and output.[68] It is important to note that although the bulk of remaining material related to intelligence on *Graf Zeppelin* stems from PR, there were other sources. Nothing can be said about their nature beyond the fact that they existed, and even if they were largely incorrect, they still shaped the overall perception.[69]

The process of concealing the carrier's appearance continued into the late autumn and eventually involved the extensive use of netting and other structural camouflage.[70] Camouflaging a warship of this size was a massive undertaking and

---

[64] Based on the PR images of *Graf Zeppelin* that have survived, one might infer that less than ten flights provided tangible material beyond visual sighting. For the earliest shots, see AIR 40/347. Some are reprinted in Price, *Targeting* and Roy M. Stanley, *Looking Down on War: Axis Warships* (Barnsley: Pen & Sword, 2011).

[65] AIR 34/44, Monthly Interpretation Review 5, June 1942.

[66] CAB 66/25/31, W. P. (42) 251, 11 June 1942.

[67] CAB 66/27/23, W. P. (42) 343, 6 August 1942.

[68] AIR 29/259, Interpretation Report No. AS23, 12.12.42.

[69] For example, at least on occasion the Soviets supplied details, ADM 223/289, Meeting with Russian Naval Officer, 14.4.42. Interestingly enough, German naval intelligence was aware that the British had obtained at least one (false) report on *Graf Zeppelin's* status, see *Seekriegsleitung Kriegstagebuch* entry for 11.11.41.

[70] AIR 29/258, Interpretation Report E40, 19.11.42.

it was reasonable to assume that this signaled work was underway. The complexity of deriving useful intelligence through PR may be seen from the fact it took numerous flights after the sighting at Stettin in September 1941 to gather photographs of sufficient quality to allow the carrier's dimensions to be established. Obtaining good resolution top down rather than oblique angle photographs was the key to this.[71] What this showed was that *Graf Zeppelin,* just like *Bismarck* or *Tirpitz,* was larger than previously believed.

The move from Gdynia back to Kiel in December represented a significant development. Although the move had occurred at the beginning of the month, it was not until 23 December that the carrier was identified as being in Kiel— and this too was only inferred as she was located under very heavy camouflage in the Southern Floating Dock.[72] The problem at Kiel was also that the Germans had installed smoke generators that could quickly obscure the targets, which meant that PR flights needed to take the Germans by surprise to gain useful images and this did not always happen.[73] Her continued presence in Kiel continued to be monitored throughout January and February, but it was not until March, when she was taken out of the floating dock and brought alongside the quay at the entrance of the inner dockyard basing, that new unobscured images could be obtained.[74]

By coincidence, she was also photographed on her last day in Kiel although this was not known at the time. At noon on 20 April, a pass over the harbor spotted her, but by the time a second pass occurred in the early evening, she had gone. Two days later she was spotted at anchor off Swinemünde.[75] A rare naval Enigma decrypt that day alerted the Admiralty to the carrier's arrival in Stettin.[76] That PR did not provide instantaneous results can also be seen in this final phase of intelligence gathering as it was not until the second half of June that A Section concluded that work on her had ceased. This was assumed because she was lying alongside an underdeveloped river bank outside Stettin and receiving no attention,

---

[71]   AIR 34/48, Monthly Interpretation Review 9, October 1942; AIR 29/258, Interpretation Report S7, 1.11.42; AIR 34/234, Evidence in Camera, p. 33.

[72]   AIR 29/261, Interpretation Report No. 4461, 28.1.43. It appears that the British had some earlier knowledge of the move from a ground-based source; what this was remains unclear. It is reasonable to assume that this was from Captain Denham, the very well-informed naval attaché to Sweden.

[73]   AIR 29/265, Use of Smoke Screens over Enemy Ports, February 1943.

[74]   AIR 29/264, Interpretation Report No. 4566, 22.2.43; AIR 29/266, Interpretation Report No. 4644, 7.3.44.

[75]   CAB 66/36/21, W. P. (43) 171, 22 April 1942.

[76]   TNA, Government Communications Headquarters file (hereinafter HW) 1/1629 CX/MSS/2471/T1.

but a more detailed assessment could not be made from imagery intelligence.[77] Only two weeks earlier, another undisclosed source reported that she was carrying out trials in the Baltic.[78] Thus, although imagery intelligence provided a considerable portion of the information, it was intermittent and only part of the intelligence picture. From then on she would occasionally still be photographed, but there was no further evidence of any attempt to bring her into service.[79] Even when in February 1944 intelligence noted that all the remaining German heavy ships (cruisers and above) were being made ready for service, *Graf Zeppelin* remained the exception.[80]

The Assessment of *Graf Zeppelin*

The British experience assessing *Graf Zeppelin* needs to be put into its contemporary context and seen through both the peace and wartime perspectives. Understanding enemy developments has always presented intelligence analysts and military planners with challenges.[81] This is compounded when such capabilities encompass weapon systems the opponent has hitherto never fielded, or that themselves are at the cutting edge of military innovation subject to unknowns in terms of their technical and operational performance. Enemy capabilities often tend to be over-or underestimated because of limited intelligence, and assessments are likely to be shaped to existing perceptions or experiences.[82] Understanding foreign capital ship development represented an increasingly difficult task as the twentieth century progressed, and the Royal Navy was not alone in this regard. The United States Navy (USN) failed to envisage that the Japanese might undertake wholescale modernization of their first-generation dreadnought battleships, putting the Americans at a disadvantage during the initial stages of the Solomons campaign.[83]

---

[77]   AIR 41/48, The RAF in Maritime War, Vol. IV, p. 353; AIR 29/284, Interpretation Report No. S41, 2.7.43.

[78]   CAB 66/37/37, W. P. (43) 237, 10th June 1943.

[79]   CAB 66/38/37, W. P. (43) 287, 1st July 1943; CAB 66/41/26, W. P. (43) 426, 30th September 1943; CAB 66/43/25, W. P. (43) 525, 18th November 1943.

[80]   CAB 66/47/31, W. P. (44) 131, 24th February 1944; CAB 66/49/4, W. P. (44) 204, 13th April 1944.

[81]   Michael I. Handel, "Intelligence and the Problem of Strategic Surprise," *The Journal of Strategic Studies* 7:3 (1984), pp. 229–81; "Technological Surprise in War," *Intelligence and National Security* 2:1 (1987), pp. 1–53; Mark M. Lowenthal, *Intelligence: From Secrets to Policy* (Washington, DC: CQ Press, 2009), pp. 111–25, 234–38.

[82]   Michael I. Handel, "The Politics of Intelligence," *Intelligence and National Security* 2:4 (1987), p. 18.

[83]   Thomas G. Mahnken, "Gazing at the Sun: The Office of Naval Intelligence and Japanese Innovation, 1918–1941," *Intelligence and National Security* 11:3 (1996), pp. 424–41.

Nor were the Americans aware of the true specifications of the *Yamato*-class super-battleships before they encountered one, *Musashi,* for the first time in the Sibuyan Sea on 24 October 1944.[84]

Understanding a foreign aircraft carrier represents another step up in terms of complexity as the capability encompasses the sum of the vessel and its equipment, the air group together with the ordnance it can deliver, and the doctrine with which the system is employed. More variables make it hard to gauge the efficacy of the whole system. The evolution of the aircraft carrier has neither been linear nor uniform, yet navies' efforts to judge their competitors has often been subject to mirror imaging. In the early 1930s, the British assumed that the high figure of seventy-four aircraft quoted for the American carriers *Lexington* and *Saratoga* included spare airframes rather than being an indicator of American intention to operate a large air group.[85] By this stage, the USN was already conducting air operations on a larger scale than the RN. Japanese success in the first six months of the Pacific War rested upon a hitherto unprecedented degree of concentration of carrier forces in the shape of the First Air Fleet, a development American and British intelligence had failed to detect or envisage.[86]

As mentioned, the Admiralty assumed from the outset that the Germans would want to acquire aircraft carriers as part of any naval rearmament program to create a modern and balanced fleet structure. The Admiralty also believed the Germans possessed the technical expertise and industrial capacity to bring carriers into service within a reasonable timeframe. While the view of the British naval attaché in Paris that the Germans would be considerably more efficient in their first attempt than the French had been was premature, it reflected the perception of German capabilities.[87] This was also based on the experience of having inspected German warships after the First World War, which had shown British and German designs to have had their own merits, but were of equal overall quality.[88] What limited information the British had up to 1939 also suggested that the German carrier design was similar to the contemporary British approach, and most likely employment, rather than that of the Americans or Japanese.

---

[84] Malcolm Muir, Jr., "Rearming in a Vacuum: United States Navy Intelligence and the Japanese Capital Ship Threat, 1936–1945," *The Journal of Military History* 54:4 (1990), pp. 482–84.

[85] Norman Friedman, *British Carrier Aviation: The Evolution of the Ships and Their Aircraft* (London: Conway, 1988), p. 114.

[86] Mark R. Peattie, *Sunburst: The Rise of Japanese Naval Air Power, 1909–1941* (Annapolis: Naval Institute Press, 2001), pp. 147–67.

[87] FO 371/18736, A 6246/22/45, 12 July 1934.

[88] D. K. Brown, *A Century of Naval Construction: A History of the Royal Corps of Naval Constructors* (London: Conway, 1983).

The practical implication of the Germans laying down carriers was that the Navy would, in turn, need to keep more carriers in home waters limiting its deployable strength to other theaters. While even the first tentative war plans against Germany from 1933 foresaw the use of two carriers in home waters, the realization in late 1934 that Germany had an interest in acquiring its own carriers now made this a necessity. If Germany possessed even just one carrier, the British would have to maintain a minimum of two in home waters to ensure superiority in the North Sea.[89] Simply put, potential German carriers limited what forces could be sent to the Far East in the event of a crisis with Japan. Following the conclusion of the Anglo-German Naval Treaty, press and international reaction focused more on the Germans being allowed to reacquire U-boats, but from the Admiralty perspective, the carriers were more problematic.[90] There was a certain paradox at work because while the Admiralty needed to concede German carrier tonnage to control overall German naval construction, this would inevitably influence British long-term planning.

The arrival of the first limited technical details from Berlin in October 1936 complicated British plans as, until this point, the Admiralty had continued to assume the Germans were interested in a medium-sized design.[91] The implications for trade protection in home and Atlantic waters were profound. Aviation was considered a greater threat to maritime communications than submarines owing to the larger number of aircraft and their ability to deploy faster.[92] If Germany was limited to land-based maritime aviation, the threat could be contained to the North Sea.[93] While commerce raiding cruisers or auxiliary warships might embark some seaplanes, their use was restricted by sea states and would also not greatly enhance the range at which reconnaissance could be conducted. However, carrier aircraft were superior in all regards and could operate in poorer conditions.[94] The larger the carrier, the more effective it was as an operating platform.[95] German carriers would greatly increase the difficulty of trade protection as, with air support, raiders could cover more ocean and operate farther from focal or assembly points.

---

[89]   ADM 1/27413, Notes on Blockade of Germany (May 33); Note 31st December 1934.

[90]   See, for example, FO 371/18736 A624922/45, 9 July 1935; press cuttings in CAB 104/29 and FO 371/18860.

[91]   ADM 116/3368, M05271/36, Notes by DoP Capt. Tom Philips, 15.10.36.

[92]   Lambert, "Seapower," pp. 93–94; Joseph A. Maiolo, "The Knockout Blow against the Import System: Admiralty Expectations of Nazi Germany's Naval Strategy, 1934–9," *Historical Research* 72:178 (1999), p. 213; ADM 1/27413, Courses of Action Open to Germany Plans Division, 20.3.35.

[93]   ADM 199/2365, Naval Appreciation (1937) of War with Germany 1939 (Volume 1).

[94]   ADM 199/3, C. B. 01764(39), Protection of Shipping at Sea 1939.

[95]   ADM 178/137, German Naval Strategy revised intelligence 1936–37.

A carrier operating in conjunction with surface raiders optimized for commerce warfare constituted the worst-case scenario.

The slight conciliation was that by 1936, delays in German naval construction were becoming apparent, and as yet, no significant progress had been made on the carriers. The pre-war assessment of German naval construction was that the existing yards had the capacity to produce the fleet afforded under the Anglo-German Naval Treaty by 1940. The principal restrictions on output might be labor, the production of armor plate, and manufacture of complex gun-mountings.[96] In this regard, the assessment was wrong and overestimated the state of German industry and resources. There were deficiencies in all areas, with major warships running around two years behind schedule. This overestimate was in line with the wider problems British intelligence had with assessing the German pre-war economy and industrial output.[97] The fact that the projected German carrier strength through to 1942 lay at three units became a factor in the Admiralty's considerations concerning capital ship, and specifically carrier, construction for the 1939–41 programs.[98] It is unclear to what extent the Admiralty began to consider how German carriers might actually be dealt with before the war. Trade defense wargames still seem to have focused on the threat posed by what the Germans actually had in service.[99] Yet at least one exercise was held at sea in which the defense of large convoys against a combination of surface, submarine, and air attacks was simulated. The profile of the attacking force, composed of fast battleships and a carrier, matched that of potential future German raiding groups. The results were not encouraging either, as the defending forces incurred heavy losses.[100] From a pre-war position, there was no reason to assume that the *Kriegsmarine* would not be able to deploy a carrier within the next few years. Outwardly, German rearmament efforts seemed on course, the launching of *Graf Zeppelin* and *Bismarck* within weeks of one another was a clear reminder.

When war broke out in September 1939, Anglo-French naval superiority over Germany was considerable; nonetheless, with a view of short-term German qualitative advantages, the Admiralty was interested in reducing German capital ship strength. This did not materialize as Allied submarines found few opportunities to attack German warships in the North Sea, proposed Motor Torpedo Boat attacks in German waters were deemed too risky at this stage, and RAF bomber attacks against German posts proved costly failures.[101] At the same time, the Germans had

96   CAB 4/24 1252-B, German Naval Construction.

97   Wark, *Ultimate Enemy*, pp. 155–87.

98   ADM 205/80, Revised Forecasts of the Cost of Defence Programme (1/1938).

99   ADM 1/9466, Atlantic Trade Protection (1938).

100   ADM 186/159, Ex Z. P. Serial 8, 14–15th March 1938.

101   ADM 1/9899, Early Reduction of German Capital Ship Strength.

sunk the carrier *Courageous* and the battleship *Royal Oak,* as well as badly damaging other major warships.[102] Throughout the autumn, considerable resources had been expended in hunting *Deutschland* and *Graf Spee.* Tracking a small number of German warships, let alone containing them to the North Sea, had proved impossible. *Scharnhorst* and *Gneisenau* had been able to slip into the North Atlantic and sunk the armed merchant cruiser *Rawalpindi.* While the immediate risk to Atlantic shipping receded with the destruction of *Graf Spee* in mid-December, and the U-boat threat was contained, the overall situation was far from favorable.[103] The situation in the Mediterranean was progressively deteriorating, and with a view to more and more powerful German warships entering service in 1940, protecting Allied maritime communications would become an increasingly complex problem. What constituted the greatest threat in the opinion of the Director of Plans, Captain Victor Danckwerts, was:

> the aircraft carrier GRAF ZEPPELIN which is likely to provide our most disagreeable problem. If this ship, accompanied by BISMARCK or one of the SCHARNHORTS [sic], were to break out, we should have to be prepared for very serious depredations on our trade. In good weather the aircraft carrier could reconnoitre some 20,000 square miles in one day and could hardly fail to locate some of our large convoys. Her reconnaissance would serve equally to defend the attackers from our hunting groups. . ..
>
> The conclusion is that the BISMARCK herself is not likely to prove the menace that would at first seem likely. It is the aircraft carrier which is going to turn the scales in favour of any raider."[104]

With *Graf Zeppelin* soon expected to be in service, it was possible that she would be an element in the German raids into the Atlantic in the coming summer. Neutralizing the carrier before this could take place became an Admiralty priority. Following the losses incurred in raids in 1939, the Air Ministry was reluctant to risk sending any further bombers over the heavily defended Schleswig area to reach Kiel. Bombing the carrier while alongside in port was precluded under the existing bombardment policy, and catching her while at sea undergoing trials would be near impossible owing to the lack of intelligence.[105] As the RAF's

---

[102]   Levy, *Home Fleet,* pp. 35–48.

[103]   Andrew Lambert, "The Only British Advantage: Seapower and Strategy," in Michael H. Clemmesen and Marcus S. Faulkner, eds., *Northern European Overture to War, 1939–1941* (Leiden: Brill, 2013), pp. 62–70.

[104]   ADM 1/10617, D. of P. (comments) 29.1.40.

[105]   ADM 1/10617, Methods of Attack on German Ships Bismarck and Graf Zeppelin, 27 March 1940.

torpedo-bombers lacked the range to reach Kiel, this left the Admiralty with little choice than prepare for a carrier strike using Swordfish torpedo-bombers. Preparation for this was underway by the time the Germans launched the invasion of Denmark and Norway in early April, and continued until at least early May. The German victories in Norway, the low countries, and France, followed by air attacks on Britain in the summer, meant that the specific threat posed by *Graf Zeppelin* declined. Following the Battle of Britain, the Atlantic campaign began in earnest in the autumn with U-boat and Focke-Wulf Condors operating from newly-acquired French and Norwegian bases. To this the *Kriegsmarine* incrementally expanded the scope of surface operations reaching its zenith with *Rheinübung* in May 1941. By this stage in the war the Royal Navy faced an ever-expanding series of tasks and the focus remained on immediate concerns in the Atlantic and Mediterranean. As it was highly unlikely that the *Kriegsmarine* would risk sailing a single carrier alone, the threat posed by *Graf Zeppelin* could be linked to the overall disposition of the German surface fleet. With most of the active *Kriegsmarine* heavy units operating from Brest in 1941, these would either have to return to Germany to pick up the carrier or she would have to come out with the as yet unfinished battleship *Tirpitz*.

Graf Zeppelin returned to the forefront of Admiralty thinking in the spring of 1942 owing to several developments. First, the loss or long-term neutralization of six British capital ships within a few weeks in November and December 1941 eroded the margin of superiority the Royal Navy had possessed, while at the same time the Japanese entry into the war had added another active theater of operations. The arrival of *Tirpitz* at Trondheim in mid-January had significant implications for the Home Fleet. Like most major German deployments to date, the battleship had to evade British detection. Only a few weeks later, the surprise dash up the English Channel by *Scharnhorst, Gneisenau,* and *Prinz Eugen* suggested that the *Kriegsmarine* was moving its base of operations for the surface fleet from France to Norway. By February, the task of running the Arctic convoys was becoming more complicated. Although *Gneisenau* was put out of the war in the aftermath of *Zerberus,* a fact not fully appreciated by the Admiralty until later, *Prinz Eugen* was sent north immediately.

From the moment *Tirpitz's* presence in Norwegian waters had been detected, Admiral John Tovey, C-in-C Home Fleet, had been forced to send a significant portion of his strength to sea. Employing the whole capital strength of the Home Fleet at sea, covering every convoy movement, would lead to a steady decline in its efficiency by interrupting refits and leave.[106] He wished to conserve his strength for the summer when *Scharnhorst* was likely to join the growing German force, and thus, whenever Arctic convoys were at sea, he wanted to keep two battleships

---

[106] ADM 234/369, Battle Summary No. 22, Arctic Convoys 1941–1945, pp. 2–7. On the background, see Roskill, *War at Sea*, Vol. II, pp. 115–46; Levy, *Home Fleet*, pp. 109–33.

providing distant cover, while another and a carrier remained in port. The Admiralty preferred a carrier at sea owing to the growing *Luftwaffe* threat, which by implication meant another one would have to be allocated to the Home Fleet in the medium term. It is important to note that neither Tovey's nor the Admiralty's concerns exclusively focused on the Arctic convoys as a German task force could just as well attempt a break-out into the Atlantic on a far larger scale than during *Rheinübung*. The raid into the Indian Ocean by the Japanese Combined Fleet in early April, and the sweep of the Bay of Bengal, demonstrated pre-war concerns of how effectively carriers could operate against maritime commerce.[107]

The build-up of forces in Norway was slower than expected, and in the second quarter, surface operations declined considerably owing to the growing oil shortage Germany was experiencing—a development British intelligence would only slowly come to realize.[108] Nonetheless, a modern and powerful German squadron, supported by U-boats and specialized *Luftwaffe* maritime strike units, represented a substantial threat by the summer of 1942. The destruction of convoy PQ17 (27 June–10 July) needs no further discussion here beyond a recognition that it represented the worst-case scenario of a combined attack against a convoy. In the immediate aftermath, Tovey thought that the Home Fleet might still be able to fight through a convoy in the face of air and U-boat attacks, albeit with heavy losses.[109] If German surface forces were used more effectively, or even augmented, another convoy might be annihilated. All that was known about *Graf Zeppelin* at this stage was that outwardly she seemed ready, and presumably, following a workup period, she would commence operations. It was in this context that No. 106 Squadron's attack on Gdynia was flown on 27 August using some of the heaviest ordnance employed to date—experimental 5000lbs Capital Ship Bombs. In the event, they failed to hit their targets and the result of the raid remained unknown.[110] In September, convoys PQ18/QP14 fared marginally better than PQ17 had, but casualties too were high, and with Operation Torch due soon, the Arctic convoys were suspended.

The attacks on the two convoys marked the zenith of German efforts against the Arctic route. The *Luftwaffe's* maritime strike units were moved on to the Mediterranean, while oil shortages hampered surface fleet operations and training. This was not something the Admiralty could have known, and owing to the summer convoys, the expectation was that 1943 would be far more problematic. *Scharnhorst* was expected in Norway imminently (in the event she would not arrive until the spring), and *Graf Zeppelin* was expected in around six months. This outlook posed

[107]   David Brown, *Carrier Operations in World War II* (Barnsley: Seaforth, 2009), p. 136.

[108]   Hinsley et al., *British Intelligence*, Vol. 2, p. 531 and *British Intelligence*, Vol. 3.1, p. 261.

[109]   ADM 234/369, Battle Summary No. 22, Arctic Convoys 1941–1945, pp. 72–88.

[110]   CAB 66/28/22, W. P. (42) 392, 3 September 1942.

a significant problem because owing to losses, global operations, and limited British yard capacity, the Royal Navy was experiencing a shortage of carriers, which in turn was paralyzing the operations of the main fleets.[111] If *Graf Zeppelin* was about to come into service, the Home Fleet needed another carrier at the expense of the Eastern Fleet.[112] Auxiliary carriers might provide fighter cover in some theaters, or act as direct escorts to convoys (as happened with PQ18), but they were no substitute for the Home Fleet that would be operating in highly-contested air environments. This in turn had ramifications for the overall disposition of British carriers. The assumption was that a German carrier air group would encompass about forty aircraft, which required the Home Fleet to have thirty fighters embarked for its defense.[113] It was also assumed that *Graf Zeppelin* would carry very efficient aircraft, and thus it was desired to increase the number of Seafire fighters—in 1942, the best fighter the Fleet Air Arm operated—covering the Home Fleet. The problem was the assigned carrier, HMS *Victorious,* could not operate Seafires as these did not have folding wings and her lifts were too small. HMS *Indomitable,* then undergoing extensive repairs owing to damage sustained during Operation Pedestal, was the only modern fleet carrier with large lifts. She had been slated for operations in the Indian Ocean and Vice Admiral James Somerville, C-in-C Eastern Fleet, was warned he might get *Victorious* instead as his third carrier.[114]

In any event, these redeployments did not occur owing to more pressing demands. American carrier losses during the Guadalcanal campaign left the USN with only one operational carrier in the Pacific at the end of October. While it was both politically and operationally advantageous for the British to send a carrier out to the Pacific following the conclusion of Torch, the Admiralty had reservations and quite clearly made these known to the Prime Minister in early November.[115] With *Graf Zeppelin* possibly in service by early 1943, two fleet carriers need to be retained at home or at Gibraltar. However, given the USN's position, *Victorious* was sent out for refit in the United States in December, and then on to the Pacific. This left the Home Fleet with no fleet carrier for the foreseeable future. Although the Arctic convoys were resumed in late December, Tovey was clear that unless he were given more resources, he would suspend them in the spring if the Germans deployed all their assets.[116]

---

[111]   ADM 205/23, PD.0992/1942, 28.06.42.

[112]   ADM 205/21, DoP to FSL; ADM 205/21, Future Employment of Carriers (October 1942).

[113]   ADM 205/23, PD.0992/1942, Annex I, 28.06.42.

[114]   Naval Historical Branch, Portsmouth, UK (hereinafter NHB), ACNS(F) Signals Vol. 5, Admiralty to C-in-C, Eastern Fleet, 2.8.42.

[115]   TNA, Records of the Prime Minister's Office, 3/163/1, Minute from FSL to PM, 5.11.42. For background, see Roskill, *War at Sea,* Vol. II, pp. 228–29.

[116]   Levy, *Home Fleet,* p. 128.

As outlined above, it was in late December that *Graf Zeppelin* was identified in a dry dock at Kiel. What added credibility to the carrier soon entering service were several *Luftwaffe* Enigma decrypts. Already in July 1942, some traffic pertaining to the carrier had been intercepted, but on 15 January, the most conclusive proof to date was obtained from a signal that suggested all carrier-qualified Ju87 would be concentrated in a single unit on 1 March.[117] If *Graf Zeppelin* was not going to be brought into service, this made little sense. This explains why the Admiralty did not rely exclusively on PR products. In March, Captain Denham from Stockholm confirmed that this had been the German intention, but that delays pushed back trials into the second quarter.

The Admiralty's concern in the spring of 1943 was that once *Graf Zeppelin* commenced operations (now estimated for the summer), she might be used to attack installations on Iceland or otherwise assist U-boat operations by disrupting the provision of VLR patrols cover to convoys.[118] An attack on her in Kiel was requested, but the RAF turned this down on the grounds that Bomber Command lacked the daylight precision strike capability to disable her in dock and that this was a task for the U.S. Army Air Forces. In the gap in confirming her location at Stettin, there was no reason to assume that the carrier was not being worked up in the Baltic given the intelligence above. This explains Hinsley's reference to the OIC still being uneasy about her after March.[119] With all available British fleet carriers being required to cover a series of operations in the Mediterranean—*Husky, Musket, Brimstone,* and potentially *Lifebelt* in the Atlantic—the Home Fleet faced another carrier gap in the late summer and autumn. In early June, the Admiralty Plans Division considered this "unacceptable especially in view of the possibility of the GRAF ZEPPELIN coming into service in August."[120] This in turn led to the request for the USN to provide a carrier and thus the USS *Ranger* came to serve with the Home Fleet from August to September.

Graf Zeppelin's presence in Stettin was only confirmed by PR some weeks later and immediately prompted the Admiralty to again request the RAF conduct an airstrike to neutralize her. The RAF again declined because this was at the extreme range for Mosquitoes, and intelligence from ground sources indicated work had been suspended owing to shortages of labor and materials. It appears, though, that the Admiralty did not consider these reports as reliable at the time.[121] As the summer progressed and more PR material showed she had neither moved from her mooring nor was there any sign of activity, it was accepted that the Germans had

---

[117]   HW 1/1319 CX/MSS/1968/T19.

[118]   ADM 205/27, "Significance of recent German. . .," 13.3.43; AIR 20/5305, Draft Memo Graf Zeppelin, 4.4.43.

[119]   Hinsley, *British Intelligence,* Vol. 2, p. 530.

[120]   ADM 1/14806, Requirements for aircraft carriers for operations in 1943, 5.6.43.

[121]   AIR 20/5305, DB Ops. 14410 29.6 and reply, 30.6.1943.

abandoned her completion for the time being. From then on she did not feature in Admiralty thinking even when the threat of German "Death Rides" by the surface fleet against Allied assault convoys during Neptune or at the end of the war were examined.[122]

Conclusion

To what degree the Admiralty overestimated the threat posed by German carriers before the war, and *Graf Zeppelin* in the war, is hard to assess. From a British pre-war perspective, it was a logical step for the *Kriegsmarine* to take, and no assessment through to 1943 questioned the German ability to bring a carrier into service. The continuous delays to completion in British assessments up to 1940, and then again in 1942–43, might have given rise to some reconsideration. This was though the first German attempt, and on the hand the British, too, experienced delays with the RN's development of carrier aviation falling behind schedule. With the benefit of hindsight and knowledge of *Graf Zeppelin's* development, it is all too easy to dismiss Admiralty concerns as alarmist. This does not reflect the position the Admiralty was in at the time.

British intelligence had no way of knowing about the two principal problems that prevented *Graf Zeppelin* from coming into operation. First, as stated at the outset, the problems and high maintenance requirements of the propulsion systems of German warships only became known after the war. PR or other sources never saw the carrier underway at sea, which might well have provided further indications about her state. The *Kriegsmarine* ceased work on the carrier in 1940 because of the growing animosity with the *Luftwaffe* over control of maritime aviation assets. The implications of this on German operations, and by extension the carrier development, were not understood until after the war.[123] Leaving aside the inter-service rivalry, the British experience of German maritime airpower was that it had a profound effect on Allied naval operations. From a limited start in 1939, the Germans fielded specialist units for long-range maritime patrol (1940), anti-ship dive-bombing (1941), torpedo-bombing (1942), and guided missile carriers (1943). Unbeknownst to the British, the RAF was regularly engaging the carrier's fighters over the North Sea, Norway, and Denmark in 1942–43.[124] They were thus quite capable of developing maritime airpower.

---

[122]   ADM 1/18989, Break-out of German Fleet PD/OL.059/45, 6th March 1945.

[123]   See post-war Allied assessments and essays by *Kriegsmarine* and *Luftwaffe* officers reprinted in David Isby, ed., *The Luftwaffe and the War at Sea, 1939–1945* (London: Chatham, 2005), and essays by senior *Kriegsmarine* officers in G. H. Bennett and R. Bennett, *Hitler's Admirals* (Annapolis: Naval Institute Press, 2004).

[124]   Francis L. Marshall, *Messerschmitt Bf 109T: Die Jäger der Graf Zeppelin* (Gilching: Marshall, 2002).

The assessment of the threat did not occur in isolation and was shaped by the overall Admiralty view of the *Kriegsmarine*. The events of 1940–41, in which the Germans overturned pre-war British strategic planning and achieved strategic and operational surprise on numerous occasions, changed the view from one of confidence to apprehension of German capabilities. The fact that warships of all types were larger and more powerful than expected, and the Germans possessed a similar level of technology when it came to sensors, weapons, or signals intelligence, reinforced this. In view of incomplete, and at times contradictory, intelligence, the tendency of worst-case forecasting is understandable, and a similar trend may be observed when it came to the overall Admiralty assessment of the next generation of U-boats between 1943–45.[125] Securing the Atlantic routes and preventing a repeat of the dislocating effects German surface raiders had had on the convoy system in early 1941 was a significant factor in Admiralty thinking. Having experienced a German ability to adapt and innovate in the war at sea, the Admiralty was sensible in taking the potential threat of a German carrier seriously until reasonable proof had been obtained that this project was not being pursued to its conclusion.

---

[125]   Llewellyn-Jones, *The Royal Navy,* pp. 46–92.

8

Meat Exports and the Limits of Wartime Multilateralism

Secretary of Agriculture Claude Wickard's Response to America's Changing Global Role

Kevin Smith

The Allied victory in the Battle of the Atlantic required managerial as well as martial successes, especially after the United States entered the global war in December 1941. Cargo-carrying capacity had to be maximized. But British shipbuilding capacity had been reduced in the preceding decade. The Great Depression and tariff increases had reduced international trade and the need for ships to carry it, while simultaneously the British shipbuilding industry had colluded to close some yards in a controversial effort to save others, sending thousands of embittered workers into unemployment or forcing them into other professions. Winston Churchill, Britain's prime minister from 1940 until 1945, preferred not to risk industrial strife in wartime by pressing the industry for reforms in production techniques and labor usage. He also prioritized naval over merchant building and repair. Britain's wartime production of merchant ships remained, as a result, at virtually the same levels as during peacetime. Churchill himself summed up the consequences of his decisions: "It is to the United States building that we must look for relief."[1] The consequences

---

[1] The National Archives, London (hereinafter TNA), Cabinet Office File (hereinafter CAB) 66/15/42, War Cabinet Paper (hereinafter WP) (41) 69, 26 March 1941 by Churchill, "The Import Programmes," Annex II, Naval Programme 1941, 27 March 1941, p. 6, reducing the target for new merchant ships from 1,250,000 tons to 1,100,000 tons, closer to peacetime levels. For a description of the problems in British shipyards, see Kevin Smith, "'Immobilized by Reason of Repair' and by the Choice 'Between Lithgow and Hitler': Class Conflict in Britain's Wartime Merchant Shipping Repair Yards," in the present volume. Ball State University provided a research leave to work on this project. Additional research funding was provided by the Benjamin Cohen Peace Studies Faculty Fellowship and the John W. Fisher Faculty Research Fellowship in American Politics. I also benefited greatly from insights into Wickard's personality gained from conversation with members of his family, especially Ann Wickard Pickart, in February 2000. They shared some clippings which are cited below as "Wickard Family Collection (WFC)." This chapter also builds on some themes initially developed in Kevin Smith, *Conflict over Convoys: Anglo-American Logistics Diplomacy in the Second World War* (Cambridge: Cambridge University Press, 1996).

of industrial limitations and political decisions were far-reaching, both for the British and Allied war effort, and for historians' efforts to study the Battle of the Atlantic and America's adjustment to global leadership. Because Britain failed to increase domestic merchant shipbuilding to the level needed to replace wartime losses, British "logistics diplomacy" would be needed to pry cargo vessels—and cargoes to fill them—from the United States for British, as well as Allied, purposes. One important subset of that overall need for cargo vessels was ships with refrigerated capacity, which were needed as cargo vessels to bring meat to Britain, but which Churchill and Britain's War Office meanwhile also demanded to be employed as fast troopships to ferry soldiers to distant battlefields. Even when Britons succeeded in negotiations that extracted promises of assistance from their American counterparts, implementation remained vulnerable to the attitudes and actions of various U.S. bureaucrats. Critical decisions were frequently made by individuals with no direct role in convoy battles, the allocation of ships, or the formulation of grand strategy. Once our viewpoint shifts from the martial to the managerial aspects of the Battle of the Atlantic, a different set of historical actors emerges as decision-makers in the conflict, including a heretofore obscure U.S. Secretary of Agriculture. By expanding our narrative of this campaign to include new individuals with responsibilities well outside maritime affairs, a broader poly-causal perspective on industrial-era maritime warfare emerges.

With Roosevelt's clear espousal of the Allied cause in 1940–41, U.S. bureaucrats promptly and publicly echoed his views, but they were emerging from the long shadow of two decades of post-Wilsonian "isolationist" rhetoric. The inescapable reality that rhetorical change was galloping ahead of shifts in actual policy implementation would be illustrated in 1942–43 by the gap between internationalist foreign policy rhetoric and nationalist U.S. Department of Agriculture (USDA) management of wartime domestic meat rationing and meat exports. Secretary of Agriculture Claude Wickard, while rhetorically committed to multilateral cooperation, responded to domestic political constraints with a nationalistic, unilateralist meat export policy. Even as he loyally reiterated the multilateralist rhetoric of the Roosevelt administration for public consumption, this "last real farmer"[2] to be Secretary of Agriculture could not easily escape the nationalist and "isolationist" habits and discourse of his rural upbringing. The Roosevelt Administration had promised to mitigate Britain's shortage of refrigerated shipping capacity by increasing America's meat exports to Britain in the winter of 1942–43; Wickard delayed fulfillment of this promise. Thus America's dramatic shift after Pearl Harbor—from unilateral political disengagement *vis-à-vis* European discord toward multilateral cooperation to engage and pacify global strife—was in reality, at best, gradual. Deeply rooted in the Midwestern heartland, Wickard turned inward amid bureaucratic strife and domestic political misfortune. This examination of the

---

[2]   Interview with Ann Wickard Pickart, February 2000.

1942–43 controversy over inter-Allied meat allocation therefore illustrates the challenge of implementing rapid policy transition, the importance of this policy-maker's rural roots, and the ongoing need for scholars to examine the managerial component that had to complement martial success in order to achieve victory in the maritime conflict we call the Battle of the Atlantic.

The Interwar Context: "Disengaged Unilateralism"

This exploration of practical continuity amid a sudden rhetorical policy shift is best contextualized by the twisted interplay in the 1930s of two themes that have long shaped the relationship between U.S. agricultural policy and foreign policy as the United States has evolved from a continental to a global power: a quest for markets and an ambivalence about political consequences. American farmers have, naturally enough, wanted to increase export markets to enhance their profits, but have sometimes been hesitant about the foreign entanglements that resulted. Perhaps that hesitation has never been as obvious as in the 1930s. In the wake of World War One, the Wall Street Crash, and European debt default, many residents of the American heartland were highly susceptible to suggestions that avaricious businessmen and foreign statesmen sought to manipulate naïve Americans into financing, feeding, and eventually fighting "their" pointless wars. Because many believed that German efforts to interfere with American trade with Britain in 1914–17 had been a primary cause of American involvement in the First World War, many Americans preferred to seek domestic solutions to the Great Depression rather than risk another ghastly war by trading with prospectively belligerent (and cash-poor) Europeans who, in any case, had defaulted on war debts. Many residents of the American heartland, therefore, were committed thoroughly to what I term a policy of "unilateral political disengagement"—what they called an "isolationist" foreign policy—in the 1930s, regardless of the loss of export markets. While the term "isolationism" is controversial among historians (though still a common pejorative in public usage) because it implies a total withdrawal that did not occur and because it has been used by politicians as a "straw man" to justify interventionism, the phrase "unilateral political disengagement" correctly reflects the reality that many Americans, in the Midwest and elsewhere, did advocate policies and legislation that would isolate the United States from European power politics while permitting some cultural and economic interaction—but only (they hoped) on American terms. Scholars have described expanded cultural and economic engagement with Europe in the interwar period, especially in the 1920s, but this contrary sentiment toward political disengagement could and did influence politicians in both parties. This was especially true from the mid-1930s onward as Europe and Asia destabilized, narrowing the sphere for trade as well as opportunity for intervention. Senator Gerald Nye (R-ND) exemplified such views as he investigated the role that so-called "Merchants of Death" had played in enticing America to enter World War One. His efforts facilitated the passage of Neutrality

Acts in 1935–37, legislation that recoiled from trade that might lead to war, and thereby "set the tone for American attitudes toward foreign affairs during the remainder of the decade." Representative Louis Ludlow (D-IN) even tried to amend the Constitution to require a nationwide referendum before a Congressional declaration of war could take effect.[3]

Because their efforts hampered President Franklin Roosevelt's struggle to assist the Allies in resisting Nazi aggression, these advocates of unilateral political

---

[3]   Wayne S. Cole, *Senator Gerald P. Nye and Foreign Relations* (Minneapolis: University of Minnesota Press, 1962), pp. 80, 97ff. Agrarians' desire for markets and their interwar quest for political disengagement has been a frequent subject of research. See William Appleman Williams, *The Roots of the Modern American Empire: A Study of the Growth and Shaping of Social Consciousness in a Marketplace Society* (New York: Random House, 1969); Joseph A. Fry, *Dixie Looks Abroad: The South and U.S. Foreign Relations, 1789–1973* (Baton Rouge: LSU Press, 2002); Betty Glad, *Key Pittman: The Tragedy of a Senate Insider* (New York: Columbia University Press, 1986); Alfred Haworth Jones, "The Making of an Interventionist on the Air: Elmer Davis and CBS News, 1939–1941," *Pacific Historical Review* 42 (February 1973), pp. 74–93; and Justus Doenecke's overview of relevant scholarship in "U.S. Policy and the European War, 1939–1941," *Diplomatic History* 19:4 (Fall 1995), pp. 669–98. Laura McEnaney provides a gendered perspective in "He-Men and Christian Mothers: The America First Movement and the Gendered Meanings of Patriotism and Isolationism," *Diplomatic History* 18:1 (Winter 1994), pp. 47–57. While as David Reynolds points out in *From Munich to Pearl Harbor: Roosevelt's America and the Origins of the Second World War* (Chicago: Ivan R. Dee, 2001), p. 9, scholars have recently looked beyond "an ethnic or regional basis," the reality of such attitudes remains salient—though not in exclusive terms either in limiting isolationism to the Midwest or in categorizing all Midwesterners as isolationists. See here James C. Schneider, *Should America Go to War?: The Debate over Foreign Policy in Chicago, 1939–1941* (Chapel Hill: University of North Carolina Press, 1989). Warren F. Kuehl diagrams the limits of any discussion of Midwestern "isolationism" in "Midwestern Newspapers and Isolationist Sentiment," *Diplomatic History* 3:3 (July 1979), pp. 283–306, using the views of newspaper editors to proclaim that it is "time to put to rest some of the hoary stereotypes regarding Middle West isolationism." Yet this is far from conclusive, especially because Kuehl's study ends (awkwardly) in 1935, precisely as the collapsing international system seemed to prove the futility of collective security. So while "isolationist" sentiment was by no means peculiar to the Midwest, it certainly was strong there. For cultural and economic engagement, see Frank Costigliola, *Awkward Dominion: American Political, Economic, and Cultural Relations with Europe, 1919–1933* (Ithaca, NY: Cornell University Press, 1988). Thomas Paterson, et al., use the phrase "independent internationalism" in the prominent text *American Foreign Relations: A History* (Boston: Houghton Mifflin, 7th ed., 2009). Reynolds (*From Munich to Pearl Harbor*, p. 4) suggests the term "hemispherism," which indirectly implies both unilateralism and disengagement to some degree. See also regarding this period Benjamin D. Rhodes, *United States Foreign Policy in the Interwar Period, 1918–1941: The Golden Age of American Diplomatic and Military Complacency* (Westport, CT: Praeger, 2001) and David M. Kennedy, *The American People in the Great Depression: Freedom from Fear*, Part One (New York: Oxford University Press, 2003).

disengagement were later viewed as unsophisticated rubes during much of the Cold War. The Cold War culture that came to shape foreign policy discourse emphasized firm deterrence of aggressors alongside allies—"multilateral engagement." In this view, unilateral disengagement had invited expansion by dictators that had, in turn, risked exposing America to defeat should Britain have fallen. Thus the Cold War mantra emphasized that not only did America have to respond to aggression, but that she had to do so multilaterally. Though Cold Warriors occasionally behaved in an essentially unilateral fashion, they generally embraced multilateralist rhetoric and (often) action for the remainder of the 20th Century.[4] They did so based upon their understanding of the perceived "lessons" of the 1930s—do not appease aggressors, and do not confront them alone.

However, this examination of the actual implementation of the 1940s transition from unilateral political disengagement to multilateral engagement with America's allies illuminates the essential continuity in administration of foreign policy after Pearl Harbor, executed by officials who had been intellectually formed in the interwar period, including some who were wary of America once again falling victim to foreigners' wiles. They had also learned "lessons" from the First World War and its aftermath. Claude Wickard, Secretary of Agriculture for Franklin Roosevelt from 1940 until 1945, had not inhabited the internationalist coastal

---

We await a full study of Ludlow. Meanwhile, see Kevin Smith, "Hoosier Statesmen and the Coming of the Second World War: Louis Ludlow, Claude Bowers, and the Impact of Jeffersonian Democracy on American Foreign Policy," *Journal of the Indiana Academy of the Social Sciences* VI (2002), pp. 42–55; Travis Ricketts, "Congressman Louis Ludlow and the War Referendum: A Test Case of Evangelical Christianity Applied to Government," Ph.D. dissertation, Kansas State University, 1998; Walter R. Griffin, "Louis Ludlow and the War Referendum Crusade, 1935–1941," *Indiana Magazine of History* 64:4 (December 1968), pp. 267–88; and two works by Ernest C. Bolt, "Reluctant Belligerent: The Career of Louis L. Ludlow," in *Their Infinite Variety: Essays on Indiana Politicians* (Indianapolis: Indiana Historical Bureau, 1981), pp. 353–408, and *Ballots before Bullets: The War Referendum Approach to Peace in America, 1914–1941* (Charlottesville: University of Virginia Press, 1977).

[4]   Thomas Risse-Kappen discusses the cooperative, multilateral aspects of the NATO allies' decision-making process in *Cooperation Among Democracies: The European Influence on U.S. Foreign Policy* (Princeton: Princeton University Press, 1995). The award of the Nobel Peace Prize to President Obama in 2009, at least in part as reaction to President George W. Bush's seeming post-9-11 shift toward unilateral engagement, illustrates how pervasive this sentiment has become among America's European allies as well as most of the American foreign policymaking "establishment." Amid controversial arguments about George W. Bush's foreign policy, John Lewis Gaddis has reminded us that a tendency toward unilateralism is by no means new, referencing John Quincy Adams' very different unilateralism in *Surprise, Security, and the American Experience* (Cambridge, MA: Harvard University Press, 2004). More recently, President Trump's election does illustrate the continuing attraction of older unilateralist ideas.

milieu that influenced Wilson's failed earlier effort to promote engaged multilater-alism. A Midwestern farmer elevated to the Cabinet, he had matured in the heart-land of "isolationist" sentiment. While he loyally and publicly embraced Roosevelt's policy of giving all available assistance to Britain both before and after Pearl Har-bor, one of his most significant practical contributions to that effort during the meat export crisis of 1942–43 revealed an ambivalence rooted in his personal encounters with America's new allies as well as in political calculation. America's transition to multilateralism had to be implemented, not merely revealed and received without question. Wickard's experience suggests that Pearl Harbor did not lead to abrupt change, and that rhetoric and party labels do not always deter-mine actual policy. The suggestion that Wickard's behavior was influenced by a residual sentiment that had previously been regarded as the natural fruit of Ameri-can patriotism and nationalism does not contradict the view of scholars who doubt that American policy was ever "isolationist." Rather, intent and sentiment varied widely in the wake of Wilson's failure in 1919, and sentiment could and did influence implementation of policy during the Second World War, in this case by hampering the Allies' effective management of the Battle of the Atlantic.[5]

Claude Wickard: The "Indiana farmer's farmer" and Loyal Democrat

Claude Wickard was a self-professed "dirt farmer" from Carroll County, Indiana, and a fervent Democratic Party activist whose father and grandfather were named after a Democratic president, Andrew Jackson. He firmly identified with the Hoo-sier heartland. He was neither an abstract theoretician nor a small-town resident who merely had worked among farmers; he himself had experienced the ups and (mostly) downs of interwar farming after persuading his traditionalist father that the new scientific approaches he had learned at Purdue University would yield results. Andrew J. Wickard turned over operations to his son, and, by 1927, Claude had been designated as a "Master Farmer" by the *Prairie Farmer*. But Wickard never truly prospered on the farm. Tough times in the 1920s were followed by the Great Depression and family tensions arose because his wife Louise, who had grown up in a nearby town, did not adapt to living with her in-laws on the farm. She wel-comed the change of scenery that accompanied Claude's political career. As dissat-isfaction with Republican policies spread, the outlook for Democrats like Wickard in rural Indiana improved, and Wickard was elected to the Indiana State Senate.

Meanwhile, Roosevelt's aggressive and controversial responses to rural poverty demanded rapid expansion of the USDA bureaucracy. Where possible, the USDA

---

[5]   Because the policies of the early 21st Century have been implemented by veterans of the Cold War era, future historians may well find gaps between pre-emptive unilateralist rheto-ric and examples of multilateralist implementation after 2001.

sought public servants who were loyal Democrats and were knowledgeable about rural problems. Such individuals were scarce among Midwestern corn-hog farmers. Wickard's impeccable credentials—as both a real corn-hog farmer who was trusted by farmers (unlike supposedly dangerous New Deal academics who had never plowed a furrow) and as a fervent Democrat—led to his appointment to a position in the New Deal's Agricultural Adjustment Administration (AAA). Wickard served in the front lines of the New Deal's war on the nation's agricultural surplus and abysmal farm income. He was gradually promoted through the ranks to "do a magnificent job" of directing the USDA's North Central Division in the late 1930s, and was appointed Under Secretary of Agriculture in early 1940. When Agriculture Secretary Henry Wallace replaced Vice President John Nance Garner in the second spot on the 1940 Democratic Presidential ticket in September of that year, Wickard was suddenly elevated to Secretary of Agriculture at a pivotal time in America's foreign policy transition.[6]

While he was certainly in line for the appointment once Wallace resigned, the particular circumstances of Roosevelt's 1940 presidential campaign against fellow Hoosier Wendell Willkie may have prompted Roosevelt to pick someone who could be portrayed in the stretch run of that campaign as an appointment based on competence rather than politics. Certainly commentator Drew Pearson thought so. "Unquestionably the fact that Wickard is a farmer's farmer, particularly an Indiana farmer's farmer, had a lot to do with his appointment as Secretary of Agriculture. The political strategy was to offer Wickard in contrast to Willkie as what a 'real' Indiana farmer should be."[7] The obvious contrast with Wendell Willkie's withered roots in the Hoosier heartland escaped no one. Willkie had not lived in Elwood or Rushville, his hometowns, for two decades, having long since migrated (after completing his law degree at Indiana University) to Akron, Ohio, and thereafter to New York City. A longtime Democrat and ardent Wilsonian "internationalist," Willkie had become best known as the charismatic spokesman for the unpopular private utilities industry in its New Deal battle with David Lilienthal and the Tennessee Valley Authority. This domestic conflict drove him out of the Democratic Party and into an awkward embrace with the largely "isolationist"

---

6   Dean Albertson, *Roosevelt's Farmer: Claude R. Wickard in the New Deal* (New York: Columbia University Press, 1961), pp. 6–7, 20–39, 125; WFC, *Time*, 21 July 1941, p. 14. The family retains strong multigenerational Democratic loyalties (interview with Ann Wickard Pickart, February 2000).

7   In his "Washington Merry-Go-Round" column for 25 September 1940, Pearson, known for his idiosyncratic, gossipy profiles of government figures, quoted a Maryland farmer: "there's only one [USDA official] who is a real farmer, and that's this one." (The WFC includes a 28 September 1940 reprint of this column in a local newspaper.) In this profile, Pearson also quoted Wickard's description of Willkie when Wickard was introduced as the newly-appointed Secretary on 21 August 1940: "a Wall Street boy trying to make good on the farm."

Republicans. After Willkie shocked the political world by winning the 1940 Republican Presidential nomination, Democrats looked for an opening. Thus reports of Wickard's September 1940 appointment that emphasized that he was a "real" farmer contrasted starkly with attacks on "that barefoot Wall Street lawyer."[8] Subsequently, following his defeat in the 1940 election, Willkie traveled to Britain in 1941 as Roosevelt's representative to suggest that America's support for Britain was bipartisan, and eventually embarked on a world tour, devoting his considerable personal magnetism to arguing for America's postwar global role in his book *One World*. Historian Howard Jones summarized his impact: "Wendell Willkie had more influence on causing the American people and government to turn away from isolationism in the years from 1940 to 1944 than anyone other than President Franklin D. Roosevelt." Roosevelt himself concluded: "we might not have had Lend Lease or Selective Service or a lot of other things if it hadn't been for Wendell Willkie. He was a godsend to this country when we needed him most."[9] As will become evident in the meat export crisis of 1942–43, Democratic loyalist Claude Wickard was a less reliable practical advocate of Roosevelt's multilateral course than Democratic heretic Willkie. Willkie's career highlights the ambivalent relationship that some natives of the mid-century Hoosier heartland had with an internationalist foreign policy: the more cosmopolitan the individual became, the more suspicious he would be in the eyes of Hoosiers—whether the aliens embraced were Britons or New Yorkers.

In contrast, though "Roosevelt's Farmer"[10] had joined the Cabinet, he did not stray from his roots. While he enjoyed being a public servant, he never stopped seeing himself as a farmer—first and foremost. His daughter recalled that "he fought for farmers because he was a farmer himself" and proudly remembered

---

[8]   Harold L. Ickes, *The Secret Diary of Harold L. Ickes,* Vol. 3, *The Lowering Clouds, 1939–1941* (New York: Simon and Schuster, 1954), p. 396. Joseph Barnes notes [*Willkie: The Events He was Part of—The Ideas He Fought for* (New York: Simon and Schuster, 1952), p. 9] that Ickes did not originate the phrase, but he certainly popularized it. While Albertson's is the only (limited) biography of Wickard, the most useful of several books about relevant facets of Willkie's career and ideas are Steve Neal, *Dark Horse: A Biography of Wendell Willkie* (Garden City, NY: Doubleday, 1984); Ellsworth Barnard, *Wendell Willkie: Fighter for Freedom* (Marquette: Northern Michigan University Press, 1966); Warren Moscow, *Roosevelt and Willkie* (Englewood Cliffs, NJ: Prentice-Hall, 1968); James H. Madison, ed., *Wendell Willkie: Hoosier Internationalist* (Bloomington: Indiana University Press, 1992); and, of course, Wendell Willkie, *One World* (New York: Simon and Schuster, 1943).

[9]   Howard Jones, "*One World*: An American Perspective," in Madison, ed., *Hoosier Internationalist*, pp. 103, 109–10. Willkie's book sold one million copies in only seven weeks.

[10]   This was the title of Albertson's biography cited above. While Albertson's evaluation of Wickard's performance is generally positive, Wickard was displeased by what his daughter referred to as Albertson's tendency to embellish details (interview with Ann Wickard Pickart, February 2000).

him in 2000 as "the last real farmer" to be Secretary of Agriculture.[11] Claude and Louise Wickard and their daughters Betty and Ann returned to their Camden, Indiana farm every summer when the girls' school term ended. Wickard's roles as plain-spoken Midwestern farmer and as Secretary of Agriculture were initially compatible in the 1940 campaign, but they would eventually conflict as he navigated among powerful USDA subordinates, men who had once been his bureaucratic equals but who had not reconciled themselves to Wickard's elevation. They envisioned different approaches to fulfilling Henry Wallace's legacy, using wartime pressures for increased production on behalf of contrary agendas unrelated to feeding Britons and Russians—to boost the welfare of more prosperous farmers, or to serve as an agent for social change on behalf of poor tenant farmers. Contrariwise, from outside the USDA, especially from (initially) Leon Henderson's Office of Price Administration, came pressure for a better standard of living for American factory workers by holding down farm prices, even though doing so risked limiting production. These domestic pressures affected Wickard's response to British pleas for meat. Even as he struggled to cope in the Washington vortex, however, his personal integrity was unquestionable. No hint of scandal ever touched him. His service as a bureau chief in the Agriculture Department's North Central Division before 1940 and as head of the Rural Electrification Administration from 1945 until 1953 was exemplary. The political circumstances of the 1940 campaign thrust Wickard into a position which demanded a ruthless, combative approach that was alien to his honest, straightforward, decent nature.[12]

Wartime Adjustments and Struggles amid Competing Demands

Efficient usage of limited shipping resources depended upon convenient and consistent access to American agricultural exports. Wickard toed the party line rhetorically after initial statements that reflected distrust of the British. Even in acknowledging the need to provide aid, as late as October 1940 he publicly said, "We may have to give food to Europe. After the last war we lent Europe money

---

[11]   Interview with Ann Wickard Pickart, February 2000.

[12]   An undated wartime letter to daughter Ann preserved in the WFC illustrates his refusal to use his position to benefit his family: "Now I don't know about gas rationing any more than you. I am going to depend on you getting the best allowance you can for your car and for the truck and tractors and I suppose you will have to work it out for Grandpa too." Albertson carefully narrates the crosscurrents of domestic conflict, divided authority, and Wickard's administrative limitations, but the nature of his book, based primarily on oral histories from Wickard and various USDA personnel, limits his discussion of the diplomatic context of agricultural policy to occasional references; there is no discussion at all of the promises of meat to fill ships for Britain in 1942–1943. This omission illustrates the primacy of internal USDA squabbling and an ignorance of British import needs, both in retrospect and at the time, among USDA officials.

to buy our food, and the money wasn't repaid. That's pretty nearly the same thing."[13] Americans bitterly resented the default, thus this nationalist sentiment emerged in Wickard's speech even as he spoke in favor of providing assistance. But he also absorbed the "lesson" that American rejection of the League of Nations was partly responsible for the current maelstrom. He quickly understood that his professional responsibility was, as a friendly *Time* magazine profile described in the summer of 1941, "to feed the United States and Great Britain during the defense emergency and the war." *Time* gave him credit for long-range foresight as well: "He has gone beyond that charge already, to take the steps which he believes will put the U.S. into a position to write the peace. He thinks the war can be won by feeding Britain and starving Europe."[14] As Louise phrased his approach to reporters in a wartime interview, his objective was to maximize food production for the war effort so that "farmers will produce enough for our armed forces, for lease-lend [*sic*], and for the people at home."[15] His language evolved as he came to embrace a specifically internationalist, multilateral perspective. In 1944, he said: "We must not sow seeds of another war and, therefore, we must not evade the responsibilities of this nation in the world of nations. We cannot isolate ourselves from the rest of the world."[16]

Indeed, Wickard cannot be categorized as a simple xenophobe. He worked to enhance production to aid Britain. But American wartime mobilization gradually created an overwhelming set of contradictory demands that hampered effective management of the resources needed for effective maritime warfare. While the U.S. domestic political climate of 1940–41 was hostile to an explicit alliance with Britain and wary that shipments risked German submarine attacks and war, efforts to fulfill British demand during this period of undeclared war did not yet force the choice between British and American consumption that arose later. Moreover, British food needs enabled Wickard to reverse course on production policy. During the Depression era, the AAA had worked to manipulate U.S. agricultural production downward so that farmers could eke out a living based on a more favorable balance between supply and demand. After France fell, as U.S. foreign policy shifted toward aid to Britain, Wickard sought to augment agricultural production to fulfill Roosevelt's Lend-Lease policy. Government intervention to restrict production was reversed to promote it. In a 1941 article extolling the USDA's ability to adjust acreage deployment, crop rotation, and storage use, Wickard emphasized that such adjustments were underway to "furnish food for Great Britain and,

---

[13]   Albertson, *Roosevelt's Farmer*, p. 178.

[14]   WFC, *Time*, 21 July 1941, p. 13.

[15]   WFC, 7 December 1942 Associated Press wire service clipping from unidentified local newspaper.

[16]   WFC, official USDA transcript of address by Secretary Wickard at the "I am an American Day" rally at Gary, Indiana, 21 May 1944, p. 5.

simultaneously, to safeguard our own domestic needs."[17] In particular, egg, milk, pork, and green vegetables would be emphasized at the expense of wheat, tobacco, and cotton. Wickard wisely anticipated that demand would increase and courageously insisted in spring 1941 in numerous public venues to skeptical audiences which had endured the consequences of overproduction that America would have to not only expand production, but also take steps to ensure that the ships carrying that food arrived in Britain. But his foresight was limited. In one such speech he insisted: "With our ability to produce, there isn't the slightest need for rationing and there isn't likely to be."[18]

As war mobilization accelerated after Pearl Harbor, Wickard faced countervailing domestic pressures that threatened quick allocation of agricultural production to exports. The Roosevelt Administration wanted the home front population satisfied and quiescent. Discontent with government activism in the economy was growing, and it played a significant role in the Democrats' loss of forty-five House seats (and eight Senate seats) in the midterm 1942 elections, resulting in a slender Congressional majority thereafter. In Wickard's home state, the only reason Republican gains had not paralleled national gains in 1942 was because they had already gained six seats in the 1938 elections (an earlier referendum on the "court-packing" plan and the 1937 recession); overall, Republicans had rebounded from holding only one of twelve seats before 1937 to nine of eleven Indiana House seats in 1943 and would not lose a Senate race in Indiana between 1940 and 1958. The war brought rising prosperity (originally facilitated by British orders, ironically) that seemed to suggest that regulatory intervention was no longer necessary to boost or control the economy.

Wickard's ongoing effort to satisfy American consumers coexisted uneasily with his fervent and understandable determination to protect the livelihood of American farmers, many of whom feared another postwar depression. Thus Wickard believed that neither a precipitous expansion of production nor a reduction in domestic consumption was desirable or politically feasible. He vividly recalled the struggles American farmers had undergone following their rapid expansion of production during World War One. Wickard himself had suffered in a glutted market as a farmer in the 1920s. As a USDA official in the 1930s, Wickard had helped oversee the painful adjustment of agricultural supply to demand. In the 1940s, as demand increased exponentially with export requests from Britain, the Soviet Union, and others, Wickard had to appease America's allies, satisfy American consumers, minimize inflation, and encourage wary producers simultaneously. In this context, policy implementation of the rhetorical shift to multilateral

---

[17]   Claude R. Wickard, "Agricultural Policy and Abundance," *Survey Graphic* 30:7 (July 1941), p. 387ff, paragraph 5. This "magazine of social interpretation" was a leading exponent of social reform from an avowedly progressive perspective.

[18]   Albertson, *Roosevelt's Farmer,* pp. 210–17, 239.

cooperation would be difficult and would prevent efficient management of shipping.

Moreover, in addition to enhanced domestic political pressures, Roosevelt's haphazard, byzantine bureaucracy strangled efficient decision-making. Wickard lacked the power to make needed decisions even if he had maintained an enthusiastic desire to prioritize food exports to allies over domestic consumption. Don Nelson's War Production Board (WPB) allocated steel for farm implements and could reverse the assignment of food by its Foods Requirements Committee, even though Wickard sat on that very committee. While the USDA's Farm Security Administration (FSA) had moved poorer farmers to areas affected by labor shortages and Wickard had negotiated the increased use of Mexican and interned Japanese-American laborers, the War Manpower Commission still controlled deferments for farm workers from military service.[19] The allotment of these critical resources directly affected efforts to maximize production, feed Americans and their allies, and efficiently route shipping. Thus in a global, total war, the outcome of the Battle of the Atlantic would be influenced by a broader, more diverse range of factors than just traditional maritime considerations.

Also, effective administration and successful policy formulation required a stature and forcefulness that Claude Wickard lacked. Government officials inside and outside the USDA remembered that Wickard had succeeded Henry Wallace by default when Wallace became Vice President. Wickard tried to fight for the farmer and the USDA, demanding unified control of matters affecting food production. He did briefly achieve this level of control, in theory, in the fall of 1942 when Roosevelt reversed his earlier view that the U.S. would not need to reprise Herbert Hoover's "Food Administration" in the Second World War. The President considered other candidates, but he could not persuade anyone else to take the position of head of the new agency. So Wickard was named the new "Food Czar," but as with so many other administrative structures in both the New Deal and the Second World War, Roosevelt prioritized control over efficiency by ensuring that divided authority would push all critical decisions onto his own desk or that of a trusted surrogate like James Byrnes, head of the Office of Economic Stabilization. So Wickard had gained no additional power to exert his will upon the American economy. He still lacked statutory authority to exercise control over prices or to defer farm workers from military service or to allocate steel for farm machinery. Moreover, ideological infighting within the USDA over the proper focus of reorganizing administration to meet production challenges distracted Wickard from taking decisive action. FSA liberals argued that the government should achieve full production by subsidizing small farmers.[20] The battle divided the department and undermined Wickard's authority. Wickard's title was meaningless, and indeed

---

[19]   Ibid., pp. 297, 313.

[20]   Ibid., pp. 230, 330, 339–83.

exposed him to public criticism. His days as War Food Administrator were numbered; he served from December 1942 until March 1943. In this context, Wickard's internationalist rhetoric took a back seat to internal rivalries and domestic consumption. Rising above these challenges would have been an enormous task even for someone with years of experience in articulating and implementing a broad, cosmopolitan view of American national interest.

Claude Wickard was not that man. Though Roosevelt had praised his work in the initial 1941–42 transition from the New Deal agenda of reducing production in order to bolster farm income to increasing production for war needs while simultaneously managing inflation, his limitations are clear from his own oral history, his diary, and from the biography that Dean Albertson published in 1961. Even as he acknowledged that Wickard was "at times paralyzed by fears he scarcely knew how to overcome," Albertson hinted in his introduction that serious omissions remained in his old-fashioned account: "There exists a line of tact and personal privacy which must not be crossed, even in pursuit of truth."[21] Albertson thus contextualized Wickard the dutiful patriot and fundamentally decent, loyal, and hard-working human being amid his family and agricultural interests; a man of rock-solid integrity who inspired respect but who lacked close friends.[22] As early as 4 December 1941, Robert Brand, head of the British Food Mission (BFM) in Washington, described Wickard's limitations and sensitivity to domestic political pressure: "He is not a man who goes into any detail or follows very closely the subject, and he is apt to go off at a tangent. What upsets him is the pressure of politicians, both senators and congressmen, and the necessity, which he looks forward to with displeasure, of having to give evidence before them . . . in connection with a new Lease-Lend Bill. Therefore he has to be dealt with with some care. . .. [His] enthusiasm for giving us foodstuffs diminishes as we appear to be better fed."[23] Dealing with the USDA and his domestic rivals posed a challenge he eventually lost; the complexities of alliance politics and global strategy were beyond his ken. The oral history, diary, and biography portray an idealistic civil servant who struggled to keep his elevated position and to do his duty amid interdepartmental backbiting and political intrigue, frequent personal criticism from farm advocates and newspapermen, and family crisis. Albertson acknowledged: "as administrator of the North Central Region Wickard had been excellent. As Secretary he was administratively over his depth."[24] In the winter of 1942–43, as he battled for control over

---

[21] Ibid., pp. vii, ix; Franklin Delano Roosevelt Library (hereinafter FDRL), Claude Wickard Papers, diary entries for 24 January 1943 and following; oral history interviews #73–76, pp. 3026–3172.

[22] Interview with Ann Wickard Pickart, February 2000.

[23] TNA, Ministry of Agriculture and Fisheries File (hereinafter MAF) 97/1388, Brand to Minister of Food Frederick Marquis, Lord Woolton, 4 December 1941.

[24] Albertson, *Roosevelt's Farmer*, p. 227.

the issues affecting production, he faced a crisis in the administration of distribution that demanded but did not receive his full attention. Distracted, he reverted to traditional Anglophobic suspicions.

Wickard's Challenge: The Meat Export Controversy of 1942–43

The meat export controversy of 1942–43 had developed gradually since Britain lost ready access to nearby European markets in 1940. Britain had not been able to maintain the merchant shipping capacity needed to feed the British people from distant sources, expand war production, and supply forces overseas. Mutton from New Zealand required more shipping capacity than Danish ham. Overall British dry cargo imports fell from a peacetime average of fifty-five million tons yearly to thirty-one million in 1941, and they catastrophically nosedived to twenty-three million for 1942 before reaching a yearly rate of seventeen million tons during the winter of 1942–43 (see Table 8.1).[25]

The strategically necessary but logistically costly decisions to fight for Egypt in 1940 and in North Africa in 1942 especially hindered meat transport because troop movement and supply demanded numerous reallocations and conversions of vessels fast enough to travel independently of convoy. Such ships were often those equipped with refrigerated capacity. Thus, both military operations and the overseas troop deployments that preceded them were in direct competition with food shipments. Efficient usage of limited space was essential, but difficult to achieve. Ships diverted to military service also were occasionally sunk, several being lost as assault vessels invading North Africa, for example.[26] Moreover, U.S. Army logisticians trying to accelerate troop movements resented a British effort to curb inefficiencies by acquiring "confirmation from U.S. authorities that they

---

[25]   The following discussion contextualizes Wickard's role in the crisis within the American bureaucracy and in interaction with British officials, emphasizing the slow adaptation of this American Cabinet official to the realities of engaged multilateralism. This assessment builds upon the analysis of Britain's shipping shortage and the decline in imports (including meat) in Smith, *Conflict over Convoys*, especially pp. 37–38, 41–43, 184–91. C. B. A. Behrens did not discuss this episode in the official history, *Merchant Shipping and the Demands of War* (London: HMSO, 1955; 2nd ed., 1978); in other official histories, R. J. Hammond did not discuss the shipping issues, but examined the issue of meat procurement in *Food: The Growth of Policy* (London: HMSO, 1951), pp. 243–45 and *Food: Studies in Administration and Control* (London: HMSO, 1962), pp. 254–57. See, in particular, CAB 123/86, a summative memorandum by civil servant J. M. Flemming, "Shipping Position," 29 December 1942.

[26]   TNA, CAB 65/15, War Cabinet Minutes (hereinafter WM) (40) 279th meeting, 29 October 1940; TNA, Ministry of (War) Transport File (hereinafter MT) 65/163, "Refrigerator Tonnage," note by Ministry of War Transport civil servant W. P. Elderton; MT 59/694, September 1942 report on "Statistical Digest E."

Table 8.1: Dry Cargo Imports, Britain, 1940–1944

Month	1940	1941	1942	1943	1944
Jan	3811	2413	2006	1177	1966
Feb	3598	2152	1867	1267	2126
Mar	3856	2386	1943	2015	2073
Apr	4207	2360	2099	2378	1992
May	4177	2767	2214	2064	2345
Jun	4054	2776	2091	2723	2352
Jul	3389	2648	2167	2748	2060
Aug	3936	2712	1919	2368	2102
Sep	2974	2816	2149	2661	2000
Oct	3208	2930	2023	2569	2216
Nov	2602	2140	1300	2186	2371
Dec	2547	2680	1235	2327	1923
Total	**41859**	**30478**	**22891**	**26372**	**25147**

Central Statistical Office, *Statistical Digest of the War* (London: HMSO, 1951), Table 161. All import figures expressed in thousands of tons and include the Ministry of Food program, the Ministry of Supply program (later Ministry of Production), munitions, and other minor miscellaneous imports.

accept principle of [food] procurement from local sources to fullest possible extent in order to economize in shipping space." General C. P. Gross, U.S. Army Chief of Transportation, saw this request as "interference with Army regulations which fundamentally cover the situation. It is a subject upon which we do not solicit nor desire any advice from the British. It would be appreciated if the British, in the future, would refrain from such interference." Lewis Douglas, U.S. Deputy War Shipping Administrator, recorded his growing awareness of the "deep anti-British sentiment among Army officers ... often throughout my conversations, Gross, Somervell and others inferred that they must have the power to restrict the British."[27]

---

[27]   U.S. National Archives and Records Administration (hereinafter NARA), Record Group (hereinafter RG) 248, File Control of Transportation, "Memorandum of Conversation with War Department" by Deputy War Shipping Administrator Lewis Douglas, 19 March 1942. The other officer referenced is Gross' immediate superior, General B. B. Somervell, United States Army Commanding General, Services of Supply.

These diversions and losses led Sir Arthur Salter, the head of Britain's Merchant Shipping Mission in Washington, to request that the United States increase construction of ships with refrigerated capacity and allocate them to British control so that Britain could import more meat from such locations as New Zealand, Australia, and Argentina. In return, U.S. Government officials sought to fend off such demands by suggesting changes in the existing refrigerated ships' routing patterns so that they could be used more efficiently by loading meat in American ports instead. This especially appealed to Army logisticians because meat production in Australia and New Zealand could be diverted to feed U.S. troops.

So during July 1942, officials from the U.S. Agriculture and War Departments, the War Shipping Administration (WSA), and the Office of Lend-Lease Administration (OLLA), backed by President Roosevelt, proposed that shipping capacity be saved by directing existing refrigerated ships to load in American ports for shorter voyages that would have the net effect of increasing shipping capacity by reducing the length of voyages and increasing utility for civilian and military purposes—by moving the maximum amount of meat on the shortest possible route. Their recommendation was adopted by the Combined Shipping Adjustment Board (CSAB) on 1 August 1942.[28]

The intensive interaction between U.S. agencies to develop this initiative and their efforts to lobby for it in response to initial British reluctance are described in the following paragraphs, highlighting by way of stark contrast the failure to implement that initiative over the ensuing months. Wickard's reaction as he gradually realized that implementation required choices he neither had the power to make, nor that he wished to make, illustrates not only his limits as an administrator, but also his underlying nationalism.

Following the 1 August CSAB recommendation to make U.S. meat available for shipment to the UK to save shipping, General B. B. Somervell, United States Army Commanding General, Services of Supply, convened a committee composed of representatives from the WSA, OLLA, the Army and the Navy, and the Board of Economic Warfare to examine more efficient use of shipping facilities in New Zealand and Australia. The committee's purview suggests that American officials intended that the diversion would serve U.S. military purposes as well as British civilian objectives. While this Griffin Committee (named after its chair, an OLLA official) deliberated, Douglas lobbied Wickard on 12 September to make the necessary meat available: "This will probably make a reduction in domestic (U.S.) consumption of some and perhaps all of the commodities inevitable and may make it more necessary than ever

---

[28]   RG 248, CSAB Minutes CSAB (L) (42) 53, 1 August 1942. The official recommendation read: "If more beef and other foodstuffs could be made available for shipment to the U.K. from the U.S.A. whether by development of supplies or restriction of consumption, important economies in shipping could be secured by further diversions to the North Atlantic route."

to take the anti-inflationary measures which the President seeks. Nevertheless, it will make possible a substantial net saving of shipping space, a goal that I am sure you realize we must reach if the war is to go well with us."[29]

Meanwhile, the Griffin Committee concurred with the need to reduce U.S. domestic meat consumption and concluded that doing so would indeed make Dominions meat available to U.S. troops in the South Pacific. It reported in mid-September that "rationing of domestic consumption has been directed by the Food Requirements Committee of the WPB, and its rationing plans . . . are such as to permit supply by this country to the U.K. of meat formerly furnished from New Zealand."[30] The need for a reduction in U.S. domestic meat consumption was unavoidable, but meat rationing would not begin until March 1943.

British shipping and food officials were hesitant to accept this arrangement. They would have to dismantle the existing frozen meat import program from southern hemisphere nations, reorienting traditional export and import ties, and to allocate more standard cargo vessels to carry outward-bound general cargo that hitherto had provided ballast on refrigerated ships but that still needed to arrive at destinations in the southern hemisphere. They also were concerned that insufficient refrigerated storage existed in U.S. east coast ports. They worried that British civilians would be reluctant to consume American pork instead of mutton. Most of all, they doubted that the Americans would be able to "provide continuous and sustained supplies."[31] As early as September 1942, BFM official Maurice Hutton complained that a refrigerated vessel had arrived in an American port only to find that the Department of Agriculture had been unable to procure frozen meat: "we are entirely in their hands . . . their incompetence must not allow space to be wasted."[32]

---

[29]   NARA, RG 248, File Conservation of Shipping, memorandum by Bernhard Knollenberg, senior deputy administrator of the United States Lend-Lease Administration in Washington, D.C., to Lend-Lease Administrator E. R. Stettinius, Jr., 18 March 1943 (hereinafter Knollenberg memorandum), Enclosure 3, memorandum from Douglas to Wickard, 12 September 1942.

[30]   RG 248, File Conservation of Shipping, Knollenberg memorandum, Enclosure 4, Griffin Committee to Stettinius, 15 September 1942.

[31]   TNA, MAF 97/1388, cable RATION X4712 from Ministry of Food (hereinafter MF) to British Food Mission (hereinafter BFM), 19 August 1942; MT 59/88, cable BILGE 2211, Minister of War Transport Lord Frederick Leathers to British Merchant Shipping Mission chief Sir Arthur Salter, 14 September 1942.

[32]   MAF 97/1388, Maurice Hutton (BFM) to Knight (MF), 14 September 1942. The confusion inherent in this fluid situation is illustrated by correspondence from December 1942 that depicts a contrary fear: that after the Department of Agriculture had made this "solemn promise" to provide cargo, Britain might not be able to deploy enough refrigerated space in the correct ports at the right time (MAF 97/1388, E. Twentyman (BFM) to Salter, 14 December 1942).

But American advocates complained to Salter of their "deep disappointment" at British hesitation—the British were "not really trying."[33] American insistence overrode British hesitation. Minister of War Transport Lord Frederick Leathers promised to make "maximum diversions" in accordance with the diversion plan in order to "secure maximum advantage on the shortest hauls on which supplies are available." But he insisted that such action was conditional on assurances that arrangements would be made to move other needed supplies to and from Australia and, most of all, "that the United States can provide continuous and sustained supplies of meat for the diverted tonnage." His worry remained obvious. He warned of the "difficulties and delays which will be involved if we disrupted the well-organized Australasian service and found ourselves later with refrigerated tonnage on the North Atlantic lacking cargo."[34]

Wickard and Brand soon responded, recommending that the shipping authorities plan for "the gradual substitution of the United States for Australasia as a source of meat supply for the United Kingdom until an amount of 263,000 tons per year, in addition to the present schedule of 195,000 tons per year, is being carried from the United States."[35] Wickard soon communicated this conclusion to Douglas, who responded on 15 October 1942 that, based upon that recommendation, "negotiations have proceeded further with the British. It now appears to be certain that the British will plan to increase their liftings of meat from the United States from the current annual rate of 195,000 tons to the annual rate of 458,000 tons . . . indicated to be feasible. As soon as the time schedule and other details of the diversion have been worked out I will furnish you with further details. May I say that I greatly appreciate the speed and decisiveness with which the Combined Food Board acted in this matter."[36] Thus Wickard promised to save shipping by increasing the availability of U.S. frozen meat exports to Britain from 195,000 tons to 458,000 tons. That new total was equivalent to a mere four percent of American production, but amounted to almost half of Britain's total meat import requirement.

In addition to correspondence among the principals of the various agencies, their subordinates also cooperated to work out the details, thus indicating that the

---

[33]   MT 59/88, cable BILGE 1188, Salter to Leathers and Ministry of War Transport Director General Sir Cyril Hurcomb, 9 September 1942; Library of Congress (hereinafter LC), W. Averell Harriman Papers (hereinafter HP), Box 165, Robert P. Meiklejohn, "Report on the Harriman Mission," pp. 208–09.

[34]   MT 59/88, cable BILGE 2211, Leathers to Salter, 14 September 1942.

[35]   RG 248, File Conservation of Shipping, Knollenberg memorandum, Enclosure 5, Combined Food Board memorandum signed by Wickard and Brand, 29 September 1942.

[36]   RG 248, File Conservation of Shipping, Knollenberg memorandum, Enclosures 6 and 7, Wickard to Douglas, 10 October 1942 and Douglas to Wickard, 15 October 1942. Wickard and Brand constituted the Combined Food Board in Washington.

diversion program was no mere casual assurance by Roosevelt or by preoccupied Cabinet officials. After referring to prior correspondence that covered the winter months, Ralph W. Olmstead of the USDA referenced detailed plans looking beyond February. He described "our expectation" that "with your cooperation in regard to the types of cuts and with some flexibility as to the types of meats which will answer your requirements we will be able to meet the program as outlined above." He cautioned that more distant prognostications could not be firm regarding the situation "nine and twelve months from now" given "all of the unknown factors in the situation" including military needs, and he took for granted that "you would not expect us to make such futile promises." But in his conclusion, Olmstead described "our expectation, however, that we can give full performance under this program. . . . It is our understanding that the quantities mentioned indicate the annual rate at which shipments will be made after we are able to get into the full program in 1943, without regard to the actual rate of shipments between now and January 1. The commitment is intended to apply until September 30, 1943, before which time we shall work out a new commitment for the following period based upon the current situation and needs."[37] Thus, his thorough examination of the early development of the diversion plan culminated with a clear USDA commitment with appropriate caveats regarding the final months of 1943. Britain's Ministry of War Transport began shifting refrigerated ships to North Atlantic routes while its Argentine, New Zealand, and Australian suppliers reoriented their operations from processing frozen meat to canning meat for the Soviet and American armies. In October 1942, they diverted refrigerated ships capable of carrying 35,000 tons of frozen meat to load in the United States in December and another 45,000 tons of carrying capacity to load in January.[38] As late as November 1942, the WSA and USDA offered joint "explicit assurances" that the complete 1943 program of 458,000 tons (averaging 38,000 tons monthly) would be fulfilled.[39]

Yet Wickard and his lieutenants had promised more than they could deliver. Well before the expected implementation of the "full program" at the New Year, the U.S. was unable to meet its commitments for that autumn, resulting in ships being wasted. By mid-November, no more than 13,000 tons was definite for December, 30,000 for January, and 38,000 for February. Douglas was already concerned that

---

[37]   RG 248, File Conservation of Shipping, Knollenberg memorandum, Enclosure 8, Ralph W. Olmstead to E. Twentyman of the British Food Mission, 23 October 1942, referencing Twentyman's prior letter. The letter's breakdown of planned meat exports into various categories matched precisely the categories and amounts listed under the "Diversion Program" in the final table below.

[38]   RG 248, File Conservation of Shipping, Knollenberg memorandum, Enclosure 9, Douglas to Wickard, 20 November 1942.

[39]   MT 59/88, cable SABWA 93, 19 November 1942; MAF 97/1388, Brand to Wickard, 22 January 1943.

the November shortfall might portend more serious problems later in the winter. While the diversion program was still theoretically alive, by late November he already feared that current performance indicated further shortfalls ahead. Douglas warned Wickard that the failure to provide cargo "has, not unnaturally, raised doubts in the minds of the British authorities about the availability in 1943 of the full 458,000 tons of meat which the Food Board had led them to expect." He asked again "whether the British can definitely count on exports of at least this magnitude throughout the year so that the total will actually be achieved and to urge as forcibly as possible that this amount be made available so that a substantial economy in shipping can be had." He reminded Wickard of the reason for his persistence:

> throughout the course of these negotiations . . . on the diversion of shipping, it has been the WSA here and in London that has consistently brought pressure on the Ministry of War Transport to take advantage of this change in the source of supply because of the possibility of economizing shipping. The British have been somewhat reluctant and have insisted that they must be able to count on the supplies promised from here. You will readily understand that any failure on our part to deliver meat in the quantities promised would be especially important in the light of these circumstances.[40]

Responding on behalf of Wickard, USDA's Leslie Wheeler offered reassurance: "I can only confirm . . . that the information that has been obtained in regard to the amount of meat that will be available during December, January, and February . . . can be taken as the best available estimates at this moment. There is still no reason to believe that the estimates on an annual basis given . . . [on] September 29 are excessive." He concluded that USDA officials "anticipate no difficulty in supplying monthly quotas beginning in February if meat production and army procurement approximate original estimates."[41] Douglas warned again that "a major change in shipping programs, such as the one now in progress in connection with this change in sources of supply for the UK, cannot be quickly and easily reversed. . . ."[42] In response to Douglas' repeated queries, Under Secretary for Agriculture Paul Appleby reiterated in mid-December that although "we have been unable to meet"

---

[40]   RG 248, File Conservation of Shipping, Knollenberg memorandum, Enclosure 9, Douglas to Wickard, 20 November 1942.

[41]   RG 248, File Conservation of Shipping, Knollenberg memorandum, Enclosure 10, Leslie Wheeler (executive officer of CFB) to Douglas on Wickard's behalf, 5 December 1942.

[42]   RG 248, File Conservation of Shipping, Knollenberg memorandum, Enclosure 11, Douglas to Wheeler, 13 December 1942.

Table 8.2:   American Frozen Meat Exports to Britain (tons)

Month	Promised Minimum Shipment	Actual Shipment
December 1942	13,000	1,676
January 1943	30,000	21,910
February 1943	38,000	12,950

TNA, MT 59/88, Combined Shipping Adjustment Board (CSAB) Washington (W) Paper # (43) 54, 6 April 1943.

the current schedule of 195,000 tons per year, shipments would from February 1943 reach the promised rate of 458,000 tons annually, "in accordance with" the allocations planned to "begin about December 1" in September's projections.[43] Thus three months after the initial projections, the escalation in shipments had been pushed back two months. Douglas was not reassured. Though he professed to be "gratified to receive this further assurance" that 458,000 tons of frozen meat would be procured for export to Britain and to "understand why there has been some delay in putting the program into effect," he repeated his insistence: "we feel it is most important to meet this commitment in view of the fact that the initiative in pressing for the diversion of British tonnage ... came from the American side."[44] Table 8.2 compares promise with performance for December 1942–February 1943.

Wickard's Response: Reasserting Unilateralism

Indeed, the Department of Agriculture was unable to fulfill the American commitment. At the end of December, even as the Griffin Committee reassured the head of the Office of Lend-Lease Administration, future Secretary of State Edward Stettinius, Jr., that the "United States will continue to make up the ... [shortfall] of meat already affected by diversions,"[45] officials in the Agriculture Department "informally advised the British Food Mission (BFM) that the previously proposed

---

[43]   RG 248, File Conservation of Shipping, Knollenberg memorandum, Enclosure 12, Under Secretary of Agriculture Paul H. Appleby to Douglas, 16 December 1942, enclosing memo from Olmstead.

[44]   RG 248, File Conservation of Shipping, Knollenberg memorandum, Enclosure 13, Douglas to Appleby, 21 December 1942.

[45]   RG 248, File Conservation of Shipping, Knollenberg memorandum, Enclosure 14, Griffin Committee to Stettinius, 29 December 1942.

quantities of frozen meat from the U.S. to the U.K. would not be provided."[46] Wickard officially informed Brand that 22,000 tons would be available in January, 55,000 tons would be available in February–April, and that no commitment could be made beyond that. Unofficially, the total would be 120,000 tons of frozen meat for the year.[47]

The development of this shortfall coincided with the diversion of escort vessels from import convoys in order to support the invasion of North Africa, a consequent acceleration in shipping losses, and a precipitous decline in Britain's overall imports. Simultaneously, Anglo-American tensions erupted over slow progress on the Algerian/Tunisian front, relations with French partners in North Africa, and divergent views of future strategy. Meanwhile, rather than allow suddenly "surplus" refrigerated ships to wait indefinitely in American ports without meat cargoes, British officials loaded some of them with non-refrigerated bulk foods and sent them to Britain. Over five million cubic feet of refrigerated shipping space had been programmed to arrive on the east coast during November–February, but they "loaded no refrigerated cargo because none was available."[48]

In the context of strategic disagreement, this improvisation to augment the overall import program amid the disruption of British meat imports heightened tensions between American and British military planners. The U.S. Joint Chiefs of Staff (JCS) believed that the movement of Allied forces into North Africa had been an unwise diversion from the proper focus on an invasion of France. Among several arguments that historians generally agree led to the correct decision to invade North Africa was the insufficiency of shipping capacity to support a landing in France in 1942, not to mention a shortage of trained troops, aircraft, and landing craft. Thus, American generals believed that this misuse of shipping demonstrated that the desired ships could be released from the British refrigerated import program for military purposes; maladministration of cargoes and shipping capacity therefore interacted with bitter strategic debates. As more refrigerated ships arrived in the United States to load nonexistent frozen meat cargoes, the JCS demanded that these ships be redeployed as fast troopships for either Atlantic or Pacific operations. Due to the distances involved, the latter would sidetrack the ships from civilian use for as much as a year. The JCS did succeed in diverting at least one such ship to deploy troops and supplies to Britain after it had sailed from India to the U.S. "solely for strengthening refrigerated shipments and in full assurance that suitable cargo would be available." British officials in Washington overseeing shipping and

---

[46]   RG 248, File Conservation of Shipping, Knollenberg memorandum, 18 March 1943, commenting on Enclosure 14.

[47]   RG 248, File Conservation of Shipping, Wickard to Brand, 22 January 1943, referenced in Knollenberg memorandum text, 18 March 1943.

[48]   RG 248, File Conservation of Shipping, undated draft letter by WSA officials Richard M. Bissell Jr. (later CIA Deputy Director) and D. F. Anderson.

food allocations insisted that President Roosevelt order Wickard to fulfill the meat export pledge. It was too late to release the ships for service on their original routes in the Southern Hemisphere because Australia and New Zealand had shifted to canning meat for the U.S. military. Britain needed American meat exports. As Robert Brand phrased it, the "withdrawal of this [American] assistance once given puts us in even greater difficulties than when we chiefly relied on other sources of supply."[49] Britain's dependence upon the United States for exports of refrigerated meat cargoes threatened Britain's import programs as surely as did the U-boat.

Newly anointed as War Food Administration "Czar," Wickard stood squarely in the public spotlight precisely where internal and external food distribution problems intersected: providing meat for export was now a critical issue that required the imposition of rationing upon American meat consumption. But domestic political difficulties and bureaucratic backbiting had intensified after the 1942 midterm election. A cartoon published by Clifford K. Berryman in *The Washington Star* on 5 March 1943 illustrated Wickard's difficulty. In February 1943, as part of his ongoing protest against British rule in India, Mohandas Gandhi began a fast, which Berryman depicted as completing "21 days without food—even canned food." While the "cartoon Wickard" points to Gandhi as a possible model for the American taxpayer, former Senator Prentiss Brown (D-MI), the new Administrator of the Office of Price Administration (whose defeat the prior November could be seen as a consequence of the electorate's dissatisfaction with Democratic policies), rejects the suggestion, recognizing taxpayers' distaste for eating canned food while shipping beef carcasses overseas. Berryman thereby paints Wickard as emblematic of a thoughtless bureaucracy that had already imposed supposedly excessive restraints upon American consumption through rationing of other commodities.[50] This caricature was utterly at variance with Wickard's real motives and actions, but its appearance could only have heightened Wickard's fears of public perception and hampered his flexibility. Wickard's public statements had always emphasized multilateral themes involving the export of American food in order to aid the war effort, but he moved very slowly to impose meat rationing because he did not want to inflame opposition to additional New Deal regulations or to hurt a Democratic Party reeling from mid-term losses in November 1942. His indecisiveness caused conflict with America's allies, especially Britain, which had imposed much more stringent rationing. Wickard's multilateral, internationalist rhetoric collided with unilateral, nationalist reality. Though a party to the promises of July and November 1942, Wickard nonetheless resisted urgent British pleas that America must fulfill its meat export pledge.

---

[49]   MAF 97/1388, cable RATION X7070 and X7149, 24 and 29 January 1943; Brand to Wickard, 11 January 1943; MT 59/88, cables AMAST 4458 and MASTA 5059, 11 February 1943.

[50]   See <http://www.nisk.k12.ny.us/fdr/1943/1943_03.html>, second cartoon in left-hand column, listed as 43030502.GIF.

Wickard certainly recognized that the United States had to augment its allies' food supply in order to help win the war; he always understood that "food will win the war, and write the peace."[51] But while Wickard was a rhetorical infantryman in the army of American officials that implemented Franklin Roosevelt's policies, his practical response to British requests reflected a traditional nationalist perspective that suggested the persistence of Thomas Paine's 1776 conception of "two spheres": the Old and New World as separate geographic and political domains—"two worlds," not Wendell Willkie's (best-selling) *One World*. Wickard's diary, his oral history, and his correspondence with British supplicants during these crucial months in late 1942 and early 1943 illustrate that America's emergence from unilateral disengagement was rocky.

Under pressure, Wickard's hopes of winning the war by producing enough food for the home front, Allied soldiers, and America's allies were crumbling. He could not extract the meat from the American economy overnight; it was impossible to impose sufficiently rigorous meat rationing quickly enough. Transportation and distribution difficulties created fear of local shortages and hoarding.[52] At the height of the meat export controversy, Wickard faced two other issues in his personal and professional lives that monopolized his attention instead. Wickard's diary for this period does not even mention British requests, even though he had demonstrated acute awareness of British needs in speeches as early as 1941. His daughter Ann was—like many other young women in 1943—determined to marry her fiancé, Jean Pickart, before he could be shipped overseas, ignoring Claude's forcefully stated preference that she graduate from Purdue before marriage. This forced an uneasy and unrealistic compromise: she would commute between Pickart's base in Pascagoula, Mississippi and West Lafayette, Indiana to complete her education. Wickard's equilibrium was also shattered by his other daughter Betty's sudden affliction with acute appendicitis.[53] The ongoing internal fight for control of American food production and distribution also continued during Brand's discussions with Wickard. It would reach its apex in March 1943 when Roosevelt reversed his appointment of Wickard as Food Administrator and stripped him of everything but his Cabinet title. He remained as Secretary of Agriculture while Chester Davis became the new War Food Administrator.[54] Even as this internal bureaucratic warfare distracted his attention, its delayed resolution left Wickard in charge of negotiations about frozen meat exports, but without the leverage he needed

---

[51] WFC, *Time*, 21 July 1941, p. 13; Albertson, *Roosevelt's Farmer*, pp. 199, 213, 234.

[52] MAF 97/1388, Hutton memorandum to Brand, 14 January 1943.

[53] Albertson, *Roosevelt's Farmer*, pp. 289, 343–44, 353. "I didn't know the pressures he was under" (Ann Wickard Pickart interview, February 2000).

[54] Albertson, *Roosevelt's Farmer*, pp. 369–83. Senator Raymond Willis (R-IN) criticized this "divided authority" in *The Indianapolis Star*, 26 March 1943 (WFC). Davis quit after just three months, frustrated by the same division of authority and responsibility that had maddened Wickard.

to make tough choices. "For the first time in my life I have a fear of a nervous break-down. I can't sleep at night and I am afraid I may be in for real trouble."[55]

Harried by family distractions, bureaucratic intrigue, and fear that the level of rationing necessary to meet British needs would provoke a backlash, Wickard seemed "muddled and frightened, on the defensive." Brand demanded action, but Wickard told Brand that fewer animals had been brought to market than expected, that black market purchases had diverted production, and that U.S. Army and Russian needs had increased. He insisted that the diversion scheme be abandoned and he refused to explain further: "we could elaborate these points very materially but feel it would serve little purpose here. Frankly, we do not believe it will be possible to handle the . . . situation until rationing . . . is invoked and is working success-fully."[56] U.S. domestic suspicion of intrusive government was hindering efficient provision of cargoes for the Atlantic run.

Brand reported to his boss, Minister of Food Lord Woolton, while preparing to beseech Wickard for aid again. Brand noted that the U.S. tended "to seek escape from necessity of supplying U.K. with critical short commodities which will soon be rationed here by arguing that our stocks are more than sufficient for us." Brand saw this as symptomatic of a failure to realize the "totally different circumstances of the two countries." America's self-sufficient domestic production and its protected distribution network contrasted vividly with British reliance on imports threatened by submarines. Still, though Britain relied on food stockpiles to safeguard against seaborne interdiction while the U.S. desired to use stockpiles in order to overcome maladministration, Britain's actual reserves seemed enormous to Americans. Thus Wickard ignored British shortages and the U-boat threat to give priority to build-ing American meat stocks so that American rationing would not be introduced under the threat of regional food shortages. He did so even though no American meat rationing plans had yet been finalized, and the proposed American ration would reduce consumption to a level about twenty-five percent higher than British consumption. When Wickard and Brand met, Wickard said he would reconsider only when rationing was in place and running smoothly. He argued: "a good many

---

55   Albertson, *Roosevelt's Farmer*, pp. 214–21, 310–83. Wickard confided to his diary: "My father's health is very bad and my mother is having a most difficult time because she is unable to get help. I have searched the country in an effort to find help but I have been entirely unsuccessful and I don't know what I am going to do to take care of my parents" (FDRL, Wickard Papers, Diary entries for 24 January 1943 and subsequently; oral history interviews #73–76, pp. 3026–3172).

56   MAF 97/1388, BFM civil servant Maurice Hutton to Brand, 14 January 1943; cable RATION 7203, 16 February 1943. In his oral history interview, Wickard emphasized that rationing "badly frightened" the American people, while "the English people . . . would have been less frightened than we were despite the fact that they were in more jeopardy" (FDRL, Wickard Papers, oral history interview #73, pp. 3032–33), because Americans were less accustomed to rationing.

people think that your people are getting more meat than ours. It isn't simply the ration that counts, there are lots of other things." He refused to specify the "other things" that supposedly provided extra meat to British consumers in wartime. This parochial, nationalist vision could not easily be contradicted, deeply entrenched as it was in suspicions that the "nation of shopkeepers" would always find a way to outmaneuver naïve "Brother Jonathan." Wickard also refused to acknowledge that the diversion scheme's failure had wasted shipping space. Brand concluded: "it is not easy to see at what point we can reach solid ground."[57]

Meanwhile, about 10,000 tons (not 30–40,000 tons) of frozen meat would be available for export monthly from the U.S., less than what had been exported before the shipping diversion. Wickard demanded that Brand accept his new, vague, and non-committal offer of 340,000 tons of all kinds of meat. Moreover, he insisted that "changing conditions of availability, transportation, and relative need make it imperative that I be in position to adjust allocations on 90 days notice"—even though reallocation of ships to alternative import sources in the southern hemisphere as necessary obviously required more lead time than ninety days. Brand's request for details of this new offer was futile: "he had no detailed knowledge of the figures at all." When Brand finally obtained details, it became clear that only 120–150,000 of the 340,000 tons could be properly compared with the previous schedule of 458,000 tons (see Table 8.3). Thus the new U.S. offer cut two-thirds from the original program.[58]

Resolution and Conclusion

Claude Wickard's nationalism, ignorance, helplessness, and descent into political insignificance forced Brand to bypass Wickard, the new War Food Administrator Chester Davis, and even "Assistant President" Jimmy Byrnes, and seek out Roosevelt's troubleshooter, Harry Hopkins. Brand needed a high-level political solution. He followed protocol by sending his request for reconsideration to Wickard, but he also sent a copy to Hopkins, and told Wickard that he was doing so. In a memorandum, he emphasized that a reduction in the British meat ration was imminent unless there was an "immediate and serious reconsideration" of the situation.[59]

Meanwhile, Wickard finally met with Douglas to explain the diversion program's collapse. USDA estimates of supply had been flawed, the black market had reduced meat availability by 20%, and Russian demands had been greater than

---

[57] MAF 97/1388, cable RATION 6769 and 7203, 19 January and 16 February 1943; MT 59/88, Wickard to Brand, 12 February 1943.

[58] MAF 97/1388, memorandum of 15 February 1943, summarized in cable RATION 7203, 16 February 1943; MAF 97/1389, Brand to Wickard, 12 March 1943; Brand to Woolton, 12 March 1943; Wickard to Brand, 18 March 1943.

[59] RG 248, File Conservation of Shipping, Brand memorandum, "U.S.A. Supplies of Frozen Meat to U.K.–1943," 8 March 1943.

Table 8.3:   Program for British Meat (including Frozen Meat) Imports from the United States

Type	Prior to Diversion (June 1942)	Diversion Program (July 1942)	Wickard's New Plan (March 1943)
Cured Pork (Bacon)	100,000–120,000	100,000	100,000
Canned Meat	120,000–240,000	120,000	120,000
Military	80,000	80,000	0
Pork Loins	125,000	185,000	
Manufacturing Meat	50,000–90,000	100,000	120,000–150,000 (combined)
Offals	10,000	15,000	
Beef, Mutton, Lamb	0	158,000	
Subtotal (Frozen Meat)	185,000–225,000	458,000	120,000–150,000
Total	485,000–665,000	758,000	340,000–370,000

TNA, MAF 97/1389, RATION 7293, 20 February 1943; MT 59/88, RATION 7202, 16 February 1943; minute by British civil servant A.K. Ogilvy Webb, 5 March 1943.

expected. He acknowledged that the British system for distributing food was "infinitely superior" and that the American system would have to improve as meat rationing went into effect. Wickard's terminology in describing events revealed his perspective. He described the diversion program as "what the British called 'commitments.'" He contended that "the British diet was about the same as ours." While Douglas was a known Anglophile, there is no reason to doubt the accuracy of the quotations, especially since the second assertion was essentially identical to what Brand had reported to Woolton as Wickard's sentiments after a separate conversation weeks earlier. These views offer insight into Wickard's perspective on the alliance. He dissociated himself from the promise to which he had been a party, suggested a false equivalence between the diets of citizens of the two nations, depicted himself as the victim of circumstance, and concluded that "radical rationing" would hurt those Americans "on the edge of not having enough."[60]

---

[60]   RG 248, File Conservation of Shipping, Douglas memorandum, "Conference Mr. Wickard re refrigerated foodstuffs," 15 March 1943. Though Wickard and his subordinates had hedged the diversion plan with caveats, it clearly did entail a commitment that the United States would supply refrigerated meat at a level far higher than was achieved.

Douglas avoided argument and merely reminded Wickard that shipping could be saved if food could be procured. But the essence of the conversation was quickly relayed to the Office of Lend-Lease Administration. Wickard's assertions elicited a detailed response that was clearly intended for Hopkins' review and that directly challenged Wickard's unilateralist perspective. Just three days later, Bernard Knollenberg, senior deputy administrator at OLLA, summarized recent developments in a memorandum written for his boss, Edward Stettinius. Knollenberg clearly objected to Wickard's conclusions. He outlined the contrast between U.S. consumption under the proposed rationing scheme and British rationing prior to the prospective cut forced by the failure of the diversion plan. While the higher consumption of fish in Britain partly offset the larger consumption of poultry in the United States, the overall comparison of meat per capita consumption remained at 182 pounds in the U.S. versus 148 in Britain. Knollenberg collected several months of correspondence, much of which has been cited above, to demonstrate his view "that there was a commitment" to Britain. He lobbied for "more stringent" U.S. rationing in order to enable the U.S. to meet its commitment, arguing that each American would have to sacrifice just three and one-quarter pounds of yearly consumption to do so. He noted, echoing Douglas' argument, that "we participated actively with the War Shipping Administration and Agriculture in inducing the U.K. to divert meat ships from the Australasian—U.K. run under a written commitment to the U.K."[61] The contrast between Knollenberg and Wickard's reactions illustrates the complexity of the evolution on the part of American officials toward a multilateralist worldview.[62]

---

[61]   RG 248, File Conservation of Shipping, Knollenberg memorandum to Stettinius, 18 March 1943, "The U.K. meat supply ration cannot be substantially increased other than from the U.S. without a serious wastage of shipping, and, even if shipping were wastefully diverted, the amount of meats needed to maintain present U.K. supplies could not be obtained outside the U.S."

[62]   Lizzie Collingham correctly notes in her recent study, *The Taste of War: World War II and the Battle for Food* (London: Allen Lane, 2011), that Britain was never in danger of starvation; an implicit comparison arises with populations elsewhere in the world who experienced actual starvation. One of Collingham's major themes is the export of hunger to colonial and neutral peoples, pursued both intentionally and unintentionally, by the various combatants. She correctly criticizes the excessively high food stocks that Britain maintained, especially when doing so created hunger and famine in the Empire. She also notes that U.S. officials suspected that British demands were exaggerated, based on experience earlier in the war. But her assertion that "American food officials had decided to implement a forced reduction in British reserves" and did so with support from WSA officials who "were suspicious of British claims" (p. 114) oversimplifies the evidence. As is clear from the evidence presented above, generalized awareness that Britain possessed large reserves did not prevent Knollenberg (OLLA) and Douglas (WSA) from making Britain's case. (The appeal of canned meat, which constituted much of the reserve, was limited.) Moreover, while

Hopkins was reluctant to force a cut in Britain's meat ration; he had seen it firsthand, since, unlike Wickard, he had visited wartime Britain. Hopkins worked out a compromise. He diverted 100,000 additional tons of frozen meat to British imports from Soviet allotments. Allocations would then increase further from September onward. Despite continuing problems throughout the summer, U.S. rationing gradually did release enough meat to help fulfill Hopkins' pledge. Even so, the revised commitment of 250,000 tons was still 200,000 tons shy of America's July 1942 promise and 70,000 tons shy of minimum stated British needs. British rations were indeed cut again awaiting American fulfillment of this new pledge.[63] Hopkins' intervention could not mitigate all the effects of the meat export program's belated and limited adjustment to multilateralism. Only military success would do so, as tactical victory in the Battle of the Atlantic in 1943 (combined with American shipbuilding production) finally provided enough new ships and preserved enough existing ones to provide the capacity to boost British meat imports near the required minimum amid an improved import outlook overall.

Even so, this episode reinforces both the importance of the near-complete reduction of the German threat to North Atlantic convoys in March–May 1943 (pending possible German introduction of new submarines) and also the incomplete nature of that victory. Victory in combat was not enough. Because the Battle of the Atlantic involved so many variable factors, such as the moving of appropriate cargoes from American farms and factories via American roads and railways to American ports, the marrying of them efficiently to promptly-arriving cargo vessels, and the escorting of them safely across the Atlantic to be unloaded and distributed from British ports into the British economy, the defeat of the submarine threat only ensured that just one of these requirements would be met. While victory at sea and in the shipyards compensated for Wickard's struggle to adjust to new diplomatic realities, and this story does recognize the timeliness of that spring 1943 victory in the Battle of the Atlantic, it also emphasizes a broader context within which maritime warfare must be situated: a managerial and diplomatic effort that affected the outcome of maritime warriors' struggles in ways they could not see at the time and in ways historians have far too often ignored since then.

In particular, the meat export crisis of 1942–43 provides another lens for situating military and maritime history in the broader context of international history

---

Wickard complained that Britain had large reserves, he did so in contrast to the American inability to develop stocks, which was rooted in domestic political concerns and administrative incompetence, not food shortages. As Collingham acknowledges, Wickard's suggestion that the diversion plan be abandoned was "cavalier" (p. 114). Wickard's reaction to the failure of the diversion plan remains an example of a narrow nationalistic perspective.

[63] HP, Box 163, Chron File February 1943, Harriman to Hopkins, 20 February 1943; MAF 97/1389, cables RATION 7861 and 8378 and RATION X8554, 27 March and 24 April 1943 (2), exchanges between Brand and Woolton.

and the national histories of Britain and the United States. The U.S. became the dominant power in the alliance during the war, but struggled to adapt to its new global role. Claude Wickard illustrates this transition. He loyally repeated internationalist platitudes in public statements throughout the war. He believed, he said, in winning the war with food. But when beset by personal and professional troubles, rather than take a multilateralist position that balanced allocation of American meat to America's allies as well as American domestic needs far from the global battlefields, he reverted instinctively to a traditional unilateral and nationalist interpretation of the proper relationship between the Old World and the New. America's domestic politics and relatively high levels of food consumption took precedence over Allied needs. Transatlantic cooperation had rhetorically blossomed, but it remained bureaucratically embryonic in 1943. The result of Wickard's labors would be eventual Allied sufficiency by a narrow margin, but the birth pangs were painful. Amid the crisis, Brand summarized wartime America's transition:

> This is a very strange country. It seems always on the verge of a crisis of major magnitude. . . . a result of the size of the country and its disparate government . . . its wealth and energy, and its lack of a common political ethos. Nevertheless, it is also a very remarkable country. The crises very rarely come to full maturity. Results, and desirable results, are in fact achieved. They are probably less than would have been achieved given a more perfect system, but nevertheless they are most remarkable in the degree to which they approach, in their own erratic and peculiar manner, the maximum goal. I would sum it up by saying that this is a country in which one should always be apprehensive regarding political developments, but never despondent.[64]

Brand found a silver lining. Nationalism, disdain for intrusive government, and managerial incompetence had combined to damage Allied management of shipping capacity, but the Allies would overcome. While Wickard rhetorically embraced Roosevelt's policy of all available assistance to Britain, his practical contributions to that effort revealed a nationalist ambivalence rooted in personal experience and internecine bureaucratic struggle. Though Cold Warriors would later construct a narrative of a seamless post-Pearl Harbor transition away from the unilateral nationalism of the interwar years, this decent, dutiful, loyal, and honest patriot struggled awkwardly, and ultimately failed, in this crucial test to move beyond the nostrums of his rural upbringing, to balance domestic and Allied food requirements, and to shift from prewar unilateral disengagement to multilateral engagement.

---

[64]   MAF 97/1389, Brand to Woolton, 26 February 1943.

9

The Other Critical Convoy Battles of 1943

The Eclipse of the *Schnellboote* in the English Channel and the North Sea

G. H. Bennett

In the historiography of the Second World War at sea, the convoy battles for SC122 and HX229 in March 1943 represent the turning point in the Battle of the Atlantic.[1] What Jürgen Rohwer has labeled "the critical convoy battles of March 1943" gave way, in a few short weeks, to Black May.[2] During that month, forty-one U-boats were lost (25% of the operational strength of the U-boat command) and, on 24 May, Admiral Karl Dönitz suspended the campaign. While scholars have focused on the mid-Atlantic and the U-boat campaign, they have largely overlooked the Royal Navy's decisive victory in the struggle to maintain the coastal convoys along Britain's south and east coasts.[3] The campaign by coastal forces

[1] This chapter has been supported by a grant from the Wheatcroft Collection and I would like to record my thanks to Kevin Wheatcroft.

[2] Jürgen Rohwer, *The Critical Convoy Battles of March 1943: The Battle for HX.229/SC122* (Annapolis: Naval Institute Press, 1977).

[3] The number of works devoted to the coastal campaign is small. See, for example, Bryan Cooper, *The E-boat Threat* (Abingdon: Purnell, 1976); Alexander McKee, *The Coal-Scuttle Brigade* (London: New English Library, 1973); Robert Jackson, *Churchill's Moat: The Channel War, 1939–1945* (Shrewsbury: Airlife, 1995); J. P. Foynes, *Battle of the East Coast* (Isleworth: self-published, 1994); Peter C. Smith, *Hold the Narrow Sea: Naval Warfare in the English Channel, 1939–1945* (Annapolis: Naval Institute Press, 1984). There is a larger volume of work dealing with coastal forces: Lieutenant Commander Peter Scott, *The Battle of the Narrow Seas: A History of the Light Coastal Forces in the Channel and North Sea, 1939–1945* (London: Country Life, 1945); Gordon Williamson, *E-boat vs MTB: The English Channel, 1941–45* (Oxford: Osprey, 2011); Gordon Williamson, *Kriegsmarine Coastal Forces* (Oxford: Osprey, 2009); Gordon Williamson, *German E-boats, 1939–45* (Oxford: Osprey, 2002); Harold Pickles, *Untold Stories of Small Boats at War: Coastal Forces Veterans Remember* (Edinburgh: Pentland Press, 1994); Leonard C. Reynolds, *Home Waters MTBs at War: Channel and North Sea MTB and MGB Flotilla Operations, 1939–1945* (Stroud: Sutton,

from 1940 to 1945 for control of the narrow seas between Britain and France was a vital part of the war at sea. The convoys that ran along Britain's south and east coasts carried the coal on which Britain's southern cities and war industries depended. The coastal convoys also represent a vital missing link in the story of the Atlantic struggle. After crossing the Atlantic, cargoes were often transhipped for movement around the coast in smaller ships. They were also, by 1943, playing a vital role in the build-up of military resources in the United Kingdom as part of Operation Bolero. To deliver Bolero requirements, the size of coastal convoys had to more than double during 1943, and larger, ocean-going ships had to be routed along the south coast of England. It was vital to ensure the safe arrival of these ships and their precious cargoes, and, in 1943, that was in question.

From 1940 until 1942, the Royal Navy struggled to come to terms with the German *Schnellboote* (S-boats) operating in the English Channel. Referred to as "E-boats" by the British (E for enemy), the tonnage of British coastal merchant shipping sunk along the east and south coast of Britain by these powerful motor-torpedo boats grew. But, in 1943, the campaign suddenly collapsed with just six merchant vessels being sunk by the S-boats. This chapter seeks to locate the coastal campaign as an integral part of the Battle of the Atlantic, analyzing the threat posed by the S-boat together with the development of countermeasures by the Royal Navy and Royal Air Force (RAF). It will examine the evolution of British tactics, the development of new weapons systems, and the intelligence struggle against the S-boats. It will also analyze critical failures and delays to respond on the part of the *Kriegsmarine*. Historians have failed to recognize that, between 1940 and 1943, the British were able to create a sophisticated, multi-layered, sea-air defense-in-depth along the south and east coasts of the United Kingdom, using a variety of weapons platforms, and utilizing real-time intelligence and electronic information sources. It was the success of this system of defense that neutralized the S-boat as a threat to the coastal convoys.

The Fall of France and the Emergence of the S-boat Threat

The *Schnellboote* first appeared as a threat to British ships during the Dunkirk evacuation in 1940 and, during that year, S-boats sank twenty-three British ships (47,985 GRT). Although in comparison to the first "happy time" enjoyed by the U-boats in 1940, these were not particularly large numbers in terms of the overall tonnage of British ships lost, but the figures were nonetheless significant. U-boat, S-boat, auxiliary raider, surface warship, mine, and *Luftwaffe* attacks against shipping each contributed to the overall tonnage war, which was the primary strategy

2000); Jean-Phillippe Dallies-Labourdette, *Deutsche Schnellboote, 1939–1945* (Stuttgart: Motorbuch, 2006); Hans Frank, *Die Deutschen Schnellboote im Einsatz: Von den Anfängen bis 1945* (Berlin: E. S. Mittler & Sohn, 2006).

of the *Kriegsmarine*. In addition, the S-boats targeted a particular sector of British merchant shipping: short coastal traffic.

At the outbreak of war, coastal shipping made up a significant proportion of the British merchant fleet. In 1937, 1,479 steam and motor vessels totaling 1,151,880 GRT and employing 21,324 British and 261 foreign seamen were primarily engaged in the British coasting trade.[4] During the war, the coastal convoys fulfilled two significant strategic functions in terms of the British economy. First, they brought coal from the coalfields in northeast England and Wales to the southeast of England (for the purposes of heating homes and fueling the power stations vital to maintain British war industries). In 1852, William Cory had initiated the use of steam colliers to bring coal into the capital. Coal carried by sea quickly came to dominate the London market, and the growth of power-intensive industries in the capital such as heavy engineering, chemicals, shipbuilding, and armaments was fueled by plentiful supplies of coal.[5] The movement of coal from the mines in the west and north of Britain depended on coastal traffic and, by 1939, London alone required 10,250,000 tons of coal per annum to maintain her "gas, electricity, water, sewerage, transportation and hydraulic power."[6] The requirements of the southeast meant that convoys along the east coast had to run on an almost daily basis, and along the south coast on the basis of every other day.[7]

The second strategic function of the coastal convoys was that they allowed the transhipment of cargoes from larger vessels that had crossed the North Atlantic and their delivery closer to their point of use. In some cases, this involved incorporating ships that had made the Atlantic run into coastal convoys; in others, it meant unloading cargoes from larger ships into small coasting vessels. This could be done

---

[4]   Board of Trade, *Statistical Abstract of the United Kingdom,* no. 82 (London: HMSO, 1938), table 272, pp. 366–67.

[5]   John Marriott, "Smokestack: The Industrial History of the Thames Gateway," in Philip Cohen and Michael J. Rustin, eds., *London's Turning: The Making of the Thames Gateway* (Aldershot: Ashgate, 2008), pp. 22–23.

[6]   Nick Hewitt, *Coastal Convoys, 1939–1945: The Indestructible Highway* (Barnsley: Pen and Sword, 2008), p. 7.

[7]   British Coastal Convoys, Late 1943

Route	Code Id.	Frequency	Av. No. Ships	Time on Passage
Nore-Methil	FN	6 days in 7	33	54 hours
Methil-Nore	FS	every 4 days	33	54 hours
Southend-Portsmouth	CW	every 4 days	20	24 hours
Portsmouth-Southend	CE	every 4 days	20	24 hours
Portsmth.-Bristol Chan.	PW	1 day in 2	16	48 hours
Bristol Chan.-Portsmth.	WP	1 day in 2	16	48 hours

Figures from The National Archives, London (hereinafter TNA), Admiralty Records (hereinafter ADM) 1/15815, "Coastal Convoys: An Appreciation," 11 October 1943.

in port or in sheltered anchorages using the derricks of the larger ships. With both coal deliveries and the onward transhipment of cargoes that had crossed the Atlantic, the coastal convoys played a vital role in easing the strain on overburdened ports and the British railway network which struggled to cope with wartime demands. Ports, starting with the Port of London in 1940, were targets of the *Luftwaffe* after the Fall of France in June 1940. Britain's inland transport system (rail, road, and waterways) simply did not have the capacity to expand to replace the cargo capacity of the coastal convoys. On both sides of the Channel, there was an acute understanding that the coastal convoys "carried the coal on which London absolutely depended."[8] The *Führer der Torpedoboote*[9] commented on 5 July 1940 that "England is forced to carry on the traffic to London in order to keep Southern England going. This will be done regardless of results."[10] The narrow and shallow confines of the English Channel placed this traffic largely beyond the reach of U-boats and major surface warships. The development of defensive minefields off the English coast placed further restrictions on the ability of the *Kriegsmarine* to target British shipping off the east and south coasts.[11]

Their most effective weapon in the circumstance was the *Schnellboot*. Capable of speeds in excess of forty knots, equipped with two torpedo tubes and two reloads together with a 20mm cannon and 40mm heavy machine guns, the S-boat was a formidable weapon of war in 1940. They were over 110 feet in length, powered by three Mercedes-Benz diesel engines (2,500 bhp). The S-boat was a heavyweight with the speed and grace of a lightweight. "Like the panther it possessed a savagery out of all proportion to its size, and leaping forward it could slay a victim twenty times its weight if its fangs [the torpedoes] found a vital mark."[12] S-boats possessed the means to sink a battleship, and the British soon learned to have a healthy respect for their devastating effectiveness against merchant shipping, especially light coastal vessels.[13] As Hans Frank has noted, during the Dunkirk evacuation, "the sinking of two destroyers, severe damage to a third, together with three steamers sunk, showed the capabilities of the S-boats despite there only ever being two or three out of a total of nine operational at a time because of engine

---

[8]   Captain Peter Dickens, *Night Action: MTB Flotilla at War* (London: Purnell, 1974), p. 28.

[9]   *Schnellboote* flotillas were commanded by the *Führer der Torpedoboote* (FdT) until 1942 when a new post of *Führer der Schnellboote* was created.

[10]   ADM 223/28, Appreciation of the Situation by FdT, 5 July 1940.

[11]   ADM 1/15815, "Defensive Minelaying Policy in Home Waters."

[12]   Theodore Roscoe, *United States Destroyer Operations in World War II* (Annapolis: Naval Institute Press, 1953), p. 357.

[13]   The scale of casualties resulting from a torpedo strike on a coastal vessel was often considerable. When MV (Motor Vessel) *Underwood* was sunk on convoy WP 457 on 6 January 1944, there were nine survivors from a crew of twenty-three.

troubles."[14] Second Officer V. P. Wills-Rust was the senior survivor from SS *Abukir*, sunk by *S-34* on 28 May 1940 after leaving Ostend. Hit by a torpedo, the ship sank in seconds, killing many of the 200 passengers on board. Rust later described the incident: "Although I was trapped, I could see everything over my head. The stern burst into flames and I saw flames forward. I could see the water coming up and over my head. The ship hit bottom and turned over, the debris was thrown off me and I was released and I came to the surface."[15]

The S-boats were able to reap a solid harvest of victims during the May-June evacuations from the continent, and, with the coast of France secured in June 1940, they were able to operate from French, Belgian, and Dutch ports until 1944. In practice, as some units were rotated to and from other theaters of operation, only three or four S-boat flotillas were operational in the North Sea and English Channel at any one time from 1940 to 1943.[16] Requiring considerable maintenance and awkward to repair, each flotilla had four or five boats ready to dispatch on any particular sortie. Despite this, the S-boats were the ideal weapon to interdict the coastal shipping lanes, and, in the summer of 1940, they combined with the *Luftwaffe* to force a cessation of daylight traffic along certain pinch-points on the coastal routes. Convoying, usually involving around twenty-five merchant ships together with attendant escorts and minesweepers, offered one way forward. But in the circumstances of 1940, there were simply not enough escort vessels to go around. Hastily converted ocean-going trawlers and whalers with crews from the Royal Navy Patrol Service had to be pressed into service as auxiliary warships to provide escort to the coastal convoys. They were no match in speed or firepower for the S-boats. Given the shortages of destroyers, makeshift escorts were frequently the best which the Royal Navy could provide in 1940–41. However, even destroyers found S-boats difficult targets to hit. First Lieutenant Peter Dickens on the Hunt-class destroyer HMS *Cotswold* later wrote: "[S-boats] presented us with new problems in tactics and gunnery. We often heard and saw them as they strove to close our convoys, but to take a damaging shot at the ghostly shadows while they shimmered fleetingly in and out of our ken seemed beyond the capability of our

---

[14] Hans Frank, *German S-boats in Action in the Second World War* (Barnsley: Seaforth, 2007), p. 21.

[15] ADM 199/2132, Survivors Report by Second Officer, V. P. Wills Rust, 5 June 1940.

[16] Flotillas Operating in the English Channel against East Coast Convoys, 1940–45

> 1940—1st 2nd 3rd
> 1941—1st 2nd 3rd 4th 5th 6th
> 1942—2nd 4th 5th 6th 8th
> 1943—2nd 4th 5th 6th 8th 9th
> 1944—2nd 4th 5th 6th 8th 9th 10th
> 1945—2nd 6th 8th 9th 10th

ponderous [fire] control system."[17] It was not until 1941–42 that the number of escort vessels began to improve, and British shipyards began to turn out an increasing number of motor launches, motor gunboats, and motor torpedo boats to defend the coastal shipping lanes. At the same time, the RAF slowly turned its attention to how air power could be used to neutralize the S-boat threat. It took time for the improving defenses to make a difference at sea. In 1941, S-boats sank twenty-nine ships totaling 58,854 GRT and, in 1942, twenty-three ships at 71,156 GRT. However, in 1943, the S-boat campaign along the Channel Coast collapsed with just six sinkings of 15,138 GRT.[18]

In academic and public perceptions, the eclipse of the S-boat campaign has been overshadowed by the changing fortunes in 1943 in the struggle in the Atlantic. It is the emergence of the motor gunboat and the development of British coastal forces which are most frequently put forward as the principal reasons for the eclipse of the S-boat, insofar as the collapse of the S-boat campaign has been analyzed at all. In reality, it was not the emergence of a single weapons system to combat the S-boat threat that brought about the poor harvest for German coastal forces along the English Channel in 1943. Tactical changes, better utilization of intelligence, and, most crucially of all, German failure to upgrade the S-boat's weapon and defensive systems brought about the crisis of 1943 for the S-boat arm of the *Kriegsmarine*. Even then it is important to recognize that, while the British had managed to largely neutralize the threat to coastal convoys by 1943, it was another thing again to eliminate the S-boat threat by the destruction of German forces. S-boats continued to trouble British shipping in the North Sea even at war's end.

Success of the Convoy System: Escort and Tactical Innovation

In 1940, especially following the losses of destroyers at Dunkirk, the British lacked sufficient escort vessels to cover both the Channel and the Atlantic convoys. The number of available destroyers, frigates, corvettes, and sloops available for Channel and east coast operations improved during 1941 and 1942, but urgent operational requirements could lead to temporary reductions. By the end of 1943, the number of destroyers available on the east coast dipped markedly as a result of requirements in the Mediterranean.[19] In addition, under the stress of wartime

---

[17]   Dickens, *Night Action*, p. 28.

[18]   Stephen Wentworth Roskill, *The War at Sea, 1939–45*, Vol. III, *The Offensive*, Part II, *1st June 1944–14th August 1945* (London: HMSO, 1961), p. 479.

[19]   Number of Destroyers Available on the East Coast

	October 1941	October 1942	October 1943
Rosyth	25	24	14
Nore	21	24	19

Figures contained in ADM 1/15815, C-in-C Nore to Admiralty, 16 October 1943.

operations, some of the older destroyers proved increasingly unreliable and troublesome. By 1943, the Town-class destroyers, four of which were allocated to the Rosyth Command, were condemned as "virtually useless" against S-boats, and there were complaints that some of the older destroyers were "subject to continual breakdowns and minor defects due to old age."[20]

There was also a recognition in late 1940 that while heavier ships possessed the caliber of guns necessary to sink an S-boat, hitting them was highly problematic. In response, a turret mounting was developed to house twin six-pounder, quick-firing guns previously developed and used as coast defense artillery. Replacing an existing turret, the twin six-pounder mounting was installed on eight destroyers operating along the English Channel.[21] Able to fire eighteen rounds a minute, the twin six-pounder could place a considerable volume of fire on any target. Although it was not until December 1944 that the twin six-pounder accounted for an S-boat, the commanding officer's report confirmed the general appreciation that it was a handy weapon against light enemy craft, noting, "This is the first time that a kill has been made by a six pounder and in my opinion at short ranges (that is below 3,000 yards) one cannot ask for a better weapon."[22] Increasingly, the larger ships operated in conjunction with light coastal forces.

During 1941, the number of light vessels available to escort the coastal convoys increased considerably, but they still faced considerable problems in trying to deal with S-boats which were faster, more heavily-armed, more capable in rough seas, and better able to survive major damage.[23] Motor torpedo boats (MTB) were in short supply in 1940, but, following the fall of France, British boatyards were remarkably successful in responding to emergency contracts for more MTBs and more fast motor launches (MLs). In March 1941, orders were placed for a new kind of fast, heavily-armed boat—the motor gunboat (MGB). The initial order was rapidly expanded to forty boats. Motor torpedo boats and motor gunboats lacked the weapons to deal effectively with S-boats in any form of high speed combat. During the course of the war, only six (out of an overall eighty-two) British MTBs and MGBs were sunk by S-boats and only eight (out of ninety-three) S-boat losses came from attacks by MTBs and MGBs. A torpedo was an effective weapon against a slow-moving merchant ship, but against a fast-moving light craft it was all but

---

20   ADM 1/15815, C-in-C Nore to Admiralty, 16 October 1943.

21   These eight destroyers included HMS *Walpole, Montrose, Mackay, Wivern, Worcester, Windsor, Whitshed,* and *Campbell.*

22   ADM 1/30193, Report by Commanding Officer, HMS *Walpole,* enclosure 1 in "Actions against E-boats on 22–23 December 1944: Recommendations for Honours and Awards," 1 March 1945.

23   The top speed of the Motor Torpedo Boat was thirty-three to forty-one knots, depending on type. The Fairmile D Gun Boat top speed was twenty-nine knots. The S-boat top speed was forty to forty-five knots, depending on hull type and engine fit.

useless. Machine guns and cannon could pepper the hull of a torpedo boat without inflicting fatal damage. In fast-moving engagements, cutting across the enemy line and dropping a shallow-set depth charge to explode underneath the next passing enemy vessel was considered more effective than gunfire in inflicting fatal hull damage. Failing that, ramming was the next best option.

The qualitative inferiority of Allied MTBs and MGBs from 1940 to 1943 placed a heavy emphasis on numbers and tactics. In April 1942, *Führer der Schnellboote* (FdS) Rudolf Petersen noted that British coastal forces were now so numerous that they were "superior in force" to the S-boats ranged against them.[24] Those tactics owed a great deal to Robert Hichens who rose to become a Lieutenant Commander in charge of the 6th and later 8th MGB Flotillas.[25] Given command of *MGB 64* in January 1941, Hichens achieved such distinction that he became flotilla leader within nine months. Hichens believed in the Nelson tradition of engaging the enemy as closely as possible regardless of the damage done to British coastal forces.[26] The damage done to the enemy might not result in a sinking, but it would disrupt their operations and repairs would take time. An S-boat damaged off the British coast might not be able to make it back to a German-held port.

With any engagement, the S-boats lost the element of surprise that was significant in the approach to a convoy or the unobserved execution of a mining operation. Gunfire was sufficient to drive off S-boats or to disrupt their attack. For example, on the night of 19–20 November 1941, a group of S-boats from 2nd S-boat Flotilla was attacked by *MGB 64* (Hichens in command) and *MGB 67*. The German vessels were returning from an attack on an east coast convoy in which three British ships had been sunk. In the process, *S-41* and *S-47* had collided. *S-41* was under tow when a group of five S-boats was attacked by British forces. The British MGBs were unable to inflict fatal damage on any of the S-boats they engaged at short-range (their heaviest armament at this stage in the war was mounted aft, which limited the chances of a fatal shot). However, German forces felt compelled to break off the tow of *S-41*. After transferring her crew and opening her seacocks, *S-41* was left to sink, which she did, but not before the vessel had been located and boarded by the MGB crews.[27] As Roskill noted in the official history, the sinking wreck yielded "large quantities of equipment—charts, log-books"

---

[24]   ADM 223/28, Führer der Schnellboote (FdS) war diary, 22 April 1942.

[25]   Robert Peverell Hichens (2 March 1909–13 April 1943), Distinguished Service Order (DSO) and Bar, Distinguished Service Cross (DSC) and two Bars, was the most highly decorated officer of the Royal Navy Volunteer Reserve. See Lieutenant Commander Robert Peverell Hichens, *We Fought Them in Gunboats* (London: Michael Joseph, 1944), for his unfinished memoir of coastal forces actions.

[26]   Bryan Cooper, *The Battle of the Torpedo Boats* (London: Pan, 1972), p. 76ff.

[27]   Stephen Wentworth Roskill, *The War at Sea, 1939–1945*, Vol. I, *The Defensive* (London: HMSO, 1954), pp. 500–01.

before she sank.[28] Hichens put it rather more directly in his unfinished wartime memoir: "The order was given to gut the boat. Sailors swarmed all over her, appearing from all the hatches with arms full of equipment. Roberts removed all the W/T equipment, gunners took what guns they could detach and pans of ammunition. Charts, books, log, compasses, searchlights, revolvers, even pictures of Hitler were bundled into the gunboats."[29] The retreating S-boats were later attacked by British fighter aircraft, and the Air Ministry erroneously claimed one sunk and one damaged.[30]

Hichens was also the inspiration in 1942 for taking the reach of coastal forces to the enemy coast. To the defensive work of coastal forces, he sought to add the weapon of blockade by trying to intercept enemy forces as they sortied from their continental bases. By March 1942, MGBs were ready to conduct offensive patrols off the Dutch coast. On the night of 14–15 March, one patrol encountered a group of S-boats as they came out from Ijmuiden to intercept east coast shipping. According to Roskill, one S-boat was lost and RAF Spitfires joined in the pursuit of the retreating boats the next morning.[31] The Air Ministry was ready to claim their share in the victory. *The New York Times* reported that "cannon-equipped Spitfire [had] set one enemy vessel afire and damaged four others."[32] By such actions, British forces felt that they were gradually getting onto even terms with the S-boat threat.

The British steadily maximized the impact of their coastal forces. In 1942, C-in-C Nore introduced the idea of a standing offshore patrol to serve as a protective screen for shipping along the east coast. "This was known as the Z-line, which was an imaginary line about 30 miles off the East Coast, running for a distance of approximately 100 miles between Cromer and Harwich."[33] Arriving on station, British coastal forces would simply cut engines and wait the arrival of the enemy. Hydrophones were used to listen for the approach of the S-boats.[34] Invariably, gaps could be found in the patrol line, but it was still a significant deterrent. Infiltrating or exfiltrating British waters, S-boat crews increasingly had to expect contact with MTBs and MGBs.

The construction of additional fixed defenses along the English coast added to the difficulty for the S-boats. The siting of seven Maunsell Army and Navy forts in

[28]   Scott, *Narrow Seas*, pp. 36–37; Williamson, *E-boat vs MTB*, p. 48.

[29]   Hichens, *Gunboats*, p. 27.

[30]   "British Rout Nazis in North Sea Fight," *The New York Times*, 22 November 1941, p. 5.

[31]   Stephen Wentworth Roskill, *The War at Sea, 1939–1945*, Vol. II, *The Period of Balance* (London: HMSO, 1960–62), p. 162.

[32]   "7 German E-boats Blasted by British," *The New York Times*, 16 March 1942, pp. 1, 3.

[33]   David Jefferson, *Coastal Forces at War: The Royal Navy's "Little Ships" in the Narrow Seas* (Sparkford: Haynes, 2008), p. 153.

[34]   Hewitt, *Coastal*, p. 169.

the approaches to the Thames estuary in 1942–43 augmented the fixed coastal defenses covering southeastern England.[35] Constructed out of concrete before being towed into position, they were searchlight and radio platforms as well as being equipped with 40mm and 3.7-inch guns. Their primary purpose was to serve as an outer anti-aircraft defense for London as well as covering the Thames estuary against German mine-laying operations. They could, of course, engage any surface target that was unwise enough to come into view.

Success of the Convoy System: Coastal Command, the Scientific and Intelligence War

Backing operations at sea level, and an increasingly important factor in combating the S-boat threat, was RAF Coastal Command. Air to Surface Vessel Radar (ASV) had been pioneered in the mid-1930s, and by the middle of 1941, around half the aircraft of RAF Coastal Command were fitted with ASV.[36] However, there were still considerable issues with the reliability and effectiveness of the Mark I and II sets. In the summer of 1941, 16 Group RAF Coastal Command started reconnaissance flights across S-boat approach routes to the British coast. The wake of a fast-moving boat was highly visible at night, while the approach of an aircraft would be drowned out by the boat's engines.[37] An S-boat, however, was unlikely to fall victim to a bombing or torpedo attack from the squadrons at the disposal of 16 Group, but at least the experiment served to demonstrate the principle.[38] In October 1941, Wing Commander Constable-Roberts, staff officer of 16 Group RAF, attached to the Royal Navy's Dover Command, began the first experiments in the use of the home chain radar network to guide Coastal Command aircraft against enemy shipping and developing S-boat attacks. Roberts reported: "The information of early approach of enemy light forces by Type 271 10cm RDF stations has allowed our own [air] forces to intercept before any damage could be done. This fortunate state of affairs has resulted in a complete cessation of enemy . . . minelaying or torpedo attack along our convoy routes in this area."[39] By 1943, 16 Group had a larger complement of squadrons and its principal weapon against the S-boats was the radar-equipped, twin-engine Whitley bomber, while the Fleet Air Arm operated Albacore and Fairey Swordfish. The role of radar-equipped aircraft was "primarily to give

---

[35]   The forts were at the Nore, Red Sands, Shivering Sands, Tongue Sands, Knock John, Rough Sands, and Sunk Head.

[36]   Chris Ashworth, *RAF Coastal Command, 1936–1969* (Sparkford: Patrick Stephens, 1992), p. 66.

[37]   ADM 223/28, Report by FdT, December 1941.

[38]   Hewitt, *Coastal*, p. 152.

[39]   Imperial War Museum, Air Commodore J. Constable-Roberts papers, Documents 1183.

warning" of approaching S-boats.[40] They were then to mark their location for surface forces by flare or flame floats. However, by May 1943, the Director of Air Warfare and Flying Training was looking forward to the installation of High Frequency Wireless Telegraph sets which would allow direct radio contact between "convoy escorts, counter attacking force and homing aircraft."[41] Some of the difficulties affecting Royal Navy/RAF cooperation against the S-boats were removed by a meeting at the Air Ministry on 20 August 1943 when the RAF agreed to dedicate ten Wellington XIII aircraft and ten Albacores. Under the control of 415 Squadron, the Wellingtons became operational at Thorney Island and Bircham Newton in October and the Albacores by the end of the year.[42]

The impact of the scientific and intelligence war on the coastal campaign is difficult to quantify as the documentary record is fragmentary at best. However, some insights can be gained from files in the British National Archives dealing with S-boats in the Mediterranean.[43] By 1941, the British were using HUMINT (agents and interrogations of captured personnel), SIGINT (signals intelligence), and photo-reconnaissance to monitor S-boat activity. The amount of information which could be derived from such sources was considerable. For example, a twenty-four page dossier of information was put together on every aspect of S-boat operations following the interrogation of survivors from *S-38*, sunk 20 November 1940.[44] Short-range radio chatter on VHF while S-boats were at sea added further detail to the Royal Navy's understanding of German coastal forces, and, in 1944, a book was opened at HMS *Hornet* (the Coastal Forces shore base at Gosport) to log every piece of information on S-boat personnel. British Naval Intelligence was able to build up remarkably detailed insights into the movements of boats, flotillas, maintenance issues, operations, and personnel. Those insights can be glimpsed on information sheets included (seemingly by accident) in one file in the British National Archives.[45]

---

[40] ADM 1/15815, Minutes by Director of Air Warfare and Flying Training, 11 May 1943.

[41] Ibid.

[42] ADM 1/15815, "Coastal Convoys: An Appreciation," 11 October 1943; Ashworth, *Coastal Command*, p. 89.

[43] ADM 223/610 and ADM 223/611, "E-boats in the Mediterranean."

[44] ADM 186/806, German E-boat S-38 Interrogation of Survivors, February 1941. Interrogation of S-boat personnel continued to reap rich rewards throughout the war, see, for example, ADM 186/809, "German E-boats S-141 and S-147: Interrogation of Survivors," July 1944.

[45] For example, the file contains collected details on *S-153* (build, length, beam, draught, height of superstructure, engines, horsepower, maximum and cruising speed, endurance, crew size, and commanding officer), making reference to the Combined Services Detailed Interrogation Centre (CSDIC). It also contains a detailed history of the 7th S-boat Flotilla. See ADM 223/611, "E-boats in the Mediterranean."

The development of Allied radar coverage off the east and south coasts had a significant impact on the S-boat campaign. Radar direction finding (RDF) had been developed on the River Debon at Bawdsey Manor during the mid-1930s. Rushed into service in early 1941, Type 287 radar towers had a relatively short range and were superseded by later models. Despite the initial problems, by mid-1941 the approach of S-boats towards the British coast was usually (but not always) detected by shore-based radar at a range of approximately eighteen miles, allowing intercepting forces to be vectored in their direction.[46] The low-lying nature of the east coast was a particular difficulty and, between Bawdsey and Cromer, the eight radar stations required 200-foot-high towers to allow them to function.[47] Despite this, gaps in coverage and breakdowns were considerable. To try to improve matters, in December 1942 C-in-C Nore proposed an alteration in the marked safe route along the east coast between Shipwash, Cross Sand, and Hearty Knoll to bring the route farther inshore and more firmly under the effective cover of the RDF stations along the coast.[48] After considerable debate and consideration of the navigational and tactical difficulties of bringing the channel inshore, the proposal was accepted and implemented in February 1943.[49] Nevertheless, in October 1943 C-in-C Nore still had to report to the Admiralty that "Conditions vary greatly on the East Coast and failures to obtain contacts, even inside the restricted range, are frequent."[50] When radar did work, and when near enough, radar-equipped vessels could find and fix S-boats. For example, the Type 271 radar was fitted to corvettes and frigates from March 1941 onwards. With refinements and upgrades, the Type 271Q was able to detect S-boats over six miles distant.[51] A frigate operating in conjunction with MTBs and MGBs could vector them towards a group of S-boats to the point where they appeared on the less-efficient radar sets of the smaller British vessels. Although the S-boats possessed the speed to evade or outrun British coastal forces, the certainty that they could not linger in any one spot deprived them of their tried and trusted means to locate a coastal convoy. As Gordon Williamson has noted: "By early 1943 it was becoming clear that the previous . . . tactic of lying in wait on a known convoy route in order to make a night-time ambush was no longer working. This was principally due to the heavy use of radar by both shore stations and Allied aircraft."[52]

---

[46]   ADM 1/15815, Minutes by Director of Local Defence, 14 January 1943, on file "C-in-C Nore: Proposed Alterations to Searched Channels."

[47]   Ibid.

[48]   ADM 1/15815, C-in-C Nore to Admiralty, 29 December 1942.

[49]   ADM 1/15815, Herbert Morrison to C-in-C Nore, 12 February 1943.

[50]   ADM 1/15815, C-in-C Nore to Admiralty, 16 October 1943.

[51]   ADM 1/30193, Recommendation for immediate award Leading Seamen Edward Dowdall (radar), 28 December 1944, enclosure in "Actions against E-boats on 22–23 December 1944: Recommendations for Honours and Awards," 1 March 1945.

[52]   Williamson, E-boats, p. 33.

Information on the position and direction of S-boats was supplemented from late 1941 onwards by intercepts from German VHF radio traffic. S-boats relied heavily on short-range VHF to coordinate their movements. The radio chatter from a group of S-boats at sea was considerable, so much so that in January 1943 Petersen ordered radio silence in the approach to target and emergency use only of VHF within forty-five miles of the enemy coast.[53] The order appears to have been entirely disregarded. In one action in September 1944, eighty-six separate messages were picked up from three S-boats in a seventy-one minute period.[54] In another action in December 1944, five British vessels detected ninety transmissions during an action lasting ninety-eight minutes.[55] Although these messages were often very short, and could consist of a single word such as "melden" (instruction to report), they were often broadcast in the clear, making only limited use of code words. They frequently contained tactical and positional information. At short ranges, the carrier wave for S-boat VHF radios could be picked up by wireless operators on Allied ships even if the Germans were not broadcasting.[56] To take advantage of the radio chatter in October 1941, a search for German-speakers who could join British coastal forces was initiated. They came from all directions, from the Merchant Navy, Women's Royal Naval Service, and from civilian life.[57] Listening stations were set up on the east coast and at key coastal forces bases. Given the short range of VHF, the amount of warning which they could provide was often fairly minimal.[58] To compensate, some coastal forces flotillas took German-speaking radio operators (known as "headache operators" after their headphone apparatus) to sea to provide real-time intelligence on S-boat movements and intentions.[59] For example, in the case of the 21st MTB Flotilla, a German Jew was used to eavesdrop on the S-boat radio channels. He could give slightly faster warning of the approach of S-boats towards the east coast convoy route. At sea, he provided a running commentary on the enemy's position and intentions.[60] This real-time tactical intelligence had considerable value, and it also allowed the British to build up a detailed picture of their adversaries even down to the level of individual personalities.

---

53   ADM 223/28, FdS memorandum on Torpedo Attacks, 20 January 1943.

54   ADM 1/29955, "Control Frigate and Coastal Force Action with E-boats," 18–19 September 1944, 14 October 1944.

55   ADM 1/30193, Enclosure 10 in "Actions against E-boats on 22–23 December 1944: Recommendations for Honours and Awards," 1 March 1945.

56   Hewitt, *Coastal*, p. 168.

57   Ibid., p. 152.

58   Dickens, *Night Action*, p. 29.

59   Jefferson, *Coastal Forces*, p. 164.

60   Dickens, *Night Action*, pp. 29–30.

By early 1942, the British had established a defense-in-depth (horizontal and vertical) for their coastal convoys. That defense started at the "Z-line" with the support of the aircraft of 16 Group and culminated with the close-in protection of the ships by their escorts. Radar, RDF, and "headache" operators provided information to respond to any attempted penetration of the "Z-line" by German forces. By the end of 1943, consideration was being given to integrating these elements with efficient air-to-sea wireless telegraphy links. Ultra decrypts and information derived from interrogations of S-boat personnel allowed the Royal Navy to build up a detailed picture of the boats and flotillas operating against the British coast.

German Responses: Weapons Systems

The Germans were acutely aware of the changing fortunes of the war at sea. The steady strengthening of anti-S-boat forces in the English Channel and improvements in British radar meant that, as early as December 1941, the *Führer der Torpedoboote* (FdT) had concluded that there was a need to take action, stating that "German defensive and offensive ability could be increased only by continual improvement of equipment and type, and the present advantage over the enemy could be maintained only if an improved type of S-boat were to be produced."[61] Within six months, the FdS, a newly-created post, was ready to conclude that his boats were "no longer master of the situation in the Western area."[62] The extent of the task now facing S-boats along the Channel coast was brought home to him after an action on 10 September 1942. *MGB 335* was captured along with her confidential books, radar, radio gear, and marked-up maps after a gun battle. The badly-damaged boat was taken to Den Helder, where Petersen and *Beobachtungsdienst,* or *B-Dienst* (the *Kriegsmarine's* naval radio intercept and decoding service), carried out an extensive examination of the boat and its secret material.[63] To keep the capture and its intelligence windfall secret, the *Kriegsmarine* claimed that the boat had been sunk. Petersen's reactions revealed his shock at the full realization of the capabilities of British coastal forces:

A) Speed less than an S-boat, probably about thirty knots.

B) Gunnery armament far heavier.

---

[61]   ADM 223/28, Report by FdT, December 1941.

[62]   ADM 223/28, Report by FdS to Group West, 25 May 1942.

[63]   Angus Konstam, *British Motor Gunboat, 1939–45* (Oxford: Osprey, 2010), p. 44, incorrectly lists this boat as scuttled by the British. Jak Mallmann Showell, *German Naval Code Breakers* (Hersham: Ian Allan, 2003), p. 59, places this incident in 1940. For additional information, see entry 11 September 1942, *Kriegstagebuch der Seekriegsleitung* (hereinafter KTB der SKL), Teil A, Band 37 (Berlin: E. S. Mittler & Sohn, 1993), p. 229, and ADM 223/28, Remarks by FdS after inspection of *MGB 663.*

C) Seaworthiness . . . not regarded unfavorably.

D) MGB has radar and radio equipment such as has been recommended for the last two years for the S-boats and which is only just beginning to be produced . . .

E) Has other equipment not yet recognized.

F) Has VHF aerial but no set. Possibly also infra-red signaling.

G) Bridge is armored . . .

H) Simple construction and engines. Appearances of having been built simply and quickly.[64]

Duly impressed, and concerned, Petersen issued an order calling for S-boats to stay together on passage to the convoy lanes and to undertake evasive routing when leaving port. He also required the introduction of armoring of bridges, weapons upgrades, and the rapid progression of the radar program.[65] Petersen's order reflected the urgent need to upgrade the defensive and offensive systems of the S-boat, to think about tactics, and to consider changes to the design. Failure to upgrade and update weapons and other critical systems would manifest themselves in the collapse of the S-boat campaign in 1943.

As early as mid-1942, Petersen had concluded that it was "vital . . . to develop new types of boats, mines, torpedoes, gunnery and signal equipment."[66] Given the demands of the U-boat war and the campaign in Russia, there was little improvement. The standard G7a torpedo with which the S-boat arm entered the Second World War was still being used by S-boats in 1945. This was despite the fact that, powered by compressed air, it left a trail of bubbles in its wake which could give away the fact that an attack was in progress. It was also an indicator to escort vessels of the approximate direction of the attacker. The G7a was designed for long-range torpedo attacks by submarines (up to 6,000 meters), whereas S-boat attacks were made at ranges of less than 3,000 meters. Developed for use by U-boats, the electric drive G7e torpedo was tried but abandoned. Operational experience in 1942 showed that the time of travel of the G7e from launch to target was too slow for hit-and-run attacks on coastal convoys, which usually consisted of quite small and easily-missed vessels.[67] The slow running speed of the G7e made it completely unsuitable as a weapon against fast-moving destroyers.

The need to upgrade the standard torpedoes used by S-boats was underlined by the fact that after 1940 torpedo attacks against British coastal convoys were

---

[64]   ADM 223/28, Remarks by FdS after inspection of *MGB 663*.

[65]   ADM 223/28, FdS War Diary, 10 September 1942.

[66]   ADM 223/28, Report by FdS to Group West, 25 May 1942 in Tactical and Staff Duties Division (Foreign Documents Section).

[67]   Entries 30, 31 October 1942, KTB der SKL, Teil A, Band 38, pp. 645–46, 665–66.

made at increased distances. Meticulous records of S-boat torpedo firings were maintained and they were later captured by the British.[68] The hit rate (number of torpedoes fired versus number of sinkings) improved from 1940 (25%) to the end of 1942 (over 50%) before falling away in 1943 (30% in December 1943). By the end of 1944, the rate had fallen to around 15%.[69] The G7a remained in operational service, although, by late 1943, homing versions of the G7e were also becoming available to S-boat flotillas.[70]

If there was a failure to update the torpedoes used by S-boats there was at least a limited upgrade of S-boat deck guns. Early examples of S-boats carried just a single 20mm anti-aircraft gun in addition to multiple light machine guns. The later S-38 class was designed with a special 20mm gun turret between the forward torpedo tubes, which gave considerable firepower forward as well as protection for the gunner. Experience in the Channel in 1941 and 1942 showed that this was insufficient, and the S-100 design (introduced in 1943) featured additional armament such as a twin 20mm cannon amidships and a heavier gun aft (37mm). Existing S-boats were retrofitted with additional and heavier weaponry (including 40mm guns in the aft position) as they became available and according to the whims of commanding officers.[71] A heavy weapon mounted aft was an effective way of dealing with pursuit by enemy coastal forces, which became increasingly common from 1941 onwards. However, they could not be mounted on some of the older S-boats. A 40mm gun produced a recoil equivalent to 1.5 tons, which the age-weakened frames of some boats could not support.[72] The

---

[68]   Average S-Boat Torpedo Firing Distances

Year	Distance
1940	900 meters
1941	1,700 meters
1942	1,800 meters
1943	2,000 meters
1944	1,700 meters

ADM 292/204, Underwater Weapons Department (Admiralty), German Torpedo Documents.

[69]   Ibid.

[70]   ADM 223/611, Admiralty to Home and Mediterranean Stations, 13 July 1944, "E-boats in the Mediterranean."

[71]   Interestingly, in 1944, a further evolution of the S-boat design was developed. The S-700 class would feature the addition of a forward-firing 3cm cannon and additional aft-facing torpedo tubes to target any pursuing vessel. Although the hulls of a number of vessels were completed before the end of the war, shortages meant that they would be finished to the S-100 specification.

[72]   ADM 223/611, S. O. Sichel to Speer, 15 May 1944, "E-boats in the Mediterranean."

fitting of heavier weapons required six weeks dockyard time, severely reducing operational availability.[73]

Defensive Systems and Target Acquisition

The purpose of increasing the number of deck weapons was primarily defensive in nature. The torpedo and mine would remain the principal weapons of the S-boats, and Allied merchant ships their principal targets, until the Normandy invasion of 1944. There were other attempts to improve S-boat defensive systems, but they did not come to full fruition. Short-range VHF radios (Type Lo 1 UK 35) together with visual signals (flag semaphore and lights) remained the principal means by which S-boats worked together, even though the British were using S-boat VHF transmissions to intercept and disrupt operations in the English Channel. S-boat navigation continued to rely on old-fashioned techniques and a wheelhouse-mounted RDF loop, which could also be used to locate enemy ships when they were transmitting. This had both offensive and defensive applications. Attempts to equip S-boats with radar were a limited success.[74] The FuMo 71 Lichtenstein B/C radar had a limited range (3,000 meters for a merchant ship) and a limited arc (thirty-five degrees ahead of the boat). They were marinized cast-offs from the *Luftwaffe* night fighter force and were fitted to a small number of S-boats during 1943. However, S-boat radar was to prove disappointing with inadequate range even in the hands of the best operators.

Introduction of radar on S-boats did lead to some attempt at tactical innovation. On the night of 7–8 March 1943, the 2nd, 4th, and 6th S-boat Flotillas attempted to put into practice the tactic of radar lurking. Boats of the 4th Flotilla used radar to monitor the convoy lanes while the 2nd and 6th Flotillas remained just beyond. If radar responses suggested an enemy convoy, the 2nd and 6th Flotillas were to approach the convoy lane. Poor visibility precluded the necessary coordination, and only the boats of the 6th Flotilla attacked. Driven off by the destroyer HMS *Mackey* and two MTBs, *S-114* and *S-119* collided, resulting in the sinking of the latter.

If radar on S-boats was not a success, then at least German scientists developed passive radar detection and ranging equipment. The FuMB 29 "Bali" multidirectional antenna and FuMB 10 "Borkum" signal detector used radar and radio emissions from Allied warships to detect their positions. Unfortunately for the Germans, it took until March 1944 for the first sets to be delivered. The poor state of German shipboard radar hurt the S-boats both defensively and offensively. In

---

[73]   ADM 223/611, Speer to Operations Group South, 1 May 1944, "E-boats in the Mediterranean."

[74]   Experiments were also conducted to see whether S-boats could be rendered invisible to Allied radar by the use of rubberized coatings known as *Tarnmatte*. Trials would begin only in 1944.

June 1942, a tactical innovation was introduced known as the *Stichansatz*, whereby a dispersed group of S-boats, acting on information from *B-Dienst* or *Luftwaffe* reconnaissance, would take station along the convoy route. On detecting the convoy, the boats were to attack. The tactic did produce some useful results, especially in a convoy action on 8 July when six merchant ships were sunk.[75] However, dispersing forces made them more vulnerable to British coastal forces. It was a measure of desperation on the part of the S-boat command that the *Stichansatz* was introduced. On 20 January 1943, Petersen ordered that it be discontinued in its present form as a result of the strength of enemy defenses.[76]

Intelligence

After 1940, *B-Dienst* had been able to expand its network of coastal stations rapidly, and the growth of marine radio traffic (including shore-to-ship) in 1942 and 1943 gave the service an increasing volume of sensitive information to decode. The *B-Dienst* remained a highly efficient service, but the difficulty of operating in the Channel deprived the S-boats of significant opportunities to pick up survivors out of the water for the purposes of interrogation. Two survivors were picked up from the 600-ton coaster SS *Angularity*, sunk on 5 February 1941 in the Shipwash Channel. Under interrogation, they gave away details of convoy organization, destroyer types in operation along the east coast, and perceptions about the dangers of torpedo and mine attack.[77] By 1943, S-boats could no longer afford to linger in the Channel to rescue survivors for interrogation.

Cooperation with the *Luftwaffe*

The importance of cooperation with the *Luftwaffe* was recognized in 1940. The *Führer der Torpedoboote* commented that "The traffic in the Channel can only be paralysed by full use of the Luftwaffe by day, and . . . [S-boats] at night."[78] However, the effectiveness of the *Luftwaffe* in the west declined markedly after 1940 as the campaign in Russia, and then the need to defend Germany's cities from aerial bombardment, drew resources farther east.[79] In a paper written in October 1942,

---

[75]   Frank, *S-boats*, p. 53.

[76]   ADM 223/28, FdS memorandum on Torpedo Attacks, 20 January 1943.

[77]   ADM 223/28, FdS War Diary, 7 February 1941.

[78]   ADM 223/28, Appreciation of the Situation by FdT, 5 July 1940.

[79]   See Sönke Neitzel, "Kriegsmarine and Luftwaffe Co-operation in the War against Britain, 1939–1945," *War in History* 10:4 (2003), pp. 448–63. See also Sönke Neitzel, *Der Luftkrieg über dem Nordatlantik und der Nordsee, 1939–1945* (Bonn: Bernard & Graefe, 1995); Sönke Neitzel, "Die Zusammenarbeit zwischen Schnellbooten und Luftwaffe," *Militärgeschichte* 4 (1995), pp. 55–63.

FdS noted tersely that "Owing to the relative weakness of the German Air Force . . . there have been gaps in the reconnaissance network."[80] The development of the *Stichansatz* was one response to the failure to secure effective cooperation with the *Luftwaffe*. By April 1943, FdS demanded "Fighter reconnaissance by aircraft equipped with radar [as the] only reliable method by which aircraft can contact convoys at night."[81] The demand brought about no significant and lasting improvement. Just as damagingly, requests to cover with fighter sweeps the dawn return of S-boats to their continental bases and to attack British coastal forces were invariably given a lower priority than the need to respond to bomber operations against the Reich.[82] In May 1943, FdS complained that, in the opening weeks of the year, his S-boats had been attacked "16 times during their operations, even though there was no moon, and visibility was bad."[83] He was convinced that S-boats would, in the near future, "be located by night fighters as soon as they left port and that . . . losses would mount accordingly." The only way to counter this growing threat was to deploy *Luftwaffe* fighters against the Coastal Command aircraft used in the anti-S-boat campaign. In summing up the S-boat campaign in 1943, the FdS concluded that "The gradual cessation of air and S-boat co-operation was one of the main reasons why S-boat successes decreased in 1943."[84]

Armoring

In response to encounters with increasingly heavily-armed British light vessels in 1942, experiments were undertaken with *S-67* to produce a design for an armored bridge that could be retrofitted to S-boats already in operational use. For the boats on the Channel coast, this work was usually done in Rotterdam and did not require a lengthy refit period. The armored design (known as the *Panzerkalotte,* or "armored skullcap") was also incorporated in new boats of the S-38 class to produce a variant of the class, the S-38b. The 1943 S-100 class continued the pattern of armoring the bridges of S-boats. However, there were limits to the process of up-armoring and up-gunning. Armoring added greatly to the weight of the vessel, placing additional strain on critical systems and decreasing performance.[85]

---

80   ADM 223/28, Report by FdS, October 1942.

81   ADM 223/28, Report by FdS, 19 April 1943.

82   See, for example, ADM 223/28, FdS War Diary, 23 April 1942.

83   ADM 223/28, Note by FdS on Enemy Air Attacks, 30 May 1943.

84   ADM 223/28, FdS Observations on S-boat Operations in the West during 1943, 31 December 1943.

85   See, for example, ADM 223/611, Speer to Operations Group South, 1 May 1944, "E-boats in the Mediterranean."

The next logical step beyond up-armoring a wooden boat was to introduce a fully-armored S-boat built in steel. A steel S-boat was better suited to mass production than the existing wood design. However, it was not until after 1945 that the German Navy would realize the goal of a steel S-boat. In the circumstances of the Third Reich, where the *Heer* and the *Luftwaffe* had control of the lion's share of Germany's industrial capacity and the annual production of steel, the *Kriegsmarine* had difficulties in securing its minimum requirements for shipbuilding. In any case, within the *Kriegsmarine* (and especially after Dönitz became its head in January 1943), U-boat construction was privileged over all other forms of construction. Moving to a steel-hulled S-boat design was simply out of the question in 1942–43. The British operated under fewer restrictions and, in early 1942, produced six examples of the Steam Gun Boat (SGB) class of motor torpedo boats. At 260 tons and 137 feet in length, and with two steam turbine engines capable of thirty knots, the steam gunboats were able to carry "one 3-in, two 6-pdrs, and three twin 20-mm guns, with two 21-inch torpedoes."[86] Reynolds' description of them as "mini-destroyers" is apt.[87] An initial lack of armor to protect critical systems was remedied by up-armoring, but it took some time to overcome early teething troubles. For example, following a night action off the south coast on 28–29 May 1943, Lieutenant T. W. Boyd, commanding *SGB 4*, reported that "Gunnery communications, already the subject of frequent correspondence, again proved a failure."[88] Nevertheless, operational experience pointed to the potential of the steel-hulled motor torpedo boat. The Germans lacked the industrial capacity to adopt the design and to turn out sufficient numbers, and so too did the British. The SGB class was halted at just seven vessels in 1942 in order to prioritize destroyer construction.

The failure to upgrade the offensive and defensive systems of the S-boat meant that FdS considered it vital to increase the number of boats available in the west. However, there could be no quick fix. In December 1941, FdT called for an operational fleet of forty S-boats in the west to strike a "decisive blow" against the east coast convoys.[89] At the same time, he recognized that, given the current rate of production, "this was not a practical possibility."[90] It was not until the introduction of the 1943 building program (seventy-two boats specified) that the *Kriegsmarine* embraced the goal of a massively enlarged S-boat force. That program, however, would not begin to bear fruit until mid-1944.

---

[86]   Leonard C. Reynolds, *Dog Boats at War: A History of the Operations of the Royal Navy D Class Fairmile Motor Torpedo Boats and Motor Gunboats, 1939–1945* (Stroud: Sutton, 1998), p. 251.

[87]   Ibid.

[88]   ADM 1/14391, After Action Report by Lieutenant T. W. Boyd, 29 May 1943.

[89]   ADM 223/28, Report by FdT, December 1941.

[90]   Ibid.

The Convoy Engagements of Late 1943

The problems facing the *Kriegsmarine's* S-boat force became manifest in late 1943. The lengthening nights in the autumn of 1943, and the build-up of supplies in Britain for the opening of the Second Front in 1944, presented significant possibilities to renew the offensive against British coastal convoys. The opportunity was particularly important, perhaps even decisive, since, on 6 July 1943, a decision was taken to increase the frequency of coastal convoys from six days to seven days a week in order to facilitate the movements of supplies under the Bolero plan.[91] With the railways "working to capacity," this was regarded as the only possible way to get the necessary supplies and equipment in place for an invasion in the summer of 1944.[92] The number of ships in convoy would also be increased and larger vessels permitted to make the passage. From September, the amount of traffic along the coast was expected to more than double, making very tempting targets for the S-boat flotillas along the French, Belgian, and Dutch coasts. Although the decision to introduce seven-days-a-week convoying was taken in July, it had still not been implemented by September. Concerns about the S-boat threat and the Royal Navy's ability to protect larger coastal convoys introduced a certain hesitancy that led to an on-going review of the situation. The need for larger and more regular convoys was set against concerns about the renewal of the S-boat campaign during the winter of 1943–44. Although there was an appreciation that British coastal defense had come a long way since 1940, there was an acute awareness of the need to deliver the Bolero cargoes. Consideration was given to improving coastal defenses, including the protective mine belts (both surface and deep-set) along the east and south coast, to guard against S-boats and also U-boats that might venture inshore in pursuit of the rich traffic.[93] The idea was ultimately rejected on the grounds that it would impede freedom of maneuver as D-Day approached.[94]

The S-boat flotillas had spent the summer months up-armoring and up-gunning the boats already in service. During this period, the operational strength of flotillas had been halved. By the middle of September, the 2nd, 4th, 6th, and 8th S-boat Flotillas were in Dutch waters in preparation for the campaign.[95] In late

---

[91]   ADM 1/15815, Cyril Hurcomb (Permanent Under Secretary, Ministry of War Transport) to Rear Admiral J. H. Edelsten (Assistant Chief of the Naval Staff), 19 November 1943.

[92]   Ibid.

[93]   ADM 1/15815, "Defensive Minelaying Policy in Home Waters."

[94]   One comment on the proposal (signature unreadable) was that: "It is likely that were every British mine in Home Waters to self-detonate to-night, we should find this less disadvantageous than their presence in the not too far distant future," ADM 1/15815, 21 July 1943.

[95]   The 2nd and 6th Flotillas were at Ijmuiden and the 4th and 8th Flotillas at Rotterdam.

September, S-boats and the *Luftwaffe* launched a joint mining campaign that was approved by *Seekriegsleitung* (SKL). On the night of 24–25 September 1943, the S-boat flotillas in Dutch waters departed from Ijmuiden and Rotterdam on a torpedo and mine-laying operation. The mine-laying phase of the operation went well but, in this opening encounter of the campaign season, the torpedo operation was a disaster. Encountering two armed trawlers, *S-96* and *S-88* of the 4th Flotilla launched torpedoes, one of which hit and sank HMT *Franc Tireur*. They were intercepted and engaged by two motor launches (*ML 150* and *ML 145*), which proceeded, in turn, to ram *S-96*, inflicting serious damage to all vessels.[96] A surface engagement followed, which ended when scuttling charges were fired on *S-96* and the crew took to the water. The seriously damaged *ML 150* was towed back to port. Five other S-boats were damaged in the action, reducing temporarily the offensive capacity of the Dutch-based flotillas. A further mine-laying operation on 7 October was successful, but, three days later, the *Luftwaffe* pulled out of the joint offensive in response to Hitler's desire to see the bombing of British cities. Despite the orders of SKL, Petersen broke off the campaign to return to mixed torpedo/mining operations.

The problems facing the S-boat flotillas were further underlined during a large operation on the night of 24–25 October when thirty-one S-boats (2nd, 4th, 6th, and 8th S-boat Flotillas) crossed the Channel to intercept east coast convoy FN1160.[97] This was an attempt to test the British defenses by a maximum effort against the east coast convoy route.[98] The operation was not supported by *Luftwaffe* reconnaissance, and it was conducted on the basis of *B-Dienst* intercepts. British forces in the vicinity included five destroyers, eight MGBs, four MLs, and nine MTBs.[99] The radar on *MGB 610* broke down, but "new centre line hydrophones" were used for the first time to locate the enemy.[100] Radar on the other boats enabled British Coastal Forces to establish contact with the S-boats at 2,000 to 3,000 yards, and the hydrophones enabled them to "roughly assess the enemy's course" and speed.[101] A series of running battles between British Coastal Forces and their

---

[96]   Scott, *Narrow Seas,* p. 170.

[97]   See maps in ADM 1/3716, Report on Coastal Forces Action on Night of 24–25 October 1943, CO HMS *Midge* to C-in-C Nore, 28 October 1943.

[98]   Mike Whitley, *Deutsche Seestreitkräfte, 1939–1945: Einsatz im Küstenvorfeld* (Stuttgart: Motorbuch, 1995), p. 65.

[99]   Admiral Sir John Tovey to Admiralty, 18 November 1943, incorporated and published in "Coastal Force Actions," *Supplement to The London Gazette,* 15 October 1948, pp. 5493–5523.

[100]   ADM 1/13716, Report on Coastal Forces Action on Night of 24–25 October 1943, CO HMS *Midge* to C-in-C Nore, 28 October 1943.

[101]   ADM 1/13716, Report on *MGB 603* (radar) and *MGB 609* (hydrophones) contained as enclosures to Report on Coastal Forces Action on Night of 24–25 October 1943, CO HMS *Midge* to C-in-C Nore, 28 October 1943.

German opponents resulted in sixteen separate engagements.[102] German attempts to attack the convoy were frustrated, and British losses were confined to HMT *William Stephen* and one MGB damaged. German forces, meanwhile, lost *S-63* and *S-88*.[103] Radar failure on *MGB 610* potentially enabled a crippled S-boat to escape destruction. There were indications that at least one of the German vessels had been equipped with passive radar detection equipment.[104] Severe storms during the rest of 1943 curtailed operations, bar one against CW221 on 4 November, which resulted in the sinking of two merchant ships.[105] Homing torpedoes were used for the first time, but the victory came at a cost. Retiring to the Dutch coast, *S-74* was lost in an attack by British Beaufighter aircraft. *Luftwaffe* fighter cover was requested but unavailable, owing to the need to intercept an anticipated raid on Germany by enemy bombers. In the opening phases of the campaign season, British defenses had held. Casualties to the coastal convoys had been minimal, while the operational strength of the S-boat flotillas in Dutch waters had been significantly eroded.

Surprisingly, the convoy battles of late 1943 occurred against a background of weakened escort forces along the south and east coast as a result of operations in the Mediterranean. There were significant problems with the defensive forces available on the south and east coast even though, on paper, they appeared formidable.[106] As early as June 1943, Captain (Destroyers) at Rosyth had raised grave concerns about the ability of weakened escort forces to cope with the larger coastal convoys required by the Bolero build-up and the expected renewal of the S-boat offensive with the long nights of winter.[107] Such was the paucity of available escorts that convoys were often sailing with just one destroyer. Convoy CW221, attacked on 4 November, was protected by a single destroyer together with lighter craft. A minimum escort of two destroyers per convoy had become the norm by 1942.[108]

---

[102]   For German accounts of the action, see ADM 223/28, KTB entry for 24 October 1943.

[103]   Reynolds, *Dog Boats*, pp. 87–88.

[104]   ADM 1/13716, Report to CO HMS *Midge* from Commander *MGB 609* on night action of 24–25 October 1943, 27 October 1943.

[105]   Whitley, *Deutsche Seestreitkräfte*, p. 66.

[106]   Escort Forces available for Coastal Convoys, Late 1943

Command	Destroyers	ML	MGB	MTB	Corvettes
Nore	12	12	15	10	6
Portsmouth	4	12	6	3	-
Dover	-	6	-	-	-
Plymouth	3	6	3	2	-
Rosyth	15	-	-	-	-

Figures from ADM 1/15815, "Coastal Convoys: An Appreciation," 11 October 1943.

[107]   ADM 1/15815, Captain (Destroyers) to C-in-C Rosyth, 13 June 1943.

[108]   ADM 1/15815, C-in-C Nore to Admiralty, 16 October 1943.

The loss of two merchant vessels from an eighteen-ship convoy was testament to the efficiency of the available forces and the defense-in-depth which had been developed along the English coast after 1940. CW221 did, however, provoke bitter complaints about inadequate escorts from the merchant seamen whose ships were involved in the convoy.[109] The mate of the SS *Fulham* explained to a security officer that visited his ship that as Merchant Navy personnel were being "sought for the much talked of Second Front [he] personally . . . would be only too pleased to take part, as he would at least get decent and reasonable protection."[110] The C-in-C Portsmouth commented, "Although the substance of these reports is from imperfectly informed persons they emphasise once again the necessity for additional escorting destroyers for Channel convoys."[111]

The C-in-C Nore was very eager for the return of the three Hunt-class destroyers that had been detached as part of Operation Husky (in total, forty-three Hunt-class destroyers were operating in the Mediterranean).[112] Although he did not receive them, an additional five Town-class destroyers were found for the Rosyth Command. Given the success of the defense in the opening weeks of the campaign season, and with the Bolero plan "lagging behind schedule" (coal stocks were estimated to be three weeks below minimum Bolero requirements for the spring of 1944[113]), on 25 November the Naval Staff instructed the commands at Nore, Rosyth, and Portsmouth to begin seven-day-per-week convoying.[114] The C-in-C Nore Command accepted the order only "on the understanding that the situation renders it essential to accept a considerably increased risk."[115] One representative of the Trade Division recorded in the minutes, "I hope that our luck with the East Coast convoys will hold until reinforcements are available."[116] The decision to undertake seven-day convoying was a sign of confidence, as well as urgency, but it was tempered with a sense that the S-boat threat remained serious.

---

[109]   See ADM 1/15815, complaints from personnel on-board SS *Fulham*, SS *Colonel Crompton*, SS *John Hopkinson*, logged by Security Officer (Portsmouth), 5 November 1943.

[110]   ADM 1/15815, Report by Security Officer (Portsmouth) in conversation with W. Johnston (First Mate, SS *Fulham*), 5 November 1943.

[111]   ADM 1/15815, C-in-C Portsmouth to Admiralty, 14 November 1943, in E-boat attack on Convoy CW211 on 3 November 1943, Complaints from Merchant Navy Personnel.

[112]   ADM 1/15815, Minutes on file "East Coast Convoys: Protection against E-boat Attack," 1 November 1943; Minutes on file "Destroyer Reinforcements for Plymouth and other Home Commands," 6 November 1943.

[113]   ADM 1/15815, Director Trade Division, 28 November 1943.

[114]   ADM 1/15815, Admiralty to C-in-C Nore, Rosyth, and Portsmouth, 25 November 1943.

[115]   ADM 1/15815, C-in-C Nore to Admiralty, 27 November 1943.

[116]   ADM 1/15815, W. Stephens (Trade Division), 15 November 1943.

The Atlantic convoy battles of March 1943 were critical in the sense that they established the capacity of the escort forces to hold off the Wolfpacks. In the English Channel against the S-boats, that same critical moment came in September-October-November 1943. The battles of late 1943 established that German forces were no longer able to cross the Channel undetected, that they could not linger around the convoy route until a passing convoy arrived, and they could expect a very hostile reception from British coastal forces prepared to press home their attacks beyond the point at which they themselves would sustain fatal damage. A badly damaged S-boat close to the convoy route was unlikely to make it home, and, with so few S-boats being built, even a low level of loss was unsustainable in the medium term. Such was the productivity of British boatyards that the British could expect rapid replacement of their losses whereas the Germans could not. That, in turn, especially with the looming prospect of invasion in 1944, fed through into a conscious policy to reduce the danger to the existing S-boat fleet in order to conserve the available resources. By 1944, this became an ingrained feature of the S-boat arm. Glimpses of it can be seen in comments such as an S-boat "carried torpedoes and mines against merchant ships. Should it meet anything else it must not become involved, but must retire behind a smoke-screen. So [S-boat] crews were instructed . . . to flee should any opposition be encountered."[117] The executive officer on USS *Frankford* observed in an after action report that S-boat "captains are seldom aggressive in the face of illumination and gunfire."[118] The battles of late 1943 established just how far British forces had come in their development of an effective system of coastal defense. The battles of late 1943 also pointed towards future developments where, by 1945, air and sea forces would increasingly operate together in the destruction of S-boats. As Admiral Tovey reflected after the successful defense of FN1160 in October:

> This action gives general proof of a great improvement in the efficiency of the Coastal Forces particularly as regards communications and the use of radar. The small number of material breakdowns also indicates a higher standard of interest and handling by the Commanding Officers and crews of boats and reflects great credit on the maintenance officers and staffs of the bases. Furthermore, it clearly demonstrates the value and essential need of constant training and practice. In addition to the successful defence of the convoy, it is considered permissible to feel a modicum of satisfaction in the number of times the E[nemy] boats were engaged. They were roughly handled six times in or near the convoy route . . . Had the RAF been able to attack them after daylight it would

---

[117]   Scott, *Narrow Seas,* p. 9.

[118]   On 8–9 June, USS *Frankford* engaged S-boats using airbursts to keep them at bay. Roscoe, *United States Destroyer Operations,* p. 359.

have been a strong deterrent to E-boats leaving their return to their bases till so late.[119]

Conclusion

Towards the end of 1942, C-in-C Nore estimated that between the start of the war and 14 November, 63,350 transits of the east coast passage had been made by merchant ship. A total of 157 merchant ships had been lost as a result of enemy action, which represented just 0.24 percent of the total number of sailings. He expressed some satisfaction with the figure, noting, "these losses cannot, in my opinion, be regarded as excessive, and compare, I believe, favourably with other convoys sailing through dangerous waters."[120] Despite these successes, the Royal Navy remained anything but complacent. In October 1943, at the start of the winter convoy battles, and influenced by the inadequate number of escorts at his disposal, C-in-C Nore wrote to the Admiralty to demand further resources. He commented, "I consider the extraordinarily small losses which have taken place over recent months must be attributed principally to good fortune and lack of enterprise on the part of the enemy."[121] He warned, "These two factors cannot be expected to continue indefinitely."[122] The coastal convoys were, in many ways, the poor relation of the bigger struggle taking place in the Atlantic.

In late 1943, C-in-C Rosyth expressed grave concerns about the lack of available escorts, writing that "while every effort is being made to win the Battle of the Atlantic and considerable success is being attained in bringing convoys safely to West coast ports, I view with alarm their passage up and down the East coast unprotected save by a single destroyer."[123] While the view of the Royal Navy on developments during 1943 might be described as cautiously pessimistic, the view on the German side was starkly worse. In his paper on the 1943 S-boat campaign written on the last day of the year, FdS described the situation as a "crisis."[124] His paper was a recognition that, since 1940, British defenses had improved considerably and rapidly. Concurrently, there had been a failure to invest and upgrade the S-boat design and its systems. The significance of the Channel convoys to the British war economy and to the Bolero build-up had not been recognized with the allocation of an appropriate level of resources. There had also been a failure of

---

[119]   Tovey, "Coastal Force Actions," p. 5505.

[120]   ADM 1/15815, C-in-C Nore to Admiralty, 30 December 1942.

[121]   ADM 1/15815, C-in-C Nore to Admiralty, 16 October 1943.

[122]   Ibid.

[123]   ADM 1/15815, C-in-C Rosyth to Admiralty, 16 June 1943.

[124]   ADM 223/28, FdS Observations on S-boat Operations in the West during 1943, 31 December 1943.

vision on the part of the German High Command to take a holistic view of the war against enemy shipping. The U-boat war and the Battle of the Atlantic were part of a wider campaign that included operations by major and minor surface vessels, *Luftwaffe* maritime reconnaissance, and bombing and mining operations. Although, in December 1943, FdS would look forward to increased numbers of S-boats promised in the 1943 building program and to a renewal of effective cooperation with the *Luftwaffe,* the reality was that the strategic value of his flotillas was shifting from the offensive to the defensive. In 1944, their principal value would lie not in the interception of coastal convoys, but as a potential threat to the Allied invasion fleet that was building in British waters. Historians have failed to recognize the significance of the coastal convoy battles of late 1943 as a key moment in the winning of the Atlantic campaign. Getting the convoys across the Atlantic was one thing—getting their cargoes to the point of use frequently required transit through another stretch of dangerous waters. The year 1943 was pivotal to both operations.

10

The Cruise of *U-188*

Special Intelligence and the "Liquidation" of Group Monsoon, 1943–1944

David Kohnen

As Allied forces consolidated the beachhead on the Normandy coast in Nazi-occupied France, the German submarine *U-188* slipped into port in Bordeaux. The skipper of *U-188*, Lieutenant Siegfried Lüdden, carried a dossier containing high-grade intelligence about German and Imperial Japanese efforts in the Indian Ocean and Pacific. On 24 June 1944, an Allied team comprised of British and American special operations forces working in collaboration with the French resistance intercepted Lüdden—seizing the intelligence found in the *U-188* dossier. Although this incident had significant influence on Allied operations, few histories have examined the capture of Lüdden and the role of Allied special operations forces in seizing intelligence sources in targeted operations on the European continent.

This chapter examines the sophistication of Anglo-American intelligence collaboration by focusing on the unique example of Lüdden and *U-188*. Documents found in British and American archives are the basis for the present study. First, a map illustrating this tale currently exists in the United States at the National Archives in Record Group 457.1 under the title of "*U-188* (Luedden) Cruise to Penang and Return: 30 June 1943–19 June 1944." The second duplicated copy provided by the U.S. Navy submarine tracking room to their Royal Navy counterparts currently exists in the British National Archives in London in Admiralty 199/2061, Section 7, Narrative Section, "'*U-188*' Cruises in the Indian Ocean." As German submarines sailed through waters falling under British and American areas of interest from the Atlantic to the Pacific Oceans, *U-188* also provides unique means to reexamine the special intelligence relationships between the Royal Navy and U.S. Navy in the Second World War.[1]

---

[1] Lawrence Paterson, *Hitler's Grey Wolves: U-Boats in the Indian Ocean* (London: Green-hill Books, 2004), pp. 68–162; Klaus Willmann, *Das Boot U 188: Zeitzeugenbericht aus dem Zweiten Weltkrieg* (Rosenheim: Rosenheimer, 2008), pp. 5–6; David Stevens, *U-boat Far from Home: The Epic Voyage of U-862 to Australia and New Zealand* (St. Leonards: Allen & Unwin, 1997), pp. 229–39; David Kohnen, *Commanders Winn and Knowles: Winning the U-boat War with Intelligence* (Krakow: Enigma Press, 1999), pp. 96–128.

Upon examining the British and American records pertaining to the voyages of German submarines to the Indian Ocean, an uninformed reader might mistakenly think that Anglo-American tracking room personnel produced the chart illustrating the cruise of *U-188* as a means of following individual submarines for the immediate purpose of locating targets. Indeed, *U-188* provided an excellent snapshot of the broader German naval strategy, as the individual submarine sailed between Europe and East Asia in 1943 and 1944. However, the actual reason why the Allies studied the voyage of *U-188* in such detail is far more interesting for contemporary historians to consider.

For the first time, this chapter will offer a fresh perspective on German submarine operations in the Indian Ocean by reexamining the adventurous tale of *U-188*. Drawing from multiple archival sources in Europe and the United States, records relating to *U-188* also provide a new perspective on Anglo-American special operations forces. Although efforts by the Allies to procure information from Axis intelligence sources have become widely known in the historiography of the Second World War, the tale of *U-188* offers a new look at the competitive nature of Anglo-American special intelligence collaboration.[2] For providing access to personal papers, the author would like to thank families of the late Royal Navy Volunteer Reserve Captain Rodger Winn, Royal Canadian Volunteer Reserve Commander John B. McDiarmid, and U.S. Navy (Ret.) Captain Kenneth A. Knowles. Former *Kriegsmarine* lieutenants, Karl August-Landfermann and Karlheinz Meenen, also provided unique personal perspectives of their experiences with Allied intelligence through their recollections of the cruise of *U-188*. For their hospitality and encouragement, the author would like to extend heartfelt thanks.

Mission Creep

The *Kriegsmarine* suffered from an inadequate strategic understanding of the global maritime arena, rendering surface and air operations irrelevant by comparison with the tactical results produced by submarines in the war at sea. *U-188* provides one example among the hundreds of German submarines which sailed under the flag of a misguided cause and fell victim to the global strategic approach of Allied "Combat Intelligence" during the Second World War. Among forty-one German submarines that deployed to East Asian waters after 1942, *U-188* was

---

[2]   David Kohnen, "Seizing German Naval Intelligence from the Archives of 1870–1945," *Global War Studies* 12:1 (2015), pp. 133–71; David Nutting, ed., *Attain by Surprise: The Story of 30 Assault Unit Royal Navy/Royal Marine Commando* (Burgess Hill: Selwood, 1997); Nicholas Rankin, *Ian Fleming's Commandos: The Story of the Legendary 30 Assault Unit* (New York: Oxford University Press, 2011), pp. 270–91; Craig Cabell, *History of 30 Assault Unit: Ian Fleming's Red Indians* (Barnsley: Pen & Sword, 2009); and Sean Longden, *T-Force: The Race for Nazi War Secrets, 1945* (London: Constable, 2009), pp. 1–38, 79, 97, 134, 230, 227–68.

among the few to slip through the noose provided by the Allied submarine tracking rooms. By tracing the cruise of *U-188*, contemporary readers may also reconsider the character of collaboration between the submarine tracking rooms of the Admiralty in London, the Naval Service Headquarters (NSHQ) in Ottawa, and the Navy Department in Washington, DC. Within these Allied headquarters existed the Operational Intelligence Centre (OIC), "Section 8S" under Winn, OIC-5 under McDiarmid, and the "F-21" Atlantic Section of Knowles.[3]

British and Canadian counterparts Winn and McDiarmid fell squarely under the intelligence subdivisions of their respective headquarters, although Knowles served in an operational subdivision of the Navy Department. In 1943, Admiral Ernest J. King reorganized the Commander in Chief, U.S. Fleet (CominCh) headquarters with a "Combat Intelligence Division" designed to support the global antisubmarine operations of the "numbered fleets." Through the "X-Com" circuit, the Combat Intelligence Division provided targeting data to the Fleet Intelligence Officers assigned to the geographic fleets in the Atlantic and Pacific. The global scope of CominCh remains an area of particular interest in examining the question of Anglo-American collaboration in the Second World War.[4]

Under the overall command of CominCh, the Atlantic and Pacific fleet commanders had authority to organize numbered fleets only when required for *offensive* operations. In particular, King retained personal control over the First Fleet and Tenth Fleet. After 1943, the First Fleet coordinated offensive "friendly" submarine operations and the Tenth Fleet focused upon *global* hunter-killer antisubmarine operations.[5] British and Canadian OIC models are completely different in considering the personal role of King and the CominCh headquarters in global U.S. Navy operations in the Second World War.

---

[3]   The National Archives, London (hereinafter TNA), Records created or inherited by GCHQ (hereinafter HW) 50/94, "U-Boat Tracking—Admiralty and United States—Memorandum for Admiral King of 7 September 1945 / Admiralty Tracking Room, 1939–1945, with covering letters," unpublished manuscript, Lieutenant Commander Eric Fiske, RNVR, comp. 26 March 1946; Library and Archives Canada, Ottowa, Department of National Defence, Record Group 24, Vol. 29163, "History of OIC 5"; U.S. National Archives and Records Administration, College Park, MD (hereinafter NARA), Records of the Chief of Naval Operations and Commander in Chief, U.S. Fleet, Record Group (hereinafter RG) 38, Crane Files, Box 35, "CominCh F-21 (Atlantic Section of Combat Intell.) War Report on U-boat Tracking, 15 May 1945," Commander Kenneth A. Knowles, USN (Ret.); and RG 38, CominCh, Crane Files, SSIC 5750/24, Box 35, F-21, Atlantic Section, F-211, "Secret Room."

[4]   Naval History and Heritage Command, Washington, DC (hereinafter NHHC), "Administrative History of CominCh Headquarters in World War II." See also, David Kohnen, "Commander in Chief, U.S. Navy: Reconsidering Ernest J. King and his Headquarters of the Second World War," Ph.D. dissertation, King's College London, 2013.

[5]   Naval War College, Newport, RI (hereinafter NWC), Manuscript Collection 22, Ernest J. King Papers (hereinafter King Papers), Box 7, Folder 6, "Tenth Fleet."

In the historiography, key organizational relationships remain largely muddled in examining the differences between the British and Canadian OICs by comparison with the unique functions of CominCh in global American naval operations. Unlike the Royal Navy and Royal Canadian Navy variant, the U.S. Navy sailed squarely under the overall command of King as he personally claimed control of global American efforts in the maritime arena. His role in coordinating submarine and antisubmarine offensive operations is an area of special intelligence interest. King remains an ambiguous figure in postwar literature, given his direct relationship in coordinating the operational functions of the "numbered fleet" commanders—and particularly the First Fleet and Tenth Fleet after 1943.[6]

The Anglo-American triangle of submarine tracking rooms ensured the steady strategic collapse of German submarine operations. On nine occasions after 1943, Royal Navy and U.S. Navy forces used information supplied by the OIC and CominCh to ambush the refueling ships and submarines associated with *U-188* in the Indian Ocean. Despite the best efforts of the Anglo-American navies, *U-188* stood apart among the four to survive operations in the Indian Ocean and return to a European port before the Allied victory. For this reason alone, the cruise of *U-188* provides a unique perspective on German submarine operations in the Indian Ocean.

Although the Indian Ocean remained central to British naval strategy, the region drew little interest from American and German historians. The official and semi-official studies by Stephen W. Roskill and Samuel Eliot Morison provide basic accounts, which also reflected special access to German and Anglo-American intelligence records.[7] Working under the supervision of the Admiralty and Navy Department in the Cold War era, German Navy Captain Günter Hessler provided additional details on remote submarine operations in East Asian waters.[8] By the 1960s, Allison W. Saville provided an authoritative study in *Proceedings*, "German Submarines in the Far East." A former Nazi propagandist, Jochen Brennecke, retold lively tales of their adventures in the Indian Ocean in *Haie im Paradies*. Ladislas Farrago offered a sympathetic portrayal of German submariners being hounded by the unseen hand of Allied intelligence in his memoir, *The Tenth Fleet*.[9]

---

[6]   NHHC, "Administrative History of CominCh Headquarters in World War II."

[7]   Stephen W. Roskill, *The War at Sea: The Period of Balance* (London: HMSO, 1956), Vol. II, pp. 406–07; and Samuel Eliot Morison, *United States Naval Operations in World War II: The Atlantic Battle Won, May 1943–May 1945* (Boston: Little, Brown, 1956), pp. 274–304. See also L. C. F. Turner, et al., *War in the Southern Oceans, 1939–45* (London: Oxford University Press, 1961), pp. 239–50.

[8]   Günter Hessler, et al., *Ministry of Defense (Navy): The U-boat War in the Atlantic, 1939–1945* (London: HMSO, 1989), pp. iii–12, 15–17, 60, and 97.

[9]   Allison W. Saville, "German Submarines in the Far East," *Proceedings* 87:8 (August 1961), pp. 80–92; Jochen Brennecke, *Haie im Paradies: Der deutsche U-Boot-Krieg in Asiens Gewässern, 1943–45* (Herford: Koehler, 1961), pp. 49–61; Ladislas Farago, *The Tenth Fleet: The Untold Story of the Submarine and Survival* (New York: Ivan Obelensky, 1962), pp. 244–78.

Other histories generally focused on grand strategic themes, often overshadowing the underlying question of German submarine operations in East Asian waters in the global war at sea. For example, John W. M. Chapman provided a useful contribution through the edited wartime recollections of Rear Admiral Paul Wenneker, the German Naval Attaché in Tokyo, in *The Price of Admiralty: The War Diary of the German Naval Attaché in Japan*.[10] Focusing on the Japanese, Carl Boyd and Akihiko Yoshida also acknowledged the presence of German and Italian submarines in the Indian Ocean in *The Japanese Submarine Force and World War II*.[11] David Stephens added to the narrative in *U-boat Far from Home: The Epic Voyage of U-862 to Australia and New Zealand*. Hans-Joachim Krug and Yōichi Harama also pooled their wartime experiences with a scholarly collaboration with Berthold J. Sander-Nagashima and Axel Niestlé in producing an authoritative history of Axis collaboration in 2001, which they titled *Reluctant Allies: German-Japanese Naval Relations in World War II*.

With declassification in British and American archives, historians enjoyed comprehensive access to the key archival sources of Anglo-American strategic collaboration in naval operations and intelligence. Despite broader access to these sources, the interrelationship between Allied operations and intelligence remained obscure in other histories of German submarine adventures to the Indian Ocean. In 2004, Lawrence Paterson relied heavily upon the familiar narratives derived from German submarine logbooks in *Hitler's Grey Wolves*.[12] Arguably the better choice in examining this complicated history, Ashley Jackson examined the underlying threat of German commerce raiding operations in the 2006 study, *The British Empire and the Second World War*.[13]

Although available histories generally covered wartime operations and tactics, few have acknowledged the central point that German adventures to the Indian Ocean reflected the broader failure of German naval strategy in general. The dramatic failure of the German surface campaign contrasted with the apparent successes of submarine operations. Under these circumstances, Admiral of the Fleet Erich Raeder stepped aside as Commander-in-Chief of the *Kriegsmarine*. Taking his place in January of 1943, Admiral of the Fleet Karl Dönitz dispatched the submarine force in an all-out surge against Allied shipping in the North Atlantic. During these operations, he lost his son, Peter, as the submarine force suffered a series

---

[10]   John W. M. Chapman, *The Price of Admiralty: The War Diary of the German Naval Attaché in Japan, 1939–1943* (Ripe: Saltire Press, 1982), Vol. I.

[11]   Carl Boyd and Akihiko Yoshida, *The Japanese Submarine Force and World War II* (Annapolis: Naval Institute Press, 1995), p. 132.

[12]   Paterson, *Hitler's Grey Wolves*.

[13]   Ashley Jackson, *The British Empire and the Second World War* (New York: Hambledon Continuum, 2006), pp. 269–350.

of withering defeats during the critical convoy battles of spring 1943.[14] German submarines largely withdrew from the North Atlantic shipping lanes after May, which influenced Dönitz and his staff to seek short-term tactical successes in other areas.[15] His memoirs, *Zehn Jahre und Zwanzig Tage,* explain in detail his role in the German naval campaign of the Second World War, but devote fewer than two pages to the entire German effort in Asian waters.[16]

Given other histories, this chapter reconstructs the remarkable story of *U-188* by examining how the Allied submarine tracking rooms in London and Washington reacted to the presence of German submarines in the Indian Ocean. To illustrate these points, this chapter will examine the broader dynamics by reconstructing the three war patrols completed by *U-188* in the Atlantic and Indian Oceans. This business was very personal. Allied analysts drew from multiple sources to track the whereabouts of individual enemy skippers, as their location often coincided with the locations of their warships. By locating individual German submarine commanders, the Anglo-American submarine tracking rooms could also orchestrate antisubmarine operations with precision. In the case of *U-188*, the unseen hand of the Allied submarine tracking rooms loomed very large. Although *U-188* survived numerous battles at sea, many of the crew did not survive the war ashore.

Intelligence collaboration served as the glue which fused the strategies of the Admiralty and Navy Department in the global war at sea. In the case of *U-188,* the Allies frequently disagreed about the tactics employed in antisubmarine operations. By sharing intelligence and discussing these differences of strategic opinion, the analysts serving in the submarine tracking rooms helped soothe the serious disagreements among their senior commanders. Closer to the front, the submarine tracking rooms also helped place Allied forces into advantageous positions to defeat their common rivals. For the first time, this chapter will highlight this close collaboration by examining how the Allied submarine tracking rooms influenced clandestine operations ashore. Shortly after the Allied landings at Normandy in June of 1944, tracking room analysts supplied critical information which inspired a mission to capture the *U-188* skipper, Lüdden, as he traveled from Bordeaux to Paris.

Documents captured with Lüdden enabled British and American analysts to complete a detailed study of *U-188* for the purposes of developing means to more efficiently defeat Axis forces in the Asiatic. In particular, they examined the two patrols *U-188* completed in the Indian Ocean. From 30 June 1943 to 19 June 1944,

---

[14]   See Jürgen Rohwer, *The Critical Convoy Battles of March 1943: The Battle for HX.229 / SC.122* (London: Ian Allan, 1977), pp. 6, 8, and 9–14.

[15]   Timothy P. Mulligan, *Neither Sharks Nor Wolves: The Men of Nazi Germany's Submarine Arm, 1939–1945* (Annapolis: Naval Institute Press, 1999), pp. 35–38, 56–64, 73–83, and 198–201.

[16]   Karl Dönitz, *Zehn Jahre und Zwanzig Tage* (Bonn: Athenäum, 1959), pp. 405–07.

U-188 sailed with ten other German submarines as the first wave to operate under the cover name of Group Monsoon. Their primary mission centered upon commerce raiding in the Indian Ocean. Only five reached the area, only able to continue the mission after refueling from M/T *Brake* on 8 September 1943. The submarines then operated separately, rather than in a cohesive group offensive. One by one, the Royal Navy monitored the individual submarines of Group Monsoon. On 16 October, Royal Air Force No. 244 Squadron from Sharjah caught *U-533* by surprise in the Gulf of Aden—leaving only four of the original Monsoon submarines to press the attack in the Indian Ocean.[17] Unable to provide logistical resources to sustain the operations or bring the four submarines home to a European port, Dönitz improvised by diverting the surviving Monsoon submarines to Penang in Malaysia. Of these, three remained stranded in the Indian Ocean. As a result, *U-188* was the only submarine of those involved with the original group to return to Europe before the German capitulation.[18]

Allied analysts drew from various intelligence sources to follow the cruise of *U-188* from Europe to the Indian Ocean. Given limited resources, Royal Navy Admiral Sir James Somerville, Commander-in-Chief, Eastern Fleet (CinCEF), used high-grade intelligence sources to maneuver shipping away from *U-188* and other Axis submarines associated with Group Monsoon. He also risked cryptographic intelligence sources to systematically sink the Monsoon refueling ships M/T *Charlotte Schliemann* and M/T *Brake* in the spring of 1944. The sinking of these two ships thwarted German submarine operations in the region and forced the Germans to request greater access to the base facilities and logistical resources in Malaysia, which fell under the immediate control of their Japanese partners, causing some tension within the Axis alliance.[19]

Anglo-American commanders sought information on future Axis submarine operations in the Indian Ocean. In the summer of 1944, Allied special operations forces briefly captured the skipper of *U-188*. Royal Navy and U.S. Navy analysts subsequently retraced the voyage by comparing captured enemy documents against intelligence sources used in tracking *U-188*.[20] This information was then depicted upon a chart for the benefit of Allied strategists—including the First Sea

---

[17]   The largely Indian crew of HMIS *Hiravati* rescued the only survivor of *U-533*, Petty Officer Günther Schmidt. British interrogators gleaned good information about the Monsoon adventure from the German sailor.

[18]   Note, the only other member of the original Group Monsoon to return to European waters was *U-532*, which surrendered in Liverpool on 13 May 1945.

[19]   Fort Meade, MD, National Security Agency (hereinafter NSA), Center for Cryptologic History, Library and Archives, GC&CS Naval History, Vol. XXIV, p. 74.

[20]   RG 38, Crane Files, SSIC 2234, Op-20-G "Translations of Intercepted German submarine Messages" (hereinafter *U-188* Intercepts), Index Card File, cross reference to F-21 Location Lists, filed under the bigram "HM."

Lord, Admiral Sir Andrew Cunningham, and the CominCh/CNO, Admiral Ernest J. King.[21] Royal Navy analysts within the OIC duplicated the U.S. Navy report on *U-188* for wider dissemination among seagoing forces at the front. The full narrative of the cruise—excluding the cryptographic details—appeared in an Admiralty summary of December 1944.[22] Information derived from *U-188* provided details of strategic significance to Allied commanders as they planned operations for the defeat of Germany and the final offensive against Japan.

Weltensegler

Typical of other German submarines of the Second World War, *U-188* participated in a variety of pivotal events in the global war at sea. For example, the skipper of *U-188*, Siegfried Lüdden, first appeared in Allied message traffic during the rescue efforts surrounding *Atlantis* and *Python*. Then in February 1942, the Allies lost immediate access to *Kriegsmarine* communications. Within the Naval Intelligence Division records of the Admiralty, Lüdden's dossier ended until his name reappeared in the text of a Prisoner of War interrogation summary in the fall. Cryptographic "Special Intelligence" sources confirmed the identification of Lüdden as the commissioning skipper of the Type IX/C40 German submarine *U-188*.[23] The identification of his first officer, Karlheinz Meenen, also appeared within these same sources. Lüdden and Meenen placed *U-188* into commission at the Finkenwerder dockyard of Deschimag Werke near Hamburg on 2 August 1942.[24]

Inside the OIC, analysts developed a relatively accurate assessment of the new threat posed by *U-188* by compiling various tidbits of information derived from multiple intelligence sources. The focus sharpened after Allied cryptographers regained access to *Kriegsmarine* communications after November.[25] The leading analyst within the submarine tracking Section 8S, Royal Navy Volunteer Reserve (RNVR) Commander Rodger Winn, began tracking Lüdden and his new com-

---

[21]   NARA, Records of the National Security Agency/Central Security Service, 1917–1998, RG 457.1, cartographic records, National Archives Identifier 783990, "*U-188* (Luedden) Cruise to Penang and Return: 30 June 1943–19 June 1944."

[22]   TNA, Admiralty Records (hereinafter ADM), 199/2061, Section 7, Narrative Section, "'*U-188*' Cruises in the Indian Ocean," pp. 14–17 [new pagination of pp. 366–69] (with separate chart located in MFQ 588, part 3(32).

[23]   Patrick Beesly, *Very Special Intelligence: The Story of the Admiralty's Operational Intelligence Center, 1939–1945* (London: Hamish Hamilton, 1977), p. 105. Beesly emphasizes that the term "ultra" was not the term used within the submarine tracking rooms for the various forms of cryptographic "Special Intelligence."

[24]   RG 38, OP-16-Z, Subject Files, Box 21, "U-Boat Officers," Lüdden, Siegfried.

[25]   *U-188* Intercepts, Index Card File, cross reference to F-21 Location Lists, filed under the bigram "HM."

mand by assigning the bigram signature of "HM"—the "H" designating a 700-ton Type IX submarine and the "M" correlating with the numerical sequence of its commissioning.[26] American submarine tracking rooms also adopted this system of cataloging German submarines after 1942.[27]

Drawing from previous work as a barrister and then as a civil servant within the British government, Winn offered a fresh approach in examining questions of naval intelligence. He had suffered from polio—a condition which typically precluded individuals from active service in the Royal Navy. Thus, his appointment as a RNVR officer reflected the level of confidence he had earned among many professionals within the Admiralty. He developed new procedures for orchestrating naval operations at the front by using intelligence to pinpoint and then forecast the future locations of enemy submarines and surface ships. Characterizing Winn, the First Sea Lord, Admiral of the Fleet Sir Andrew Cunningham, explained: "[H]is knowledge of the U-boats, their commanders, and almost what they were thinking about, was uncanny. I must not go into details; but every submarine leaving an enemy harbour was tracked and plotted, and at every moment Captain Winn could give the numbers, likely positions and movements of all the U-boats at sea. His prescience was amazing."[28] Winn shared his novel approach with his American understudies then serving inside the OIC in the fall of 1942. He helped establish similar tracking rooms for the Royal Canadian Navy and U.S. Navy by training Royal Canadian Volunteer Navy Lieutenant John B. McDiarmid and retired Lieutenant Commander Kenneth A. Knowles. Having earned a Ph.D. in the classics from Johns Hopkins University, McDiarmid gained seagoing experience aboard HMS *Hurricane* during the transatlantic voyage from America. Knowles was a professional naval officer, but had been medically retired in 1937. He returned to active service in 1941 and then received the assignment to London in July of 1942. By the spring of 1943, Winn trained McDiarmid and Knowles to improve their counterpart organizations on the other side of the Atlantic.

Tracking the whereabouts of German submarines required analysts to know the most intimate details of their subject. For example, British analysts compiled a very detailed biographic profile of Lüdden from interrogation summaries, spy reports, and communications intelligence. Within OIC in London, such details helped track the whereabouts of specific targets as well as the personalities associated with individual submarines. German naval messages were frequently

---

[26]   RG 38, Crane Files, SSIC 5750/24, Box 37, "F-21 War Report," p. 18.

[27]   Ibid. Note, the submarine bigram signatures remained uniform until the final months of the war, when the Allies revised the original system to include the newer German submarine designs, such as the Type XXI.

[28]   Andrew B. Cunningham, *A Sailor's Odyssey: The Autobiography of Admiral of the Fleet Viscount Cunningham of Hyndhope* (London: E. P. Dutton, 1951), p. 578.

addressed to individual submarines by side number, like *188*, radio call sign, or by the name of the commander—Lüdden.[29]

Allied submarine tracking room analysts focused on seemingly unimportant details to pinpoint German submarines. For example, the *U-188* crew christened their submarine as the "*Weltensegler*," or "world sailor," with the logo of a submarine silhouetted against the globe. They also painted the 10th U-boat Flotilla cross insignia on the front of the conning tower. Reports describing these logos helped analysts identify *U-188*.[30] Survivors from vessels sunk by *U-188* later described these markings in reports, which then correlated with the information found in other references maintained by the submarine tracking rooms.[31] Such levels of detail illustrate the commanding knowledge Anglo-American tracking room analysts acquired after refining their methods and studying their subject over an extended period.[32]

The major hindrance to Royal Navy and U.S. Navy antisubmarine operations in the Atlantic reflected their differing strategic objectives in the global war at sea. Conflicts between the Royal Navy and U.S. Navy centered upon questions of control, the competition for resources, differences of doctrine, and their various opinions over the proper focus of operations. Within the naval intelligence subsections, however, the strong personal connections established among individual personalities—like Winn, McDiarmid, and Knowles—helped unify the efforts of the Allied navies through the free exchange of intelligence. Although they often debated about the relationship between naval operations and intelligence, Winn and Knowles helped unify the efforts of their respective navies through forthright discussion. Beesly later characterized their relationship as "probably closer than between any other British and American organizations in any [s]ervice and in any theater."[33]

Soldiering Work

Winn and his American counterparts anticipated the arrival of *U-188* at the North Atlantic front. However, Lüdden provided the definitive proof by dutifully transmitting his whereabouts in messages to Dönitz and his staff. These intercepts enabled Winn, McDiarmid, and Knowles to maneuver Allied convoys and naval

---

29   RG 38, Crane Files, SSIC 5750/24, Box 37, "F-21 War Report," p. 18.

30   RG 38, OP-16-Z, Subject Files, Box 21, "U-Boat Officers," Lüdden, Siegfried.

31   RG 38, CominCh/CNO, Tenth Fleet, Analysis and Statistics, Subject File, USN Liaison Officer—Eastern Fleet, Commander Clark Lawrence Green, comp., "Submarine Intelligence Summary," Intelligence Report 11–44, 3 April 1944, Survivor Statement, SS *Chung Cheng*.

32   RG 38, Crane Files, SSIC 5750/24, Box 37, "F-21 War Report," p. 13.

33   Beesly, *Very Special Intelligence*, p. 192.

forces—thwarting German submarine operations in the North Atlantic through the critical convoy battles of March 1943. During this spring surge, the *U-188* crew became seasoned in submarine wolf pack operations with groups *Seeteufel* and *Adler*. Operating in April with group *Meise*, Lüdden nurtured his reputation with Dönitz by claiming four torpedo hits against convoy Outbound North (ON)-176 on 11 April. Skirting the fringes of the convoy, Lüdden observed the hazy sinking silhouette of HMS *Beverley* (H 64).[34] The sounds of crushing metal confirmed the kill.[35] Only four survived out of a crew of 155 British sailors.[36]

Having gained confidence to offer firsthand opinions from the front, Lüdden transmitted a series of messages to German submarine headquarters ashore. Lüdden complained about the *U-188* engines. He reported shoddy workmanship as the engines constantly broke down. He also emphasized the weather conditions in the North Atlantic caused further problems, describing the hardships as "soldiering work."[37] He then suggested shifting German submarine operations farther to the south in another signal. In response, Dönitz admonished Lüdden for transmitting so many signals and copied his response to other submarines at the front.[38] Despite Lüdden's public rebuke, Dönitz had also recognized that the situation in the North Atlantic had become untenable. He ordered German submarines to rendezvous with their submersible support vessels (known as "U-Tankers" in the Allied submarine tracking rooms), refuel, and withdraw from the North Atlantic shipping lanes. During the month of May, forty-one German submarines sank during combat operations in the area.[39]

Allied air cover improved in more remote areas where German submarines had previously experienced success. During the voyage to Lorient, Lüdden reported the appearance of "unfamiliar aircraft" of the type typically associated with aircraft carriers.[40] He also noted unidentified periscopes closer to British waters. Then, on the approaches to the Bay of Biscay, Lüdden suffered a chest wound after the sudden appearance of a "Whitley" Mark V bomber, which flew out of a cloud with the engines idling to catch *U-188* by surprise.[41] Lüdden ordered the crash dive, dragged a fellow crewman who was shot through the spine below, and then placed Meenen

---

[34]   *Beverley* was formerly the USS *Branch* (DD-197), a Clemson-class destroyer.

[35]   *U-188* Intercepts, 1612/11 April 1943.

[36]   Hours before the sinking, the anti-submarine detection equipment aboard *Beverley* failed after a collision with the merchant ship SS *Cairnvalona*.

[37]   *U-188* Intercepts, 0753/15 April 1943.

[38]   *U-188* Intercepts, 1353/15 April 1943.

[39]   Axel Niestlé, *German U-Boat Losses during World War II: Details of Destruction* (Annapolis: Naval Institute Press, 1998).

[40]   *U-188* Intercepts, 1511/20 April 1943.

[41]   *U-188* Intercepts, 1203/2 May 1943.

in temporary command aboard *U-188*. Meenen later recalled that the situation seemed particularly bad in the Bay of Biscay, where Allied aircraft maintained a constant presence. He suggested *U-188* might not have survived during another surprise attack in the Biscay. As an Allied aircraft prepared to deliver the *coup de grâce,* four *Luftwaffe* escorts arrived overhead to fend off the attack.[42] Meenen brought *U-188* into the safety of the submarine bunker at Lorient on 4 May 1943. In the following weeks, messages transmitted by 10th U-boat Flotilla suggested *U-188* as a likely candidate to participate in the surge to Asian waters.[43]

Wireless exchanges between *U-188* and the German submarine headquarters ashore provided the basics for the submarine tracking rooms in London and Washington. While Allied cryptographers had intermittent access to German naval messages during the summer of 1943, they eventually solved the messages to gain a clear understanding of the German point of view. By August, British cryptographers helped the U.S. Navy perfect the "high-speed" four-rotor *Bombe,* an analog computer designed to solve messages encrypted on the German naval four-rotor M4 Enigma cipher, which enabled the Allies to read German messages within twenty-four hours of first interception.[44] Given this tremendous advantage, the U.S. Navy launched an all-out offensive to sink Axis refueling ships and submarines—the "U-Tankers."[45]

Having regained access to *Kriegsmarine* codes and ciphers, British and American strategists disagreed about the practice of using information derived from such sources in targeted attacks. Yet, during a series of attacks between June and August 1943, U.S. Navy hunter-killer groups sank eight out of nine U-Tankers and a number of combat submarines during refueling operations. These operations seriously curtailed German submarine operations in the Atlantic during the build-up for the invasion of Europe. Yet, Winn disagreed with the U.S. Navy practice of using Special Intelligence in hunter-killer operations. Knowles explained: "Ro[d]ger had the feel of the British, naturally, of protecting ULTRA at all costs. So they were very cautious in utilizing ULTRA. They made very indirect moves in order to support it with an operational program so that it was completely submerged in this operation. Whereas, over in my area, being younger at the game and also being somewhat aggressive we were using ULTRA more aggressively. There's quite a difference in philosophy here."[46] Winn and Knowles articulated the policies of their superiors and resolved differences during daily conversations on their

42   Karlheinz Meenen correspondence with the author, 2 August 1996.

43   *U-188* Intercepts, Index Card File, cross reference to F-21 Location Lists, filed under the bigram "HM."

44   Ralph Erskine, "Naval Enigma: The Breaking of Heimisch and Triton," *Intelligence and National Security* 3:1 (1988), pp. 162–83.

45   RG 38, CominCh, Atlantic Section War Report, p. 4.

46   NSA, NSA OH-22–86, Kenneth A. Knowles Oral History, declassified on 21 July 1998, pp. 5–6.

scrambled telephone system.[47] In essence, the Royal Navy had previously used intelligence to stage overt attacks against Axis targets. This practice influenced the Germans to change their communications procedures and adopt the M4 Enigma, which caused the cryptographic blackout of 1942.[48]

Admiralty strategists were horrified by the CominCh scheme to use Special Intelligence for a precision campaign against *Kriegsmarine* targets in the Atlantic. Having endured the cryptographic blackout at Bletchley Park, the Admiralty warned CominCh against using Special Intelligence in overt attacks. Cunningham cautioned his counterpart, King, to safeguard cryptographic sources. As the U.S. Navy largely perfected the technology required to solve M4 Enigma, British leaders anticipated the Americans would take too many risks in exploiting information derived from *Kriegsmarine* communications. Cunningham argued that the plan to stage Special Intelligence-driven ambushes would inevitably "result in our shipping losses going up by anything from 50 to 100 percent."[49] King responded, "I am equally concerned with you as to the security of ZEBRA [codename for M4 Enigma]." He then emphasized, "it is my belief [that] we are not deriving . . . the fullest value [from ZEBRA]."[50] Pressing the point with Cunningham on the strategic question of using Special Intelligence at a tactical level, King argued that the "risk of compromise would be a matter of lasting regret to all if ZEBRA security were [sic] jeopardized in some less worthy cause."[51] Given British concerns about handling Special Intelligence, King essentially chose to use such sources to the maximum extent possible—even at the prospective risk of tipping off the enemy and possibly losing access to high grade intelligence sources.

In essence, Cunningham feared losing cryptographic access while King favored using all available information for immediate results in antisubmarine operations. To avoid an unnecessary argument with Cunningham and his staff, King simply initiated the Special Intelligence attacks by using jeep carriers in hunter-killer attacks within sectors controlled by the U.S. Navy in the central and south Atlantic. Following the Atlantic Convoy Conference, the Admiralty no longer held immediate responsibility for defending Allied shipping in these waters. This enabled the CominCh/CNO staff under King to operate unilaterally within their sectors of responsibility. The U.S. Navy also had perfected new tactics to exploit technological innovations in electronic sensors, long-range communications, and precision weapons like the Mark 24 "Fido" acoustic homing torpedoes.[52] Given these

---

[47]   RG 38, CominCh, Atlantic Section War Report, p. 4.

[48]   Erskine, "Naval Enigma," pp. 162–75.

[49]   RG 38, CominCh, Tenth Fleet, Box 33, 27 April 1943/281628, CominCh to Admiralty.

[50]   Ibid.

[51]   Ibid.

[52]   William T. Y'Blood, *Hunter-Killer: U.S. Escort Carriers in the Battle of the Atlantic* (Annapolis: Naval Institute Press, 1983), pp. 1–10 and 280–83.

developments within the context of the U.S. Navy solution to the four-rotor (M4) Enigma cipher system, Knowles argued that the

> present availability of certain R. I. information provides us with a power-ful weapon against the enemy which we have so far used only in a defen-sive manner—i.e. convoy diversions. While these tactics are proving fairly successful they do not lessen in any way the ever present, ever growing U/B menace. It is therefore proposed that we utilize this R. I. information in a more active fashion by engaging the enemy offensively with our sub-marines . . . the main objection against directing attacks solely on refuel-ing submarines is the possibility of the enemy shortly suspecting that his codes are compromised with the resultant loss to us of this vitally impor-tant information. This risk continues in any event and can be lessened considerably if U/Bs in general are attacked instead of going after refuel-ing subs only. Another point in favor of a regular all-out sub hunting U/B campaign is the almost certain cracking of enemy morale. Sudden destruction of U/Bs carried over a protracted period of time is bound to weigh heavily on the nerves of U/B personnel. In consideration of the above it is urgently recommended that an appreciable number of subma-rines be assigned to CominCh to wage a vigorous offensive against Ger-man U/Boats, utilizing R. I. information to dispose our submarines and to direct them to exact locations of enemy refueling operations. Control of such submarines should remain with CominCh in order to protect sources of information and direct operations expeditiously.[53]

Knowles convinced his superiors that "such use would not jeopardize, beyond risk taking, the sources of ULTRA information, provided all projected operations were controlled directly from CominCh."[54] The question of control persistently influ-enced the focus of discussions between Royal Navy and U.S. Navy headquarters, as Allied forces pursued a decisive victory over the Axis.

To coordinate these operations while safeguarding the original intelligence sources, King reorganized his headquarters in Washington. In June of 1943, he fused the operations and intelligence functions performed under the separate CominCh and the CNO organizations by establishing the Tenth Fleet. This bureau-cratic entity served as a clearinghouse within the CominCh/CNO headquarters, which then disseminated information of concern to subordinate antisubmarine commanders and Allied forces at the front. It is important to note that the Tenth

---

53   RG 38, CominCh, Crane Files, SSIC 3840/2, Box 37, "F-21 Memoranda Regarding Sub-marine Tracking and Operations, June 1943–June 1945," Memorandum, circa April 1943, "Offensive Action against submarines," p. 3.

54   Ibid.

Fleet was nothing more than the antisubmarine subsection of the CominCh/CNO headquarters. As one memoir of the Tenth Fleet explained, it "had no ships. It had no armament. But it had the greatest weapon of all—the human brain."[55] The Tenth Fleet provided a clearinghouse for all information relating to antisubmarine missions within the CominCh/CNO headquarters. Unlike the popular myth of a fleet without a ship, King employed the Tenth Fleet to orchestrate the operations of every ship associated with Allied antisubmarine efforts and convoys.

The U.S. Navy held significant advantages in antisubmarine weapons technology and intelligence. Mimicking the hunter-killer group tactics first employed by the Royal Navy in the North Atlantic, King formed hunter-killer task groups comprised of jeep carriers and between four and six destroyer escorts in the summer of 1943. These units operated independently in the vicinity of Allied shipping lanes or wherever German submarines tended to operate. Beginning in June, King identified German refueling vessels as primary targets for U.S. Navy forces. He also targeted enemy submarine concentrations and vessels of interest, such as the *Yanagi* ships running strategic cargos between Asia and Europe.[56]

The British warned the Americans against risking their best sources of cryptographic intelligence on the *Kriegsmarine*. From 1943 to 1945, the Admiralty and CominCh submarine tracking rooms claimed seventeen surface vessels (fifteen blockade runners and two U-Tankers). Winn, McDiarmid, and Knowles also collaborated to achieve the "liquidation" of more than ninety-three Axis submarines (fifty-four to U.S. Navy hunter-killer groups).[57] Knowles later described the U-Tankers as "the pivots which, upon being dislodged, made of B.d.U.'s [*sic*] moving structure a disjointed frame, sagging here, hastily bolstered there, [and] gradually crumbling to inevitable collapse."[58] Given the situation in the North Atlantic, Winn and Knowles agreed in their predictions of a German submarine offensive in remote coastal waters in the central and southern Atlantic. As early as July 1943, Special Intelligence had also confirmed German and Japanese discussions to collaborate against Allied shipping in the Indian Ocean.[59]

The prospective expansion of Axis naval operations in the Indian Ocean caused grave concern within the Admiralty. After withstanding early Japanese

---

[55]   Farago, *The Tenth Fleet,* p. xi.

[56]   Carl Boyd, "U.S. Navy Radio Intelligence During the Second World War and the Sinking of the Japanese Submarine *I-52*," *The Journal of Military History* 63:2 (April 1999), pp. 339–54.

[57]   RG 457, SRMN-051A, Vol. II, "OP-20-GI Memoranda to CominCh F21 on German submarine Activities," Appendix I, "submarines Sunk by U.S. Forces with the Aid of Radio Intelligence."

[58]   NSA, CCH, GC&CS Naval History, Part 6, p. 344.

[59]   NSA, CCH, GC&CS Naval History, Part 6, pp. 25–26 and 27.

attacks, Churchill feared Britain was in "real danger of losing our Indian Empire."[60] The Royal Navy also struggled to provide sufficient resources to the Eastern Fleet under Admiral Sir James Somerville. Having played a key role in the sinking of the battleship *Bismarck*, Somerville had unique experience as a commander skirting the nexus between operations and intelligence. Shortly after he assumed duty as the Commander-in-Chief, Eastern Fleet (CinCEF), he masterfully exploited intelligence to maneuver the Eastern Fleet to safety—thereby thwarting a potentially devastating Japanese surprise attack potentially "akin to a Pearl Harbor in the Indian Ocean."[61] In fact, intelligence provided the best means for Somerville to employ his forces as efficiently as possible against the Axis in the Indian Ocean. Yet, he also faced the realities of having "totally inadequate air and sea escort and patrol forces and was unable to form convoys."[62]

Group Monsoon

The situation in the Atlantic shifted decisively against the German submarine force, which set the stage for a surge into the Indian Ocean. This strange campaign marked the utter failure of Dönitz as a supreme commander. In the quest to prove the basic assumption of tonnage warfare strategy after 1943, he wasted costly resources in warships and trained personnel in waters as far afield as the southeastern Australian coast and into the Japanese home waters. Moreover, this effort did not represent a cohesive strategy designed to establish better collaboration with Axis partners. Instead, one Royal Navy and U.S. Navy assessment suggested "it actually represents the conclusion of the German policy of diversion rather than an attempt at joint operations with the Japanese."[63]

German submarine operations in the Indian Ocean helped Dönitz nurture the reputation of the Navy in relations with fellow strategists. For example, the patrols of *U-181* in the fall of 1942 and spring of 1943 resulted in the sinking of twenty-two Allied ships and a claimed estimate of 103,702 gross registered tons.[64] Such promising numbers enabled Dönitz to distract conversations within the high command away from the problematic situation on the European front.

Having recovered from injuries sustained during the spring convoy battles, Lüdden reassembled the *U-188* crew at Lorient. The crew found *U-188* retooled for

---

[60]   Michael Simpson, ed., *The Somerville Papers: Selections from the Private and Official Correspondence of Admiral of the Fleet Sir James Somerville* (Aldershot: Scolar Press/Navy Records Society, 1995), p. 355.

[61]   Ibid.

[62]   Ibid., p. 376.

[63]   NSA, CCH, GC&CS Naval History, Part 6, p. 26.

[64]   Kenneth Wynn, *U-Boat Operations of the Second World War* (Annapolis: Naval Institute Press, 1998), Vol. 1, pp. 135–45.

a patrol far from home, with ballast tanks reconfigured to accommodate more fuel, new (and experimental) Radar detection equipment, and an extended conning tower to accommodate additional ammunition and a larger anti-aircraft battery.[65] These hasty modifications to *U-188* reflect the unpreparedness of the German submarine force for global operations, such as their effort to launch an offensive in East Asia. At the time, the ultimate destination for the next patrol of *U-188* remained unclear to the crew. Their training had not prepared them for operations in East Asia, although they received tropical uniforms in anticipation of departure from Lorient. By 30 June 1943, Lüdden signaled *U-188* was sailing in company with *U-155* during the passage through the Bay of Biscay.[66] In response, he received a query from the 10th U-boat Flotilla stating that he had forgotten a key codebook required for properly configuring M4 Enigma settings.[67] Without this document, *U-188* would be unable to communicate during its patrol. As a result, the 10th U-boat Flotilla sent a copy of the codebook with another submarine destined to operate with *U-188*—the *U-168*.[68] This would require the two boats to meet somewhere in the Atlantic.

The Biscay transit proved very difficult, as Allied aircraft forced the two submarine skippers aboard *U-155* and *U-188* to expend fuel while sailing at high speed on the surface. During the day, they sailed at a slow pace and, for the most part, submerged. During this time, Lüdden informed the crew of their mission to operate with ten other German submarines and one Italian submarine in the Indian Ocean.[69] The original operations order designating *U-188* as a member of Group Monsoon revealed the scope of the German surge into the Asiatic. Lüdden held orders to operate in tandem with *U-168* between Mauritius and the Gulf of Aden. Eight days following their departure from Lorient, additional submarines followed in waves with *U-183*, *U-200*, *U-506*, *U-509*, *U-514*, *U-516*, *U-523*, *U-532*, and *U-847*. The Italian submarine *Ammiraglio Cagni* also sailed with orders to join the German effort in Asian waters.[70] The pacing of these submarine departures reflected careful planning by Dönitz and his staff, as they coordinated the movements of the U-Tanker *U-487* to support *U-188* and the other submarines of Group Monsoon.[71] Yet, this complex plan began to crumble almost immediately with the loss of the U-Tanker *U-487* and *U-847*, the latter of which carried the

---

[65]   Meenen correspondence with the author.

[66]   *U-188* Intercepts, 0812/30 June 1943 (OIC Serial 544).

[67]   *U-188* Intercepts, 1732/5 July 1943 (OIC 544).

[68]   Ibid.

[69]   Meenen correspondence with the author.

[70]   This submarine surrendered to Allied forces after the Italian capitulation in September 1943.

[71]   NSA, CCH, GC&CS Naval History, Part 6, p. 78.

commander intended to lead the operations of Group Monsoon, Lieutenant Herbert Kuppisch.[72]

Drawing insight from Special Intelligence inside the submarine tracking room of CominCh/CNO in Washington, Knowles recognized that *U-487* and *U-847* were key to the entire Monsoon adventure. In August 1943, he transmitted the locations of the Monsoon submarines to the hunter-killer groups centered on the USS *Core* (CVE-11) and USS *Card* (CVE-13). He further identified the key targets by identifying the locations of the "U-Tankers."[73] U.S. Navy hunter-killer skippers understood the meaning of such information, and acted accordingly in orchestrating the operations against Group Monsoon. They then systematically sank the remaining submarines associated with the group. By the end of August 1943, Royal Navy and U.S. Navy forces sank five Monsoon submarines and forced another to return to port—*U-188* being among the five remaining boats. In efforts to salvage the operation, Dönitz directed the remaining Monsoon boats to cannibalize fuel and provisions from other submarines in order to make the voyage around Cape Horn.[74] In this case, *U-155* supplied the provisions required for *U-188* to continue the voyage to East Asia.

U-188 and the other survivors of Group Monsoon entered the Indian Ocean with a blunted edge. On 8 September 1943, as *U-188* steamed to meet a refueling ship at a clandestine rendezvous in a remote area, the crew received news of the Italian surrender. As a result, the German skippers feared the prospect of betrayal by former allies aboard *Cagni*. The same day, the Monsoon skippers rendezvoused in a remote area of the Indian Ocean to discuss their situation aboard the refueling ship M/T *Brake*. The reserve skipper of *Brake*, Captain Heinz Kölschbach, provided the latest update of intelligence along with cold beer and cigars.[75] These perks were gifts of the Imperial Japanese Navy and the German Naval Attaché in Tokyo, Rear Admiral Paul Wenneker.[76] Following their meeting during the clandestine rendezvous with *Brake,* the Monsoon submarine skippers sailed to various choke points where Allied shipping concentrated in the Indian Ocean. Although the Gulf of Oman remained Lüdden's assigned area, he received orders from Dönitz diverting *U-188* to conduct a reconnaissance mission in the shallows of Mauritius. Lüdden failed to find any evidence of Allied shipping and considered this effort to be a waste of time.[77]

---

72   Ibid.

73   RG 38, CominCh/CNO, Tenth Fleet, dispatches to CinCLant and CTGs.

74   Ibid.

75   Meenen correspondence with the author. See also Heinz Kölschbach, *Der Blockadebrecher mit der glüchlichen Hand* (Herford: Koehler, 1958), p. 200.

76   *U-188* Intercepts, 1938/1 September 1943.

77   ADM 199/2061, "'*U-188*' Cruises in the Indian Ocean," p. 15 [366].

The directive sending *U-188* on the reconnaissance of Mauritius had appeared in Special Intelligence. Between Winn and Knowles, information derived from German naval and Imperial Japanese communications provided a clear picture of the situation from the enemy point of view. This information enabled the CinCEF, Somerville, to limit the potential Axis submarine threat. He maneuvered Allied shipping away from danger. He also organized Eastern Fleet warships into three primary escort groups. The Aden Escort Force (AEF) had a total of ten vessels, the Kilindini Escort Force (KEF) had six vessels with four more expected to arrive from the Mediterranean Theater, and the Aden-Bombay-Columbo (ABC) was comprised of five vessels. Somerville hoped to "put as much shipping as possible into convoy."[78] However, his decision to establish convoys drew questions from the Admiralty. Convoy operations required more transit time for ships sailing in formation between ports. "It seems incredible that the hardly-learned [sic] lessons of the Atlantic battle," one Royal Navy officer exclaimed, "were thus regarded as inapplicable in the Indian Ocean."[79]

Somerville faced significant challenges marshalling the resources required to safeguard Allied merchant shipping in the vast expanses of the Indian Ocean. One biographer suggested that "because of circumstances or conviction, Somerville favored the formation of hunting groups, though again he rarely had sufficient ships."[80] Many of the officers in the CinCEF headquarters also remained convinced that hunter-killer tactics wasted scarce resources, which could be better utilized to provide escort support for convoy operations. Royal Navy Captain Stephen W. Roskill characterized the British concept of convoy operations as an effort to provide "live bait which attracted submarines [as] the only effective form of trade defense and counter attack."[81] Yet, the Eastern Fleet escorts lacked proper equipment and proficiency in antisubmarine operations.[82] The danger to Allied shipping was mitigated somewhat, as German submarine skippers complained about the environmental challenges found in the Indian Ocean.

German submarines lacked the technical capacity to conduct sustained operations in waters far from a friendly port. Aboard *U-188,* the crew exhibited signs of intense exhaustion.[83] Bridge watch personnel also saw mirages of ships, where the mist of the heated sea blended with the horizon.[84] Lüdden documented the stresses endured by his crew in the *U-188* logbook. For example, he described how the

---

[78]   Simpson, *Somerville Papers,* p. 474.

[79]   Roskill, *The War at Sea,* Vol. III, p. 348.

[80]   Ibid., p. 376.

[81]   Ibid.

[82]   Ibid.

[83]   Meenen correspondence with the author.

[84]   Ibid.

extreme phosphorescence and mirror-calm sea made him fearful of detection. He also noted that phosphorescence trailed the course of torpedoes, thus betraying the position of the submarine. Moreover, the *U-188* engines and other machinery required constant attention.[85] The *U-188* crew also discovered clear evidence of sabotage—likely by French dockyard workers—in examining the torpedoes loaded at Lorient.[86] Torpedoes seemed to run on their own and potentially ran in a circular course, thus threatening the submarine.[87]

Despite these frustrations, the *U-188* crew reported sighting numerous convoys with sparse escort protection. The convoys ranged between six and ten ships, while the escorts exhibited poor proficiency in antisubmarine operations.[88] Lüdden also reported a number of independently sailing merchant ships. For example, he sank an American Liberty, SS *Cornelia P. Spencer,* between Mogadishu and the Seychelles islands on 21 September 1943. During this attack, Lüdden noted that the *U-188* conning tower came under fire when it broached the surface. The weight of the torpedoes had changed the ballast causing difficulty for the crew to compensate against the dense salinity of the Indian Ocean.[89] Running low on fuel, *U-188* again happened upon an unescorted tanker, M/T *Britannia,* which he claimed to sink. However, this vessel survived after the crew returned to the hulk and patched the ship together with chains and cables—barely reaching the safety of port Bandar Abbas.[90] The disappointing results reported by *U-188* matched those of the other four surviving submarines of Group Monsoon.[91]

Dönitz and his staff had hoped for better results in undertaking the initial surge into the Indian Ocean. According to their original plan, the Monsoon submarine skippers expected to return to Europe upon completing combat operations in the Indian Ocean. However, they failed to anticipate the difficulties involved with coordinating the logistical support for the Monsoon adventure. By 16 October 1943, only four of the original Monsoon submarines survived—after Royal Navy forces surprised *U-533* in the shallows of the Arabian Gulf. Having now lost seven submarines in the Monsoon adventure, Dönitz ordered the remaining Monsoon submarines to Penang in Malaysia. In turn, he directed the German Naval Attaché in Tokyo to request assistance from the Japanese. The Monsoon submarines required overhauls to survive the voyage back to Europe. The crews also required rest for the long journey. In a postwar analysis, a U.S. Navy analyst

---

[85]   *U-188* Intercepts, 1645 and 1857/7 October 1943.

[86]   Meenen correspondence with the author.

[87]   Ibid.

[88]   *U-188* Intercepts, 1645 and 1857/7 October 1943.

[89]   ADM 199/2061, "'*U-188*' Cruises in the Indian Ocean," p. 15 [366].

[90]   Ibid.

[91]   *U-188* Intercepts, 1645 and 1857/7 October 1943.

characterized the decision to divert the Monsoon submarines as "part of the welter of improvisation which characterized the effort [in the Indian Ocean]."[92]

The beleaguered submarine crews of Group Monsoon experienced frustration in dealings with their Japanese allies. For instance, a Japanese soldier waved *U-188* away from the docks at Penang. As they threw a line over to the pier, the Japanese soldier kicked it back into the water. He then pointed to the adjacent pier.[93] Lüdden later learned of a clear delineation between the Japanese Army and Navy commanders concerning access to the dockyard facilities.[94] The lack of spare parts and basic support facilities in Penang forced the Germans to accept compromises in making preparations for the return voyage to Europe. Having sailed in combat operations for over 121 days, *U-188* had covered in excess of 19,000 nautical miles—submerged for 925 nautical miles. The crew and the submarine required attention.

In this respect, the Japanese did provide special accommodations for the officers and submarine crews of Group Monsoon. "As German soldiers," the first officer of *U-188* recalled, "we wore tropic uniforms with a little [swastika] badge and submarine pins."[95] This uniform helped the Japanese identify Germans from the British prisoners engaged in work details in the streets of Penang. German officers also received an automobile and invitations to interact with civilian women who had been captured with the surrender of British, French, and Dutch forces in East Asia. "Out of it," the first officer of *U-188* emphasized, "communication with women was forbidden."[96] Enlisted German submariners billeted in an abandoned schoolhouse and enjoyed liberty in off hours at the Shangri La Hotel, where the Japanese had made arrangements for them to interact with girls from India, Malaysia, and Korea.[97]

The tropical conditions and inadequacies of the base facilities at Penang amplified the fatigue experienced by the German submariners of Group Monsoon. The emphasis Japanese officers placed upon rank and bureaucratic position also hindered the *Kriegsmarine* liaison officers in Penang. For example, the officer in charge

---

[92]   NSA, CCH, GC&CS Naval History, Part 6, p. 78.

[93]   Meenen correspondence with the author.

[94]   Bundesarchiv-Militärarchiv, Freiburg, Germany (hereinafter BAMA), German Submarine Logs, RM 98/392, *Seekriegsleitung,* Logbook of *U-188,* Special Report, "*Erfahrungsbericht,*" compiled at sea by Lieutenant Commander Siegfried Lüdden, Commander of *U-188* (*U-188* Report of Experiences in East Asia). After this document was captured by the FFI, it was cataloged in the Captured Documents Section of NID-24 as "PG/7337." As a subsection of the *U-188* logbook, the Report of Experiences in East Asia appears on pages 158 through 171.

[95]   Meenen correspondence with the author.

[96]   Ibid.

[97]   Ibid. See also Paterson, *Hitler's Grey Wolves,* p. 29.

of the situation ashore, Lieutenant Commander Wilhelm Dommes, earned the Knight's Cross and held status as a submarine war hero within the *Kriegsmarine*. Yet, he suffered from "Biscay Sickness"—a prevalent reference to combat fatigue within the German submarine force.[98] Dommes suffered a nervous breakdown as the skipper of *U-178* during operations in the Indian Ocean and had been sent to Penang in a hasty effort to remove him from command.[99] He then created problems with the Japanese police by amassing a gambling debt while serving on a brief assignment on the German Naval Attaché staff in Tokyo.[100] In turn, Wenneker banished Dommes to serve as a liaison officer in Penang.

The situation in Penang reflected the utter failure of the *Kriegsmarine* to establish basic facilities for serious offensive operations in East Asian waters. Complicating matters further, the skipper of *U-183*, Lieutenant Commander Heinz Schäffer, died suddenly of acute appendicitis.[101] German and Japanese physicians collaborated in an emergency surgical procedure, but lacked the medical resources to save the patient during the recovery.[102] Lieutenant Fritz Schneewind, who earlier delivered *U-510* as one of the two submarine gifts from Hitler, flew from Kobe to Penang to assume command as the new skipper of *U-183*—only to be killed shortly thereafter by the American submarine USS *Besugo* (SS-321) in an attack facilitated by Special Intelligence in the Java Sea.[103]

Special Intelligence and Group Monsoon

By momentum, rather than sound military planning, the Indian Ocean became the only theater in which the Axis Tripartite operated together against the Anglo-American and Soviet lines of maritime communications. For the Allies, the presence of German submarines in East Asian waters represented an annoying diversion from the primary theaters of the Atlantic and Pacific. On the other hand, the Indian Ocean also connected the two fronts and featured shipping lanes leading to the oil and economic interests of the Middle East and East Asia. Moreover, Churchill viewed India as the key to the future of the British Empire.[104] To defend the region, the CinCEF, Somerville, organized plans to conduct combined operations with Royal Navy and U.S. Navy warships against Japanese bases in Malaysia and Indonesia in the spring of 1944.

---

[98] RG 38, OP-16-Z, Subject Files, Box 21, "U-Boat Officers," Dommes, Wilhelm.

[99] Ibid.

[100] Ibid.

[101] *U-188* Intercepts, 1423/4 January 1944.

[102] Ibid.

[103] RG 457, SRH 008, "Battle of the Atlantic," Vol. II, pp. 173–74.

[104] Simpson, *Somerville Papers*, p. 355.

Somerville envisioned a decisive campaign to destroy German and Japanese forces in East Asian waters. These plans became the basis for Operation Transom, during which Somerville formed Task Force 65 of the Eastern Fleet. The CominCh/CNO, King, specifically approved the deployment of U.S. Navy Task Group 58.4, featuring the aircraft carrier USS *Saratoga* (CV-2), serving under the immediate command of Somerville. Such examples of Anglo-American naval collaboration contrasted with the popular myth of King's frustration with the Royal Navy in supporting strategic efforts requiring operational support by the U.S. Navy. From his point of view, the destruction of the Axis base facilities in East Asia represented a legitimate strategic target—worthy of the forces required for the effort.[105]

Within the submarine tracking rooms of OIC and CominCh, Winn and Knowles monitored the movements of the Monsoon submarines with great interest. Special Intelligence provided unique insight into the enemy point of view. On the other side of the hill, Dönitz had improvised another scheme to secure maximum benefits from the commitment of submarines to the Indian Ocean adventure. He transmitted orders to *U-188* and the other surviving Monsoon submarines to travel from Penang to Singapore to embark cargoes, which he described as "crucial to the German war effort."[106] However important the cargo may have seemed to Dönitz and his staff, this directive required the Monsoon submarines to risk the dangerous transit through the gauntlet of the Malacca Strait—running on a zigzag course at high-speed on the surface during the passage to the port facilities in Singapore, Surabaya, and Jakarta. One U.S. Navy report suggested that the Japanese had the "common saying in Singapore that you could walk from that port to Japan on American periscopes."[107]

The Japanese offered limited assistance in the form of conscript labor to assist the German submarine crews in the *ad hoc* effort to stow cargo aboard. To this end, the Germans removed deck guns, unloaded keel ballast, reconfigured stowage compartments, and then replaced this weight with cargo before beginning the voyage back to Europe.[108] After making a brief port visit during the transit from Singapore to Penang, *U-188* returned with a fresh payload of torpedoes and prepared for combat operations on the way home to Europe. *U-188* also carried a rich cargo of 100 tons of tin, 24,000 pounds of rubber, 1,000 pounds of quinine, four chests of opium, and 40,000 pounds of wolfram.[109] Beyond the threat of *U-188* and the

---

[105]   RG 38, CominCh/CNO, Tenth Fleet, Box 35, Antisubmarine Measures Division, Subject File, 10 April 1944 "Memorandum for the Admiral," Francis S. Low comp. for King.

[106]   *U-188* Intercepts, 1407/19 November 1943.

[107]   RG 457, SRH 306, "Contribution of Communication Intelligence to the Success of Submarine Operations against the Japanese in World War II," Charles A. Lockwood, comp., p. 44.

[108]   ADM 199/2061, "'*U-188*' Cruises in the Indian Ocean," p. 15 [366].

[109]   Ibid.

other Monsoon submarines to Allied shipping, the cargoes alone sparked significant interest within the submarine tracking rooms of Winn and Knowles.[110]

Somerville and the Eastern Fleet struggled to marshal forces to thwart the anticipated return of the Monsoon submarines in the Indian Ocean. Once again, the operations of *U-188* in the spring of 1944 illustrate the vulnerability of Allied defenses in the region. From 21 January to 12 February, *U-188* sailed on a rampage against Allied shipping—sinking eight merchant ships and at least twelve native dhows carrying cargoes deemed to be legitimate targets for destruction. Having expended remaining torpedoes in the Gulf of Aden, *U-188* turned southward to refuel. Within the submarine tracking rooms, Special Intelligence revealed that Lüdden had been rewarded with a Knight's Cross for his *claimed tally* of ten ships for 91,054 Brutto Registered Tons (BRT) and for his exploits in the Indian Ocean.[111] With this message, his stature as a German submarine commander also increased. Winn and Knowles took special interest in sinking German skippers holding this particular medal.[112] Further elevating the symbolic importance of Lüdden to the German submarine campaign, propagandists dubbed him *"Ritter von Socotra"* (Knight of Socotra).[113] During this period, *U-188*, with three other Monsoon submarines, claimed twenty-one Allied ships for a total haul of 119,000 gross registered tons.[114]

Additional German submarines continued sailing into the Indian Ocean, which severely taxed the resources of the Eastern Fleet. Facing few alternatives, Somerville devised an aggressive plan to restrict future German submarine operations by concentrating on the refueling ships—a tactic employed against *Bismarck* earlier in the war. Drawing from his previous experience against German com-

[110]   RG 38, CominCh, Crane Files, SSIC 3840/2, Box 37, "F-21 Memoranda Regarding submarine Tracking and Operations, June 1943–June 1945," Summary of U/B capabilities and prob. operations in Indian Ocean, 4 January 1944.

[111]   *U-188* Intercepts, 2201/11 February 1944 and 1048/12 February 1944. In hindsight, *U-188* actually sank an *estimated claimed* tally of 60,893 Gross Registered Tons (GRT). However, the actual tally would be closer to the number equating to nine ships for 50,915 GRT—excluding *Britannia* (which survived the attack) and the dhows, for which available records fail to provide details of the estimated tonnage, cargo, or flag of national association. The discrepancy in tonnage figures also illustrates the underlying strategic problem in examining the emphasis Dönitz placed upon commerce raiding tactics. In essence, his approach could be compared to the practice of evaluating body counts as a metric in determining success—or failure—in evaluating wartime strategy.

[112]   RG 38, CominCh, Crane Files, SSIC 3840/2, Box 37, "F-21 Memoranda Regarding submarine Tracking and Operations, June 1943–June 1945," 14156 CominCh F-21 for Action OIC, regarding "HM KCIC."

[113]   Ibid.

[114]   NSA, CCH, GC&CS Naval History, Part 6, p. 80.

merce raiders in the Atlantic, Somerville planned to use high-grade Special Intelligence to pinpoint the surface refueling ships supporting the German operations in the Indian Ocean. Draft concepts for these operations reflected the ultimate objective—with the working cover name Thwart. In execution, Somerville dubbed Operation Canned as being focused on M/T *Charlotte Schliemann,* while Operation Covered centered on M/T *Brake.*[115]

Having participated in previous hunter-killer operations involving high-grade intelligence sources, Somerville orchestrated an elaborate plan to fill the ether with Radar signals. He also dispatched aircraft to the expected rendezvous sites between the Monsoon submarines and their refueling ships, *Charlotte Schliemann* and *Brake.* He hoped to convince the Germans to blame Radar and air escorts for the loss of their refueling ships. Basing these operations primarily upon Special Intelligence, Somerville orchestrated the sinking of these ships in February and March of 1944. It was a major *coup* against German submarines in East Asian waters. Given the timing of these hunter-killer attacks, one of the German submarine skippers transmitted an unencrypted message stating his belief that their communications had been "systematically compromised."[116] This transmission caused concern particularly after the Germans introduced the *Schatten* procedure in a hasty effort to restore communications security.

The sudden appearance of Royal Navy forces in remote rendezvous areas of the Indian Ocean provided clear evidence of a cipher compromise among the Monsoon skippers. Their confidence in the M4 Enigma deteriorated after the sinking of *Brake.* Dönitz also acknowledged the likelihood of a cipher compromise with the introduction of the *Schatten* procedure. Yet, the Germans faced few alternatives other than to press forward and return to a friendly port as quickly as possible.[117] Having completed replenishment with *Brake* before the sudden appearance of the Royal Navy at the scene, *U-188* was the only submarine of the remaining Monsoon submarines with sufficient fuel and provisions to attempt the voyage back to Europe. The other three received orders to return to Penang.[118]

Royal Navy and U.S. Navy hunter-killer formations subjected Axis naval forces to an unrelenting war of attrition. High-grade cryptographic intelligence facilitated precision attacks to destroy roughly eighty Axis submarines and refueling vessels in the Atlantic between June of 1943 and June of 1944. Yet, following the sinking of *Charlotte Schliemann* and *Brake,* the Admiralty issued instructions to

---

[115]   ADM 199/1388, documents relating to Eastern Fleet operations Thwart, Covered, and Canned.

[116]   RG 38, Crane Files, SSIC 2234, Op-20-G "Translations of Intercepted German submarine Messages," *U-532,* intercept 2236/12 March 1944.

[117]   Meenen correspondence with the author.

[118]   Allied submarines ultimately sank *U-168* and *U-183* in the Malacca Strait, leaving *U-532* as the last survivor to surrender after the German capitulation in May of 1945.

reemphasize the importance of safeguarding Special Intelligence sources among commanders at the front. The directive stipulated that this particular "source must never be jeopardized by carrying out a tactical operation which might arouse the enemy's suspicion."[119] The restrictions instituted for Royal Navy forces drew a response from the U.S. Navy. In the spring of 1944, Cunningham received messages from King applauding the aggressive use of Special Intelligence: "During the past month I have noted with satisfaction the marked increase in U-boat kills in areas of U-boat concentration off southeast approaches resulting from the sustained coverage and vigorous action of your surface support groups. Please be good enough to convey my congratulations to those responsible."[120] Given the circumstances of the time, Cunningham perceived such messages as a condescending nudge. Acknowledging the achievements of Somerville and the Eastern Fleet against the Monsoon refueling ships, King then transmitted a message stating "congratulations on Indian Ocean successes."[121] This exchange centered upon a brewing controversy between the Admiralty and CominCh.

The *Charlotte Schliemann* and *Brake* incidents amplified British concerns about the use of Special Intelligence sources in orchestrating hunter-killer operations at the front. Cunningham transmitted a message to King exclaiming, "as a result of German suspicions of compromise of their cyphers . . . The Germans have reacted by a modification of their cyphering system. It is of vital importance that their suspicions be allayed."[122] Cunningham continued, "I think that for the present it will be most advisable to suspend operations against U-boats at or near any known rendezvous in the Atlantic."[123] Such messages from the Admiralty seemed overly cautious within the CominCh headquarters. British efforts to influence American tactics also proved counterproductive. Cunningham received a sharp response from King: "From [the] enemy's reactions[,] it is evident that his suspicions were aroused as a direct result of the *Brake* episode[,] the precision of which operation so closely [to] that of the *Schliemann* [clearly] left little doubt in his mind regarding [the] compromise [in cryptographic communications] . . . abruptly terminating the use of ULTRA for attack purposes might in itself tend to confirm the cipher compromise."[124] King concluded, "it is my opinion that continued use of

119   ADM 223/88, "Admiralty Control in Operations," p. 45.

120   RG 38, Crane Files, SSIC 3840, Box 24, 291315 CominCh to Admiralty, 29 February 1944.

121   RG 38, Crane Files, SSIC 3840, Box 24, 14456 CominCh to Admiralty, 14 February 1944.

122   RG 38, Crane Files, SSIC 3840, Box 24, 171739A Admiralty to CominCh, 17 March 1944.

123   Ibid.

124   RG 38, Crane Files, SSIC 3840, Box 24, 191548 CominCh to Admiralty, 18 March 1944.

special intelligence for operational purposes does not in itself involve undue risk."[125] King criticized the Admiralty practice of using Special Intelligence to route convoys away from the known positions of enemy forces. He preferred to use such information in an overt manner, subjecting the enemy to a relentless offensive strategy of attrition. King discounted criticism of offensive hunter-killer operations in offering the counterpoint that "consistently diverting North Atlantic convoys around u/boat concentrations has caused the enemy grave concern [about the security of their communications]."[126] King believed the Admiralty tactic of routing convoys on evasive courses "appears potentially one of the most dangerous operational uses of such intelligence in the Atlantic Theatre."[127] Cunningham and King agreed about the strategic importance of defeating the *Kriegsmarine* as quickly as possible, but they disagreed somewhat about the sequence of general operations and the tactical methods required for achieving their common objectives in the war at sea. Both also hoped to establish the most advantageous position for their respective navies in anticipation of the postwar reconstruction.

Operation Bergamotte

Intelligence collaboration helped unify the Anglo-American navies, and helped to defeat common Axis rivals in the global war at sea. However, the Royal Navy and U.S. Navy also competed to control the course of postwar reconstruction in Europe and Asia. The fall of the Axis Tripartite represented the conclusion of one war, but also the beginning of a new era in military policy and strategy. The British Empire increasingly fell under the shadow of America in global maritime affairs. The bureaucratic process of analyzing information to produce intelligence evolved from the British school. By 1943, the Americans adapted these methods in the interest of developing superior organizations, technological dominance, and doctrinal means to harness strategic capabilities with tactical actions at the front. The competition to acquire German intelligence on the Japanese—and the Soviets—during the final months of the Second World War provides an excellent means to analyze these broader questions of intelligence.

Within the submarine tracking rooms, Winn and Knowles carefully monitored the progress of *U-188* from the Indian Ocean. Sailing into the southern Atlantic, one transmission revealed the increasingly desperate situation developing aboard. Lüdden reported the chief engineer, Lieutenant Max Kiessling, suffered from frayed nerves—amplified by failing engines and inadequate stores of spare parts to fix the mechanical breakdowns. In response, Lüdden received orders to rendezvous with *U-181*—outbound from France—to receive assistance from the highly-

---

[125]   Ibid.

[126]   Ibid.

[127]   Ibid.

seasoned chief engineer, Lieutenant Carl-August Landfermann.[128] Among German submarine engineers, he had earned the rare distinction of being one of the few awarded a Knight's Cross.[129]

Allied submarine tracking room analysts monitored the location of German submariners with the Knight's Cross. Winn and Knowles took particular interest in the rendezvous culminating in the transfer of Landfermann from *U-181* to *U-188*. From an analytical perspective, they thought that the skills of an experienced chief submarine engineer would prove more useful aboard an outbound submarine, *U-181*, by comparison with the homeward bound *U-188*.[130] The transfer of Landfermann in the central Atlantic illustrated the importance Dönitz and his staff placed upon the safe return of *U-188*.

The radio exchanges between these German submarines and their headquarters ashore drew the close attention of Winn and Knowles within the Allied submarine tracking rooms. Knowles hoped to sink *U-188* with its precious cargo and the two German submarine heroes, Lüdden and Landfermann. From another message transmitted on 1 May, Knowles soon discovered an opportunity. The message from Dönitz directed *U-188* to rendezvous with *U-66* in the central Atlantic.[131] The positions and most likely courses of these German submarines appeared in messages compiled by Knowles within CominCh, which then filtered through the Tenth Fleet within dispatches transmitted to U.S. Navy hunter-killer skippers. In turn, Captain Francis M. Hughes, commanding USS *Block Island* (CVE-21), Task Group 21.11, maneuvered to interrupt the rendezvous between *U-66* and *U-188*. On 5 May 1944, Hughes directed USS *Buckley* (DE-51) to investigate Radar and High-Frequency Radio Direction Finder (HF/DF, or "Huff-Duff") contacts.

U.S. Navy hunter-killer groups in the Atlantic perfected the doctrinal procedures for exploiting intelligence to unify surface and air forces in antisubmarine operations. For example, the skipper of *Buckley*, Lieutenant Commander Brent M. Abel, U.S. Navy Reserve, recounted that these indications "fitted admirably with information to the effect that enemy refueling operations were being carried on in this area."[132] As expected, Abel found *U-66* loitering under a bright moon on the

---

[128]   *U-188* Intercepts, 1246/15 April 1944, 2305/15 April 1944, 1506/16 April 1944, and 1149/22 April 1944.

[129]   Roughly thirteen engineers or technical ratings received the Knight's Cross out of an estimated total of 144. See Rainer Busch and Hans-Joachim Röll, *Der U-Boot-Krieg, Die Ritterkreuzträger* (Mittler: Hamburg, 2003).

[130]   RG 38, Crane Files, 3840/5, Box 75, "U-boat Intelligence Summaries 17 March 1944–19 May 1945," "Special U-boat Invasion Summaries," 22 April 1944.

[131]   *U-188* Intercepts, 0523/1 May 1944.

[132]   RG 38, CominCh/CNO, World War II Action and Operational Reports, USS *Buckley* (DE-51), 8 May 1944, Action Report of Engagement with German Submarine, 6 May 1944.

surface and awaiting the arrival of *U-188*. During an engagement of approximately fifteen minutes, Abel rang-up to full-speed and rammed *U-66* amidships, which bent the bow of *Buckley* in the process. "Men begin swarming out of submarine and up on *Buckley's* forecastle," and Abel described that "machine gun, tommy gun, and rifle fire knocks off several [Germans] . . . ammunition expended at this time included several general mess coffee cups . . . two of the enemy were hit on the head with these."[133]

The sinking of *U-66* illustrates the unique combination of mechanized violence and human carnage which characterized antisubmarine combat in the war at sea. The *Buckley* action report features commentary comparable to that found in accounts from the trenches of the First World War or from various fronts of the Second World War. Observing the battle from afar, Lüdden described the scene in the *U-188* log as a *"schlag ins gesicht"* (a punch in the face).[134] He watched the destroyer trolling the water, logging the sound of explosions in the distance. In a twist of luck, the transmitter aboard *U-188* failed immediately following the sinking of *U-66*. Queries from *Kriegsmarine* headquarters remained unanswered from *U-188*. Then, on 18 June 1944—roughly six weeks after the sinking of *U-66* and two weeks following the Allied landings on Normandy—*U-188* suddenly emerged in a transmission to the 12th U-boat Flotilla, requesting an escort into Bordeaux.[135]

Winn and Knowles took particular interest in the sudden reappearance of *U-188*, as they attempted to confirm the veracity of the intercepted message. In previous cases, other Axis submarines sunk in combat reappeared within the text of intercepted messages. Such ghosts fouled their tally of kills, which Winn and Knowles used to examine other raw sources of intelligence in order to track other Axis targets. Inside the CominCh/CNO submarine tracking room, Knowles and his team referred to these reference files as the "morgue."[136] After some deliberation, Winn and Knowles ultimately concluded that *U-188* had somehow survived. Nearly twelve hours following the original request for escort, the 12th U-boat Flotilla directed *U-188* to rendezvous at "Point Garden" in the approaches to Bordeaux.[137] By 22 June, Winn and Knowles received firm evidence within a series of messages from the 12th U-boat Flotilla to the Commander of Submarines, Naval Group West.[138]

---

[133]   Ibid., p. 4.

[134]   BAMA, RM 98/392, *Seekriegsleitung,* Logbook of *U-188,* entry of 5 May 1944.

[135]   RG 38, CominCh/CNO, Crane Files, Box 166, "Translations of Intercepted Enemy Radio Traffic," 0028/0157 18 June 1944 (OIC 1183).

[136]   RG 38, CominCh, Crane Files, SSIC 5750/24, Box 35, F-21, Atlantic Section, F-211, "Secret Room," p. 2.

[137]   *U-188* Intercepts, 1103/18 June 1944.

[138]   *U-188* Intercepts, 1643/23 June 1944.

Confirmation of the existence of *U-188* appeared in dispatches transmitted from the OIC and CominCh to subordinate Allied headquarters. Winn and Knowles continued to monitor *Kriegsmarine* traffic for additional details about the potential return of *U-188* to the front. Their interest in *U-188* again peaked with the solution of a message transmitted on 23 June. Having visited key ports in East Asia, the skipper of *U-188*, Lüdden, compiled a comprehensive report about Japanese forces and facilities.[139] He referred to this unique document in a series of radio transmissions to the *Kriegsmarine* high command.[140] The details of Lüdden's traveling route from Bordeaux to Paris also appeared within the text of another encrypted message from the 12th U-boat Flotilla. These messages were intercepted and within roughly twenty-four hours the deciphered text reached Winn and Knowles inside the OIC and CominCh.[141]

Analysts serving under Winn and Knowles sifted the tidal wave of raw data flowing from the European front. Allied forces specifically disrupted telephone communications to isolate the Normandy beachhead along the French coast, which resulted in an increased volume of radio communications among *Kriegsmarine* headquarters. In turn, British and American cryptographers benefited from access to the cryptographic material captured aboard the German submarine *U-505* on 4 June 1944. One ranking U.S. Navy cryptographer described the haul from *U-505* as "particularly important [enabling cryptographers] to read all messages as soon as the Germans sent them."[142] This report quantified the assertion that:

(a) 4,000 extra bombe hours were run by Op-20-G on Mediterranean keys which would normally have been run on British bombes. This permitted GC & CS to spend an equivalent amount of time on Army and Air Force keys.

(b) Op-20-G ran 9,000 extra bombe hours on Army and Air Force keys.

(c) The total net gain was 13,000 bombe hours devoted to Army and Air Force keys which permitted many such keys to be solved which would otherwise not have been possible. This was particularly important, as such bombes became available on D+9 day.[143]

---

[139] RG 38, CominCh/CNO, Division of Naval Intelligence, Folder 24309-H, F-6-E, PG 7337–40, "*Erfahrungsbericht-U.188.*"

[140] RG 38, CominCh/CNO, Crane Files, Box 166, "Bigram File on the Movement of Blockade Runners and U-boat Groups," H-WT953, Filed under "HM" [Lüdden's Enigma bigram signature].

[141] RG 38, "Translations of Intercepted Enemy Radio Traffic," Box 166, Index Cards, 1059/23 June 1944 intercept, Lüdden intention to travel in a van from Bordeaux to Paris with request for sleeping coach from Paris by train to Berlin.

[142] RG 38, CominCh, Crane Files, Box 149, "Benefits Gained from *U-505* Documents."

[143] Ibid.

The *U-505* capture yielded M4 Enigma settings that remained valid through the fall of 1944, allowing American cryptanalysts to solve other Axis communications during the critical months following the Allied landings at Normandy.[144] These messages helped Winn and Knowles monitor the whereabouts of Lüdden and *U-188* into the spring of 1945.

Although Winn and Knowles specialized in naval operations at sea, they also supplied intelligence about *Kriegsmarine* targets to Allied forces on the ground. This information filtered from the OIC in London and the CominCh/CNO headquarters in Washington to the Combined Intelligence Objectives Committee (CIOS) of the Combined Chiefs of Staff (CCS), which directly supported the Supreme Headquarters Allied Expeditionary Force (SHAEF) under General Dwight D. Eisenhower.[145] In the weeks following the Allied landings in Normandy, the CIOS coordinated Allied intelligence-gathering operations on the European front. Units specially trained in identifying enemy intelligence sources included those of the Special Operations Executive (SOE) of the United Kingdom and the Office of Strategic Services (OSS) of the United States. Target Intelligence Committee (TICom) units focused on cryptographic targets, with teams four and six focusing on *Kriegsmarine* communications technology and personnel.[146] Also at the front, the Royal Navy wing of 30 Advanced Unit (AU) and U.S. Navy counterparts of the Forward Intelligence Unit (FIU) also scoured the European continent for raw German naval intelligence sources.[147]

The chaos on the French front created the ideal conditions for Allied forces to obtain fresh intelligence from the Germans about the Japanese. For example, as Lüdden and Landfermann traveled from Bordeaux to meet their train to Paris, they drove into an ambush on 24 June 1944. Operating on the outskirts of Bourganeuf on 24 June 1944, Colonel Albert Fossey-François of the French Forces of the Interior (FFI) ambushed Lüdden along with the chief engineer from *U-181*, Landfermann.[148] In conjunction with Operation Bergamotte, a combined SOE and OSS team, lead by U.S. Army Lieutenant Colonel Jack T. Shannon, parachuted into the Bourganeuf area with FFI Major Jacques Robert-Rewez on 26 June.[149]

---

[144]   Ibid.

[145]   RG 38, Crane Files, 3840/5, Box 75, "U-boat Intelligence Summaries 17 March 1944–19 May 1945," "Special U-boat Invasion Summaries," 18 June 1944.

[146]   RG 457, Entry 9037, Box 168, Target Intelligence Committee, "Narrative and Report of Proceedings of TICom Team 6," 5 September 1945, pp. 1–24.

[147]   RG 313, Records of the Operating Forces, Commander, U.S. Naval Forces in Europe (ComNavEu), Box 1, Folder 5, "History of ComNavEu Forward Intelligence Unit—Part I," 30 December 1944, comp. by Lieutenant Commander George T. O'Neill to Commodore Tully Shelley, pp. 1–10.

[148]   RG 38, Box 166, Index Cards, 1059/23 June 1944 intercept, Lüdden intention to travel in a van from Bordeaux to Paris with request for sleeping coach from Paris by train to Berlin.

[149]   RG 226, "Bergamotte" Mission, Entry 190, Box 740, Folder 1466.

Shannon reported that Lüdden and his entire dossier featured intelligence about German submarine operations. Perhaps more importantly, Lüdden and the material he carried contained detailed information about Japanese forces in East Asia. Winn and Knowles, in turn, requested copies of the captured documents and details of the interrogation with Lüdden.[150] Though the FFI generally failed to take prisoners, they spared ranking officers for interrogation purposes. As both wore the Knight's Cross, Lüdden and Landfermann were taken prisoner and held for nearly three weeks by the FFI.[151] Their satchel also held German intelligence about the Japanese, *Kriegsmarine* communications, and details on the Axis strategy in the Pacific. On 10 July 1944, U.S. Army Colonel James R. Forgan of the OSS requested assistance to evacuate Lüdden and Landfermann from the front.[152]

The Germans found the FFI to be amateurish, but viewed the British and American intelligence officers as seasoned professionals. Recalling his brief incarceration in a 1999 interview, Landfermann explained that the FFI had summarily executed other passengers in the van they were riding in outside of Limoges.[153] However, they spared Lüdden and Landfermann. Recalling the experience fifty-five years later, Landfermann suggested that the FFI had spared them from execution because of their Knight's Crosses.[154] He also believed that the FFI thought them to be high-ranking members of the *Kriegsmarine* High Command, as they had just returned from Japan. The FFI bound, gagged, and blindfolded the Germans, then placed them in the basement of a chateau in Bourganeuf. During the following days, Lüdden and Landfermann were treated well during interrogations with Shannon, François, and Rewez.[155]

The FFI secured the secret documents captured with Lüdden and Landfermann, but failed to control their prisoners. Landfermann explained that an FFI member named "Roger" had given them a Bible and writing paper. Then, the FFI forced Lüdden and Landfermann to write letters to the local German authorities. The FFI used the letters in an attempt to limit the prospect of German reprisals against French civilians.[156] Colonel François required Lüdden and Landfermann

---

[150] Ibid.; and OIC Serial 1228, 1119/29 June 1944.

[151] Schwelm, Germany, 2 December 1999, Carl-August Landfermann interview with the author.

[152] RG 226, "Bergamotte" Mission, Entry 190, Box 740, Folder 1466.

[153] Landfermann interview with the author.

[154] Ibid.

[155] Ibid.

[156] BAMA, RM7/1828, *Seekriegsleitung*, 13 August 1944 report from MVO-Vichy to the OKM 1/SKL, "*Anwesenheit amerikanischer und englischer Offz. im Maquis*" (Presence of American and English Officers among the *Maquis* Resistance Forces). The OSS notebook of U.S. Army Major Jack T. Shannon was captured by German forces during the surprise attack. This document contained details of the OSS organization in France, individual names of

to state that the FFI had treated them in accordance with proper military protocol. Landfermann recalled that the FFI reviewed their letters very carefully.[157] However, the FFI had failed to notice the true meaning of the letters scribbled on the postcard placed inside the Bible, which revealed the address of the chateau. Lüdden and Landfermann wrote their letters in the IRLAND officer code.[158] In their letters, they embedded their location in Bourganeuf. Shortly thereafter, German forces came to the rescue. Lüdden and Landfermann escaped into the woods and were ultimately repatriated.[159] According to Landfermann, they were rescued by *Waffen-SS* forces dressed in civilian clothing.[160]

Conclusion

Anglo-American analysts in London scoured the documents captured from Lüdden in France. From these materials, they discovered new targets from which to procure *Kriegsmarine* intelligence sources. Information about the Imperial Japanese Navy also appeared within the text of the *U-188* logbook, communications digest, and cipher log. Such material provided excellent foundations for planning the final victory in Asia. In particular, the *Erfahrungsbericht* (Report of Experiences), compiled at sea by Lüdden, detailed weaknesses affecting the Imperial Japanese Navy. U.S. Navy analysts took great interest in the Lüdden report, as it

---

OSS and SOE agents, and the key FFI officials involved with the capture of Landfermann and Lüdden. Following its capture, the *Kriegsmarine* Liaison officer to Vichy described the book as being titled with the operational covername Bergamotte. Paraphrasing the captured notebook, the German Liaison to Vichy explained that the "American writer explains his satisfaction that soon after his arrival valuable intelligence was obtained from Kaptlt. Lüdden and Landfermann . . . the diary confirms the survival account of Kaptlt. Lüdden. The American writes about the execution of French Militia, as well as women and men in the care of the *Sicherheitsdienst*. The American also does not approve of the neck shots at the back of the head type executions by the FFI against French collaborators, however the sentence describing the FFI reprisals are described as an 'internal-French affair,' into which the American cannot mix officially."

[157]   Landfermann interview with the author.

[158]   *U-188* Intercepts, 1018/12 July 1944, Grey Series (OIC 1231), regarding Lüdden and Landfermann letters featuring IRLAND officer code; BAMA, RM7/1828, *Seekriegsleitung*, Lüdden Survival Report; and Landfermann recollections from 2 December 1999 interview with the author.

[159]   BAMA, RM7/1828, *Seekriegsleitung*, 13 August 1944 report from MVO-Vichy to the OKM 1/SKL.

[160]   BAMA, RM7/1828, *Seekriegsleitung*, 1/Skl 24427/44g Kdos., 30 July 1944 report from *Deutscher Marine Verbinungs-Offizier Vichy* (MVO-Vichy), "*Erlebnisbericht*," submitted by Siegfried Lüdden to the German Navy Liaison Officer in Vichy ("Lüdden Survival Report").

revealed details about the capabilities and limitations of Japanese forces.[161] Such information drew the attention of Allied planning officers at the highest levels of the Admiralty and Navy Department.[162]

In planning offensive operations in Asia, Anglo-American collaboration was the foundation for achieving common strategic objectives. Sharing raw intelligence sources, and the conclusions derived from analysis, provided the basic elements of victory against the Axis powers. To facilitate combined operations in Asia, the First Sea Lord, Cunningham, endorsed the selection of Somerville to serve as the ranking representative of the British Admiralty Delegation (BAD) in Washington. The CominCh/CNO, King, welcomed the appointment. Somerville's decision to sink the Monsoon refueling ships pleased King and his staff. As the leading representative of the BAD, Somerville thus helped soothe differences between the Admiralty and the Navy Department during the final months of the Second World War.

The final collapse of the *Kriegsmarine* reflected the fundamental failure of Dönitz as a strategic commander. His decision to send submarines to the East Asian warfront has been portrayed as an example of creativity. The efforts of German submariners associated with the Monsoon adventure have furthermore contributed to a heroic mythology not dissimilar to other lost causes of past wars. As this chapter has demonstrated, Dönitz sacrificed strategic results in favor of operations designed to deliver short-term tactical success. In the process, he supervised the destruction of the German submarine force in the pursuit of an unrealistic Nazi fantasy. In this respect, military professionals may still find lessons to be learned from examining examples such as the Monsoon adventure.

On a more intimate level, the fate of Lüdden and *U-188* illustrates the strategic bankruptcy of the German submarine operations on the grandest scale. As Allied forces pressed across France to the German border during the fall of 1944, the first officer, Meenen, helped scuttle the hulk of *U-188* inside the channel leading into the German submarine bunker complex at Bordeaux. He was unable to sail the boat under its own power, as the batteries no longer held a charge and, despite significant effort, the *U-188* diesels failed to turn over.[163] Meanwhile, after Lüdden escaped from the FFI, he received an assignment on the staff of Dönitz. Although his war had ended, Lüdden suffered a tragic death aboard the barracks ship SS *Daresalem*—moored in the north German anchorage at Kiel. On 13 January 1945,

---

161 BAMA, RM 98/392, *Seekriegsleitung, Logbook of U-188*, Special Report, "*Erfahrungs-bericht*," compiled at sea by Lieutenant Commander Siegfried Lüdden, Commander of *U-188* (*U-188* Report of Experiences in East Asia). After this document was captured by the FFI, it was cataloged in the CIOS Captured Documents Section as "PG/7337." As a subsection of the *U-188* logbook, the Report of Experiences in East Asia appears on pages 158 through 171.

162 U.S. Naval Institute, Annapolis, MD, Reminiscences of William J. Sebald, pp. 290–340.

163 Meenen interview with the author.

Figure 1.   Inside the F-21 "Atlantic Section" submarine tracking room on the third deck of the Navy Department, April 1944. Women from the Combat Intelligence Division of the Headquarters of the Commander in Chief, U. S. Navy, Fleet Admiral Ernest J. King, provided the information required to win a global victory at sea. (Image courtesy U. S. Navy)

he died while watching a Nazi propaganda film with twelve other highly-decorated officers assigned to the personal staff of Dönitz. This audience of German submarine heroes was unable to escape when the celluloid suddenly burst into flames—Lüdden died of asphyxiation in the fire.[164]

In the final analysis, the Monsoon adventure mimicked the damage caused in the violence of a tropical storm. German submarines in the Indian Ocean caused noteworthy damage within a very short amount of time. Yet, these operations proved strategically flawed and unsustainable at a more basic level. The cruise of *U-188* drew the attention of Allied analysts during the final months of the Second World War, as they planned for the defeat of Japan and anticipated the prospect of problems during the reconstruction. The dramatic events surrounding the cruise of *U-188* also provide fresh insight into the war at sea. Through the Monsoon adventure to the Indian Ocean, one can revisit and examine new aspects in the history of antisubmarine operations, the broader role of intelligence in the war at sea, and the interaction of key personalities within the bureaucracies of Allied and Axis powers. Given the scope of the subject, this chapter has shown how the cruise of *U-188* also affected the course of battle in other theaters. Furthermore, it has also identified new opportunities for additional research within archival records of the Second World War.

---

[164]   Ibid.

Figure 2. On the conning tower of *U-188* upon arrival in Penang in 1943, Lieutenant Karlheinz Meenen stands to the far left with Lieutenant Siegfried Lüdden with the white cap second from right. (Image courtesy Karlheinz Meenen)

Figure 3. *U-188* required significant repairs in order to make the return voyage to Europe. As the dockyard facilities in Penang proved insufficient, *U-188* sailed the Malacca Straits on the surface to Singapore. As Allied submarines sank a number of Axis submarines and merchant vessels in the Malacca Straits, the *U-188* crew sat with their life rafts on the top deck during the voyage to Singapore. (Image courtesy Karlheinz Meenen)

Figure 4.   At sea in *U-188,* Lieutenant Karlheinz Meenen (right) with Lieutenant Siegfried Lüdden, who had just been awarded the Knight's Cross. Photo taken somewhere in the Indian Ocean in 1944. (Image courtesy Karlheinz Meenen)

Contributors

Christopher M. Bell is Professor of History at Dalhousie University in Halifax, Nova Scotia. He is the author of *Churchill and the Dardanelles* (Oxford: Oxford University Press, 2017); *Churchill and Sea Power* (Oxford: Oxford University Press, 2012); and *The Royal Navy, Seapower and Strategy between the Wars* (Stanford: Stanford University Press, 2000); and co-editor, with John Maurer, of *At the Crossroads between Peace and War: The London Naval Conference of 1930* (Annapolis: Naval Institute Press, 2014); and, with Bruce Elleman, *Naval Mutinies of the Twentieth Century: An International Perspective* (London: Frank Cass, 2003). http://christophermbell.ca/

Tim Benbow is Reader in Strategic Studies in the Defence Studies Department of King's College London at the UK Defence Academy. He is the author/editor of numerous works, including *The Magic Bullet? Understanding the Revolution in Military Affairs* (London: Brassey's, 2004); *Naval Warfare, 1914–1918: From Coronel to the Atlantic and Zeebrugge* (London: Amber Books, 2011); *British Naval Aviation: The First 100 Years* (Farnham: Ashgate, 2011); and *Operation Neptune: The D-Day Landings, 6 June 1944* (Solihull: Helion, 2015).

G. H. Bennett is Associate Professor in History at the University of Plymouth. The majority of his research concentrates on the Second World War and he is particularly interested in maritime history (both civilian and military) and the on-going relevance of the past to an understanding of today's maritime/naval issues. He has contributed numerous articles to journals and magazines and is the author of more than twenty books, including *Destination Normandy: Three American Regiments on D-Day* (Westport, CT: Praeger, 2007); *The RAF's French Foreign Legion: De Gaulle, the British and the Re-emergence of French Airpower, 1940–45* (London: Bloomsbury, 2011); and *Admiralty Despatches: The Story of the War from the Battlefront, 1939–45* (Stroud: Amberley, 2017). Professor Bennett has appeared frequently on television programs on the BBC and other channels.

Marcus Faulkner is an international historian with interests in the development of navies and seapower in the twentieth century, intelligence, and strategic history. His current projects include a history of German naval intelligence between the world wars and a volume on the German aircraft carrier *Graf Zeppelin*. He holds a BA in War Studies (2000) from King's College London and an MA in Politics,

Security and Integration from the School of Slavonic and East European Studies, UCL (2003). He completed a PhD entitled "Intelligence, Policy and the *Kriegsmarine* in the Interwar Period" with the Department of War Studies, King's College London in 2008. He is the author of *The Great War at Sea: A Naval Atlas, 1914–1919* (Barnsley: Seaforth, 2014); *War at Sea: A Naval Atlas, 1939–1945* (Barnsley: Seaforth, 2012); and, with Michael H. Clemmesen, editor of *Northern European Overture to War, 1939–1941* (Leiden: Brill, 2013). He currently teaches in the Department of War Studies, King's College London.

Rear Admiral James Goldrick had sea service around the world in the RAN and on exchange service with the British Royal Navy. An anti-submarine specialist, he commanded HMA Ships *Cessnock* and *Sydney* (twice), the Australian Surface Task Group and the multinational maritime interception force in the Persian Gulf in 2002, Australia's inter-agency Border Protection Command, the Australian Defence Force Academy (ADFA), and the Australian Defence College. He is an Adjunct Professor in the Strategic & Defence Studies Centre at The Australian National University and at UNSW Canberra (ADFA). He has published in many academic and professional journals and contributed chapters to more than forty books. He is the author of *Before Jutland: The Naval War in Northern European Waters, August 1914–February 1915* (Annapolis: Naval Institute Press, 2015), which is a much revised and extended version of his earlier work, *The King's Ships Were at Sea: The War in the North Sea, August 1914–February 1915* (Annapolis: Naval Institute Press, 1984); *No Easy Answers: The Development of the Navies of India, Pakistan, Bangladesh and Sri Lanka, 1945–1996* (Hartford, WI: Spantech & Lancer, 1997); and, with Jack McCaffrie, *Navies of South-East Asia: A Comparative Study* (London: Routledge, 2012).

Ben Jones is a Senior Lecturer in Naval History at the University of Portsmouth and is based at the RAF College, Cranwell. He specializes in naval history and British defense policy. Current research interests include maritime air power, naval logistics during the Second World War, and defense policy East of Suez in the postwar period. He is co-author, with David Gates, of *Air Power in the Maritime Environment: The World Wars* (Abingdon: Routledge, 2016), and editor of *The Fleet Air Arm in the Second World War,* Vol. I, *1939–1941* (Farnham: Ashgate, 2012) and *The Fleet Air Arm in the Second World War,* Vol. II, *1942–1943* (Abingdon: Routledge, 2018). Dr. Jones has been General Editor of the Navy Records Society since 2013.

David Kohnen is the Director of the John B. Hattendorf Center for Maritime Historical Research at the U. S. Naval War College. Having served in the U. S. Navy, he earned a PhD under the supervision of the Laughton Professor of Naval History in the Department of War Studies, King's College London. He is the author of *Commanders Winn and Knowles: Winning the U-Boat War with Intelligence, 1939–1943* (Krakow: Enigma, 1999); *Two Kings and a Navy: Fleet Admiral Ernest J. King and* *the Fifty Years War for Global Command at Sea, 1897–1947* (Annapolis: Naval Institute Press, forthcoming); and editor of *21st Century Knox: Influence, Sea Power, and History for the Modern Era* (Annapolis: Naval Institute Press, 2016).

Marc Milner is Director of the Brigadier Milton F. Gregg VC Centre for the Study of War and Society and Professor of History at the University of New Brunswick. His articles have appeared in numerous journals and scholarly publications and for years he wrote a regular column on Canadian naval history for *Legion Magazine*. Professor Milner is the author of several works, including *North Atlantic Run: The Royal Canadian Navy and the Battle for the Convoys* (Annapolis: Naval Institute Press, 1985); *The U-Boat Hunters: The Royal Canadian Navy and the Offensive against Germany's Submarines* (Annapolis: Naval Institute Press, 1994); *Battle of the Atlantic* (Stroud: Tempus, 2003); and *Stopping the Panzers: The Untold Story of D-Day* (Lawrence: University Press of Kansas, 2014).

Kevin Smith is Associate Dean of the College of Sciences and Humanities at Ball State University; he served as chairperson of Ball State's History Department from 2010 to 2016. He is the author of *Conflict over Convoys: Anglo-American Logistics Diplomacy in the Second World War* (Cambridge: Cambridge University Press, 1996) and several journal articles, including "Reassessing Roosevelt's View of Chamberlain after Munich: Ideological Affinity in the Geoffrey Thompson–Claude Bowers Correspondence," *Diplomatic History* 33:5 (November 2009).

Index

AAA. *See* Agricultural Adjustment Administration
Abel, Brent M., 279–80
Abukir (SS), 229
Achilles (HMS), 130
acoustic homing torpedoes, 17–18, 145, 147
Activity (HMS), 141
ACV. *See* auxiliary carriers
Acworth, Bernard, 100–101
Aden Escort Force, 270
Adler U-boat group, 262
Admiral Graf Spee, 130, 172, 188
Admiralty: Anglo-American debates on the use of Ultra and, 263–65, 276–78; Anglo-American special intelligence collaboration and the case of *U-188*, 254 (*see also* Anglo-American special intelligence collaboration); assessment of Churchill's grand strategy and its impact on the Battle of the Atlantic, 41–45; Bay of Biscay Offensive, 40–41; British grand strategy from July 1941 to May 1943, 27–41; British grand strategy from June 1940 to July 1941 and, 21–27; closing of the air gap and, 36–37, 39, 41; components of the trade defense system, 7–9; Corbettian approach to the Battle of the Atlantic, 6–7; disputes with the Air Ministry over the uses of air power and air resources, 27–35, 36–37, 39–41, 79–81, 84, 98–113, 123–24; escort carriers, 36–37 (*see also* escort carriers); Essential Work Order for Shipbuilding and Shiprepairing, 55; failure to prioritize merchant ship repair, 61; formula for convoy escorts in 1943, 137; impact of the sinking of *Bismarck*, 172–73; legacy of the

inter-service dispute over the Battle of the Atlantic and, 124; *Monthly Anti-Submarine Reports*, 156; postwar interest in U-boats, 171; prewar assessment of German naval construction, 184–87; prewar consideration of German aircraft carriers, 174–75; prewar doctrine of trade defense, 125–27; wartime view of German aircraft carriers and *Graf Zeppelin*, 170–74 (*see also* Graf Zeppelin). *See also* Fleet Air Arm; Royal Navy
Agricultural Adjustment Administration (AAA), 201, 204
agricultural production: wartime adjustments to and competing demands on in the U.S., 203–6. *See also* meat export crisis of 1942–1943
aircraft carriers: in anti-submarine hunting groups, 127–29; auxiliary carriers, 125n1, 135–37, 191; British prewar consideration of German aircraft carriers, 174–75; in British prewar trade defense doctrine, 126–27; Churchill's wartime reversals of course concerning, 120–21; cruiser-carrier hybrids, 174–75; early air cover for convoys, 133–34; escort carriers, 36–37, 41, 86 (*see also* escort carriers); Merchant Aircraft Carriers, 37, 41, 86 (*see also* Merchant Aircraft Carriers); opinion of air power theorists regarding, 89. *See also* Fleet Air Arm; Graf Zeppelin
aircraft transport ships, 142
air gap: activity of U-boats in late 1942, 14, 36–37; Allied closing of, 17, 36–37, 39, 41, 86; assessment of Churchill's grand

New Perspectives on the Second World War

Series Editor: Robert von Maier

an imprint of the University Press of Kentucky

Brécourt Academic